PATHS OF GLORY

Paths of Glory

*The Life and Death
of General James Wolfe*

Stephen Brumwell

hambledon
continuum

Hambledon Continuum is an imprint of Continuum Books

Continuum UK
The Tower Building
11 York Road
London SE1 7NX

Continuum US
80 Maiden Lane
Suite 704
New York, NY 10038

www.continuumbooks.com

First published 2006 in hardback
This edition published 2007 in paperback

ISBN 1 85285 553 3 (hardback)
ISBN 1 84725 208 7 (paperback)

British Library Cataloguing-in-Publication Data
A catalogue record for this book is available from the British Library.

Typeset by Carnegie Book Production, Lancaster
Printed and bound by Cambridge Printing, Cambridge

Contents

For my son Ivan,
and for my nephews Daniel, David, Todd, Guy and Max

Illustrations

Acknowledgements

I am most grateful to Her Majesty the Queen for gracious permission to cite material from the Hawley-Toovey Papers, held in The Royal Archives, Windsor Castle (with transcripts in the National Army Museum, Chelsea). I also wish to thank the Earl of Dalhousie for allowing me to draw upon his important family papers, the Dalhousie Muniments, in the National Archives of Scotland, Edinburgh. Sincere thanks are also due to Mr and Mrs John Warde, of Squerryes Court, Westerham, for courteously allowing me to study the originals of the extensive correspondence from Wolfe to his parents in their possession, and likewise to Pam White, Administrator at Squerryes Court, for her patient help.

Martin West, the Director of Fort Ligonier, Pennsylvania, very generously allowed me to reproduce – for the first time in colour – Edward Penny's *The Death of General Wolfe*, one of many outstanding paintings in his museum's collection of art; coming from a direct descendant of Penny's competitor Benjamin West, Martin's support was all the more welcome. I am also most grateful to Penny West for her assistance with this. For help with assembling illustrations from the exceptionally rich John Clarence Webster Canadiana Collection at the New Brunswick Museum, Saint John, I am much obliged to Janet Bishop. At the McCord Museum of Canadian History, Montreal, Curator of Collections Conrad Graham was most generous with his time and knowledge regarding the caricatures attributed to George Townshend.

Thanks are also due to Randolph Vigne of the Huguenot Society, for sharing his research on Wolfe and Lord Ligonier; Lawrence Power, MD, of Ann Arbor, Michigan for some extremely illuminating thoughts on the question of Wolfe's health, and for allowing me to see a copy of his paper, 'A Good Spirit Carries'; to Marijke van der Meer for providing precise translations of French-language sources; to Lt-Col Ian

McCulloch of the Canadian Defence Headquarters for a fascinating and enlightening 'staff ride' around Quebec sites associated with the siege of 1759, and also for giving me a copy of his unpublished manuscript on the battle of the Plains of Abraham; and to Peter Harper for his fine maps. For their help and friendship I am also most grateful to Walt and Sue Powell, John Houlding, Robert Andrews, Gerry Embleton, Nicholas and Virginia Westbrook and Carl Crego.

Lyrics from The Stranglers song, 'No More Heroes' (written by Burnel / Cornwell / Duffy / Greenfield), are used here by kind permission of Complete Music Ltd. Bill Speck and Ian Mason, the editors of *The Historian: the Magazine of the Historical Association*, kindly allowed me to draw upon material from my article, 'The First Trans-Atlantic Hero? James Wolfe and British North America', published in 2004. Some of the arguments presented here were first aired in papers given to the Historical Association Border Conference, at the University of Northumbria, Carlisle in July 2003, and the Annual French and Indian War History Seminar held at Jumonville, Pennsylvania, in November 2005. I remain grateful to the organizers of both events for inviting me to participate, and also to the conference delegates for their thought-provoking questions.

As a writer and 'independent' historian working outside the academic mainstream, I have especially valued the interest of scholars whose research overlaps with my own. Thanks are owing to Geoffrey Plank, who generously shared references, and also to Fred Anderson, whose encouraging response to my previous writings on 'the Great War for the Empire' has been sincerely appreciated. Whilst my own view of Wolfe diverges from that held by both of these scholars, I have benefited from their stimulating work, and enjoyed engaging with it. I have also very much appreciated the continuing encouragement of two British historians with a strong interest in the eighteenth century, and particularly the relationship between war and society during that era, Stephen Conway and Jeremy Black.

This book has had an unusually protracted gestation. Above all, therefore, I must acknowledge my debt to Martin Sheppard and Tony Morris of Hambledon & London, publishers of rare vision and integrity. Without their patience, support and friendship this project would never have been completed. Crucial encouragement in the early stages came from Patrick Bell, whilst the project received a timely boost in 2004 when I was awarded the Elizabeth Longford Grant for historical biography by the Authors' Foundation. The generosity of the award's sponsors enabled me to undertake research in Canada that was fundamental to the book.

Just as the completion of my last book coincided with the arrival of my daughter Milly, so *Paths of Glory* was finished just days before the birth of my son, Ivan. I hope that he will grow up to relish books as much as his big sister, for whom, happily, mention of the 'W word' still prompts no more than an expectant 'huff and puff?' To my wife Laura, I owe, as always, an immense debt for all of her support, understanding and tolerance – not least at those times when James Wolfe cast his long shadow upon family life. I am also very grateful to my parents, who first nurtured my interest in history, and who have been supportive ever since. I would like to dedicate this book to my son, and to my nephews Daniel, David, Todd, Guy and Max: serving respectively in the Royal Navy and British Army, Daniel and David are well qualified to mount a 'combined operation' of their own.

Addendum

As this book was going to press, it was confirmed that the house near Montmorency Falls, long believed to have been James Wolfe's headquarters during the 1759 siege of Quebec, is actually of a later date. However, as this tradition has only recently been disproved, I believe that my observations about the condition of the building (see p. xxi) remain valid. The house *now* thought to have been occupied by Wolfe (Maison Vézina) which is located nearby, has been renovated as a cultural and artistic centre and contains an exhibit highlighting its historical significance. I am grateful to David Boston, of the Wolfe Society, and to Hélène Quimper, at the National Battlefields Commission (Quebec City), for this information.

S. B., Amsterdam, 2006

Prologue

All was ready. The first wave of red-coated infantrymen had long since clambered down from the transport ships into the landing boats. Wedged together and facing each other on benches running the length of each narrow craft, they now sat waiting in silence, muskets clamped between their knees. Besides his firearm and bayonet, each man carried seventy rounds of ammunition, two days' rations of salt pork and hard bread, and a canteen filled with watered rum. The soldiers' regimental coats were faded and tattered, their faces leathery from prolonged exposure to the elements. All were veterans of the savage war against New France. If they felt any nervousness at the prospect of what lay ahead of them this night, their demeanour did nothing to betray it.

Oars jostling the backs of the stolid redcoats, pigtailed sailors swore under their breath as they struggled to steady the boats against the mounting strength of the ebb tide. Naval officers in blue uniforms that merged with the darkness of the night consulted pocket watches and stole frequent glances towards the looming bulk of the *Sutherland* man-of-war. It was from high above her bristling gun decks that the signal to depart would come.

Of the thousands of men now assembled upon the surface of the great river, none awaited that moment more keenly than their commanding officer, Major-General James Wolfe. At just thirty-two years of age, he was young for the great responsibility that rested upon his narrow shoulders. James Wolfe was acutely aware of the high hopes placed in his proven courage and leadership: in the course of a gruelling and frustrating summer campaign that burden had come close to shattering his frail constitution. The strain of command, exacerbated by painful illness, had left its mark upon Wolfe's pale, pointed features. Yet it had failed to extinguish his confidence in himself and the men around him.

On this, the last day of his short life, James Wolfe had chosen, as usual, to wear a plain scarlet coat of distinctly old-fashioned cut; it was devoid of lace, marks of rank, or any other decoration save for a black scarf bound around the left arm in token of mourning for his recently deceased father. As was his custom, Wolfe's flaming red hair was unpowdered and tied back in a long queue with a black silk ribbon. Like the rank and file around him, he cradled a musket and carried a bayonet on his hip: under the hazardous conditions that his own orders dictated, even a general officer might have to use both in his own defence.

Now the tide began to ebb in earnest. Two lanterns rose, one above the other, high up into the rigging of the *Sutherland*'s mainmast. It was the signal. The sailors shipped their oars and released the ropes that tethered the boats to the transports. Cast loose at last, the close-packed craft gently slipped away with the current. Swiftly gathering momentum, they followed the band of moonlight that paved the dark river. It stretched like a highway, down and onwards to Quebec.

Introduction: The Changing Reputation of James Wolfe

Whatever happened to,
all of the heroes . . .

The Stranglers, 'No More Heroes', 1977

In 1794, when a British expeditionary force hesitated to assault the Corsican port of Bastia, the young Captain Horatio Nelson posed a simple question: 'What would the immortal Wolfe have done?' Nelson had his answer ready: 'As he did, beat the enemy, if he perished in the attempt.'

Britain's most celebrated naval hero was born in 1758 – the year before James Wolfe was killed in action whilst winning the battle that changed the destiny of North America. Nelson matured during an era when Wolfe's exploits at Quebec remained fresh in the nation's memory; like his own childhood hero, Nelson too would die gaining a famous victory for his country.

Although separated by nearly half a century, by a strange coincidence the last minutes of both men were to be captured on canvas by the same artist. Benjamin West had created a sensation when he exhibited his *Death of General Wolfe* in London in 1771. In 1802, after West had risen to become President of the prestigious Royal Academy and Nelson was already fêted for his victories at the Nile and Copenhagen, artist and admiral conversed over dinner. Whilst confessing his general ignorance of art, Nelson assured West that there was one notable exception to this rule. He explained: 'I never pass a print-shop, where your *Death of Wolfe* is in the window, without being stopped by it.' In response to Nelson's questioning, West explained that he had refrained from painting anything similar owing to lack of suitable subjects, although he feared that the admiral's legendary intrepidity might yet provide him with 'another such scene'; if that opportunity arose, he would not let it slip. West's macabre offer, with its promise of immortality akin to Wolfe's, caused Nelson to exclaim: 'Then I hope I shall die in the next battle!'[1]

When Nelson fell at Trafalgar, three years later, West honoured his pledge. But whilst West's *Death of Wolfe* remains an iconic image of patriotic self-sacrifice, his rendering of Nelson's last moments aboard the *Victory* is a curiously wooden affair, dismissed by most critics as the swansong of a jaded genius. Yet if West's *Nelson* failed to match his *Wolfe*, in all other respects it is the sailor, rather than his soldier role model, who has emerged victorious in the battle for posthumous fame.

Today, as the Trafalgar bicentenary demonstrated, Nelson's 'immortal memory' remains as dear to Britons as a grieving Vice-Admiral Cuthbert Collingwood predicted it would in 1805: critics may have periodically damaged Nelson's rigging, but they've never holed him below the water line. In 2002, a BBC poll to find the greatest Britons of all time ranked Nelson ninth. By contrast, James Wolfe failed to fight his way into the top hundred. Why? A general once hailed as the very embodiment of the military virtues of courage, leadership and strategic flair, allied to a selfless patriotism and becoming modesty, is now more likely to be described in very different terms: ruthless, incompetent, cantankerous, bloodthirsty, vainglorious.[2]

The debunking of Wolfe is a relatively recent phenomenon: for more than a century and a half after his death his public image remained as invulnerable as Nelson's. Biographers and historians on both sides of the Atlantic extolled Wolfe's virtues, often bequeathing him saintly qualities that he never possessed in life. This deification began within months of the young general's death. A rough template for much that followed was cut in 1760 with the publication of a slim volume entitled *The Life of General James Wolfe, the Conqueror of Canada: or The Elogium of that Renowned Hero Attempted According to the Rules of Eloquence*. As the florid subtitle suggests, this book was an unabashed panegyric. Its two-dozen pages, frustratingly thin on hard biographical detail, were thick with what one contemporary critic dismissed as 'fustian eulogium'. These stylistic shortcomings may explain why the author, who readily confessed his inequality to the task in hand, chose to identify himself only as 'J.P.' The initials designated John Pringle, who, whatever his deficiencies as a writer, enjoyed a well-deserved reputation for scientific research. His efforts in that field gained him not only the rank of baronet, but also the presidency of the Royal Society. Pringle's most significant contribution – one that would surely have earned the approval of Wolfe himself – was his pioneering reform of hygiene and medical care within the British Army. And for all its failings, Pringle's tribute achieved wide circulation: in January and February 1760 it was serialized in a popular newspaper, *Read's Weekly Journal or British Gazetteer*, whilst the book itself was soon reprinted in Boston, Massachusetts.[3]

Given Wolfe's celebrity during the generations following his death, it is surprising that the first full-scale 'Life' only emerged a full century after Pringle's effort. Early biographers appear to have been discouraged by an apparent dearth of manuscripts upon which a more substantial biography could be founded. One attempt that came to nothing provides yet another link between Wolfe and Nelson. The Poet Laureate Robert Southey completed an acclaimed *Life of Nelson* in 1826; having tackled the sailor, he now contemplated the heroic soldier. Southey began the task, and the work was even advertised as forthcoming in a publisher's catalogue; but it was never finished.

Southey abandoned his project after failing to unearth enough primary sources. In fact, as Robert Wright demonstrated in 1864 in his *Life of Major-General James Wolfe*, the raw material for a detailed account of Wolfe's life has never been lacking. Wright was the first author to make use of the extensive surviving correspondence between Wolfe and his family, and to publish many other key documents; half a century later, hundreds of these letters were republished by Beckles Willson in a work that has provided a handy quarry for subsequent biographers.[4]

In 1884, the general's transatlantic fame was rekindled when the Harvard historian Francis Parkman published his masterly chronicle of the French and Indian War. Fusing extensive archival research with powerful prose, Parkman's *Montcalm and Wolfe* consolidated Wolfe's reputation as the heroic protagonist in an epic struggle. Popular writers and novelists reinforced this image.

The stirring events before Quebec exerted an irresistible lure, not least for the prolific G. A. Henty, whose *With Wolfe in Canada: or The*

Winning of a Continent (1880) merged with a seemingly endless stream of juvenile fiction calculated to inculcate plucky Victorian lads with a proper sense of Britain's imperial destiny. As Henty's title indicates, Wolfe's continuing celebrity hinged upon his credentials as the man credited with adding Canada to the British Empire. Much the same criteria were reflected a generation later in Sir Harry Johnston's *A Gallery of Heroes and Heroines* (1915). In its pages both Wolfe and Nelson feature amongst a dozen British empire-builders: these range from the Elizabethan seadog Sir Francis Drake to the Antarctic explorer Robert Falcon Scott. A decade later, Wolfe and many of these same figures again took their place in the cavalcade of stalwarts lauded for painting the globe red who were pictured upon the promotional poster for the 1924 British Empire Exhibition at Wembley: according to the accompanying slogan, this frieze-like procession constituted 'A Glorious Company – The Flower of Men – To Serve as Model for the Mighty World'.

In the years following the Second World War, as Britain began its messy and humiliating withdrawal from empire, the values that had once justified the glorification of such leaders no longer mattered. The subsequent fortunes of Sir Harry's *Gallery* are instructive: some, like Nelson and the Pacific explorer James Cook, survived the twentieth century with their reputations intact or even enhanced. Others have been obliged to weather the onslaughts of revisionists: Captain Scott, whose stoicism in the face of impending death struck such a chord with Edwardian Britons, has since endured castigation as a stubborn bungler, whilst Drake has been obliged to share credit for the defeat of the Spanish Armada. Most telling of all is the fate of another of Johnston's heroes, the Victorian general and avenging scourge of mutinous sepoys, Sir Henry Havelock. By 2000, London's Mayor, Ken Livingstone, could propose the removal of Havelock's weathered statue from its plinth in Trafalgar Square on the grounds that nobody longer knew – still less cared – who he was.[5]

Unlike Havelock, Wolfe has at least been spared the ultimate ignominy of obscurity. An upsurge of scholarly interest in the crucial American phase of the Seven Years' War, and in the 'First British Empire' that it defined, has kept him within the rarefied academic limelight. More significantly for Wolfe's profile amongst the wider public, Benjamin West's ground-breaking painting remains a familiar image. So firmly has it become embedded in popular consciousness that Margaret Atwood, herself a Canadian, could award it a choice slot in her best-selling satirical novel *The Robber Bride*: the office of one of her characters, the history lecturer Tony, includes a bad reproduction of West's 'lugubrious picture'. To Tony, Wolfe looks as 'white as a codfish belly, with his eyes rolled piously upwards and many necrophiliac voyeurs in fancy dress grouped around him'.[6]

As Atwood's mischievous prose suggests, though he is far from forgotten, Wolfe's current reputation provides a sorry contrast to the one he enjoyed a century ago. To some extent, the backlash has been a natural reaction against not only the jingoistic output of imperialist historians, but also the cloying eulogies of early biographers. For them, Wolfe was often 'our hero' – a saintly soldier deemed incapable of anything less than the highest standards of personal conduct. Their desire to uphold Wolfe's reputation at all costs even extended to the suppression of original correspondence – innocuous enough by modern standards – deemed to cast a slur upon his character; as recently as 1902, Arthur Doughty felt obliged to prune a lengthy passage in a 1749 letter from Wolfe to a close friend, in which he frankly discussed his marriage prospects. Doughty justified this policy on the grounds that these were 'private matters, which must be held sacred'. Seven years later, Beckles Willson's edition of Wolfe's correspondence printed the entire text of the same letter; but Willson himself was not above editing material judged to be undesirable: for example, the published version of a letter written by Wolfe to his father in 1752 omits revealing paragraphs dealing with James's health, and joking about the sexual exploits of a brother officer. Here the later volume of transcripts accompanying the original letters carries a damning pencilled verdict: 'very disagreeable'.[7] By burdening 'their' Wolfe with superhuman virtues, and raising him dizzyingly high upon a pedestal, such well-meaning enthusiasts manufactured a paragon all too vulnerable to counter-attack from commentators keen to knock him down to size.

Given this tempting target, it is unsurprising that published assaults upon Wolfe's reputation actually predated the end of the British Empire. The first – and most devastating – of these came in 1936, when E. R. Adair delivered the presidential address to the annual meeting of the Canadian Historical Association. Adair opened by observing that

Wolfe's reputation had 'so far survived practically untarnished'. He swiftly altered that state of affairs with a blistering critique of the general's character and military capabilities. In Adair's forceful paper, not only was Wolfe depicted as an unpleasantly vain, smug and humourless young man, but his reputation as a soldier of genius came under concerted attack. On this point Adair's conclusion was unequivocal: Wolfe did *not* possess the qualities of a great general.[8]

Following Adair's strident lead, publications triggered by the 1959 bicentenary of Wolfe's death included not only the anticipated crop of laudatory narratives, but also revisionist works. Respected historians on both sides of the Atlantic produced treatments that were highly critical of Wolfe. In a lively and popular work, Christopher Hibbert painted Wolfe in an overwhelmingly unsympathetic light – ruthless, neurotic, priggish and probably a repressed homosexual to boot; and one of Canada's foremost military historians, Colonel Charles P. Stacey, published a meticulous account of the Quebec campaign that was equally damning of Wolfe's generalship on the St Lawrence.[9]

Colonel Stacey's unflattering conclusions also underpinned his lengthy reassessment of Wolfe in the prestigious *Dictionary of Canadian Biography*. But, as that same publication made clear, by the closing decades of the twentieth century it was not only Wolfe who had suffered at the hands of the iconoclasts: his antagonist at Quebec, and the dual hero of Parkman's great narrative history, had also come under sustained attack from Canadian historians. Once celebrated as a gallant Frenchman maintaining a creditable rearguard action in the face of overwhelming odds, the Marquis de Montcalm could now be branded a homesick defeatist. Like Wolfe, Montcalm has been lambasted as a shortsighted strategist who foolishly threw away the advantages he possessed. Men once regarded as honourable enemies in an epic struggle were dismissed by professional historians as overrated mediocrities – minor figures who would have been long forgotten were it not for the high drama surrounding their deaths.[10]

As the robust verdicts of Canadian scholars show, there is one place above all where James Wolfe is unlikely to be forgotten. The young soldier whose victory on the Plains of Abraham sounded the death-knell of the French regime in Canada continues to exert a powerful influence upon that country's politics. More than two centuries after his death, Wolfe and his final victory remain matters of extreme sensitivity and potential division within Canadian society. For Quebec's French-speaking majority, Wolfe is less a hero than a symbol of oppression – one whose memory continues to arouse strong emotions amongst anglophobe separatists. 'The Maple Leaf Forever', a song through which generations of Canadian schoolchildren recalled how

> Wolfe the dauntless hero came,
> And planted firm Britannia's flag,
> On Canada's fair domain

is now seen by many *Québecois* as triumphalist and provocative. French-Canadian feelings towards the 'conquest' still run so high that history itself must be rewritten to match the modern mood. In 1999, a re-enactment staged to commemorate the 240th anniversary of the momentous encounter on the Plains of Abraham was tactfully declared a 'draw': descendants of Wolfe and Montcalm shook hands afterwards in a well-publicised gesture of reconciliation.[11]

Wolfe's name will always be linked with the city where he found a hero's death, yet there is scant interest in perpetuating his memory there. Visitors to Quebec must search long and hard for concrete evidence that the famous siege of 1759 yielded a British success. The first battlefield obelisk, inscribed HERE DIED WOLFE VICTORIOUS, was repeatedly defaced. It was eventually replaced by another column now marooned within a traffic roundabout. The current monument's inscription mirrors the original's, with one significant omission – that last unpalatable word. Again, although the tiny house occupied by Wolfe during much of the Quebec campaign survives intact, it remains unremarked by the tourists who flock to marvel at the nearby Montmorency Falls. It lacks even a plaque to mark its historical significance, and instead stands neglected, dilapidated and graffiti-covered. Quebec's citizens may be forgiven a reluctance to commemorate the architect of their ancestors' downfall, but the decision to site an ugly public toilet block just yards away from Wolfe's former command-post suggests that something worse than indifference is at work.

In his blistering 1936 address to the Canadian Historical Association, Professor Adair argued that Wolfe's reputation rested upon his posthumous fame rather than his earthly exploits: he acquired a celebrity in death – 'an anachronistic glory' – that he had never achieved in life. It was on this very point that one of Nelson's foremost biographers drew a crucial distinction between the admiral and his soldier hero: Nelson's *enduring* fame resulted from the fact that, unlike Wolfe, he 'became a national hero in his own lifetime'.[12]

It is apparent that the imagination of Wolfe's contemporaries was fired, to an almost unprecedented degree, by his final hours on the Plains of Abraham. In 1760 John Pringle asked his readers: 'If we search the records of history for a death like that of Wolfe, shall we find one, in all respects, so noble?' The remarkable public response to the bittersweet news of Quebec's conquest and Wolfe's fall also made a deep impression upon that cynical man of letters, Horace Walpole. As he recalled in his *Memoirs of King George II,*

> Joy, grief, curiosity, astonishment were painted in every countenance: the more they inquired, the higher their admiration rose. Not an incident but was heroic and affecting![13]

Neither is there any doubt about the extraordinary outpourings of official and public sentiment that greeted the reports of Wolfe's death, and the proliferation of patriotic ballads, poems, paintings and artifacts that kept his memory alive down the decades. In scale, intensity and longevity, these reactions prefigured those following Nelson's fall at Trafalgar. Taken together, they granted Wolfe what one scholar has characterized as a cultural 'life after death'.[14]

But all of this emphasis upon the celebration of Wolfe as *posthumous* hero misses an important point: how can these remarkable phenomena be explained unless Wolfe, like Nelson, *already* enjoyed an extraordinarily high reputation amongst his countrymen? Does Wolfe's fame rest upon the circumstances surrounding a single dramatic and significant victory, or is there a deeper explanation for his great contemporary reputation? These questions lie at the heart of this book.

James Wolfe was first and foremost a professional soldier, one who spent all of his adult years as an officer in the British Army. Wolfe's career spanned a pivotal era in the evolution of that institution: when he gained his first commission, the reputation of British soldiers had never been lower; at the time of his death seventeen years later, it stood higher than ever before. These same years also witnessed the emergence of Great Britain as a leading global power. This book considers Wolfe's significance for the rise of both the British Army and the empire that it fought to create and safeguard.

That first British Empire was a genuinely transatlantic community: James Wolfe became a hero not only to Britons of the Mother Country, but also to their 'children' in the burgeoning colonies ranged along the eastern seaboard of British North America. This was an unprecedented feat, and one that would never be repeated. Wolfe's emergence as the first truly *transatlantic* celebrity is a remarkable and hitherto neglected aspect of his career: it provides another key theme here.

In reassessing General James Wolfe, illustrious warrior and precocious imperial hero, this book builds on the work of many other writers; the debt that it owes them will be readily apparent from the notes. In particular, no researcher approaching this topic can ignore the collections of Wolfe family correspondence published by Robert Wright and Beckles Willson. Whilst undeniably valuable, particularly for the insights they offer into Wolfe's personality, these 'domestic' letters have their limitations. The occasional suppression of 'unsavoury' material in the published versions has already been noted, but there are also other problems. Many of the letters are from Wolfe to his parents, and especially to his mother. It is all too clear that their length and frequency increased in direct proportion to the amount of time that Wolfe had on his hands: when busy, he wrote less – and less often. Ironically therefore, whilst the boring and frustrating interludes of peacetime soldiering generated numerous rambling and introspective letters that record Wolfe's thoughts and experiences in minute detail, other key episodes remain unchronicled in his own words.

To compensate for this marked imbalance in Wolfe's surviving family correspondence, every effort has been made to examine the widest possible spectrum of evidence. This reflects not only the opinions that Wolfe expressed to a range of correspondents, but also what his contemporaries thought and wrote about *him*. Priority has been given to previously neglected voices. Some of them are published here for the first time. It is hoped that all will help the reader to decide whether there was indeed more to James Wolfe than a famous death.

Note on Dates and Quotations

Until 1752, the English system of reckoning dates followed the Julian, or 'Old Style' calendar, as opposed to the 'New Style' Gregorian system adopted elsewhere in Europe. This meant that dates used in England were eleven days behind those employed across the Channel. For example, the battle of Dettingen in Germany was fought on 27 June 1743: this equated with the Old Style date of 16 June. Confusingly, Britons abroad sometimes followed their own national calendar, or flitted between the two systems. In addition, under the Julian calendar, the year started on Lady Day, 25 March. In September 1752, England finally fell into step with the rest of Europe; an Act of Parliament decreed that 2 September would be followed by 14 September. Here, unless noted otherwise, Old Style (OS) dates are used for events within Britain before the changeover, and New Style (NS) for those on the Continent. Throughout, the year is taken to start on 1 January.

To ease readability, in quoted material, all eighteenth-century capitalizations and abbreviations have been modernised; in the interest of consistency, this policy has been applied to manuscript and published sources alike. With the same aim, in some instances punctuation has been slightly amended. In all cases, great care has been taken to preserve the precise meaning of the quoted material. Original spellings, however eccentric, are retained throughout. Editorial insertions have been kept to a minimum and are enclosed within square brackets.

1

False Start

Come all you brave soldiers wherever you live,
Come listen a while and the truth I will give,
There are great rogues and small rogues, to us do belong,
And there's nothing but roguery in the whole song.

Anon, 'The Soldier, A New Song'

As 1726 gave way to 1727, all England shivered in the grip of a cruel winter. MPs from the far-flung North Country and Wales wrote to London apologizing that the roads were too snow-bound to permit their attendance at the House. Many other letters failed even to reach their destinations. Some sent from London to Plymouth were found fluttering forlornly amidst the drifts at Crookham in Somerset: of the rest of the mail, or of the post-boy and his horse, there was no trace. From Bristol, too, there came 'several melancholy accounts' of travellers who'd lost their bearings in the driving snow; and in London itself, a 'poor woman' who lay down to sleep in the streets after supping too much Geneva at a Barbican gin shop was found stiff and dead next morning.

Such harsh weather befitted hard times. Beneath its surface façade of restrained elegance – epitomized by the neoclassical couplets of the poet Alexander Pope, the artfully landscaped vistas of Lancelot 'Capability' Brown, and the Palladian frontages of countless country houses – early Georgian England was a rough and lawless place.

A random sampling of London-based newspapers from those same weeks that saw out the old year of 1726, and ushered in the new, reveal a society dominated by violence. In Wiltshire, troops were called out to deal with disgruntled weavers. On New Year's Day 1727, a party heading for Devizes in a 'riotous manner' clashed with mounted dragoons. The wild weavers responded with insults to the 'good advice given them' by the soldiers, and shots were fired before they dispersed. A fortnight later, near Dartmouth in Devon, it was the forces of law and order that came off worse. The port's customs boat encountered a heavily laden smuggling vessel close to shore near the Mew Stone. The five 'tidesmen' ignored warnings to keep off. Their zeal cost them dear: no sooner had one of them swung a leg over the smuggler's gunwale than a vicious scrimmage erupted. Before it ended four of the revenue men had been shot or cut about. One of them died on the spot, another was so badly injured that his life was 'much despair'd of'. Only the steersman escaped unscathed.

Even public entertainment could prove a bloody business. At 'Mr Stokes's Amphitheatre', near London's Sadler's Wells, Boxing Day 1726 certainly lived up to its violent name. There, five bouts were to be fought with the backsword: this was a yard-long stave of stout ash, with a basketwork hilt giving some protection for the wielder's hand. The 'sport' involved two men whacking each other about the unguarded head and shoulders until one of them considered that he'd had enough. As the *Weekly Journal*'s jovial Christmas Eve advertisement put it, 'he that breaks the most heads' would earn himself a silver-laced hat to adorn his own. There was more backswording on 27 December, this time for the prize of a fine Holland shirt. Next day the wrestlers had their turn, with the foremost grapplers of Moorfields and Harrow-on-the-Hill disputing possession of a pair of buckskin breeches.

For 'gladiators' tempted to test their mettle and skill in Stokes's Amphitheatre, the dangers were all too obvious. But it wasn't only participants who risked life and limb there. During one bare-knuckle boxing match, William James – himself 'a boxing fellow and horse-courser' – took umbrage when a hapless spectator clambered clumsily up into the viewing galleries. James lashed out, kicking 'one Mr Caroon', a biscuit-maker, under the left jaw so violently that he dropped dead on the spot, 'leaving a wife and three children behind him'. The hot-tempered James promptly left the scene, his departure no doubt speeded by the recent fate of his brother-in-law, a convicted murderer whose rotting corpse was currently hanging in chains as a grim warning to others.

Such sorry episodes provided the bread and butter fare that filled the columns of Britain's numerous metropolitan and provincial newspapers. But December 1726 also produced a choice morsel that journalists

and their readers relished for weeks. The story concerned 'the imposture of the Rabbit Woman'. It was widely reported, and almost as widely
believed, that Mary Tofts, from Godalming in Surrey, had given birth
to seventeen rabbits. Tofts's case created a sensation. On 3 December, as
the *London Journal* informed its readers, the Rabbit Woman had been
brought to London at the express command of King George I himself.
She'd been lodged in the Bagnio in Leicester Square, where 'great numbers of the nobility' had called to see her. Many prominent physicians
were also in attendance, 'another birth being soon expected'.

In its next edition of 10 December, the same newspaper revealed that
it was all a hoax. Those who had swallowed the scam entire included
leading surgeons. Some of *them* were now frantically backtracking in
a futile effort to salvage their tarnished professional reputations. As
the *Journal* gleefully added, Nathaniel St André, anatomist to the royal
household itself, 'who published an account of her wonderful delivery',
had since 'promised a particular account of the frauds she used, and by
what means she impos'd upon him and the public'.

The Rabbit Woman herself remained tight-lipped, refusing to say
anything more without a promise of His Majesty's pardon for herself
and her accomplices. On the 17th, the *Journal* provided its readers with
full particulars of the story. Its gynaecological approach left little to the
imagination: Tofts's confidence trick was no more than a variation upon
the magician's standby of pulling rabbits out of a hat. The correspondent who supplied these details trusted that they would expose fully the
'imposture of this wicked woman' who had so terrified and abused
the 'weak and credulous'. Tofts spent Christmas 1726 incarcerated in the
Bridewell, where 'infinite crowds' of people flocked to gawp at her. In
the New Year she faced prosecution in the court of the King's Bench.[1]

At Westerham in Kent, these same weeks produced nothing to rival
the strange case of the Rabbit Woman. Its births were unremark-
able enough by the standards of the age. But one at least would be
remembered long after Mary Tofts had become nothing more than an
embarrassing footnote in medical history. On 2 January 1727 a child
was born to Edward Wolfe, a middle-aged lieutenant-colonel of Foot
Guards, and his much younger wife, Henrietta Thompson. The boy was
soon after christened James.[2]

Once he had undergone his dramatic transformation into 'The late brave General Wolfe', the popular *London Magazine* felt able to state with confidence that the hero of Quebec was by birth a Yorkshireman. North of the border, the canny journalists of the *Scots Magazine* proved more circumspect. Whilst also reporting that James Wolfe was born in the venerable city of York, that newspaper hedged its bets by at least acknowledging the rival claim of Westerham. The Wolfe family's ties with Yorkshire were certainly strong enough to justify the speculation that followed James's death, but, as one of many bad poets later crowed, the future conqueror of Canada was indeed 'the man of Kent'.[3]

Passing through Westerham earlier in that decade, the celebrated and well-travelled writer Daniel Defoe found it to be 'a neat handsome well built market-town ... full of gentry, and consequently of good company'. Colonel Wolfe and his dark-haired bride swiftly found their niche in these congenial surroundings. The Wolfes set up home in the gabled Tudor mansion of Spiers on the Maidstone road. James however, was born in the nearby vicarage, where his mother had been invited to stay during the final stages of her pregnancy whilst her husband was away on regimental business. Almost exactly a year later, the family was completed when Henrietta Wolfe was safely delivered of another son, named Edward like his father.[4]

James's birth fell within the last year of the reign of His Britannic Majesty King George I, and the first in the far longer rule of his son. In fact, the thirty-three-year monarchy of George II would coincide almost exactly with the life of James Wolfe himself. The kingdom that George II inherited on 20 June 1727 was in a state of transition. Three years before, when he introduced the first volume of his remarkable *Tour through the Whole Island of Great Britain*, the indefatigable Defoe had emphasized the bewildering pace of the changes then taking place throughout the land: the steady decline of old towns, families and industries was matched by the equally dramatic rise of new; indeed, these fluctuations were so widespread and rapid that he had no doubt that commentators who followed in his footsteps would not lack fresh material for their own accounts.

In Defoe's eyes, the land that he criss-crossed so thoroughly on horseback was 'the most flourishing and opulent country in the world'. Although its economy remained predominantly agricultural, a long-established manufacturing sector was poised upon the brink of massive growth. James Wolfe's lifetime witnessed the beginnings of a process that would underpin Britain's emergence as the first industrial nation. This gradual transformation rested upon a unique combination of circumstances: rich mineral resources; dramatic population growth; the evolution of a viable transport infrastructure of canals and turnpike roads; and a thriving overseas trade. This last factor was itself largely a consequence of the fact that the kingdom formed the hub of what Defoe could already describe as 'this great British Empire'.[5]

In 1727, in striking contrast to the situation a century later, Britain's overseas possessions lay to the westward, across the Atlantic; they embraced several West Indian islands and the teeming colonies lining the east coast of the North American continent. The colonies not only provided prized raw materials, such as tobacco, sugar and furs, but also offered crucial markets for Britain's manufactures.

Originating in the tenuous Virginian and Massachusetts bridge-heads of the early seventeenth century, by the accession of George II these, and the other colonies that followed in their wake, had matured into populous and sophisticated societies with their own cities, own newspapers – and own elected governments. Although subject to royal authority, and regarding themselves as loyal British subjects, they had grown accustomed to a high degree of autonomy.[6]

To the intense chagrin of their more respectable inhabitants, the American colonies had recently become a convenient dumping ground for British felons – like Defoe's own fictional Moll Flanders – who had been marked down for transportation after escaping the hangman's noose. But many others crossed the Atlantic voluntarily: the booming colonies exerted a powerful lure for those keen to build a new life in the New World.

The opening decades of the eighteenth century heralded a steady flow of emigrants from the kingdoms of Great Britain and Ireland, and also from Europe. The sheer scale of this largely one-way traffic did not go unnoticed by contemporaries. Citing letters from New York dated 20 October, the London Journal of 10 December 1726 reported how 'in the two preceding months, above a thousand passengers from England, Holland and Ireland, had arrived there, and at Philadelphia'. In coming years, this vast folk movement showed little sign of slackening. By the middle of the century, the British colonies already held a population of one and a half million – no less than a quarter of the estimate for England and Wales.[7] During those same decades, the concerns of North America came increasingly to dominate British foreign policy. They would also shape the destiny of James Wolfe.

Precious little is known of Wolfe's childhood, although biographers have naturally speculated about his boyish pastimes and the friendships forged amidst the wooded hillsides surrounding his birthplace. It is possible that both James and his brother Edward were sickly lads who suffered from chest complaints. This is certainly suggested by a noxious recipe for the treatment of consumption recorded in Henrietta Wolfe's household book: green snails and earthworms variously pricked, sliced, pounded, washed in beer and baked before being distilled in milk with roots, herbs and spices; the resulting potion to be administered in dosages of two spoonfuls.[8]

In a painting of 1777, Benjamin West imagined the young James Wolfe surrounded by armour, military treatises and a plan depicting the Duke of Marlborough's great victory over the French at Blenheim in 1704. West's canvas was as fanciful as his earlier and more celebrated *Death of Wolfe*, but James and his younger brother no doubt grew up in an environment in which military matters loomed large. After all, their father was a career soldier who had served under Marlborough in Flanders and against the Jacobites in the rebellion of 1715. Lieutenant-Colonel Wolfe was himself the son of an army officer, also named Edward, who'd been wounded in the service of William III.

Genealogical opinion divides over the identity of James's paternal great-grandfather. Romantics favour Captain George Woulfe of Limerick, an ardent Royalist who was lucky to escape with his life when that city fell to Parliament's forces in 1651. Given George's Catholicism – a creed at direct odds with the staunch Protestantism espoused by the later Wolfes – a more likely, if less glamorous, candidate is Lieutenant-Colonel Edward Wolfe, who came to Ireland in 1649 with Cromwell's New Model Army.

Whether the great-grandson of Cavalier or Roundhead, soldiering ran in James Wolfe's blood. Through his mother, who belonged to the old-established Yorkshire family of Tindal of Brotherton, he could likewise claim descent from warrior stock. Indeed, Wolfe's remote ancestors included two of medieval England's most celebrated paladins – King Edward III, vanquisher of the French at Crécy and founder of the Order of the Garter; and Henry Percy, the hero of the old border ballad of *Chevy Chase*, and immortalized by Shakespeare as 'Harry Hotspur'.[9]

In 1738, when James was eleven, the family moved to Greenwich. In the opinion of Defoe, who had so admired Westerham, the Wolfes could not have made a better choice. Greenwich was, he wrote, 'the most delightful spot of ground in Great Britain; pleasant by situation, those pleasures increased by art, and all made completely agreeable by the accident of fine buildings, the continual passing of fleets of ships up and down the most beautiful river in Europe; the best air, best prospect and the best conversation in England'.[10]

Besides such recommendations, Greenwich possessed other, more practical, advantages. In Westerham the Wolfe boys had received rudimentary lessons at the local school; now they were able to benefit from the more extensive curriculum available at Reverend Samuel Swinden's recently opened establishment for the sons of the army and naval officers who clustered in the town. The move also brought Lieutenant-Colonel Wolfe closer to the heart of government at Westminster, and to the sources of influence and patronage that might reactivate his stalled military career.

The Wolfes' relocation was timely. A long era in which the 'Prime Minister' Sir Robert Walpole had sought to keep Britain free from entanglement in costly and disruptive foreign wars was now drawing to a close. Throughout the 1730s relations with Bourbon Spain had grown increasingly strained. Britain had captured Gibraltar in 1704, and its subsequent refusal to relinquish the Rock represented a continuing affront to Spanish dignity. Across the Atlantic, the foundation of Georgia in 1732 had created a fresh zone of friction between Britain's thriving North American colonies and Spanish Florida to the south.

Above all, an illicit trade between English merchants and Spain's American territories had prompted a draconian response from exasperated Bourbon officials. Lurid tales of Spanish atrocities against honest English tars were seized upon by Walpole's political opponents and a vociferous anti-government press to whip up the popular clamour for war. Exactly when Captain Robert Jenkins of the *Rebecca* lost his ear to brutal Spanish coastguards, and whether he actually presented the pickled organ to a horrified House of Commons, are both matters of debate. The massive publicity surrounding Jenkins's case nonetheless reflected the root causes of the conflict and gave it the curious name by which it remains known, 'The War of Jenkins's Ear'.

No longer able to stand against the jingoistic tide, Walpole was obliged to accept the inevitable: on 30 October 1739, amidst widespread rejoicing, Britain formally declared war upon its old enemy. For many Englishmen, the prospect of hostilities in Spanish America was an alluring one. It stirred patriotic memories of Elizabethan sea-dogs like Drake and Raleigh, and such buccaneers as Henry Morgan, whose assaults upon the Spanish Main in the 1670s offered yet another tempting precedent.

Initial tidings from the Caribbean had done nothing to dash these expectations of easy plunder at the expense of the hapless 'Dons'. News that Rear-Admiral Edward Vernon had captured Porto Bello, on the Isthmus of Panama, reached England in March 1740 and sparked universal jubilation. Vernon's exploit was credited with reviving 'British Glory' after humiliating years in the doldrums: the admiral became Britain's first popular hero, and his victory was commemorated in an extraordinary proliferation of public addresses, odes, medals, Toby jugs and street names.[11]

Such overtly patriotic responses prefigured those that would greet the news of Quebec's conquest nineteen years later. It was therefore apt that the mood of optimism engendered by Vernon's triumph should lead to James Wolfe taking the first teetering steps upon his own path to glory.

Tidings of Porto Bello's fall encouraged the administration to build on this promising beginning by ordering a substantial expedition to reinforce Vernon's squadron in the West Indies. The combined force would then strike against Spain's Caribbean possessions.

A powerful fleet commanded by Sir Chaloner Ogle was to rendezvous at Spithead, whilst the neighbouring Isle of Wight provided the assembly point for a landing-force of redcoats under Lord Cathcart. British North America was invited to join this assault upon the common enemy. Orders were dispatched to the royal governors of the colonies or 'provinces' to begin raising an 'American Regiment' of 4000 men. Their proclamations met with an enthusiastic response as volunteers from Massachusetts to North Carolina stepped forward to share in the spoils of the Spanish Empire.[12]

For all the enthusiasm that surrounded its outbreak on both sides of the Atlantic, this 'War of Jenkins's Ear' found Britain ill-prepared to wage a major conflict. After a quarter century of peacetime retrenchment, its armed forces now struggled to place themselves upon an effective war footing. On paper at least, Britain was Europe's leading naval power in 1740, with more warships than the French and Spanish fleets combined. Yet this apparent maritime superiority, seemingly demonstrated by Vernon's swift seizure of Porto Bello and celebrated soon after in Thomas Arne's 'Rule Britannia', was deceptive. Britain's wooden walls were useless without experienced crews to man them, and at the onset of war with Spain such trained seamen were in short supply.

During the summer of 1740, as the West Indian expeditionary force assembled, this manpower crisis was exacerbated by a typhus epidemic that swept through the ports of southern England. Despite the high public expectations of its capabilities, it was scarcely surprising that the undermanned and overstretched Royal Navy failed to prevent the departure of Spanish and French squadrons bound for the projected theatre of operations in the Americas.[13]

Nor were Britain's land forces ready to wage a major colonial war. Unlike the Royal Navy, which at least enjoyed popular approval as the bulwark of English liberties and trade, the army was viewed with a suspicion that impaired its effectiveness. To those who recalled the political upheavals of the previous century, the very notion of a permanent, or 'standing', army kindled fears of military despotism, whether imposed by a republican like Oliver Cromwell or an 'absolute monarch' such as James II. After James was ousted by William of Orange in the 'Glorious Revolution' of 1688, the new king was obliged to bow to his English subjects' ingrained fears of militarism by accepting stringent parliamentary controls over the size of his regular army. Although the army underwent massive expansion during the long wars against Louis XIV that straddled the turn of the seventeenth and eighteenth centuries, it was swiftly pruned to the bare minimum after the peace of 1713.[14]

Despite Marlborough's famous victories over France's hitherto invincible armies, and the danger to domestic security highlighted by the Jacobite rebellion of 1715, Britain's peacetime army was thereafter maintained at a level that any self-respecting continental power would have sneered at. At the onset of the War of Jenkins's Ear, the regular establishment totalled just 35,000 men: of these, a quarter languished in foreign garrisons ranging from Minorca to Antigua, whilst no less than half provided a strategic reserve that was hidden from prying eyes on an entirely separate Irish Establishment. In 1739, a scant 9000 soldiers were actually based in the kingdom of Great Britain itself.[15]

War with Spain brought only a modest augmentation of these paltry forces: six new regiments of marines were authorized in November, although parliamentary concern over the size of the standing army ensured that the bulk of their manpower was actually drafted from existing regiments. For experienced and ambitious officers like Edward Wolfe, however, the looming hostilities brought long-awaited opportunities for active service and advancement; he secured promotion to colonel of the first of the new marine regiments.

As the priority placed upon raising such 'sea soldiers' suggests, Walpole's administration envisaged a war dominated by amphibious operations. Unlike Britain's last major confrontation, the War of the Spanish Succession, this would be an overwhelmingly maritime conflict, waged over issues of trade and aimed squarely at Spain's prosperous colonial possessions. It has therefore been viewed as Britain's first clear-cut war for empire, and as a trial run for the Seven Years' War of 1756–63.

In July 1740, Colonel Wolfe joined the troops assembling for the West Indian expedition. He duly departed for Portsmouth, taking the thirteen-year-old James with him as a 'volunteer'.[16] Such young officer cadets could expect to gain valuable insights into the workings of military life. Attached to individual regiments, volunteers were also well placed to impress senior regimental officers with their potential, and so to compete for ensigns' commissions when vacancies arose. Whilst officers' commissions were customarily bought for fixed prices under the established 'purchase' system, a volunteer who distinguished himself by gallantry in action might achieve his crucial first step on the promotion ladder without paying anything.

As their coach reached the crest of Portsdown Hill, Colonel Wolfe and his eldest son would have witnessed a spectacular panorama. To either side spread the flat Hampshire and Sussex coastline, indented with creeks and harbours like a vast jigsaw. Prominent on the right were the sturdy Norman keep and Roman bastions of Portchester Castle, where Henry V had mustered another English expedition in 1415 before leading it to victory at Agincourt. Directly ahead and across the salt flats of Portsea Island stood the formidable ditches and ramparts of Portsmouth and its fortified dockyard. Beyond lay the bristling masts of Ogle's fleet, the silver band of the Solent and the gentle hills of the Isle of Wight.

The troops encamped around the island's leading town of Newport included the half dozen regiments of marines and two of line infantry – Brigadier-General Thomas Wentworth's 24th Foot and Colonel William Blakeney's 27th Foot. Since the declaration of war, recruiting parties had been busy in an effort to complete these units. As always, the recruiting sergeants faced an uphill task: whilst the Spanish war was popular enough with the population at large, the British Army was not. The meagre pay and brutal discipline endured by the rank and file ensured that recruits were typically confined to the most adventurous or desperate amongst the 'lower orders'.

It was not only the notoriously harsh conditions of life in the ranks that discouraged enlistment. 'Thomas Lobster' – as the redcoated British soldier had recently been nicknamed – seldom enjoyed the esteem that his civilian countrymen lavished upon his naval counterpart 'Jack Tar'. For the humble labouring classes who provided the army with the bulk of its manpower, the decision to 'go for a soldier' represented a shameful loss of caste. With no barracks beyond a handful of traditional garrison towns, most battalions were lodged in alehouses and livery stables amongst resentful and suspicious civilians. Many units pursued a semi-nomadic existence as they footslogged across Britain from one wretched billet to another. Regiments were habitually scattered over wide swathes of the country – with dire consequences for their training and discipline.

The duties required of these redcoats merely reinforced their unpopularity. There was no professional police force to maintain law and order, so soldiers were often obliged to quell the era's endemic rioting.

For example, during the autumn of 1738, Henry Harrison's 15th Foot had occupied Bristol, where they had been sent to tackle rioting coal-heavers. Such duties ensured that the redcoat was all too easily cast as the state's enforcer – a tool of tyranny rather than a symbol of national pride.[17]

In an age when hunger usually offered the most powerful incentive to take the king's shilling, dearth resulting from the hard winter of 1739 and the poor harvest that followed probably helped to lure likely lads to the colours. The physical standards required of recruits were never high, and were lowered further in wartime when the demand for manpower became acute. Some of those enlisted in 1740 nonetheless failed to match even these specifications. Youngsters drummed up for Blakeney's battalion were so scrawny that they could barely shoulder their muskets. Lord Cathcart refused to allow the regiment to join the expedition; it was replaced by Harrison's 15th Foot, fresh from its stand-off with the truculent coal-heavers of Bristol.[18] Brigadier-General Wentworth showed great zeal in disciplining the troops assembled for the expedition; this earned him the respect of the commander-in-chief. Yet Wentworth lacked combat experience: Cathcart's faith in this tireless drillmaster was destined to have disastrous consequences.

The first of many surviving letters that James Wolfe wrote to his mother during his military career was sent from Newport camp. By then the troops had already embarked aboard the fleet and James and his father were about to join them. James Wolfe enjoyed a close relationship with his mother, and his letter expresses an affection that goes beyond the merely dutiful. Having failed to reply to her last letter as swiftly as she expected, he was now at pains to assure her of his sincere love. He continued:

> I am sorry to hear that your head is so bad, which, I fear, is caused by your being so melancholy; but pray, dear Mamma, if you love me, don't give yourself up to fears for us. I hope, if it please God, we shall soon see one another, which will be the happiest day that ever I shall see. I will, as sure as I live, if it is possible for me, let you know everything that has happened, by every ship; therefore pray, dearest Mamma, don't doubt about it. I am in a very good state of health, and am likely to continue so ...[19]

Despite this confident declaration, James was far from well. He had expected the fleet to sail within a fortnight, but the expedition was dogged by continuing manpower problems and contrary winds. It did not finally get under way until October. By then the troops had spent the best part of two months packed into transport ships, tormented by seasickness and obliged to subsist upon their salted rations. This was the worst possible preparation for a force facing a winter crossing of the Atlantic with a Caribbean campaign at the end of it. James Wolfe was a life-long martyr to seasickness: it was scarcely surprising that he became so ill that he had to be put ashore at Portsmouth and sent home to Greenwich before the fleet had even weighed anchor.

Although this must have represented an acutely embarrassing outcome for the teenager, it probably saved his life. For all the high hopes that sailed with it, the expedition that eventually rendezvoused with Vernon at Jamaica in the spring of 1741 met a dismal fate: in a pattern that would be repeated with depressing regularity for as long as the Caribbean continued to count in British strategy, a formidable expedition arrived in the tropics, only to melt away in a matter of months as malaria and yellow fever swept through crowded decks and filthy encampments. Nine out of every ten soldiers who sailed from Spithead in October 1740 never returned to England: it is unlikely that Colonel Wolfe's sickly son would have been numbered amongst the survivors.

James Wolfe played no part in this unfolding tragedy, but the factors behind the failure of Britain's West Indian operations of 1741–42 deserve analysis here, not least because their disappointing outcome instilled a widespread belief that the British Army and Royal Navy could never work together.[20]

At the outset, the delayed departure of the expedition greatly reduced its chances of success. The hiatus of more than a year between Vernon's triumph at Porto Bello and the arrival of the reinforcements from Britain and North America gave the Spaniards ample opportunity to perfect their already formidable shore defences. In addition, by the time the fleet reached the West Indies, soldiers and sailors alike were weakened by scurvy and in a poor condition to resist the ravages of tropical disease.

Before then, Cathcart had himself succumbed to dysentery. His successor, the inexperienced Wentworth, suffered from a chronic lack of self-confidence. Although the army and navy commanders were expected to exercise a joint command, it was the bullish Vernon who dominated proceedings from the start. When the force sailed from Jamaica in early March, the objective was Vernon's own favoured target of Cartagena. For the admiral, the fleet's needs were always paramount. When sickness devastated his crews, Vernon browbeat Wentworth into providing replacements from his own depleted regiments, so weakening the army before the land campaign had even begun.

The troops were disembarked near Cartagena on 22 March 1741, after the warships' broadsides had pummelled two small forts guarding the harbour entrance. Despite this encouraging start, subsequent operations were blighted by hesitation and bungling. On 20 April, a night-time assault on the crucial fort of St Lazarus was repulsed with heavy casualties. Both the planning and execution of this attack were botched: there was no artillery battery to breach the defences or provide covering fire for the assault columns; the scaling ladders were too short to reach the ramparts; and most of the grenades hurled by the storming parties failed to explode because their shells were too thickly cast. The British rank and file fought bravely enough, but the attack lost momentum after their equally raw officers insisted upon drill-book tactics. Drawn up in close formation, they were mown down by musketry and cannon fire.

The novelist Tobias Smollett experienced the full horrors of Cartagena as a surgeon's mate aboard the fleet, and recalled them sardonically in the pages of *Roderick Random*. He likened the stolid redcoats to 'their own country mastifs, which shut their eyes, run into the jaws of a bear, and have their heads crushed for their valour'. More than six hundred men were killed or wounded before the attack was called off. Edward Wolfe's marines covered the retreat of the survivors.[21]

These included the eighteen-year-old private Duncan Cameron, who enjoyed a lucky escape on the bloody slopes before St Lazarus. He stumbled and fell, so avoiding the cannon ball that passed overhead and killed the man behind him. In his published memoirs, Cameron provided a brief but accurate summary of subsequent developments at Cartagena:

> Our men at this place grew very sickly, and died very fast, and the rainy season coming on, it was thought most expedient to raise the blockade, which we did, without doing much further damage to the enemy, than

battering down and ruining several strong forts going into the harbour. And indeed the difference that was known to subsist between the general and admiral I apprehend was a great cause of our miscarriage.[22]

The inter-service friction identified by Cameron was the overriding factor in the expedition's failure: such animosity denied the venture the ungrudging cooperation crucial for the success of any combined operation. When the joint force returned to Jamaica, projected descents upon Cuba and Porto Bello were also abandoned amidst mutual recrimination. The grand expedition intended to humble Spanish pride in the Caribbean petered out in early 1742. It had achieved nothing. But the human cost was appalling: out of some 14,000 Anglo-American troops who ultimately participated in the campaign, no fewer than 10,000 died, the vast majority victims of tropical illness. Losses amongst the ships' crews have never been tallied but must have added thousands more to the casualty lists.

Back in Britain, dismay at the scale of the disaster was fuelled by a wave of pamphlets written by jaundiced veterans. Admiral Vernon's partisan dispatches placed blame for the débâcle squarely upon the indecisive Wentworth and his redcoats. His views carried the day and, to James Wolfe's contemporaries, Cartagena became a byword for British military ineptitude. Indeed, the disastrous West Indian expedition of 1740–42 provided an object lesson in how *not* to conduct an amphibious campaign. This damning verdict influenced perceptions and expectations of Britain's armed forces that go some way to explain the euphoria that would later greet the very different results achieved by a new generation of commanders that included James Wolfe himself.

Amongst the expedition's disillusioned survivors was Colonel Edward Wolfe. His bitter recollections left a strong impression upon his eldest son. Writing from the Caribbean, the Colonel had emphasized not only the mortality amongst the officers but also the 'utmost discouragements' that had resulted 'from the want of simple prudence and unanimity'. Reporting his father's comments, James now acknowledged that providence had undoubtedly played a role in his own ignominious return from Spithead. 'As for me,' he told his friend William Weston, the assistant schoolmaster at Swinden's Academy, in January 1742, 'I am sufficiently thankful that my carcase was not equal to my zeal else the good collonel would soon have been put out of all anxiety on my account.' James revealed that he was now hopeful of securing an ensign's commission in Colonel Scipio Duroure's 12th Regiment of Foot.[23]

In fact, at that time James *already* held the equivalent rank of second-lieutenant in his father's regiment of marines. Wolfe's first commission was dated 3 November 1741, and reached him in the following month whilst he was spending Christmas at Westerham with his old friend, George Warde of Squerryes Court. But as James had ruefully informed Weston, despite this 'formal entrance into a military career', he was 'not in the least puff'd up at the near prospect of cutting a martial figure'. Although his father had wished him to enter the marines, his mother was resolved that he should never serve in that corps, 'owing to the peculiarity of my constitution, which makes salt water and me bitter enemies'. In any event, there was precious little prospect of joining a regiment that remained on active service in the remote Americas; and, in truth, Edward Wolfe can scarcely have wanted his son to join him amongst the disease-ridden human wreckage of the doomed Caribbean expedition. There was also another factor to be considered: like all newly raised wartime units, the marines were likely to be disbanded at the end of hostilities. For a young man determined to make the army his career, an old-established 'line' regiment of foot offered a more promising foundation. With that end in mind, the remarkable Henrietta Wolfe was busy lobbying on her son's behalf; but, until a new commission was forthcoming, James would be obliged to play the 'stoic', preparing for his chosen profession by struggling to improve his grasp of Latin and mathematics. Wolfe begged Weston to exercise discretion regarding this latest hitch in his plans; having plainly suffered the jibes of his classmates following his inglorious return from the Isle of Wight, he 'could not easily bear to be teas'd again on that score'.[24]

On 27 March 1742, Wolfe's hopes were fulfilled when he was exchanged into Duroure's Regiment with the rank of ensign. By then, the inglorious War of Jenkins's Ear had already become subsumed within a broader conflict that would complete James Wolfe's transformation from callow youth to seasoned veteran.

2

First Campaign

Oh Polly, oh Polly, the rout has now begun,
And we must march away at the beating of the drum,
Go dress yourself all in your best and come along with me,
And I'll take you to the cruel wars in High Germany.

Anon, 'High Germany'

The events that led James Wolfe to undergo his baptism of fire on the plains of 'High Germany' stemmed from the actions of another ambitious young soldier. Although not yet known to history as 'the Great', the newly crowned Frederick II of Prussia was nonetheless impatient to take his place amongst Europe's power brokers. Frederick's chance came in October 1740, at much the same time that Britain's ill-fated West Indian expedition finally sailed from Spithead.

The death of the Holy Roman Emperor, the Habsburg Charles VI, on 19 October 1740, rocked the balance of power on the Continent. His family domains centred upon Austria, Bohemia and Hungary, but were scattered as far afield as the Netherlands and Italy. When Charles died, the disparate Habsburg territories were inherited by his young and inexperienced daughter, Maria Theresa. Scenting weakness, the Bourbon powers of France and Spain, and the rising military state of Prussia, closed in for the kill. Prussia struck first, mounting a devastating invasion of Silesia. Austria was Britain's valued ally on the Continent, where Habsburg power had long provided a counterweight to the influence of France. Britain's primary foreign policy objective was to prevent France from becoming the dominant European land power. Walpole's government responded to the crisis by raising subsidies for Austria's defence.

Yet the situation was complicated by the fact that George II was not only king of Great Britain and Ireland but also elector of the north-west German state of Hanover. George's notorious obsession with the well-being of his hereditary Electorate added an awkward twist to Britain's foreign relations and was the cause of much ill-feeling amongst opposition politicians, who argued that Hanover's interests were being placed above Britain's. Such criticisms were not without grounds: to guarantee Hanover's neutrality during the looming conflict, George was obliged to cast his own vote as one of the electors for Holy Roman Emperor in 1741 in favour of France's nominee, Charles Albert of Bavaria.[1]

Discredited by the disastrous outcome of the Spanish war he had never wanted, Walpole was finally forced from power in 1742. Foreign policy now fell under the control of the King's favourite John Carteret, Earl Granville. He sought to construct a coalition strong enough to counter France. To this end, Maria Theresa was to be persuaded to accept Prussia's annexation of Silesia, securing Frederick's withdrawal from hostilities and relieving pressure on the Austrian army.

As Carteret pursued his diplomatic objectives, Britain's role in the conflict escalated from financial support to military intervention. A mixed force of infantry, cavalry and artillery was assembled for foreign service. On 27 April 1742, the troops were inspected by the King and his sons, Frederick, Prince of Wales, and William Augustus, Duke of Cumberland. A vast crowd of Londoners descended upon Blackheath to view the colourful array. Those on parade included the lanky fifteen-year-old James Wolfe, now resplendent in the scarlet coat, yellow facings and gold lace of an ensign in Duroure's Regiment.

Marching directly to Woolwich and Deptford, the regiments embarked aboard transport ships which carried them down the Thames and across to the Austrian Netherlands. Roughly akin to modern-day Belgium, this low-lying region was already known to generations of redcoats by the evocative name of 'Flanders': its strategic importance guaranteed that many more British soldiers would become acquainted with the mud and blood of this same 'cockpit of Europe'.

The convoy reached Ostend on 10 May and next day proceeded inland to its quarters in the historic cities of Bruges and Ghent. Although the British contingent was in Flanders to fight for the Empress, the redcoats were scarcely perceived as liberators by her indifferent subjects. In Ghent, where Wolfe was billeted, mutual dislike between the soldiers and their reluctant hosts soon escalated into violence. One lethal fracas erupted after a misunderstanding in the city's market place. An off-duty soldier picked up a piece of meat from a stall to sniff it for freshness, his comrades claimed; or to steal it, according to the local butchers. The hapless redcoat was slashed across the face with a butcher's knife, and the stallholder skewered for his pains. A vicious mêlée ensued as irate butchers and burghers attacked the soldiers with cleavers and spits: the beleaguered Britons were only rescued after a dozen dragoons spurred into the mob, cutting down everyone in their path and scattering the rest. Major-General Henry Hawley blamed alcohol for a situation that had threatened to provoke a full-scale battle between townsfolk and troops: it being the infantry's payday, 'allmost the whole garrison was drunke'. With few officers present, the troops had been about to run riot when the cool-headed Major-General Charles Howard took control and shepherded them back to their barracks.[2]

James Wolfe's earliest surviving letter from Ghent is dated 27 August 1742; it was evidently not the first he wrote home from his new quarters, and fails to provide his initial impressions of what was clearly a lively period.[3] Luckily, it is possible to fill this gap through the diary of another young subaltern who was quartered in nearby Bruges. An accident-prone but observant native of County Durham, Ensign Hugh McKay chronicled the chequered relations between the men of the British expeditionary force and their surly Flemish hosts during the summer and winter of 1742–43. McKay's journal also offers a vivid insight into the British Army of the mid eighteenth century. In particular, it illuminates the outlook, character and customs of the close-knit officer corps within which James Wolfe was destined to spend his adult life.[4]

At Bruges, like Ghent, there was friction between soldiers and civilians: on 26 June, in revenge for an unspecified 'affront', the mob pelted the guard with stones. These 'creatures' were dispersed, and the ringleaders confined. According to McKay, the locals had employed similar 'tricks' against the Hungarians who had formerly garrisoned the town, 'which being never reported they imagined they might with impunity play the same tune over again to the English; but beware of broken pates the next attempt'. On 1 July British troops were once again a focus of attention, albeit for a very different reason. That afternoon Sir Robert Rich's Dragoons rode into town complete with their black

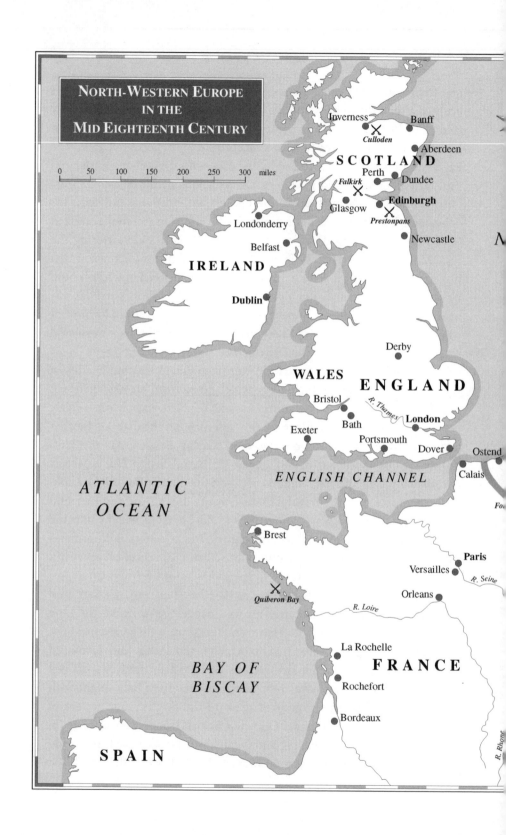

NORTH-WESTERN EUROPE
IN THE
MID EIGHTEENTH CENTURY

0   50   100   150   200   250   300   miles

SCOTLAND

Inverness
✕ Culloden
Banff
Aberdeen
Perth
Falkirk ✕
Dundee
Glasgow
Edinburgh
✕
Prestonpans
Newcastle

Londonderry
Belfast
IRELAND
Dublin

Derby

WALES   ENGLAND

Bristol
R. Thames
London
Bath
Exeter
Portsmouth
Dover
Ostend
Calais

ATLANTIC
OCEAN

ENGLISH CHANNEL

Brest

Paris
Versailles
R. Seine
✕
Quiberon Bay
Orleans
R. Loire

BAY OF
BISCAY
La Rochelle
FRANCE
Rochefort
Bordeaux

SPAIN

R. Rhône

kettle-drummers. Musicians of African descent were a long-established feature of British regimental life, but 'the people stared like bewitched, wondring to see blacks amongst the English soldiers'.

All eighteenth-century armies were plagued by desertion, and those facing each other in the Low Countries were no exception. That autumn witnessed a steady interchange of manpower between British units and the neighbouring French garrison of Dunkirk. On 7 October, no fewer than seven French deserters arrived at Ghent; six others followed on the 10th. All were 'set at liberty'. Two British deserters, who had enlisted with the French but then changed their minds and sought a passage to England, were not so lucky. They were 'snap'd up' at Ostend, and brought back to Bruges to face military justice. Both were sentenced to death by a general court martial. Trained soldiers were valuable commodities, and the British Army could ill afford to lose two lives when one would provide an example. Early on 20 December, a detachment of the garrison formed up on the Grand Parade to witness a grim lottery as the pair drew straws to decide which of them would face the firing squad. The youngest went first and picked 'the fatall billet'. He died so bravely that even his executioners wept.[5]

When arrested, these deserters had been wearing the uniform ('red turn'd up with black plush') of Claire's Regiment. This unit formed part of the French Army's famous 'Irish Brigade'. Originally recruited from exiled supporters of the ousted James II in the 1690s, it continued to draw heavily upon Ireland's disadvantaged Catholic majority. With its sizeable Irish Establishment, the British Army also recruited many Irishmen; although 'papists' were theoretically proscribed, the red-coat battalions undoubtedly included Irish Catholics. When such men tired of King George's service, the Irish Brigade provided convenient alternative employment.[6]

James II had died in 1701, but his son James Francis Edward, 'the Old Pretender', remained a figurehead for those Jacobites who hoped that this 'King over the Water' would one day return and replace the upstart Hanoverians with the rightful Stuart dynasty. Expressions of pro-Jacobite sentiment were widespread within British society, and not unknown within the British Army itself: on 19 October Ensign McKay noted that a private of Cornwallis's Regiment received the second of two instalments of four hundred lashes 'for drinking the Pretender's health'.

In accordance with the court martial's sentence, he was drummed out of the garrison with a halter around his neck. On 31 January 1743, the same seditious toast cost another soldier a thousand lashes, to be laid on 'at four different times'.

Despite the undoubted brutality of army discipline, in which such floggings with the cat-of-nine-tails featured all too regularly, British officers could display a paternalistic concern for the ordinary soldiers under their command. For example, on 15 August a collection was taken at church for the dependants of an infantryman whose musket had detonated whilst he was loading it. This accident blew 'away one of the poor creature's fingers and in a most terrible maner shatter'd another'. As McKay reported, 'the whole congregation (except a certain officer's wife and sister) contributed something towards so good an undertaking'. And it was through the intercession of his officers that another private, who had been sentenced to death for desertion, was pardoned on 12 January 1743 by the British contingent's commander, Lord John Stair.

Regardless of rank and responsibility, British officers remained notoriously touchy about their 'reputation'. They were quick to fight each other in defence of their honour, although such encounters often owed more to gutter brawling than the etiquette of the formal duel. On 24 August, when a camp was held outside the town, Colonel John Campbell generously provided the officers with 'an elegant cold entertainment'. This, combined with the excessive heat of the day, may have contributed to an ugly quarrel between two field officers who, 'in the hight of their passion', drew their swords and fell upon each other with such fury that one weapon was 'broke to pieces and the other very much bended'. The antagonists themselves fared little better: one was wounded in three places, the other slipped and broke his arm.[7]

Tempers were scarcely cooled by the frustrating months of 'phoney war': on 31 August, odds of five guineas to two were laid against any battle being fought that year. Yet, for McKay at least, garrison life was far from dull. Heavy drinking sessions, usually leading to 'harmless mirth and jollity', provide a recurring theme in his diary. On 11 September, whilst on an excursion to Ghent, a friend invited him 'to the wetting of his commission'. The evening's celebrations grew rowdy: there were 'great wagers laid at billiards' with 'some gentlemen prodigiously out of humour at the balls and table because they had lost their money, and swore mightily they had never plaid so ill in their lives'. McKay had planned an early night on 18 September but thought better of it and instead pocketed the key to his lodgings and sauntered down to the regimental 'club': he was admitted as a member that night, and when 'the reckoning was called for, the colonel was so kind as to pay my share of it'.

Wednesday 29 September saw one of the many elaborate processions that punctuated the Catholic religious calendar. A dean was installed amidst the Baroque ostentation of the church of Notre-Dame, but McKay's thoughts were on earthly matters: 'I never in my life long'd so much to speak French as to day', he wrote, 'for I stood by one of the prettiest girls in town and had not a word to say to her.'

How did the gangling young James Wolfe fit into this boisterous society of hard-drinking and hot-tempered 'gentlemen'? Not surprisingly, Wolfe's letters home to his parents offer a rather different perspective upon garrison life in the Low Countries than that provided in the pages of McKay's candid personal journal: if Wolfe encountered scenes of drunkenness and depravity, he evidently chose not to report them.

As related to his highly-strung mother, the teenaged ensign's pleasures were innocent enough: he had acquired a flute, and often played upon it; he spent much time with his old Westerham friend George Warde, who was now serving at Ghent as a cornet of dragoons; and, yes, he was eating well but had little taste for drink, although 'there is very good rum and brandy in this place, and cheap, if we have a mind to take a little sneaker now and then at night just to warm us'. Like Bruges, Ghent offered plenty of company. And, unlike the frustrated McKay, Wolfe was at least able to subject the local females to his schoolboy French.[8]

Whilst youngsters like Wolfe and McKay grew acquainted with the routines and rituals of army life, generals and diplomats were debating the direction of the Allied war effort. As the summer of 1742 dwindled away in indecision and inactivity, Lord Stair grew increasingly frustrated at the curbs that George II and his advisers placed upon him. Stair was an experienced soldier who had fought at the bloody battle of Steenkirk in 1692, and subsequently participated in all four of Marlborough's great victories. Although now nearing seventy, the years had done little to mellow him: he wanted nothing less than an assault upon the fortified port of Dunkirk, followed by a march inland against Paris itself. Events favoured Stair's audacious plan. In June, Prussia's withdrawal from the conflict in exchange for Silesia had freed Austrian troops to deal with an isolated French force in Bohemia; the despatch of further French regiments to extricate this detachment left France's own northern frontier dangerously denuded of manpower.

Stair was reminded, however, that just as the French were only participating in the conflict as 'auxiliaries' of Bavaria, so Britain's troops served merely as auxiliaries of Maria Theresa. As Britain was not even at war with France, any assault upon French territory would be perceived as blatant aggression. The cautious George opposed such a provocative and risky endeavour, instead preferring a march into Germany that would both safeguard his beloved Hanover and support Austrian efforts against the French.

The wrangling over strategy continued until autumnal rains finally extinguished Stair's hopes of invading France. The commander of the Austrian troops, Léopold Philippe de Ligne, Duc d'Aremberg, now travelled to London in person to secure Whitehall's backing for a German campaign. Having seen his own advice repeatedly spurned, the exasperated Stair contemplated resignation before reluctantly accepting the situation and grappling with the logistical preparations for a spring offensive in the east.[9]

The British component of what would become known as the 'Pragmatic Army' finally left its winter quarters at the beginning of February 1743. Duroure's was amongst the first units to take to the road. By now the fifteen-year-old Edward Wolfe had also secured an ensigncy in the regiment and would quite literally be following in his brother James's footsteps.

It was a punishing march under harsh weather conditions. Neither of the Wolfe brothers possessed a robust constitution, and they suffered accordingly. After just five days of foot slogging James was already showing the strain. Though he never marched into quarters without 'aching hips and knees', he remained nevertheless 'in the greatest spirits in the world'. With supplies uncertain, both Wolfes had tasted the tough 'ammunition bread' issued to the private soldiers. By April they had acquired a horse, taking turns to ride it, although Edward had been obliged to dismount to negotiate knee-high snowdrifts near Bonn. Just months out of school, the younger Wolfe was already accustomed to bedding down on straw.[10]

As the British pursued their laborious progress eastwards, Stair still hoped to deal the French a vigorous blow where they least expected it. With thoughts of emulating his old chief Marlborough's celebrated march from Flanders to the Danube in 1704, Stair now urged a junction with the Austrian forces on that river. Once again, Stair's aggressive strategy was vetoed. The orders he finally received from London were less ambitious: he was to occupy the high ground dominating the junction of the rivers Rhine and Main, where the Allies would be conveniently placed to throw their weight behind King George's own nominee for the vacant electorate of Mainz.[11]

Although increasingly hampered by a lack of forage, by early May the Allied forces were strung along the north bank of the Main to either side of Frankfurt. To the south, a powerful French force of 70,000 men under the command of Marshal Adrien Maurice, Duc de Noailles had concentrated at Speyer on the Rhine ready to support their countrymen in Bavaria. Bullish as ever, Stair crossed the Main to confront Noailles as he advanced along the high road to Frankfurt. Noailles declined the challenge. Anxiously monitoring developments from Hanover, King George feared that the Allies would engage the enemy before he could assume personal command. At his frantic bidding, Stair reluctantly recrossed the Main. With the French now controlling the river's southern bank, the Allies could expect no further supplies by water.

On 19 June George finally arrived to take charge of the British and Hanoverian troops camped around the village of Aschaffenburg. Here a bridge spanned the Main, but French forces barred the way across. Over the next week, whilst George dallied in his camp, the supply shortage became a crisis. The starving redcoats resorted to plundering the countryside: on 26 June, as discipline threatened to collapse, the army began retreating to Hanau in hopes of securing provisions.

The morning of 27 June 1743 found the Pragmatic Army in a predicament. Word that the Allies were on the march had reached Noailles in the early hours. He lost no time in arraying his forces to snare them in what he later described as a 'mousetrap'. When the Allies quit Aschaffenburg, a strong force of French infantry was ordered to cross the Main and dog their heels. Ahead of the Allied column, an even larger body of foot, horse and artillery crossed the river at Seligenstadt on pontoon bridges and deployed to bar the way forward. This wing of the French Army was placed under the command of Noailles's young nephew, the Duc de Grammont; it occupied a formidable defensive position screened by the Forchbach and Haggraben streams and the boggy ground that bordered them. The sole bridging point lay at the village of Dettingen, which was swiftly occupied by the French.

Dawn revealed batteries of heavy cannon on the far side of the Main: these were well posted to bombard the Allied march. As a glance at the sketch-map shows, the Pragmatic Army was now boxed in by the enemy on three sides; on the fourth, escape was effectively blocked by the wooded Spessart Hills. As they slogged down the narrow corridor that remained open to them, the Allies came under a galling cannonade from the flanking batteries across the river. With casualties mounting, the Pragmatic Army's situation now appeared more perilous than ever. Noailles's methodical dispositions presented the Allies with an unenviable choice: ignominious surrender; or a determined effort to prise open the jaws of the trap. For a soldier-king like George II, the first option was unthinkable. His army therefore began the laborious process of deploying from column of march into line of battle.

The Allies would fight, although a frontal assault upon the French Army beyond Dettingen was a daunting proposition. Yet for reasons that remain unclear, Grammont now abandoned his strong position behind the Forchbach stream and marched through Dettingen to fight in the open. It is possible that he hoped to catch the Allies off guard as they altered front; perhaps he believed they intended to take their chances in the hills; but whatever the logic behind it, Grammont's decision shortened the odds against the Pragmatic Army. Across the Main, Noailles looked on aghast as his careful plans went awry.[12]

Dettingen was a bottleneck; like a popping cork, the leading French battalions proved incapable of resisting the pressure mounting behind them as ever more white- and blue-coated troops poured through its streets. When the foremost regiments spilled into the open countryside beyond they were in considerable confusion. A thousand yards away, the British, Hanoverians and Austrians had finally shuffled into fighting formation. Contrary to convention – which prescribed an infantry

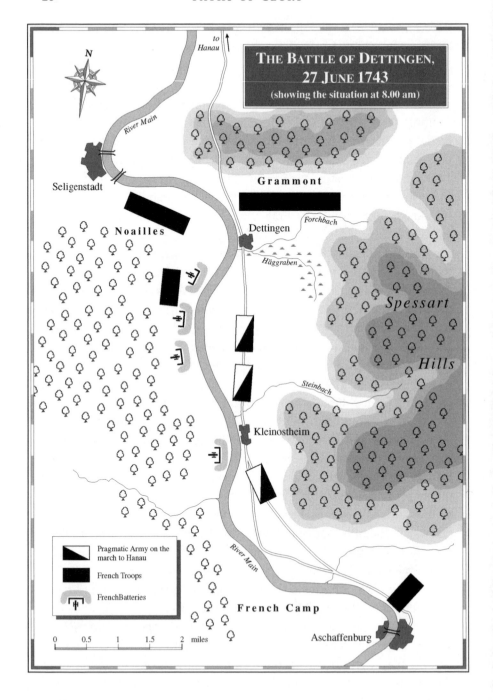

THE BATTLE OF DETTINGEN,
27 JUNE 1743
(showing the situation at 8.00 am)

centre and cavalry wings – lack of space forced their commanders to place the horse *behind* the foot.

No less cramped than their opponents, Grammont's disordered battalions now launched an uncoordinated attack over the marshy terrain dividing the armies. The Allies marched to meet them but were themselves soon obliged to halt and correct their alignment. When the advance resumed, the British and Austrian infantry opened fire without orders. The unscheduled fusillade startled King George's horse, sending it galloping to the rear as the mortified monarch frantically attempted to draw rein. Finally dismounting, and thereafter trusting to his own two feet, George joined his beloved Hanoverians on the right of the line; with drawn sword in hand, he would be the last British monarch personally to command his soldiers in battle.

It was not only the Pragmatic Army's horses that had reason to be skittish that day: many of its officers and men were likewise steeling themselves for their first taste of action. By a remarkable coincidence, those about to undergo their baptism of fire included not only James Wolfe but also a trio of subalterns destined to loom large in his future: Lieutenant Jeffery Amherst, who acted as *aide-de-camp* to Lieutenant-General John Ligonier, was to lead the expedition against Louisbourg in which Wolfe would gain his first taste of popular fame; and two aristocratic youngsters, Ensign Robert Monckton of the Third Foot Guards and George Townshend, who was serving as a volunteer on the staff of Lieutenant-General Lord Dunmore, would both serve under Wolfe as brigadiers at Quebec.

For them and many others, Dettingen provided a bewildering introduction to the realities of eighteenth-century warfare. The precise evolutions and clockwork volleys of the drill-book and parade ground were exchanged for a chaotic free-for-all in which the rank and file fired as fast as they could load, prime, and pull the trigger. Soon the battlefield was wreathed in the dense banks of smoke that inevitably resulted from the mass ignition of black powder weapons.

As the advancing redcoats swiftly discovered, the sheer volume of fire emanating from the Allied line was effective enough in its own irregular way. An officer in the Royal Welch Fusiliers reported that 'when the smoak blew off a little, instead of being among their living, we found their dead in heaps by us'. The first line of French infantry was eventually repulsed. A second likewise recoiled after what another British officer described as 'a very bloody and well-fought battle on both sides'.

The French cavalry offered even tougher opposition. Eager for action, the elite household brigade attacked the Allied left. Bland's Dragoons spurred forward to bar their way. Although badly outnumbered, they fought tenaciously, losing some three-quarters of their strength in killed and wounded. Most of the British cavalry proved less resolute. They attacked impetuously, only to be thrown back in confusion and obliged to shelter behind their own scornful infantry. These battalions of foot now confronted the victorious Gendarmes of the Maison du Roi. In the words of one British officer, they trotted forwards 'most charmingly'. Brandishing a brace of pistols apiece and with broadswords dangling from their wrists, they discharged their firearms, flung them at the stolid red-coated ranks, and charged home with cold steel. Courage and momentum carried many clean through the Scots Fusiliers, but in the close-quarter fighting that followed their saddles were swiftly emptied. Under pressure from fresh British and Austrian dragoons, what remained of the Maison du Roi was forced back.

With both infantry and cavalry rebuffed, the French army now began to give ground; a hail of case shot from a rapid-firing Hanoverian battery on the British right helped them on their way. In theory, Grammont's men could have resumed their former position and continued to contest the vital Dettingen bridge. But many of the French infantry battalions had suffered heavily during the recent campaigning in Bohemia, and the replacements drafted into them from the militia were raw and ill disciplined. Disorder spread swiftly through their ranks and retreat soon escalated into rout. Hundreds drowned in a panicked scramble for safety across the Main. Presented with this unexpected outcome, and despite the urgings of Stair, King George hesitated to risk what he had gained by authorizing a vigorous pursuit. According to the cynical young George Townshend, 'the scene of action and military ardour was suddenly turned into a Court circle' as the King 'was congratulated by every military courtezan on horseback'. Meanwhile the French escaped unmolested.[13]

Dettingen was not the decisive victory that it might have been, but it was enough. Disaster had been averted. Indeed, had George II and his

son William been snared in Noailles's 'mousetrap', the national humiliation would have been unthinkable, rivalling that inflicted upon the
French by the Black Prince at Poitiers back in 1356. Across the Channel
the news was greeted with palpable relief and wild celebration. George
Frideric Handel marked his patron's triumph by composing the *Dettingen Te Deum*, whilst the general populace needed no prompting to get
roaring drunk. Following the disappointments of the Caribbean campaign, Dettingen provided a tonic for the jaded national morale. As one
contemporary pamphlet bragged, the outcome would 'convince foreign-
ers, and the *French* in particular, that Englishmen are as brave as ever'.

Britons had faced the hereditary foe and proved themselves worthy
of their forefathers under the immortal Marlborough. Both James and
Edward Wolfe had emerged unscathed from this brutal rite of passage.
They were lucky to do so. Duroure's Regiment had occupied the centre
of the first line and was in the thick of the fight; it suffered ninety-six
casualties – the highest of any British infantry battalion engaged that
day.

Something of Dettingen's confusion and horror is reflected in a letter from James to his father. Although just sixteen years old, he was
already fulfilling the key function of regimental adjutant. As such, he
had started the battle on horseback, only to be thrown when his mount
was wounded. Like other British officers, Wolfe subsequently did all
he could to persuade his men to hold their fire until the French were
within effective range: he ordered, he pleaded – but they blazed away
just the same. Composed a week later in a detached and almost non-
chalant style, his letter nonetheless provides a graphic account of the
carnage inflicted by the French round shot as it bounced through the
close-packed ranks of redcoats: 'I sometimes thought I had lost poor
Ned, when I saw arms, legs and heads beat off close by him', he wrote.
The stress of combat seemingly left James both mentally and physically
exhausted: soon after the battle he grew 'very much out of order' and
was obliged to keep to his tent for two days.[14]

For many other Britons, the immediate aftermath of the glorious
victory was equally depressing. That night, as a private in the Life
Guards recorded, 'there fell as heavy a rain as ever I saw'. The army
lay under arms and within half an hour all were soaked to the skin.
In the cold light of dawn, the extensive battlefield presented a dismal

prospect. One British cavalryman found the whole area 'cover'd with dead and mangled bodies, limbs, and wounded men'. The horror of the scene was only compounded by the 'deplorable condition' of the injured horses. He confessed: 'Though I can truly say, that I was not the least discouraged in the action, yet this sight shock'd my very soul!'[15]

French casualties and prisoners were estimated at 5000. The Allies lost about half that number in killed and wounded. The latter included Trooper Thomas Brown, of Bland's Dragoons, who had disregarded multiple sword cuts to rescue one of his regiment's fallen guidons. Missing two fingers, with a brace of bullets in his back and his face hacked like a butcher's block, Brown was rewarded with promotion and popular celebrity. The disfigured hero subsequently received a pension with which he bought a tavern in his native Yorkshire. But for Thomas Brown the scars of Dettingen were not merely physical: within three years he had drunk himself to death.[16]

On the afternoon following the battle the Allies arrived at Hanau, where badly needed supplies were waiting, along with 12,000 fresh Hanoverian and Hessian troops. Despite these reinforcements, George ignored Stair's plea to maintain his moral advantage by crossing the Main and severing the French line of retreat to the Rhine. In a now familiar scenario, the commanders of the polyglot Allied contingents remained at loggerheads over strategy. It was not until the end of July that George could be persuaded to agree to a joint offensive in conjunction with Austrian troops under Prince Charles of Lorraine. So sluggish was the Pragmatic Army's advance that it required thirty days to march as many miles to Worms. Here, news that the French had established a strong defensive position on the River Queich, and that Prince Charles had yet to pass the Rhine, convinced George that he had gone far enough.

Seeing his advice repeatedly spurned, and exasperated by these continuing delays, Lord Stair finally resigned his command on 4 September. In mid September, the tardy Dutch contingent at last joined the Pragmatic Army. Heartened by this development, and intelligence that the French had abandoned their lines, George inched forward once again, reaching Speyer on 27 September. The campaign now over, the Pragmatic Army dispersed to its old billets in the Low Countries.

For all its frustrations, the campaign of 1743 had at least yielded concrete results. Grumbling British taxpayers received a victory for their money and the French were bundled out of Germany; operations would thereafter focus upon the traditional, and more convenient, battlegrounds of Flanders. For the Wolfe brothers there had also been compensations for the hardships and dangers endured. Both were now veterans; indeed, young Edward had been dubbed 'The Old Soldier' by his men. Within a month of Dettingen, James not only received a commission confirming his appointment as adjutant to Duroure's Regiment but was also promoted to the rank of lieutenant.[17]

He remained keen to build upon this promising start by forging contacts amongst the powerful and influential. Having witnessed the Duke of Cumberland's coolness under fire at Dettingen, even speaking with him as the cannon balls fell around them, James had already identified at least one potential patron. Writing to his father from Worms, he voiced his admiration for the King's favourite son, hoping 'some day or other to have the honour of knowing him better than I do now'.[18]

That winter, Duroure's battalion was quartered at Ostend. Whilst many other officers, including his own younger brother, crossed the Channel for a spell of leave, James Wolfe remained with his regiment. As a bantering but rather wistful letter to Ned back in London suggests, the minutiae of regimental administration was not the only thing on his mind:

> I'm glad you find the mantua-maker pretty; I thought so, I assure you. I give up all pretensions. Pray use her kindly. Doubtless you love the company of the fair sex. If you should happen to go where Miss Seabourg is, pray don't fall in love with her. I can't give her up tamely. Remember I'm your rival. I'm also in pain about Miss W— Admire anywhere else and welcome (except the widow Bright). Miss Patterson is yours if you like her, and so is the little staring girl in the chapel, with £20,000. Pray give my duty to my mother. I hope she is well. The plum-cake she gave me was very good, and of singular service to me.[19]

For all its sacrifices, Wolfe's dedication to his chosen career was now paying dividends. On the 3 June 1744, he secured a captain's commission in one of the British Army's senior infantry units, Lieutenant-General John Barrell's 4th, or 'King's Own' Regiment of Foot. Even allowing for James's unusual zeal, this was a rapid rise indeed. Such accelerated promotion no doubt owed much to the influence and purse of his father, who had now progressed to the rank of brigadier-general. Edward Wolfe junior, who returned to Duroure's with the rank of lieutenant, certainly attributed his own promotion to the general's generosity.[20]

By the spring of 1744, the Wolfe brothers were both serving with their units in the Allied army on the banks of the River Scheldt. After the high drama of the Dettingen campaign, the next year was a sorry anti-climax. Stair's baton as field-marshal in command of the British contingent passed to another seventy-year-old, George Wade. It was not a happy choice. Like Stair, Wade had fought bravely during the wars of King William and Queen Anne; he had subsequently supervised the building of a remarkable network of roads through the rugged and lawless Highlands of Scotland. In contrast to his predecessor, however, Wade lacked the initiative and strategic vision necessary for high command in the field. The result has been condemned as 'one of the dingiest campaigns ever waged by British arms and nourished by British gold'.[21]

In fairness to the aged and ailing Wade, he faced a task that would have taxed the genius of Marlborough in his prime. Now that the United Provinces had finally been persuaded to take the field against Louis XV, he was required to cooperate not only with d'Aremberg's Austrians but also a Dutch contingent under the Prince of Nassau. Ranged against these uneasy partners was a powerful French army commanded by one of the ablest generals of the day, Marshal Maurice de Saxe.

When the Allies finally opened their campaign, in May 1744, they lacked both unified command and common objectives. Saxe reacted with decision: within weeks the French had reduced Menin, Ypres and Furnes. In July, when Prince Charles of Lorraine invaded Alsace, so obliging Louis XV to divert troops from Flanders, George II urged Wade to exploit the situation by mounting an offensive. An advance towards Lille was eventually organized, but it subsequently stalled amidst logistical problems and acrimonious councils of war. This frustrating lack of progress began to take its toll on discipline. In August, Sir John Ligonier grew concerned at the 'dirty and ill dressed' appearance of the troops encamped at Anstain. For the future, majors and adjutants were to ensure that all men sent on duty should appear with their tricorne hats 'well cocked' and 'cravats well rolled', in 'marching gaiters' and with the long skirts of their regimental coats neatly hooked back.

But slovenliness was the least of the problems now besetting Wade's army. That same month General Orders railed against 'unheard of disorders ... committed by soldiers of all nations' against the local peasants. Houses had been pillaged, cattle rustled, and the 'country people' robbed 'in every shape by which the army is in danger of perishing by famine and the honest and orderly soldiers suffer for the crimes of the disorderly'. As such behaviour was a 'shamefull reproach on the king's arms' and would hamper future military operations, Wade was 'resolved to punish the guilty with the utmost severity'. Such warnings were ineffectual. Two weeks later further orders were issued for roll-calls to be held *four* times a day, whilst patrols would be out after 9.00 p.m. in a bid to stop soldiers 'straying'.[22]

In late October the British retired to winter quarters in Ghent. As one acerbic eyewitness commentator put it: 'Thus ended this inglorious campaign, to the satisfaction of none abroad, and I fear to the satisfaction of few at home.'[23] That same month Field-Marshal Wade resigned his command. He subsequently provided a convenient scapegoat for the Allies' lamentable showing, but his performance had been hampered by poor health, obstructive colleagues and the unsettling interference of Stair. King George, who preferred superannuated generals, expressed 'the most perfect satisfaction' in Wade's services; as events would soon show, even now old Wade had not yet earned his retirement.[24]

Whilst the campaigning season of 1744 produced no punishing marches or bloody encounters to match those of the previous year, it undermined the health of Edward Wolfe, who died, possibly of consumption, early that autumn. For James, the loss of his cheerful and devoted sibling was a source of grief and self-reproach. Although quartered within reach of the brother who had always 'pined' after him, James had been absent from the deathbed. As he explained to his mother, the knowledge that he *could* have been on hand to comfort 'Poor Ned' was the cause of 'many uneasy hours'. Here, the surface formality that typifies Wolfe's correspondence with his parents is punctured by outbursts of unrestrained emotion. He wrote:

God knows it was being too exact, and not apprehending the danger the poor fellow was in ... I know you won't be able to read this paragraph

without shedding tears, as I do writing it; but there is a satisfaction even
in giving way to grief now and then. 'Tis what we owe the memory of a
dear friend.[25]

That winter James Wolfe once again remained with his regiment in
Flanders. It was a dreary and depressing interval that nonetheless provided him with further opportunity to study the theory and practice
of his profession.

The Allies' failure to deliver concrete results in 1744 had contributed
to the downfall of Carteret, although the new ministry headed by Lord
Harrington continued the previous policy of hefty financial aid to
Maria Theresa combined with the maintenance of a sizeable continental
expeditionary force to cooperate with the Austrians and Dutch. There
had also been changes on the military front. The elderly Wade was
replaced by the twenty-four-year-old Duke of Cumberland. Although
nominated Commander-in-Chief of the Allies, the inexperienced Cumberland remained subject to the restraint of a general three times his
senior, the Austrian Marshal Königsegg. With the spring, the British
Army prepared for a fresh campaign. The Allies now mustered some
50,000 to set against the 75,000 French under Saxe.

Before the end of April, Saxe commenced operations by laying siege
to the fortress city of Tournai on the Scheldt. The Allies immediately
marched to its relief, but Barrell's Regiment stayed in garrison at Ghent,
and James Wolfe therefore missed one of the bloodiest days in the history of the British Army. Leaving a detachment to maintain pressure
on Tournai, Saxe prepared to confront the Allies from an extremely
strong defensive position at Fontenoy. Cumberland's reconnaissance
of the French army was inadequate, failing to detect a crucial redoubt
that defended the left flank of Saxe's line. When the armies engaged,
on 11 May, the Duke's tactics were unsophisticated. His frontal assault
came close to clinching victory, thanks largely to the spirit and discipline of his redcoated British and Hanoverian infantry. These battalions
advanced through a murderous crossfire to puncture the very heart of
the French position. There they remained under raking artillery fire
from the flanks, and were only repulsed after a desperate struggle in
which the fresh battalions of the Irish Brigade played a prominent role.
Their final retreat was conducted in good order.

The Hanoverians – hitherto the focus of bitter jealousy – now earned the ungrudging respect of the British Army. By contrast, the lacklustre performance of the Dutch, who had conspicuously failed to match the high reputation they had acquired during Marlborough's wars, generated much resentment. Indeed, the Dutch contingent's reluctance to push home the attack on the fortified village of Fontenoy was widely blamed for the defeat. Although composing half of the Allied force, their 1500 casualties were just a quarter of those sustained by the Anglo-Hanoverians. Amongst the worst hit of the British units was Wolfe's old regiment, Duroure's 12th Foot, which lost no less than eighteen officers and 300 men killed and wounded. Given the size of the butcher's bill, not least amongst the 'officers of lower rank', Wolfe could 'thank Providence' that Barrell's was not present.[26]

For James Wolfe, the slaughter at Fontenoy was itself providential. Barrell's Regiment was ordered to replace one of the battalions mauled in the battle, joining Cumberland's command on 21 May. In consequence, it escaped ignominious capture when the French followed up their seizure of Tournai by soon afterwards surprising Ghent and its garrison. It is also likely that the vacancies resulting from Fontenoy's bloody pruning of the British officer corps expedited Wolfe's own career: on 23 June, General Orders announced that 'Captain Wolf is appointed Brigade Major to Pulteney's Brigade'.[27] Although not actually an advance in rank, this was an important staff post that entailed day-to-day administrative responsibility for several infantry battalions. The appointment suggests that the precocious abilities and dedication of this gawky eighteen-year-old had not gone unnoticed by his superiors.

The costly rebuff of 11 May, and the French conquests that swiftly followed, provoked accusations of rashness against Cumberland. George Townshend, who served at Fontenoy on Lord Dunmore's staff, was amongst the most outspoken of the Duke's critics. By replacing the aged and experienced Wade with the young and inexperienced Cumberland, he postulated, the ministry had hoped that such contrasting qualities would produce opposite results. This was true enough, but not in the way envisaged. Indeed, 'An army, superior by half, attempted nothing in open plains last campaign; an army, in the same proportion inferior, attacked entrenchments, in this.' In Townshend's opinion, the ensuing defeat had been all too predictable.

Yet the punishing encounter at Fontenoy had done little to diminish the spirits of Cumberland's men. As they debated events around their campfires, Dettingen and Fontenoy were 'only game and game'. They remained confident of 'winning the rubber'.[28] But the anticipated rematch between Cumberland and Saxe in Flanders would have to wait. Britain's recent setbacks in the Low Countries had breathed new life into the moribund Jacobite cause. On 25 July, Charles Edward Stuart, the 'Young Pretender', landed at Moidart in south-west Inverness-shire. His aim was to eject the Hanoverian dynasty and reclaim the throne of Great Britain and Ireland for his father. Charles Edward had arrived with just half a dozen devoted supporters, but within weeks he was leading an army of several thousand Highlanders. For the immediate future, the first priority for James Wolfe and his comrades would be the suppression of rebellion within Britain itself.

3

Rebellion

Our Soldiers so brave, with rage being fired,
Had what they desired, with the rebels to fight;
For they never would flinch, nor give back an inch,
Till they made them fly,
For noble Duke William, for noble Duke William,
They'll conquer or die.

Anon, 'The Soldier's Praise of Duke William', 1746

News that the Stuarts had once again raised their banner in the far-flung Highlands did not at first arouse undue concern at Whitehall. For some time it was doubted whether the 'Young Pretender' himself had even landed at all, although the Lords Justices gave at least some credence to the rumours when they issued a proclamation on 1 August offering a reward of £30,000 to whoever should apprehend him in the event that he had the temerity to set foot upon British soil.

Once it was established that stories of the Prince's arrival were founded upon fact, the royal commander in Scotland, Sir John Cope, received orders to assemble all available troops and nip the rebellion in the bud. As a further precaution, the Dutch were asked to honour the treaty clause by which they were obliged to provide 6000 troops to safeguard the Hanoverian dynasty when required. No orders were yet issued for the recall of British troops from Flanders, but the Duke of Cumberland was warned to prepare for them.

Cope's command in Scotland totalled just 3850 men. In England there were no more than 6000 troops – most of them based in and around London. Writing in August, Lord Stair, who now commanded the forces in England, considered that these and the anticipated Dutch contingent would prove sufficient to quell the rebellion. But revolt in the distant Highlands was not the only threat facing the Hanoverian regime. If rebellion in the North were combined with invasion from France or Spain, as now seemed imminent, the danger would become acute.

On 20 August, in the light of this double hazard, the Lords Justices reappraised the situation. Concluding that the regular troops in Great Britain were inadequate for home defence, they sent immediate orders to recall the British garrison of Ostend. Given the precarious Allied position in the wake of Fontenoy, Cumberland was reluctant to part with a single man before Saxe had himself announced a formal suspension of hostilities by withdrawing into winter quarters. Surely, the Duke argued, the French had encouraged the 'Pretender's son' to embark upon his crazy venture with that very object of distracting British troops from Flanders?[1]

Yet it was all too soon apparent that the Young Pretender's appearance was no mere feint. In coming weeks General Cope struggled to contain the escalating insurrection in Scotland. Cope's dilemma owed more to a lack of resources than to his own shortcomings. Although doomed to eternal ridicule through the words of a rousing Jacobite song, 'Johnny Cope' was in fact an experienced professional soldier with nearly four decades of service behind him. He had played a creditable role in the German campaign of 1743, and had prevented the capture of Lord Stair after his escort was caught off guard by enemy hussars. Amongst those who noted Cope's gallant conduct on that occasion was James Wolfe himself. Cope served as a lieutenant-general at Dettingen, and in the mood of euphoria following that unexpected victory was amongst those created a Knight of the Bath.[2]

Even though his regular troops were few and of poor quality, Cope was persuaded to advance into the Highlands and tackle Charles Edward Stuart without delay. Concentrating at Stirling, he marched on Fort Augustus. Hearing that the Jacobites intended to defend the perilous Corrieyairack Pass, on 26 August Cope called a council of war; he accepted its recommendation to avoid confrontation and head for Inverness instead. Although understandable in the circumstances, Cope's decision permitted the Jacobites to advance into the Lowlands; ironically, their progress was expedited by Marshal Wade's fine new roads. On 17 September they captured Edinburgh itself.

News that the Young Pretender's bid for the throne was gathering momentum – and fears that this might finally tempt the French into mounting a full-scale invasion of Britain – increased the pressure upon Cumberland to release a substantial detachment from his Flanders army. On 4 September he was sent positive orders to return ten battalions without delay. Commanded by the veteran Sir John Ligonier, these reached the Thames on 23 September. Their arrival was timely. On the following day, shocking intelligence reached London: Cope's command had been utterly routed by the Highlanders in a bloody pitched battle.

During the previous weeks, events in Scotland had moved rapidly. Following Cope's controversial decision to make for Inverness, naval transports had rendezvoused with him at Aberdeen and ferried his little army down the coast to Dunbar. Cope's force disembarked on 18 September and, on the following day, marched towards Edinburgh. The Jacobites advanced to meet him. On 20 September the two armies made contact near Prestonpans, where Cope arrayed his troops in a strong defensive position.

That night a local Jacobite sympathizer indicated a route by which Cope's flank could be turned. The rebels' approach was detected by the general's outposts, so allowing him time to organize a formal line of battle. But when the Highlanders launched their broadsword charge, at daybreak on 21 September 1745, Cope's redcoats bolted with scarcely a show of resistance. After striving in vain to rally his panic-stricken infantry, Cope rounded up 450 dragoons and retreated to Berwick.

Prestonpans was over in minutes, but in that brief span the royal army lost some 800 killed and wounded from a total strength of around 2700. The carnage inflicted by the Highlanders' broadswords and Lochaber axes upon Cope's hapless troops lost nothing in the telling; if eyewitness accounts are to be credited, little exaggeration was necessary. Grisly descriptions of the battlefield are verified by the applications of Prestonpans casualties who eventually sought pensions from Chelsea's Royal Hospital. Wounds sustained by soldiers like Thomas Wattson of the 46th Foot – a forty-two-year-old 'scholar' from Colerane who received 'fifteen cuts in his head at Prestonpans' – suggest a frenzied assault that continued long after resistance had ceased. The horror aroused by such methods gave the Highlanders a psychological edge over their opponents; it would provide the British Army with an excuse to perpetrate barbarities of its own.[3]

News of Prestonpans caused consternation in London, although the providential arrival of Ligonier's command in the Thames helped to prevent alarm from escalating into panic. Orders were promptly issued for *another* eight of Cumberland's seasoned battalions to sail from Flanders directly to Newcastle-upon-Tyne; as the source of the coal that fuelled London's fires, that port was identified as a prime Jacobite objective.

Barrell's Regiment was amongst those embarked from Helvoetens-luys on 13 October, and Brigade-Major James Wolfe no doubt sailed with it. The convoy was scattered by North Sea gales, but the storm-tossed transports all limped into port within a fortnight. The troops assembling on Tyneside were to be commanded by Field-Marshal Wade, the very same general who had incurred so much criticism for his failures in Flanders during the inglorious campaign of 1744.

Wolfe was now serving alongside his father, whose declining health had done nothing to retard his own steady ascent of the promotional ladder. Now a major-general, Edward Wolfe was amongst a detachment of troops sent up the East Coast towards the fortified border town of Berwick; his gout obliged him to travel by post-chaise. Writing to his wife on 3 November, the sixty-year-old veteran had no doubt that the 'Pretender's Rabble' would soon be crushed, and that both he and James, who was 'well and eager for active service', would be home in time for Christmas. On 14 November, James wrote to reassure his mother about the general's safety 'for 'tis the opinion of most men that these rebels won't stand the King's troops'.[4]

The rebels constituted a far more formidable threat than either of the Wolfes appreciated. But rather than encounter Wade's sprawling army, the Jacobites avoided him altogether by taking a western route into England. Whilst the marshal struggled to impose order upon his heterogeneous command, half of which consisted of unenthusiastic and riotous Dutch and Swiss auxiliaries, the rebels' artillery battered the dilapidated medieval ramparts of Carlisle.

When Wade, on 16 November, finally began his march westwards from Newcastle, it was already too late. His sickly and dispirited troops made slow progress over bad roads in appalling weather. Their hardships were only exacerbated by inadequate supplies of bread, bedding and fuel. Each morning the benevolent Brigadier-General James Cholmondeley filled his pockets with sixpences, which he distributed in an effort to encourage the frozen and ravenous rank and file. Encountering heavy snow, the marshal's shivering troops plodded on as far as Hexham, only to learn that Carlisle had already fallen to the rebels. After a day of rest, Wade and his jaded army retraced their laborious steps, arriving back in Newcastle on 22 November.

Wade had turned back in the belief that the Jacobites would advance no further into England; he was again proved wrong when they proceeded unopposed into Lancashire. By the end of the month the Duke of Cumberland himself had been ordered to counter the threat; he was to coordinate operations with Wade, but if the two armies met the Duke would take command.[5]

Cumberland gathered a force of 8000 men in the midlands; they stretched along a straggling line centred upon Lichfield. Wade's own wandering army, including Brigade-Major Wolfe and Barrell's Regiment, began a sluggish progress south from Newcastle. With substantial royal forces arrayed to contest their advance and retreat, the 5000 Jacobites theoretically risked destruction in the claws of a pincer movement. But their leaders remained unperturbed. Marching through Cheshire, the wily Lord George Murray led one column on a westward feint: convinced that the Highlanders were bound for Wales, Cumberland swerved to counter the threat. Having sent the Duke marching in the wrong direction, Murray rejoined Prince Charles on the open road to Derby.

The only government force that now remained between the fleet-footed rebels and their goal of London was assembling north of the city at Finchley. It consisted largely of militia, although, as William Hogarth's lively and irreverent depiction of the preparations reminds us, these amateurs were stiffened by regular regiments, including the King's own Foot Guards.

Just *what* would have happened had the Jacobites pursued their march to London must remain one of the most intriguing 'what ifs' in British history. In the event, the motley Finchley army was never put to the ultimate test of a battlefield confrontation. Instead, Derby marked the limit of the Prince's advance into England. His commanders were

crestfallen at the conspicuous lack of support for the Jacobite cause
south of the border: although the rebel army had so far faced little
opposition, neither had its presence provoked the anticipated mass rising of Englishmen against the Hanoverian dynasty. In addition, there
was no evidence of the major French landing that had always been
considered fundamental to the venture's viability. Following an acrimonious council of war on 5 December, it was resolved that the Highland
army should withdraw to Scotland.

Unknown to the Prince and his officers, in their absence French
forces *had* landed on British soil, although the 800 or so regular troops
and half a dozen heavy guns that ran the Royal Navy's gauntlet to
reach the Highlands scarcely matched Jacobite expectations. Nominally
'French', these units – the Royal Ecossais Regiment and detachments
from the famous Irish Brigade – were in fact composed largely of Scots
and Irishmen. These tough and disciplined Celtic mercenaries added
another distinctive strand to the increasingly variegated fabric of the
Pretender's army; indeed, whilst the force that Prince Charles Edward
led into England consisted largely of Highlanders, the second Jacobite
army that coalesced in Scotland that winter included large contingents
of men drawn from the Lowland shires. Well armed with French-sup-
plied muskets, they too were far from despicable.

Cumberland chivvied the retreating Jacobites as best he could. Most of
his infantry were too exhausted from their recent forced marches to follow; 1000 of the fittest were set awkwardly upon horseback and joined
with the cavalry to form a flying column. It was hoped that Wade would
now block the Young Pretender's road to the north. But just as the aged
marshal had failed to catch the nimble Highland army on its southward
march, now he proved equally incapable of intercepting its subsequent
retreat. When Wade eventually reached Wakefield, on 10 December, it
was to discover that the Highlanders were at least three days ahead of
him. Sending a force of cavalry across the Pennines in the hope of severing Prince Charles Edward's route to Preston, the marshal returned
to Newcastle with his long-suffering infantry.

With the Highlanders now in open retreat before the royal forces,
pro-government commentators began to portray them as hunted ani-
mals. Yet Cumberland's quarry was far from defenceless. Turning at bay

at Clifton near Penrith, the Highland army staged a defiant rearguard action in which clansmen and dragoons crossed swords in the moonlight. After this savage little scrimmage – the last military engagement to be fought upon English soil – the Highlanders recrossed the border into Scotland.

As the threat from the north subsided, Cumberland was recalled to London, where lingering fears of a French invasion required his presence to head the army; frustrated at abandoning the chase, he obeyed with extreme reluctance. Though the Jacobite tide had receded to Scotland, the rebellion was far from over. For King George and his ministers, the presence of Charles Edward Stuart as regent or ruler of an independent northern kingdom was unthinkable: the disaffection must be cut out at its very source.

Alarmed by the sluggish reactions of 'Grandmother Wade', Cumberland urged the principal Secretary of State, Thomas Pelham-Holles, Duke of Newcastle, to replace the marshal with a more dynamic general of his own nomination. The royal troops destined to follow the Young Pretender across the border were therefore led by Lieutenant-General Henry Hawley – a man whom Brigade-Major James Wolfe was destined to know all too well.

Hawley was a hard-riding and coarse-grained cavalryman who hailed from a dynasty of tough professional soldiers. Now in his late fifties, he had received his ensign's commission in 1694 when just a boy. William III had felt honour-bound to provide in that way for the three orphaned sons of Colonel Francis Hawley, who had been killed at Steenkirk two years before; at the time, the eldest of them was only *eight* years old. As a captain, Hawley had been wounded at the disastrous battle of Almanza in Spain in 1707, and again, as a lieutenant-colonel of dragoons, at the indecisive encounter of Sheriffmuir during the Jacobite rebellion of 1715. Hawley was single-minded in his pursuit of lucrative appointments and notoriously tight-fisted. By his own admission, he spurned the chance to become a Knight of the Bath after Dettingen because he didn't believe that the honour justified the expense.[6]

But the dominating trait in Hawley's character was a brutality that had long since earned him the grim soubriquet of 'Hangman'. According to one observer, Hawley, 'if not a good soldier, studies to be thought so, by his severity of manners, and strictness of discipline'.

It was a matter for debate whether 'his rigour proceeds from a zeal for the service, or a sourness of temper; from a desire to rectify, or a delight to blame, as there are those, who think him better pleased, in finding those beneath him in fault, than in doing their duty, and escaping his censure'.[7]

Assembling his command at Edinburgh, Hawley marched to the relief of Stirling Castle. That crucial strongpoint guarded the traditional thoroughfare from the Highlands to the Lowlands; it was now held for King George by the ageing Cartagena veteran, General William Blakeney. As a young man, Hawley had seen the backs of Highlanders at Sheriffmuir and deemed them to be 'the most despicable enimy that are'. Yet he remained realistic enough to appreciate that this perspective was not shared by all of his men, particularly those demoralized by tales of the butchery at Prestonpans. In his orders of 12 January 1746, Hawley therefore sought to reassure them that there was 'nothing so easy to resist' as the 'Highlanders' way of fighting' – provided that the 'officers and men are not preposessed'd with the lyes and accounts which are told of them'.

In what remains a useful analysis of Jacobite tactics, Hawley explained that the 'True Highlanders' – the well-born and well-armed gentlemen who formed the enemy's shock troops – were invariably outnumbered four to one by 'Lowlanders and arrant scum'. The elite front-rank fighters usually opened fire when 'within a large musket shot, or three score yards', before discarding their unloaded firearms and charging home with the broadsword, all the while 'making a noise and endeavouring to pearce the body, or battalions before them'.

Hawley offered a 'sure way to demolish' the dreaded Highland onslaught. In theory at least his sovereign remedy was simple enough. Like those that had been issued to Cumberland's men at Lichfield in December, Hawley's orders emphasized disciplined, close-range musketry: indeed, his men were to hold their fire until the enemy came within just ten or twelve paces of their muzzles. Timing was everything, and Hawley drummed home the point in blunt words than can have done little to bolster his men's shaky morale:

> If the fire is given at a distance you probably will be broke for you never get time to load a second cartridge, and if you give way you may give your foot for dead, for they [the Highlanders] being without a firelock or any

load, no man with his arms, accoutrements etc can escape them, and they give no quarters.[8]

Hawley's 'directions' assumed cast-iron composure on the part of those obliged to face the howling clansmen. Yet, as events would soon demonstrate, it was this very quality that many of his men still lacked.

As he contemplated tackling the rebels besieging Stirling, Hawley established his army in a strong camp at Falkirk. Like Prince Charles Edward Stuart, the 'Hangman' headed about 8000 men. He was confident that this position ran no risk of surprise from the Jacobites, who lay encamped some three miles off. On the morning of Friday 16 January 1746 he therefore saw no reason to forgo breakfast at nearby Callendar House, home of the staunchly Jacobite Lady Kilmarnock.

At about 11.00 a.m., when, in Hawley's own words, his men 'were all boyling their kettles', outposts reported that the rebels were on the move. Major-General Cholmondeley saw them plainly enough through his telescope, although intervening hills masked their subsequent movements. The troops were called to arms; but, when another report claimed that the rebels had halted and appeared to be lighting fires, they were ordered to resume their disrupted dinner. It soon became clear, however, that the Highlanders were in fact marching swiftly for the summit of Falkirk Moor, which dominated the royal camp. Finally convinced that his presence was required, a hatless Hawley galloped to the scene; agitated and dishevelled, his appearance did little to inspire confidence. He immediately ordered his dragoons to ascend the rough hillside. The slower-moving infantry and artillery followed. The guns got no further than the lower slopes, but the infantry slogged onwards in a grim race for the high ground. It was hard going in the teeth of driving rain and an icy wind: 'as we march'd, all the way up hill, and over very uneven ground, our men were greatly blown,' recalled General Cholmondeley. Benefiting from their head start, the lightly equipped Highlanders reached the summit first, obliging Hawley to marshal his forces downhill from them.

At this moment, as Hawley remembered, 'there fell the most heavy rain that ever was seen with a hard gale of wind at West ... 'twas difficult to see or hear'. He nonetheless sent his cavalry against the Jacobite right wing. The clansmen there, under the command of Lord George Murray, held their fire before unleashing a devastating close-range volley. A handful of the surviving dragoons charged home but were worsted in a confused mêlée. The rest broke and fled in a human and equine avalanche that swept the indignant Hawley to the bottom of the hill. Sword in hand, the exultant Highlanders of the Jacobite right wing dashed after them.

Demoralized by the ignominious flight of the cavalry, panting from their recent climb, and with most of their cartridges now soaked and useless, many of the royal infantrymen offered little resistance in the face of the oncoming Highlanders. According to Cholmondeley, they 'gave a feint fire, and then faced to the right about, as regularly as if they had had the word of command, and cou'd not be rallied, 'till they got a considerable distance'.

But not all of Hawley's redcoats were inclined to turn tail at the mere sight of broadswords and tartan. Over on the British right, where a ravine screened the line, several battalions held their ground. Led by Cholmondeley and the popular Brigadier-General John Huske, these stopped the rebels in their tracks before calmly covering the army's retreat towards Linlithgow. Cholmondeley lavished praise upon the officers of Barrell's – Wolfe's own regiment – and Ligonier's 'for the spirit they shew'd'. Without their stand, he believed the royal army would have been 'cut to pieces'.[9]

In the gathering darkness many Jacobite units remained too dispersed to pursue effectively. But they occupied Falkirk and Hawley's abandoned camp, securing not only such traditional martial trophies as kettledrums and standards but also badly needed supplies of arms, ammunition and clothing. Jacobite casualties had been light, totalling scarcely one hundred killed and wounded. Hawley reckoned his own losses at 280 killed, wounded and missing; this was certainly too low and probably reflected the slain alone.

Falkirk was a tactical success for the Jacobites, but poor discipline amongst the rank and file, and an absence of coordinated leadership across the battlefield, prevented it from becoming anything more decisive. Yet the outcome undoubtedly represented another demoralizing reverse for King George's army. Like Cope's men at Prestonpans, too many of Hawley's redcoats had once again run like sheep before a Highland charge. To an experienced professional soldier like Cholmondeley, Falkirk was a 'scandalous affair'.

Reporting events to his friend and patron Cumberland, Hawley played down his own failure to read the Jacobite manoeuvres for what they were, and instead blamed the setback squarely upon the cowardice of the troops. True to form, he set about curing that deficiency by summoning courts martial. Consequent upon their verdicts, several officers were cashiered; some of their less privileged subordinates paid a higher price at the hands of Hawley's hangmen. The disgraced Cope took some satisfaction in the outcome: according to gossip, after the rout at Prestonpans he'd wagered that his successor would fare no better against the Highlanders: he collected a handsome £10,000 when Hawley was duly beaten in his turn.[10]

Unlike Hawley, James Wolfe had no reason to reproach himself for the setback at Falkirk: although hard evidence for his precise whereabouts is lacking, it is likely that he served with his own regiment and was amongst the officers who earned Cholmondeley's fulsome praise. But he shared his commander's desire to minimise the significance of the clash. Writing to his uncle William Sotheron, he refused to even dignify the 'encounter' with the title of 'battle', because 'neither side would fight'. As Wolfe viewed things, the check administered to the royal army was merely temporary. Indeed, it was 'now making all necessary preparations to try once more to put an end to this rebellion'.[11]

Although George II accepted Hawley's explanation of his rebuff, the 'Hangman' was swiftly replaced as commander-in-chief by Cumberland. The King's decision to entrust the eradication of the Jacobites to his son won widespread approval in military circles. Despite his conspicuous lack of headway against the French in Flanders, the bluff young Duke enjoyed the respect of his troops: he cared for their welfare; and, if no inspired military genius, was at least dogged and fearless under fire. Cumberland was genuinely popular with officers and men alike, and his appearance at Edinburgh on 30 January injected a badly needed boost to their morale.

Shortly before Cumberland's arrival, Brigade-Major Wolfe received a staff appointment as one of Hawley's *aides-de-camp*. What Hawley thought of his fiery young assistant is not recorded. If a later letter of Wolfe is any indication, he himself cannot have formed a very high opinion of his superior's character or generalship. He observed: 'The troops dread his severity, hate the man, and hold his military knowledge in contempt'.[12]

Under Cumberland's command the royal army marched once again to the relief of Stirling Castle. Abandoning the half-hearted siege, Prince Charles Edward withdrew and concentrated the bulk of his forces at Inverness. Cumberland advanced as far as Perth, where he halted to rest his troops and await the arrival of 5000 Hessians. These mercenaries were posted to guard the rivers Forth and Tay, whilst Cumberland pushed on to Aberdeen. There his infantry took a badly needed breather. After weeks of futile footslogging under Wade, and the loss of much clothing and equipment at Falkirk, many of them were now 'almost naked'. New shoes, breeches and waistcoats were brought in by sea, along with the provisions required to mount the next phase of the campaign.

The Duke made Aberdeen his headquarters for the following six weeks. Hawley lodged next door to Cumberland, in the house of Mrs Gordon of Hallhead and Esslemont. During this interlude an incident occurred that provides a rare glimpse of the young Wolfe – one that has caused some embarrassment to his devotees. According to Mrs Gordon's detailed statement, 'Major Wolfe' had called upon her one evening 'to tell me that by the Duke of Cumberland's and General Hawley's order I was deprived of everything I had, except the cloaths upon my back'. After delivering this disconcerting message, the major had reassured Mrs Gordon that Hawley was satisfied that she 'had no hand in the Rebellion' and would therefore allow her to keep 'any particular thing' that she wanted – and which she could prove actually belonged to her. In Mrs Gordon's recollection, however, it had not proved that simple:

> I then desired to have my tea, but the Major told me it was very good, and that tea was scarce in the army; so that he did not believe I could have it. The same answer was made when I asked for my chocolate. I mentioned several others things, particularly my china. That, he told me, was, a great deal of it, very pretty, and that they were fond of china themselves; but as they had no ladies travelled [sic] with them, I might perhaps have some of it.

But when Mrs Gordon asked after a painting of her son, Wolfe's professional interest was kindled. Haggling over household goods now became interrogation in earnest. Where was the boy? How old was he?

Fourteen? Then he was not a child at all, and would have to be produced. And so Mrs Gordon and the major parted.

On the following evening Brigade-Major Wolfe returned bearing Cumberland's assurance that Mrs Gordon would not be robbed. Yet whatever she sent for – breeches for her son, tea for herself, flour to bake bread – was refused her. Instead, her house was systematically looted. Some of Mrs Gordon's cherished china later turned up in the hands of a London antique seller; he had bought it from a prostitute to whom it had allegedly been given by Cumberland. But even the disgruntled Mrs Gordon felt obliged to record one small act of contrition by Hawley's young *aide-de-camp*: 'I should have mention'd above that Major Wolfe did one day bring me my son's picture, but without the frame, and he then told me that General Hawley did with his own hands take it out of the frame, which was a gilt one and very handsome'.

The sordid tale has prompted much soul-searching amongst James Wolfe's admirers. Surely the avaricious Hawley's brusque henchman could not be one and the same with the gallant hero of Quebec? In fact, as Wolfe's first serious biographer concluded, there is no reason to doubt the identification. But Robert Wright also emphasized that there were ample grounds for Wolfe's uncompromising stance: Mrs Gordon's husband George was actually serving in the Jacobite Army as secretary to Lord Pitsligo at the time, whilst, by the standards of the age, her son was mature enough to bear arms; Wolfe himself was scarcely older when he first embarked for Flanders. In addition, Wright argued, the fact that some of the goods pilfered from Mrs Gordon's house weren't even her own suggests that she was concealing the property of rebel friends.[13]

Leaving Mrs Gordon to contemplate her ransacked home, Cumberland and his army resumed their march northwards towards a final confrontation with the Young Pretender and his increasingly demoralized followers. Intelligence reports suggested that the Jacobites would contest the passage of the River Spey, so obliging the Duke to undertake 'a bloody piece of worke'; but the crossing on 12 April was unopposed. Two days later the royal army reached Nairn, where Cumberland issued extra cheese, biscuit and brandy so that the men could celebrate his twenty-fifth birthday on the following day.

Hoping to find the royal army sleeping off the consequences of this junketing, the rebels attempted to surprise Cumberland's camp on the night of 15–16 April. When it became clear that the Jacobites would not reach their destination before dawn, they were recalled amidst scenes of bickering and confusion. The long march merely exacerbated the exhaustion of men already weak from hunger. Reports that the Highlanders had intended to slaughter the royal troops as they slumbered drunkenly in their tents soon had sinister repercussions.

Early on the morning of 16 April, Cumberland's army finally came face to face with the rebels on the boggy expanse of Culloden Moor near Inverness. The bloody and lopsided encounter that followed remains one of the most emotive episodes in British history. With the benefit of hindsight, it is all too easy to view Culloden as the inevitable demise of a romantic but outmoded tribal culture at the hands of a modern state fielding the latest in military technology. Yet the royal ranks included hundreds of men who had recently fled from the Highlanders at Falkirk: there was no guarantee that they wouldn't do the same again.

As contemporaries on both sides recognized, however, there was no worse place for the deployment of Highlanders – and none better for a conventional force of infantry, cavalry and artillery. Cumberland's command also enjoyed a marked numerical superiority, of nearly 8000 to no more than 6000. In addition, many of the Jacobites were now dog-tired from their aborted march on Nairn. It was the wrong time and place to fight: that knowledge undermined the rebels' resolve and decided the outcome of the battle before a shot was fired.

The bare bones of what followed were described in a letter that James Wolfe wrote to his uncle, William Sotheron, on the day after the battle. In his recollection, the action began at about 1.00 p.m. and lasted for just an hour before the rebels were routed. As Wolfe wrote:

> The cannon in particular made them very uneasy, and after firing a quarter of an hour, obliged them to change their situation and move forward some hundred yards to attack our front line of Foot, which they did with more fury than prudence, throwing down their firearms and advancing with their drawn swords. They were however repulsed, and ran off with the greatest precipitation, and the Dragoons falling in amongst them completed the victory with much slaughter.[14]

As *aide-de-camp* to Hawley, who commanded the cavalry on the left flank of Cumberland's army, Wolfe's personal perspective was necessarily limited. Had he remained with his own regiment that day, his experience of Culloden would have been very different. Barrell's held the extreme left of the royal front line. This was the one point on the moor where the clans charged home through the storm of musketry and case shot to tackle the redcoats at close quarters. Barrell's had already stood firm before the Highlanders at Falkirk. If the Jacobites were unlucky at Culloden, it was not least because the weight of their charge fell most heavily upon the one battalion that was least likely to crumble before it. The regiment's experience that day nonetheless suggests that the outcome of Culloden might have proved very different if more Jacobite units had succeeded in reaching the royalists.

Barrell's buckled under the Highland onslaught, but it did not break: as Wolfe noted with pride, his regiment had resisted 'in a most obstinate manner'. Officers and men alike fought back doggedly. A savage mêlée ensued in which bayonet and musket butt were pitted against broadsword, axe and dirk. The price was heavy. Of Barrell's 350 officers and men, more than 120 were killed or wounded. Lord Robert Kerr was found covered in wounds and with his head split from crown to collar bone; Lieutenant-Colonel Robert Rich had his right hand lopped off and the left almost severed; Private Duncan Cameron, who had survived the expedition to Cartagena and the battles of Dettingen and Fontenoy without a scratch, was now 'cut and hack'd in a miserable manner'. It is unlikely that the brave but spindly Wolfe would have fared any better against the brawny Highland swordsmen.

Wolfe witnessed bloodshed enough at Culloden, but at less personal risk than his hard-pressed comrades in Barrell's. Hovering out on the flank, Hawley held back his dragoons until it was clear that the Jacobites were already broken. In eighteenth-century warfare, that moment – when the defeated ran and the victors unleashed their cavalry in pursuit – often produced the heaviest casualties of the day: excited troopers had a tendency to sabre helpless fugitives before their bloodlust abated. At Culloden, the customary chase was conducted with unusual ruthlessness. As one eyewitness reported, several troopers of the Duke of Kingston's Light Horse – a volunteer unit that had recruited heavily amongst the butchers of Nottingham – 'killed their fifteen and sixteen a piece'. By Hawley's own account, his dragoons 'cleared all the country for three miles before them and … made great slaughter every way'.

Although the French regulars were granted quarter, the rebels were not so fortunate. According to 'Hangman' Hawley, when Cumberland arrived at Inverness, he discovered that Major-General Humphrey Bland's troopers had 'taken about a hundred of the Irish officers and men prisoners but not one Scotchman'.[15]

The British Army's culpability for 'war crimes' at Culloden has generated considerable debate. Although the scale of the butchery was later exaggerated by Jacobite propagandists, enough atrocities *were* perpetrated against the helpless to lend substance to their claims. One pro-government writer, Andrew Henderson, actually conceded that Cumberland's soldiers 'stabbed some of the wounded men, and a party meeting others at Culloden House brought them forth and shot them'. Henderson sought to excuse this brutality on the grounds that the royal troops were 'warm in their resentment' at the ghastly wounds resulting from the Highlanders' penchant for cold steel. They also believed that the Jacobites had received specific orders 'to give no quarter to the Elector's troops on any account whatever'. This allegation was always hotly denied by the Jacobite army's leaders, and a 'copy' of the orders amongst Cumberland's papers that includes this clause looks like a crude forgery. But, whatever the truth of the matter, few royal soldiers doubted that the orders were genuine. In his letter to his uncle, James Wolfe cited them himself to justify the royal army's ruthlessness; he wrote approvingly that 'as few prisoners were taken of the Highlanders as possible'.[16]

Wolfe's uncompromising stance is at odds with a well-known anecdote concerning his conduct at Culloden. This remains amongst the most famous of all the stories told about him, so it deserves detailed consideration. The best-known version only appeared in print in 1802. It relates how, when crossing the battlefield, Cumberland noticed a wounded Highlander staring up at him. At this defiance the Duke ordered Wolfe to 'shoot me that Highland scoundrel, who thus dares to look on us with such contempt and insolence!' Wolfe replied: 'My commission is at your Royal Highness's disposal, but I never can consent to become an executioner'. From that day forward, the story goes, Wolfe declined in Cumberland's favour.

In another version of what is surely the same episode, recorded soon after Culloden and included in Bishop Forbes's pro-Jacobite collection

The Lyon in Mourning, the wounded Highlander was Charles Fraser of Inverallochie. According to Forbes's informant, James Hay, first 'one officer of distinction and then another' was ordered by Cumberland to shoot Fraser. When both refused, Cumberland asked a 'common sogar' if his musket was loaded. On the private answering that it was, the Duke ordered him to shoot Fraser, 'which he did'. In this earlier and more convincing version, which was told to Hay by 'the sogars' themselves, neither of the British officers was named.[17]

Of course, in refusing to play the role of executioner, a British officer and 'gentleman' may have been acting from motives of dignity rather than humanity. But alongside the well-documented brutalities committed after Culloden, there is also evidence that at least some British soldiers, both officers and men, risked the wrath of their superiors to perform acts of genuine compassion. It has been suggested that the incident actually happened, with the proviso that, as Wolfe served on Hawley's staff, it was the 'Hangman' who uttered the callous directive. There is certainly no indication that Wolfe fell out of favour with Cumberland after Culloden, or that he lost his own respect for the Duke: writing from Inverness on the day after the battle he praised Cumberland as 'a great and gallant General'.[18]

Given the half-century hiatus between the genesis of the story and the first mention of Wolfe's role, it is possible that his subsequent celebrity prompted the retrospective use of his name. Although now impossible to verify, the anecdote is intriguing – not least for what it reveals about Wolfe's high reputation at the onset of the nineteenth century.

Cumberland remained in the Highlands for three months after Culloden. In that time he proved himself the zealous servant of a regime that was determined to eradicate the threat of Jacobite insurrection once and for all. The aftermath of the '15 had seen surprisingly little retribution against the rebels. Many in government circles believed that this leniency had contributed to the fresh outbreak of rebellion three decades later. In 1746, the Duke of Newcastle and his colleagues were adamant that the same mistake should not be repeated.

Throughout that spring and early summer, Cumberland's victorious redcoats formed an army of occupation that scoured the Highlands in quest of the fugitive Young Pretender and those who had espoused his cause. If discovered in arms, rebels were to be killed and their property confiscated or destroyed. In theory at least, those rank and file Jacobites who voluntarily surrendered their weapons to royal patrols would be issued with certificates and allowed 'to return unmolested to their homes'. Such guidelines were sometimes ignored during the dragnet operations that ensued. Major-General Bland was not the only senior officer to advocate a more ruthless application of fire and sword. As the British Army and its auxiliaries drawn from the loyalist militia visited indiscriminate retribution upon countless Highland communities, the innocent suffered alongside the guilty. Following upon the brutal treatment of the rebel wounded at Culloden, the murders, rapes and beatings in the glens ultimately bequeathed Cumberland the nickname by which he remains known to posterity – 'Butcher'.[19]

The harrying of the rebel heartlands was an ugly business. Like other British officers, James Wolfe was required to play his part in this brutal pacification. Some indication of Wolfe's role in orchestrating punitive expeditions surfaces in a series of letters that he wrote from Inverness and Fort Augustus to Captain Charles Hamilton of Cobham's Dragoons at Forfar. At that time Wolfe remained as Hawley's *aide-de-camp* and provided a conduit for the general's orders. On 19 May he informed Hamilton that Cumberland approved of his 'assiduity' in hunting-down rebels. Wolfe added:

> You know the manner of treating the houses and possessions of rebels in this part of the country. The same freedom is to be used where you are as has been hitherto practised, that is seeking for them and their arms, cattle and other things that are usually found.

That Captain Hamilton was enthusiastic in the execution of his orders is indicated by the petition of Thomas Ogilvie of Coul. In June, when Ogilvie was in gaol under suspicion of Jacobite sympathies, he complained to magistrates that Hamilton had plundered his house and offices, driven off his cattle, grazed horses in his park, and even harvested and sold his crops. Hamilton soon after descended upon the Forfar estate of John Watson. The captain was happy to remove his troopers – at a price of sixty guineas. Although there was insufficient cash at Watson's house, the captain was not an unreasonable man: he agreed to accept a cheque instead.

Cumberland did little to discourage such extortions. A further let-ter from Wolfe to Hamilton relayed the information that the Duke was 'very well satisfied' with the captain's conduct, and had given him leave to dispose of Watson's belongings. In the same despatch, 'Hangman' Hawley contributed advice that reveals just how carefully the pilfer-ing was regulated: whenever seizures of livestock or other goods were made, the officers and men responsible would receive shares of the loot in proportion to their army pay.[20]

Having extinguished the last embers of rebellion in the Highlands, the Duke of Cumberland left Fort Augustus on 18 July. He arrived in London a week later to a rapturous welcome. His successor, William Anne Keppel, Earl of Albemarle, reluctantly assumed command of the British troops in Scotland. The regiments remaining in that distressed country included Barrell's. Wolfe, whose appointment to Hawley's staff had ended with the general's return to England in July, rejoined his unit at Linlithgow. He was soon after returned to the Highlands to garrison the crumbling but strategically important post of Inversnaid.

Sited at the head of Loch Lomond, the old fort provided a bulwark against the notoriously rebellious MacGregors. Here Wolfe remained until November, when he was given six weeks' furlough. This respite – Wolfe's first real spell of leave since he had entered the army four years before – enabled him to spend Christmas with his parents at their new London town house in Old Burlington Street.

For all its dramatic fluctuations of fortune, the tragic and bloody rebellion of the '45 was no more than a sideshow in the wider War of the Austrian Succession. Now that the Jacobites had been eradicated, Cumberland and his veteran 'Flanderkins' prepared for the next round of their match with Saxe. With the New Year, units that had fought at Falkirk and Culloden were gradually withdrawn from their remote Scottish garrisons and sent back to the Low Countries. In early Janu-ary 1747, after celebrating his twentieth birthday, Brigade-Major James Wolfe embarked once more for Flanders.

Whilst Cumberland and his redcoats were preoccupied in confront-ing and crushing the Jacobites, the armies of Louis XV had exploited their absence to make deep inroads into the Austrian Netherlands. In February 1746, Marshal Saxe seized Brussels; by the end of the summer, the famous fortress towns of Mons and Namur were also in the Bourbon bag. Saxe's triumphant progress was capped in October, when he roundly defeated another motley British, Dutch and Austrian force, this time commanded by Prince Charles of Lorraine, at Rocoux, near Liège. By the end of that year's campaigning season, the marshal's troops were poised to push north and invade the Dutch Republic.

The Allied war effort had long been nourished by British gold, but as the conflict rolled on into 1747 there was growing doubt that Austria's share of the military burden gave true value for the hefty subsidies it received from London. More ominous still was a distinct lack of Dutch enthusiasm for the fight. But when Saxe launched his anticipated invasion of Dutch territory in the spring of 1747, the Republic's craven stance prompted a dramatic and unexpected reaction: a wave of nationalistic feeling and resentment against the overly pacific government of the States-General led to an upsurge of popular support for the House of Orange. By early May, William IV of Orange – Cumberland's brother-in-law – had been declared 'stadtholder', or lieutenant, of the various provinces and commander of the Republic's forces. Optimistic British observers now anticipated that the galvanized Dutch would fight a vigorous patriotic war in defence of their homeland.

For the coming campaign, it was resolved that the redcoats and their allies alike should all serve under the command of Cumberland, the young royal hero of Culloden; this choice sought to avoid the disunity that had crippled their recent efforts. But national jealousies were not easily surmounted; in practice, Cumberland's authority over his Dutch and Austrian confederates was far from supreme. In addition, the enemy confronting the Duke was far more formidable than the outnumbered and demoralized clansmen who had faced him across the sleet-lashed expanse of Culloden's Drummossie Moor. His old rival Saxe was once again at the head of a powerful field army – one that was now convinced of its own invincibility.

That spring, Cumberland slowly moved his troops eastwards towards Maastricht. Regarded as the key to Holland's defence, the fortress city was now menaced by the right wing of Saxe's great army. In mid June, the marshal's forces began moving north from Liège. In response, Cumberland issued orders for his own disparate contingents to concentrate for the protection of Maastricht.

On 2 July 1747 the rival armies confronted each other in their fourth set-piece encounter of the conflict. The resulting battle of Lauffeldt was one of the fiercest clashes of the 'Second Hundred Years' War', but it remains largely forgotten outside the ranks of military historians. It deserves to be better remembered. Involving a total of more than 200,000 troops, the engagement that unfolded in the rolling countryside beyond the walls of Maastricht was a confrontation of truly Napoleonic proportions. It also embraced episodes of high drama to rival any enacted at Austerlitz, Borodino or Waterloo.

As at Fontenoy two years before, Cumberland's army included large contingents of Austrian and Dutch troops. Once again, the brunt of the fighting was borne by the Duke's British and Hanoverian regiments. These redcoats – including Brigade-Major James Wolfe – held the left wing of the Allied line, which was anchored upon the sprawling hamlets of Vlytingen and Lauffeldt. The ensuing battle was dominated by a ferocious struggle for their possession. It was here, in the very vortex of the action, that Wolfe fought.[21]

According to George Townshend, who was now an *aide-de-camp* to Cumberland, the Duke had at first failed to appreciate that Lauffeldt itself was the linchpin of the Allied line. There had been considerable confusion over whether or not the village should be occupied. Shortly before the action began, Townshend complained, 'it was once ordered to be *burnt*, and twice to be *evacuated* and *repossessed*'. Although Cumberland finally installed a garrison, nothing was done to strengthen the position. But to the French troops ordered to storm the village, Lauffeldt looked formidable enough; one officer compared the hamlet to a 'citadel'. Like other local settlements, it was ringed by orchards, themselves enclosed by six-foot-high mud walls topped with thickly planted hedges. These barriers were defended by a determined force of British and Hanoverians.[22]

Wolfe's future commander, the meticulous Jeffery Amherst, noted that the first gun was fired at about 10.00 a.m. Soon after the French attacked 'the hamlet of Laval [Lauffeldt] ... moving up to it in column'. This massive formation provided a tempting mark for the Allied gunners. They poured in a rapid and murderous fire, but the French infantry came on regardless. A volunteer in the Royal Artillery could not help admiring the courage of the men he glimpsed as targets down the hot barrel of his twelve pounder: 'they really behaved very well', he wrote, 'though we cut them down with grapeshot'.[23]

Cumberland's changing dispositions at Lauffeldt had left an undefended gap that enabled the French to secure a vital foothold. Townshend believed that this oversight was fatal, as 'from the first, they were as much masters of the village as we'. But it required some five hours of savage fighting before Saxe's infantry secured undisputed possession. During that time Lauffeldt became a maw into which brigade after brigade was fed and chewed to bloody shreds. The first French attack involved eight battalions; by the fifth and final assault, no fewer than forty-nine had been committed to the fight. One of the redcoats defending the village, Major Adolphus Oughton of Dejean's 37th Foot, maintained that, despite these overwhelming odds, the garrison did not retire 'while there was a cartridge left' to fire.

Conspicuous amongst the French troops sent against Lauffeldt was the same Irish Brigade that had turned the tide at Fontenoy. One British officer conceded that this formation once again 'fought like devils'. He reported the belief – widespread at the time but without foundation – that the Young Pretender had served at Lauffeldt as a volunteer, exhorting his followers to exact vengeance upon Cumberland. The exploits of the 'Wild Geese' permitted the same officer to offer his own countrymen some small consolation for their latest disappointment. Indeed:

> as what advantage the French had at Fontenoy as well as now, was owing to the desperate behaviour of this brigade, it may be said that the King of France is indebted for his successes to the natural-born subjects of Great Britain.

After Fontenoy, many British pundits had accused the Dutch of shirking their share of the fighting; at Lauffeldt, their performance drew more bitter criticism. Not only had the Republic's troops on the right wing stood idle whilst the redcoats contested the hedges and orchards of Lauffeldt and Vlytingen, but at a crucial moment six squadrons of Dutch cavalry simply turned tail, trampling their way through British units marching up from the reserve. In the confusion resulting from this 'monstrous tide of Dutch cowardice', Cumberland's army was split in two.[24]

The consequences would have been yet more serious save for a desperate cavalry charge that checked the French advance. Gathering up the Scots Greys, Inniskilling Dragoons and the Duke of Cumberland's Dragoons, Sir John Ligonier spurred forward, to be 'lost immediately, by the eye, in the middle of the French squadrons'. Like their regimental descendants in the celebrated attack of the Union Brigade at Waterloo, the battle-crazed Scots and Irish troopers charged too far and suffered accordingly when confronted by fresh French infantry. Their casualty lists, which reported an unusually high ratio of killed to wounded, testified to the ferocity of the fighting. Cumberland's Dragoons were likewise shattered. This unit mustered many former troopers of the disbanded Kingston's Light Horse. Men who had hounded fleeing Highlanders at Culloden now encountered stiffer opposition as they struggled to extricate themselves from deep within Saxe's position. Days later, many of them remained unaccounted for.[25] The gallant Ligonier, who came from Huguenot stock, was captured but treated with scrupulous courtesy by his estranged countrymen. That other tough old cavalryman, Henry Hawley, only escaped thanks to 'the goodness and activity of his horse', which carried him to safety amidst a storm of pistol balls.[26]

Ligonier's epic charge was widely credited with saving Cumberland's army. Mauled but defiant, it retreated in good order until it reached the sheltering guns of Maastricht. The Allies had sustained some 6000 casualties, with the majority falling amongst the Anglo-Hanoverians. But the victors' losses were heavier still, totalling about 10,000. The brave Irish Brigade alone suffered more than 1700 officers and men killed and wounded. Louis XV, who witnessed this great cull of FitzGeralds, Hegartys, O'Briens and Sullivans, compensated the survivors through a lavish distribution of pensions and decorations.

Lauffeldt was by far the largest battle in which James Wolfe fought; yet no detailed account of his own experiences survives. However, from what is known of Wolfe's duties that day, it is possible to place him in the very thick of the fight. Wolfe was major to Sir John Mordaunt's Brigade, which comprised the regiments of Crawford, Fleming and Pulteney: as their casualty lists reveal, these formations were amongst the most heavily engaged of all the British infantry units present on the field.[27]

Some hint of Wolfe's experience as a conspicuously mounted staff

officer in the midst of a protracted infantry firefight survives in a letter written four years later. Extolling the virtues of his trusty servant
Roland, Wolfe recalled that:

> He came to me at the hazard of his life in the last action with offers of his
> service, took off my cloak and brought a fresh horse; and would have con-
> tinued close by me had I not ordered him to retire. I believe he was slightly
> wounded just at that time, and the horse he held was shot likewise.

As at Dettingen four years earlier, Wolfe apparently had a horse shot
beneath him. On that occasion, and in subsequent fights, he had
escaped unscathed. This time he was not so lucky: the *London Gazette*
listed him amongst the wounded. The exact nature of Wolfe's injury is
unknown, although it cannot have been life-threatening. A letter from
Flanders dated just nine days after Lauffeldt reported that 'Wolf' was
wounded 'but will do well'.[28]

After Wolfe's death it was reported that he had served with distinction at Lauffeldt. An obituary notice claimed that 'he exerted himself
in so masterly a manner, at a very critical juncture, that it drew the
highest encomiums from the great officer then at the head of our
army'.[29] If Cumberland did indeed single out Wolfe for special praise,
the Duke's words went unrecorded in his own official orders. Those
written two days after the battle offered a more general acknowledge-
ment of the army's performance, announcing that 'His Royal Highness
thanks the officers and men for their bravery and good conduct in the
late action'. Alongside the casualty returns a list of the volunteers who
had fought in the battle was to be sent to Lord Albemarle that evening,
with certificates of each man's behaviour signed by their commanding
officers; these were to make recommendations for filling vacancies by
the following morning.

Rewards for the deserving were matched by retribution against those
who had failed in their duty. Orders issued three days later declared
that Captain Robert Cholmondely of the Third Foot Guards had been
'cashiered His Majesty's Service for quitting his platoon in the action of
the second instant'. It was Cumberland's pleasure that he should leave
the army immediately. For a young man of Cholmondely's privileged
background, this sentence was crushing enough. But he escaped lightly
compared with another soldier who lost his nerve at Lauffeldt: orders

of 9 July recorded that Private William Bell of the Scots Fusiliers, 'tryed and condemned for leaving his party on the day of action and presenting his firelock at Lieutenant Levison when he orderd him to return', would hang next morning.[30]

The futile bloodbath outside Maastricht left both sides licking their wounds; it provided powerful ammunition for those who argued that the war had now dragged on for long enough. Proponents of peace included Louis XV himself, who was sickened by the carnage he had witnessed at first hand. The French King used his illustrious captive Sir John Ligonier as a mouthpiece for overtures to Cumberland. The gallant old Huguenot brought back nothing in writing, but transmitted a clear message that any meaningful settlement between France and Britain would hinge upon the mutual restoration of *all* conquered territories.

Whilst the old enemies made their first tentative efforts to halt hostilities, the killing continued. The impotence of the Dutch Republic was underlined that September when the French took the crucial fortress of Bergen-op-Zoom by storm; then, as was their right under the laws of war, they ran bloodily amuck. The once-proud Republic now teetered upon the brink of total collapse, and the prospect of Dutch ports in French hands only encouraged British efforts to orchestrate a ceasefire.

When winter brought the year's hostilities to a close, Wolfe secured leave to return to England. He celebrated his twenty-first birthday with his parents at their London home. Wolfe had clearly recovered from his Lauffeldt wound; as he later confided to his good friend Captain William Rickson of the 47th Foot, during his time in the capital he began a dalliance with Miss Elizabeth Lawson, a royal maid of honour and the niece of General Sir John Mordaunt. But, as Wolfe explained, the prospect of yet another campaign in Flanders, 'battledore and dangerous, left little thought for love'.[31]

Although peace negotiations began at Aix-La-Chapelle on 17 March 1748, the British Army and its increasingly apathetic allies continued to face the French in the Netherlands. There Marshal Saxe maintained his designs upon Maastricht. In the following month Brigade-Major Wolfe was at Osterhout, near Breda. His views on the campaign's outcome were pessimistic, but he took encouragement from a conversation with the Adjutant-General, Colonel Joseph Yorke, which revealed that the

Duke of Cumberland himself was keen to promote his professional prospects. In the previous May, the Duke had sung Wolfe's praises in a despatch to Philip, Lord Chesterfield, recommending that he be allowed to buy a vacant lieutenant-colonelcy in the Eighth Foot. Nothing came of that, probably because Wolfe was only a major by brevet and therefore too junior for such a promotion.[32]

But according to Yorke, Cumberland remained anxious to do his best for Wolfe: indeed, he was willing to give him the major's commission in Bragg's 28th Foot 'for nothing'; this would be a stepping stone to becoming lieutenant-colonel of that unit. In the course of the war Bragg's had acquired notoriety as a disorderly and inefficient regiment. It needed a firm hand to whip it into shape, and it is likely that Cumberland regarded the zealous Wolfe as the ideal man for the job. Having seen his hopes of promotion dashed in the past, Wolfe took a resigned view of the scheme. Writing to his father on 12 April he observed: 'I'm sure the thing is yet far off, [and] possibly may fail as heretofore; but with sincerity I assure you, I am out of the reach of disappointment'. This philosophical stance was just as well. When the long war finally ground to a halt, Wolfe remained a humble captain – albeit one with friends in high places.[33]

The British, French and Dutch signed preliminary peace terms on 30 April. As it approached the negotiating table, Britain's position was stronger than its depressing string of continental setbacks suggested. These were counterbalanced by recent naval triumphs and unexpected developments across the Atlantic.

Despite a sluggish start as it struggled to adopt a war footing, by 1747 the Royal Navy had gathered full sail and notched up some notable victories. That May and October, admirals George Anson and Edward Hawke both savaged French squadrons off northern Spain's Cape Finisterre. But it was North America that produced Britain's most clear-cut success of the entire war. In June 1745, as Cumberland's army in Flanders was recuperating from its blooding at Fontenoy, a force of Massachusetts volunteers captured the coveted French fortress of Louisbourg, on Cape Breton. This 'Dunkirk of America' not only shielded the entrance to the St Lawrence River – a waterway penetrating to the very heart of French Canada – but also offered a haven for the privateers that preyed upon Anglo-American shipping.

The significance of the New Englanders' dramatic conquest had not gone unnoticed by the growing body of British politicians, led by the outspoken William Pitt, who believed that the best way to curb French power was to eschew involvement in costly and indecisive European campaigning. In future, they argued, Britain should instead deploy its sea power to ravage France's vulnerable colonies, hitting hard at the trade upon which so much of its strength depended.

To the chagrin of many Britons on both sides of the Atlantic, as peace negotiations gathered momentum, the ministry promptly agreed to surrender Cape Breton in exchange for Madras, a key British trading post captured by the French in September 1746. The American colonists were understandably mortified that politicians an ocean away could undo all their efforts at the mere stroke of a pen.[34]

It was not only the New Englanders who were irate at the peace terms finalized in October 1748. After all of Saxe's victories, bought at such conspicuous human cost, many Frenchmen were astounded by their government's swift agreement to evacuate the Netherlands. More humiliating still was France's willingness to recognize the House of Hanover as Great Britain's legitimate rulers – and to ignominiously eject the popular hero Prince Charles Edward Stuart from their territories. Empress Maria Theresa of Austria, who had scarcely been consulted as the diplomats from London and Paris honed the treaty clauses, was outraged that Frederick the Great of Prussia was permitted to keep Silesia. Considering itself betrayed by Britain, Austria would soon seek consolation in the arms of its traditional enemy, France. Contented or dissatisfied alike, none of the protagonists believed that the peace amounted to anything more than a wary truce in an increasingly bitter Anglo-French struggle for global dominance.

The convoluted and seemingly pointless War of the Austrian Succession witnessed Wolfe's transformation from raw subaltern to hardened veteran. By the age of just twenty-one he had already served through six campaigns and fought in four pitched battles. During this mixed bag of victory and defeat Wolfe had held responsibilities far beyond his youth. The marching, fighting and grinding paperwork all took its toll: in those six years, James Wolfe matured rapidly. In addition, he had become accustomed to the horrors of war: the bloodshed that so shocked him at Dettingen left him unmoved at Culloden. In that same conflict he'd lost a much-loved brother and had himself been wounded in one of the fiercest fights of the century. But for an ambitious career soldier like James Wolfe, a bloody war offered the best prospects of promotion. He now faced the far more dispiriting prospect of peace.

4

The Frustrations of Peace

War is over, peace is come,
Sheath the sword, unbrace the drum;
Soldier sing thy warlike tale,
Kiss thy doxy, quaff thy ale ...

Anon, 'Extempore on an Officer'

During six years of active service James Wolfe had established a formidable professional reputation. Now, as John Pringle put it in his
biographical sketch, 'peace lulled to rest the horrors of war, and cut
short his fond hopes of getting fresh laurels'.[1] Although the cessation of
hostilities ended Wolfe's dreams of distinguishing himself on the battlefield, it did nothing to halt his steady ascent of the promotional ladder.
On 5 January 1749, Captain James Wolfe was commissioned major in
Lord George Sackville's 20th Foot. This long-sought step took him to
Stirling, where his new regiment was posted to guard the gap between
the Scottish Lowlands and the volatile Highland zone to the north. It
was more than two years since James Wolfe had last served in Scotland.
During his absence there had been a methodical campaign to ensure
that the Stuarts never again raised the standard of rebellion there. The
British Army's ruthless forays into the Highlands in the wake of Culloden had paved a way for the subtler, but no less devastating, inroads of
the lawyers. Cumberland's redcoats had harried countless communities
in their efforts to stamp out rebellion; it required an equally systematic
programme of legislation to unpick the very fabric of the clan system
that had provided the Jacobites with their staunchest fighters.

In fact, this determined legal offensive was already under way before
Wolfe had left the ravaged Highlands for the battlefields of Flanders. On
12 August 1746, the royal assent was given to a Disarming Act intended

to strengthen existing legislation and draw the claws of the clans by depriving them of their traditional weaponry once and for all. Any man or woman who carried or concealed arms – including the broadswords and dirks that many Highlanders considered to be part of their every-day dress – faced a hefty fine, with a month's gaol for non-payment. Those still unable to pay after that time was up, and who were fit for military service, would be sent to reinforce Britain's skeleton army in the Americas; the weak and elderly could expect a further six months in custody. Searches might be made at any hour of the day. The same Act made it illegal for anyone not serving in the British Army to wear tartan clothing, thereby stripping the Highlanders of their distinc-tive garb. Despite understandable protests from those clans who had remained faithful to the Hanoverians during the '45, the Act was applied throughout the Highland zone, embracing rebels and loyalists alike.

Alongside this attack upon the outward trappings of rebellion, the legislators also struck at its social and ideological roots: new laws banned the 'heritable jurisdictions' by which clan chiefs had wielded life or death powers over their people, and sought to suppress non-juring meeting houses, insisting that Episcopal ministers qualify themselves by taking oaths and praying for King George and his family by name. It was widely believed that a previous failure to do this had helped foment a spirit of disaffection against the King and his ministers.[2]

It was one thing to pass laws in London, another to impose them upon the hostile and resentful inhabitants of a mountainous zone some 500 miles away. Indeed, not only the Highlands, but Scotland in general, remained a turbulent region with more than its fair share of the era's usual law and order problems. The sullen redcoats who tramped the glens in search of skulking Jacobites, or who reinforced customs officers in their ongoing guerrilla war against violent and well-organized gangs of smugglers, were not the enforcers of some omnipotent martial law, but rather the agents for the magistrates and justices of the peace who would actually interrogate and try offenders. As the detailed standing orders for officers posted to 'North Britain' made all too clear, the army's powers were circumscribed by a Gordian knot of rules and regulations. Fear of military rule was so ingrained throughout Great Britain that even in those recently rebellious regions civil authority must be seen to be paramount. Soldiers who swapped kid gloves for the mailed fist could expect dire retribution. As their instructions warned them: 'In the execution of all or any of the above orders, or any which you may hereafter receive, you are to take care that no person be injured either in his person or property, on pain of the severest penalties the civil or military law can inflict on the person offending.'[3]

Wolfe's latest promotion brought with it a heavy burden of responsibility, and the task that now faced him was doubly daunting. In the absence of the 20th's lieutenant-colonel, Edward Cornwallis, who had been appointed as governor of Britain's newly established naval base and settlement at Halifax, Nova Scotia, Wolfe was the regiment's acting commander. Not only did he face the challenge of enforcing King George's will upon his resentful Scottish subjects, but he was also obliged to stamp his own authority upon a battalion of more than 800 men, many of whom – officers and rank and file alike – must have regarded their young major with a mixture of curiosity and suspicion. Would he prove to be a tyrant, ready to flog men bloody for the slightest misdemeanour, or a dilettante, happy to leave the running of his battalion to the adjutant and sergeants?

The twenty-two-year-old Major James Wolfe was certainly distinctive enough to command attention. At six foot, he was exceptionally tall by eighteenth-century standards, his height only accentuated by a scrawny physique. Wolfe was redheaded, and unequivocally so; a contemporary poem by his friend John Mason, jovially recommending potential Greenwich suitors for a Miss Sally Brett, includes amongst the soldiers, 'Jemmy, whose *hair* is with passion aflame'. That ginger hair framed a pale, freckled complexion and blue-grey eyes. Wolfe's lips were full, his nose long and pointed – a feature only emphasized by a pitifully weak chin and a high, backward-sloping forehead. Viewed from the front – the perspective of the formal portrait painter – Wolfe's face was unexceptional. But his profile was singular, resembling a tilted triangle.[4]

Those who judged Wolfe by his exterior alone soon learned the error of their ways: beneath the unpromising surface beat the heart of a born soldier. It was swiftly apparent that the major intended to take an unusually close interest in the efficiency, discipline and welfare of his new unit. No sooner had he arrived in Stirling than a steady stream of orders began to emanate from his headquarters inside the formidable castle up on its rock. Before a week was out, Wolfe had issued a directive that underlined his determination to maintain discipline: two men had been tried by court martial for handling counterfeit money and were to be punished accordingly, so that others might be deterred from 'such infamous and villainous practices'. Indeed, Wolfe was 'determined to discourage as much as possible every act of knavery that may tend in the least to the discredit of the corps'. Neither officers nor men were to be left in any doubt that he intended Sackville's to become a crack battalion.[5]

Wolfe's stay at Stirling was brief. Within weeks, the regiment marched west to occupy new quarters in Glasgow. Already a bustling port of some 20,000 inhabitants, Glasgow's phenomenal growth was fuelled by a thriving transatlantic trade with British North America; in a pattern that epitomized the powerful commercial bonds between mother country and colonies, local woollen and linen goods were exported in exchange for tobacco from Virginia and Maryland. The arrival of Wolfe and his men coincided with the 'golden age' of Glasgow's tobacco trade. Within a decade, Scottish tobacco imports would eclipse those of London and all other English ports combined.[6]

Wolfe was initially unimpressed by Glasgow and its industrious citizens. Writing to his good friend Captain Rickson, he characterized the merchants as 'designing and treacherous', their energetic pursuit of trade resulting from nothing more than 'the baseness of their other qualifications'. Glasgow's women fared no better, being 'coarse, cold and cunning' and obsessed with 'men's circumstances'. This harsh verdict reflected a deeper despondency: truth to tell, the prospect of watching helplessly as his 'youth and vigour' drained away during dreary years of peacetime soldiering filled Wolfe with dread. He also feared the effect of such frustrations upon his mercurial temperament. As Wolfe confided to Rickson, the daily mood swings provoked by discontent risked transforming him into 'a martinet or monster'.[7]

This blend of resentment, self-pity and irritability coloured James Wolfe's first reaction to his Glaswegian neighbours. But here, as so often in Wolfe's personal correspondence, such outspoken verdicts can be misleading: intemperate language must be balanced against subsequent, more considered, reflections. His rapidly changing opinion of Glasgow's inhabitants is a case in point. Within a fortnight of his arrival amongst them, Wolfe had clearly mellowed, informing his mother that Glasgow was 'very far from being so disagreeable as it appeared at first'. The ladies in particular were both 'very civil ... and not so desperately afraid of a soldier as formerly'. But there remained limits to Wolfe's charity. He grudged the loss of two precious hours spent attending church each Sunday morning because 'the generality of Scotch preachers are excessive blockheads, so truly and obstinately dull, that they seem to shut out knowledge at every entrance'.[8]

Although staunchly loyalist during the '45, Glasgow remained an unruly billet. Sackville's regiment had scarcely arrived on the Clyde before it was called upon to quell a serious riot. Trouble had erupted on Saturday 4 March following a body-snatching incident involving students from the college that would later become Glasgow University. Scotland's surgeons already enjoyed an international reputation for excellence, but their cutting-edge knowledge of anatomy rested upon the ready availability of corpses for dissection. The officially approved supply of bodies – dead foundlings or executed felons whose corpses remained unclaimed by kinfolk – failed to satisfy the demands of students keen to work upon fresh subjects rather than ancient body parts fished out of brine buckets. They therefore sought other, unofficial – and illegal – specimens.

While the heyday of Scottish body-snatching lay far ahead, with the murderous careers of William Burke and William Hare during the 1820s, the mid eighteenth-century did not lack 'resurrectionists' of its own. In Edinburgh, it was customary for the university's professors to supply cadavers; in Glasgow, by contrast, the students were often expected to find their own subjects. Although the resulting grave robbing sought to advance the frontiers of medical knowledge, and thereby benefit humanity, it nonetheless affronted the highly conservative social code of the labouring classes. In London, there were scrimmages around the Tyburn gallows as sympathetic mobs battled to keep the bodies of the hanged from the clutches of the surgeons' henchmen.[9]

For Wolfe, the body-snatching riot provided welcome excitement. He reported the day's events in a long and lively letter to the commander-in-chief in Scotland, Lieutenant-General George Churchill. This was duly forwarded to Secretary at State Henry Fox. Indeed, whilst Wolfe's family letters are often rambling and introspective, his official reports

to his superiors could be direct and forceful enough to demand attention. They reinforced Wolfe's reputation as an officer to be watched.

Enraged at the sight of an open grave, Wolfe reported, the 'monster
of a mob' had assembled at the college to hunt for the missing body.
Convinced that the surgeons or students of anatomy were behind this
outrage, the rioters roughed up the sheriff sent to disperse them. When
he called for military assistance, an officer and twenty-five redcoats soon
cleared the college and barred the gates. Outside, the crowd increased,
smashed the windows and attempted to storm the building. The efforts
of Baillie Brown 'to pacify the Hydra, by mild intreaty' only prompted
a volley of stones that left him badly bruised. Glasgow's nervous magistrates now implored Wolfe for reinforcements. No doubt recalling his
recent experiences amidst the bloodstained orchards and lanes of Lauffeldt, the major sardonically reported how he placed himself at the head
of three companies and marched to the scene,

> with all that solemnity and dreadfull preparation, proceeding an attack.
> And in order to terrify the enemy (tho late in the evening) we beat our
> drums, and with no small success, for by the time we got to the Coledge,
> many of the scoundrels had sneeked of.

An officer and two soldiers were injured during the fracas, and Wolfe
himself was struck by stones as he passed through the mob. It was only
with difficulty that his men were restrained from retaliating against
their tormentors.

Wolfe called for the Riot Act to be read, but the sheriff and his
officers were reluctant to take a step that might lead to lethal bloodshed;
the grim fate of Captain John Porteous, who was lynched after opening
fire upon Edinburgh rioters in 1736, offered a stark warning against
overreaction. In any event, the troops' firm front eventually overawed
the 'giddy multitude'. Two of the ringleaders were arrested and clapped
into the Tollbooth, and by midnight all was quiet. As the corpse
remained missing, however, and it was rumoured that the colliers and
'other banditti in the neighbourhood' were gathering to find it, soldiers
continued to guard the college. Wolfe had assured the magistrates of
his protection, but had advised them to 'exert their legal authority with
more vigour, and not suffer themselves and their office to be debas'd by
this abject crew'.[10]

A very different aspect of the military's expansive law and order role was highlighted on 3 June, when a fierce fire swept through the Gorbals district. Nearly 200 poor families were left homeless. Three days later the *Edinburgh Evening Courant* reported that 'Major Wolfe and the other officers of Lord George Sackville's Regiment, were present all the time, and were of singular use by placing guards upon the Bridge, and at all the avenues, to keep off the crowd and prevent the stealing of the effects belonging to the poor sufferers'. Besides baffling the looters, many of the soldiers had exerted themselves in battling the flames and saving life and property.[11]

Meanwhile, the unglamorous routine of peacetime soldiering ground on. Like the legionaries of imperial Rome, Georgian Britain's infantry-men spent much of their time on back-breaking construction projects, receiving extra pay for their pains. That June, Sackville's regiment supplied 320 men to work on the roads between the pass of Lancey and the head of Loch Earn. These gangs of soldier-labourers were kitted out with coarse work shirts to save their linen from wear and tear. Regimental orders specified that on no account should these be of a checked pattern; *that* would have been too suggestive of the proscribed tartan.[12]

During that same summer of 1749, the 20th Foot received a personal visit from its colonel, Lord George Sackville. The third son of the Duke of Dorset, Sackville was a close friend of Cumberland and had been badly wounded under his command at Fontenoy in 1745. Arrogant and stubborn, his career was to prove unusually chequered: within a decade, events would cast him in the role of coward and villain, a disgrace alike to his country and its army.[13] But in 1749 Sackville's reputation was untarnished, and he remained a powerful and influential figure in army circles. Lord George was obviously impressed with the condition of his regiment, which reflected well upon its conscientious young major. As Wolfe informed his mother, Sackville offered to secure him a three-month furlough that winter. Lord George had also stressed the importance of networking for Wolfe's career prospects – 'of keeping up my present acquaintance amongst the heads of our trade and procuring new ones that may be of use'. And Wolfe wrote to his father that, even though Sackville was soon expected to gain the colonelcy of a more senior cavalry regiment, his patronage would continue: 'I may expect his assistance whether he is with the Regiment or not; he has given me such strong marks of esteem, that there can be little doubt'. Sackville proved true to his word. In coming years he was destined to be a staunch friend to Wolfe – one who would spare no pains to expedite his promotion.[14]

Sackville quit his regiment that August, leaving Wolfe once again in overall command. Wolfe was acutely aware of the continuing challenge this posed for a man of his youth and relative inexperience – and of the potentially corrupting influence of such power: 'You can't conceive how difficult a thing it is to keep the passions within bounds, when authority and immaturity go together,' he confessed to his mother. It was his task, he added, to act as an impartial judge and role model 'employed in discouraging vice and recommending the reverse at the turbulent age of twenty-three, when it is possible I may have as great a propensity that way as any of the men that I converse with!'[15]

In a bid to stimulate his mind, Wolfe had taken up the study of mathematics with a tutor at the college. As he confessed with rueful self-mockery, progress had not been spectacular; indeed, this belated return to the classroom had blunted rather than sharpened his wits:

> I don't know how the mathematics may assist the judgment, but they have a tendency to make men dull. I, who am far from being sprightly even in my gaiety, am the very reverse of it at this time. I'm heavier in discourse, longer at a letter, less quick at apprehension, and carry all the appearances of stupidity to so great a height, that in a little time they won't be known from the reality; and all this to find out the use and property of a crooked line, which, when discovered serves me no more than a straight one ...[16]

As autumn approached, Wolfe's frustrations mounted. He now faced the prospect of spending the winter in distant Perth, and chafed at the enforced inactivity. Rather than squander the 'very blooming season of our days', and risk going to seed in Scotland, he would rather campaign against the Ottoman Turks. He also feared the influence of his hard-drinking regimental companions. For Wolfe, their roistering lifestyle clearly held dangerous attractions: 'I dread their habits and behaviour,' he told his mother, 'and am forced to an eternal watch upon myself, that I may avoid the very manner that I most condemn in them.' For all his priggish pronouncements, James Wolfe was struggling to rein himself in.[17]

Before leaving Glasgow for Perth, Wolfe's regiment was embroiled in a scrimmage that reflected another facet of the era's endemic lawbreaking. Smuggling was rife throughout mid-Georgian Britain; Scotland, with its extensive and indented coastline, was a problem region, and Glasgow's thriving port a notorious black spot. The very first of the General Orders issued to officers posted to 'North Britain' had enjoined them to assist the customs or excise officers in seizing 'run goods, or to prevent an illicit trade being carried on, so prejudicial to His Majesty's revenue and the fair trader'. Adherence to these orders led to a bloody little encounter with Highland smugglers on the night of 2 October. Wolfe reported that the port's customs officers had taken a corporal and a dozen men about a mile down the Clyde to seize a boat laden with rum. The smugglers resisted, and a soldier who attempted to board their craft was knocked into the river. At the urging of an exciseman, the redcoats opened fire. Two of the smugglers were wounded, one of them mortally.[18]

In mid October the 20th Regiment duly marched for Perth; in the following month, it was announced that George, Viscount Bury, was to replace Sackville as colonel. Like his predecessor, Bury was an aristocratic crony of Cumberland – such a great favourite that he had been given the plum of carrying the Duke's Culloden victory despatch to London. But there the similarities ended. For all his faults of temperament, Sackville was a conscientious and hard-working professional; as Wolfe soon came to realize, young Bury, by contrast, was a showy place-seeker, reluctant to stray too far from St James's and with no more than a passing interest in the regiment that now bore his name.

As Edward Cornwallis showed no sign of returning from Nova Scotia, the lieutenant-colonelcy of the 20th remained vacant. Sackville had sent Wolfe the first information of that development, along with the 'strongest assurances of his aid and service'. Wolfe told his father that Lord George was 'very sincere' and that he therefore relied 'chiefly upon him'. But Wolfe had other friends in high places. Cumberland himself had recommended Wolfe's promotion to his father the King, and on 29 March 1750 Wolfe learned that the proposal had been confirmed.

At the age of just twenty-three, he was appointed lieutenant-colonel of Bury's 20th Foot.[19]

This was recognition that the ambitious Wolfe had long sought, but it came at a price. The strain of command was now heavier than ever. It was only exacerbated by his determination to lead by example, always playing the paragon whose behaviour was beyond reproach. Wolfe's task was made all the more onerous by his unusually close interest in the day-to-day running of the battalion. At Stirling, his regimental orders had revealed a tough disciplinarian, and those issued subsequently showed no relaxation. Savage discipline was a harsh fact of army life, and accepted as such by the hard men who wore the red coat. But whilst King George's officers were ready to resort to the lash to keep their men in check, as already noted, this brutal system of corporal punishment was theoretically balanced by paternalistic care for the rank and file. No officer took this latter responsibility more seriously than James Wolfe. The very first of his regimental orders, issued at Stirling on 12 February, 1749, demonstrated a concern for the well-being of the ordinary soldier that would become a Wolfe trademark. The men were strongly recommended to keep their quarters clean, as the major himself was convinced 'that nothing conduces more to their health'; and NCOs were instructed to bear that in mind during their daily visits to the men's billets, in case Wolfe or his officers might suddenly decide to inspect them in person. His subsequent orders were full of practical attempts to improve discipline – and thereby remove the need for punishment – not least by reminding his officers of *their* crucial role in supervising their men, so preventing them from getting into scrapes in the first place. The importance of this relationship was made crystal clear in orders issued at Perth, on 30 May 1750:

> The shameful drunkenness observed among the men, on pay days in particular, is thought in a great measure to proceed from their not putting a proportion of their pay regularly into their messes: the officers are to remember they have been more than once required to be very exact in this part of their duty, and that there is a standing order in the regiment for frequently visiting the quarters and messes; they are likewise desired to consider that any neglect on their part brings the men to disorders and crimes, and consequently to punishment, which would be avoided by proper care of them, and watch upon their conduct.[20]

Wolfe later described himself as a 'military parent', and this paternalism extended to a keen interest in the fate of individual soldiers. For example, in March 1750 he had written to the Lord Justice Clerk, Charles Erskine, on behalf of one of his grenadiers. Donald Fraser was suspected of murder, but from what *he* knew of him, Wolfe couldn't credit his guilt. He provided Private Fraser with a handsome testimonial: 'The man's behaviour since he came amongst us has been irreproachable and I have not been able to observe either in his look, conduct, or demeanour, any symptom of so black a vilainy, and shall be greatly deceived, if he appears to have been concern'd in an act of such bloody nature.' Wolfe cited a special circumstance in favour of Fraser's innocence. He had been confined in a hospital for almost two months, suffering from a venereal disease. As Wolfe reported, this ailment had required 'a very violent remedy'. However, 'notwithstanding the low condition he was brought to, or the torture it was necessary for him to undergo, he bore everything with a manly resolution, and uncommon firmness by the surgeon's account; methinks he wou'd have trembled, if the guilt of murder had hung upon him'. It was this kind of personal intervention – more characteristic of an idealistic subaltern on the Western Front in 1916 than his Georgian counterpart – that earned Wolfe his enduring reputation as 'the Officer's Friend, and Soldier's Father'.[21]

Immersion in the minutiae of regimental life was one strategy by which Wolfe aimed to combat a mounting sense of frustration and isolation; he looked upon his Scottish service as a 'confinement' and himself as an 'exile'. This bleak outlook was only heightened by the increasing remoteness of his regimental postings. Perth was bad enough, but in October 1750 the 20th's headquarters were switched to dour Dundee; soon afterwards it was ordered to more distant Banff, a tiny windswept township further up the north-east coast.

Wolfe did not accompany his battalion to Banff that autumn. At long last, he had been granted leave, although it was hedged in by restrictions that left him bitterly disappointed. Since the spring, Wolfe had held high hopes of securing permission to travel abroad, so finally providing an opportunity to 'acquire the common accomplishments' that had previously been denied to him by long years of warfare. Wolfe wanted to perfect his French, and to improve his professional knowledge by visiting the military academy at Metz in Lorraine. After spending the winter there, studying artillery and engineering, he intended to 'ramble' along the Rhine into Switzerland then return through France and the Netherlands. Wolfe believed that his proposed itinerary of eight or ten months – a modest version of the 'Grand Tour' customarily undertaken by young gentlemen as part of their education – would administer a badly needed restorative. As he told his father, 'nothing is more necessary towards doing one's part well than a little respite at convenient times'. He clung onto his dream far into the autumn, even though it was increasingly clear that both Bury and Cumberland were strongly opposed to any thought of his leaving Great Britain. Wolfe lobbied the Duke three times, only to be told 'that a lieutenant-colonel was an officer of too high a rank to be allowed to leave his regiment for any considerable time'. This stance was blinkered and short-sighted, Wolfe grumbled, encouraging a potentially disastrous 'ignorance of military affairs'.[22]

Although long anticipated, the dashing of Wolfe's hopes nevertheless dealt him a crushing blow. When he finally arrived in London that November, after breaking his journey to visit relatives in Yorkshire, his mood was prickly. Wolfe stayed with his parents in Old Burlington Street, although the reunion was far from happy. The relationship between the Wolfes was unusually close, but that winter it failed to prevent a major rift. The exact cause of the tension within the devoted family is unclear from the surviving correspondence; but it is likely that an underlying factor was Wolfe's sporadic courtship of Elizabeth Lawson – a dalliance that had provoked fierce parental opposition.

Elizabeth Lawson was the niece of General Sir John Mordaunt. Wolfe had first met her in 1747 whilst on leave to recuperate following his Lauffeldt wound, and had then seen her again during Christmas 1748. In the following April, whilst in Glasgow, Wolfe had confessed to Rickson that he remained 'smitten'. Miss Lawson, who was Wolfe's age and shared his tall, thin physique, had succeeded in winning all of his affections. Elizabeth Lawson was reckoned handsome (although Wolfe rather ungallantly claimed that he did not himself regard her as a beauty), sweet-tempered, sensible and polite – and was not short of suitors. She had already turned down a clergyman with an annual income of £1300, and was currently receiving the addresses of a 'very rich knight'; but luckily for Wolfe, that particular rival was quite mad.

Miss Lawson came with a dowry of £12,000, a sum that Wolfe considered ample. He had already sounded out General Mordaunt and Miss Lawson's mother about a possible match, and the auspices looked favourable. If circumstances permitted, Wolfe intended to propose within a year, but, if he remained sequestered in Scotland, he feared that the fire Miss Lawson had kindled within him would burn out. As he put it to Rickson: 'Young flames must be constantly fed, or they'll evaporate.' But physical distance was not the only, or even the greatest, barrier to the match. Ever eager for the future of their sole surviving son and heir, Edward and Henrietta Wolfe were angling for bigger fish: they had their sights fixed firmly upon a Miss Hoskins of Croydon, who was worth a cool £30,000.[23]

More realistic than romantic, Wolfe's parents reflected the pragmatism of an era in which marriage – particularly amongst the upper and 'middling' classes – was first and foremost a commercial contract. Views were gradually beginning to change, but in the mid eighteenth-century love – whether it existed at the outset or grew gradually over the years – was a bonus rather than a prerequisite on the bourgeois marriage market. A passing infatuation was no substitute for a hefty dowry bringing lasting economic security. True, money-minded arranged matches had recently come under fire, notably from the six prints of Hogarth's *Marriage à la Mode* (1745). The shift from 'interest' to 'affection' was, however, only slowly gathering momentum. In 1749 – the very year that Wolfe was courting Elizabeth Lawson – these conflicting views of marriage were central to the plot of Henry Fielding's novel *Tom Jones*. When all the factors were weighed up, parental pressure might tip the balance: it was not to be sneezed at, particularly when exerted upon heirs destined to inherit the bulk of the estate; and Wolfe was an unusually dutiful son.[24]

Despite these factors, Wolfe persisted in regarding Miss Lawson as a potential bride. He told his mother that whilst her high-profile position of maid of honour at court was 'but the genteeler way to wickedness', in his opinion, she did not need such public exposure 'to be taken notice of, admired and married'. That winter – perhaps because of the distance that Wolfe had already identified as a likely hindrance – the affair apparently foundered. Indeed, as he informed his mother, 'This fresh disappointment in love has changed my natural disposition to such a degree, that I believe it is now possible I might prevail upon myself not to refuse twenty or thirty thousand pounds, if properly offered!' Henrietta Wolfe now took advantage of events to promote her own favoured candidate for daughter-in-law. One of Wolfe's officers, and her neighbour in Croydon, had delivered Miss Hoskins's compliments, sung her praises as 'a complete woman' and offered the friendly advice that he should 'make up to her'. Reporting this development to his mother, Wolfe could not resist adding that the officer in question was obliged to confess that he did *not* know Miss Lawson.[25]

By February 1750, Mrs Wolfe felt sure enough of her ground to write James a letter casually mentioning that Miss Lawson was due to wed another, and that only ill-health prevented the match. Her son's impassioned reply showed that Elizabeth Lawson was anything but forgotten. He chided his mother for raising those matters with such indifference: 'How could you tell me that you liked her, and at the same time say her illness prevents her wedding? I don't think you believe she ever touched me at all ...' In the face of this blind devotion to what had seemed like a lost cause, General Edward Wolfe pitched in alongside his wife in an effort to make his stubborn son see sense. The general's letter does not survive, but James's reply leaves little doubt that it contained a severe rebuke: he explained that he had never intended to cause his father 'any uneasiness by obstinacy, or perseverance in an error'. Within weeks, the customary harmony between the Wolfes had been restored. By 29 March 1750, James could tell his mother of his 'happiness to be so far in your esteem'.[26]

The storm had apparently blown itself out by the time Wolfe was reunited with his parents in London that November. It is possible that he now sought to renew his suit of Miss Lawson in person, only to be spurned; or that, in bitterness and frustration at failing to gain foreign leave, some dismissive mention of her by his parents led to harsh words. Whatever the spark, the results were dramatic.[27]

For months, as he struggled with the burden of command, Wolfe had been straining to hold his instincts and emotions in check. Now his customary self-control finally snapped. As Wolfe confided to his friend Rickson, he promptly careered off the rails and into trouble:

> I went to London in November and came back in the middle of April. In that short time I committed more imprudent acts than in all my life before.

I lived in the idlest, dissolute, abandoned manner that could be conceived, and that not out of vice, which is the most extraordinary part of it. I have escaped at length, and am once again master of my reason, and hereafter it shall rule my conduct, at least I hope so.[28]

In his devastating 1936 assault upon Wolfe's reputation, Professor Adair memorably dismissed this episode as 'one meagre fling amidst the snares of London, one small wild oat amidst a large field of carefully tended wheat'.[29] But it was clearly much more than some lost weekend. Wolfe was in London for *five months*, although whether he indulged in Boswellian excesses, or was content with a more modest level of debauchery, must sadly remain a matter for speculation. Whatever the case, Georgian London certainly offered ample opportunities and temptations for a frustrated young bachelor with money in his pockets. There were pleasure gardens, coffee houses, theatres, taverns and, not least, brothels. The world of the era's high class prostitutes and their clients had been vividly depicted in John Cleland's pornographic best-seller, *Fanny Hill*, published in two volumes during 1748–49. All in all, mid-eighteenth-century London was the perfect playground for a young man looking to forget his sorrows.

Back with his regiment in Scotland, a contrite Wolfe apologized to his father for his recent misdeeds. The old general had ridiculed the situation in which James had placed himself during this London inter-lude; he, in his turn, acknowledged the criticism to be fully justified, although in his own defence he pointed out that his plight was hardly unique, and the effects of such experiences often were 'very extraor-dinary'. Exactly *what* Wolfe's 'situation' entailed is unclear from his correspondence, although he was possibly recalling an embarrassing fit of lovesick pique at his failed courtship. The following month, when Wolfe renewed his plea for paternal forgiveness, he alluded to his recent 'indiscretion'. Here, too, the precise nature of the lapse is unspecified. This enigma has encouraged speculation that Wolfe's spasm of licen-tiousness went beyond conventional whoring and instead embraced a homosexual liaison. In support of this theory, his failure to win and wed Elizabeth Lawson has been cited as evidence that his interest in women was never more than lukewarm and superficial, and that his real preferences lay elsewhere: if not actively homosexual, it has been suggested, Wolfe was at least latently so.[30]

Although certainly intriguing, this is pure conjecture, uncorroborated by any statement of Wolfe or his contemporaries. As has been
seen, Wolfe's pursuit of Miss Lawson was anything but half-hearted. In
addition, his surviving letters contain many expressions of interest in
the opposite sex. Writing to his mother in August 1751, for example, he
gave fulsome praise to the women of Peterhead, of whom some were

> of good understanding, others of great vivacity and others very handsome;
> so that a man could not fail to be pleased with such variety to choose out
> of; and for my part, I always think a pretty maid either has all the other
> beauties or does not want them.[31]

Of course such statements, particularly when made by a man to his
mother, do not rule out the possibility that his true instincts are actually being suppressed. But a stronger argument against the contention
that Wolfe was gay lies in the rampant homophobia of his countrymen:
such unorthodox behaviour was all very well for Italians and other such
hot-blooded races, but it could scarcely be countenanced amongst true
Britons; those placed in the pillory following conviction for 'unnatural
acts' could expect savage and potentially fatal treatment at the hands of
vindictive mobs. In the bigoted climate of the age, if Wolfe had revealed
even a suspicion of homosexual tendencies, they would undoubtedly
have been noted. When Wolfe ultimately achieved high command he
faced criticism that was both vocal and personal – yet a trait which
would have opened an obvious chink in his armour was never mentioned by even his most outspoken detractors.

Regardless of its details, Wolfe's London spree left him exhausted and
ill. For some time, James had suffered from a scurvy that erupted on
his hands during the summer; antiscorbutic spas, drafts of goats' whey
and a Spartan regimen of cold baths had all failed to cure the problem.
But this was a minor, if persistent, complaint. In fact, since his arrival
in Scotland, Wolfe's health had been generally sound, and long months
in the Highlands, where recreation consisted of arduous hunting in the
glens, had left him fitter than ever before. James Wolfe was tougher than
he looked: although resembling 'a skeleton in motion', his gaunt frame
was capable of considerable endurance. Writing to his father from Perth
in July 1750, he recounted how he went 'three days successively a-shoot-
ing in the hills from five in the morning till night'. Wolfe had never

known 'such fatigue', though such exercise clearly worked wonders. Two months later, he could declare himself 'as hard as flint' and indifferent to whatever Scotland's climate could throw at him.[32]

But soon after returning from the south Wolfe experienced symptoms of an illness that would make his previous ailments seem like mere irritations. By the early summer of 1751 he was suffering from 'the gravel' – an excruciating bladder complaint caused by the accumulation of crystals, or 'stones', in the urinary tract. The timing of this illness, and its established link to infections of the bladder, invite speculation that this was an unwelcome reminder of Wolfe's leave in London and may have been triggered by a sexually transmitted disease. That August, Wolfe had tried to treat himself by imbibing the famous mineral waters of Peterhead; they eased his gravel, only to cause a violent reaction in the lungs and stomach, plus persistent chest pain. When he turned to a renowned physician for advice Wolfe had been recommended a treatment of soap; he was willing to swallow that revolting remedy, and undertake whatever else was necessary to stop the pain. As Wolfe told his mother, he was hardly the stoical type: 'my temper of mind is not fashioned for much suffering; patience is not the leading virtue there'. His naturally fiery disposition had always left him liable to fly off the handle; but in coming years the agony of the gravel would make him still more irritable. It helps to explain the explosive rants that pepper Wolfe's later letters, and which have provided such choice quotations for critics keen to demonstrate his utter disdain for most of humanity.[33]

Lingering embarrassment and painful illness were not the only legacies of Wolfe's months in London. Before succumbing to the lure of the city's livelier attractions, he had attended the House of Commons, listening from the public gallery to the debates on the security of British North America. There had never been any doubt that the peace of 1748 was merely a breathing space in the long-running struggle for supremacy between Britain and France; by the winter of 1750–51, there were growing signs that the next, inevitable, conflagration would be sparked by friction between their rival colonies across the Atlantic.

Fed by steady immigration, Britain's North American possessions along the eastern seaboard were now bursting their boundaries. Attempts to ease the pressure, by sending expeditions beyond the frontiers in search of new lands to settle, had raised the hackles of the Native American tribes who still occupied the interior and had set alarm bells ringing at Versailles. The colony of New France was composed of two widely separated territories: Canada, concentrated along the St Lawrence River in the north; and, far to the south, Louisiana, at the mouth of the Mississippi. British schemes to push into the Ohio Valley raised fears that a wedge would be driven between them. For their part the British colonists did not doubt that France was determined to check their expansion – indeed, to corral them behind the natural barrier of the Appalachian Mountains – by cultivating alliances with the Indians and exploiting that influence to construct fortified trading posts on an arc curving from Louisiana to Canada.

Such concerns prevailed despite a striking disparity in the populations of the rival colonies. Although its origins likewise lay in the early seventeenth century, by 1750 New France could muster just 70,000 inhabitants to pitch against the one and a half million contained within Britain's territories. Yet in a succession of vicious clashes since 1689 – each of which paralleled the formal European hostilities between the parent powers – the outnumbered French colonists had demonstrated a proficiency in backwoods warfare that left their opponents intimidated and demoralized. And unlike the fourteen separate English colonies, whose autonomous governments too often struggled to present a united front against the common enemy, New France was a centralized regime subject to the orders of a single governor-general. If, as all the signs now suggested, a fresh bout of Anglo-French warfare flared up in North America, its outcome would depend upon more than mere numbers.

When Wolfe wintered in London, it seemed that the flashpoint would be far to the north, where British Nova Scotia faced French Acadia. Ceded by France in 1713, Nova Scotia was a precarious possession, very different from the thriving colonies to the south. Its scanty population was largely composed of the original French-speaking and Catholic settlers and their descendants; understandably resentful at the imposition of alien rule, these Acadians and their Indian neighbours, the Micmacs, were theoretically kept in check by a puny British garrison at Annapolis Royal. Britain's restoration of Louisbourg to France in 1748 – an act that so outraged the enterprising New Englanders who had captured it three years earlier – only increased the threat to Nova Scotia and the lucrative Newfoundland fisheries. It was to counter this menace that Britain soon after established her own naval base and civilian settlement at Halifax, named after George Dunk, Earl of Halifax, the vigorous new head of the Board of Trade which was theoretically responsible for colonial administration.[34]

Even before sitting in on the parliamentary debates, Wolfe had taken a keen interest in the fate of Nova Scotia. His faithful correspondent William Rickson of the 47th Foot had sailed with the troops sent to defend Halifax, and Wolfe lost no time in pumping him for information. Writing from Dundee in the autumn of 1750, he was hungry for the smallest detail. How was the community organized? And what of the climate and soil?

The same letter included an extraordinary declaration of Wolfe's unswerving belief in the benefits of British rule: these flowed naturally from 'the excellent nature of our Government, which extends in full force to its remotest dependency'. He contrasted the freedoms enjoyed by Britain's American colonies with the 'despotism and bigotry' of their French and Spanish neighbours. 'Within the influence of our happy Government', he added, 'all nations are in security.' It would be difficult to find a clearer statement of faith in Britain's imperial mission – a confidence that 'the British way' was quite simply the best. Without changing a syllable, Wolfe's words could easily have been uttered more than a century later, at the very apogee of the sprawling Victorian empire for which he was to become a heroic prototype. Indeed, whilst James Wolfe's posthumous role as imperial icon owed much to the enduring popularity of Benjamin West's painting of his last moments, it was singularly appropriate, fully reflecting the beliefs that he had espoused in life.[35]

Wolfe had no doubt that North America would soon become a cockpit of Anglo-French conflict. To meet that challenge, he told Rickson, Britain's colonies should possess both a large regular garrison and 'inhabitants trained to arms'. But whilst Parliament had granted substantial sums of money for colonial defence, there was no decision to send reinforcements across the Atlantic: in Wolfe's recollection of that winter's parliamentary debates, the Prime Minister, Henry Pelham, had spoken 'very faintly upon the subject', warning of the need to think carefully about actions likely to instigate hostilities 'with our ever lasting and irreconcilable adversary'.[36]

Although understandably reluctant to become embroiled in a costly war with France, the ministry was not as heedless of colonial security as Wolfe believed. In the summer of 1750, Pelham's elder brother, Thomas Pelham-Holles, Duke of Newcastle, had left no doubt of his determination to maintain the integrity of Britain's American possessions and to resist French encroachments. Writing to John Russell, Duke of Bedford, he emphasized that the issue at stake was not simply 'the fate of Nova Scotia, but of all the Northern Colonies; which are of so infinite importance to Great Britain'.[37]

As low-level Anglo-French conflict smouldered away in Nova Scotia, a frustrated Wolfe remained in Scotland, reflecting upon his recent behaviour, and bemoaning his continuing inactivity. That autumn, Wolfe's battalion shifted its quarters yet again, this time to the Highland capital of Inverness, long notorious as a hotbed of Jacobitism. Wolfe's disconsolate mood was not improved by the lack of opportunities for hunting and shooting – both 'healthy and manly diversions' in which he now delighted. He was instead obliged to content himself with riding out to Fort George, a vast strongpoint that was under construction where the point of Ardersier jutted far into the Moray Firth, and the battlefield of Culloden. Surveying that ground at his leisure, and revisiting the bloody events of five years before, Wolfe now felt that things might have been handled differently. There were lessons to be learned, he told his father: 'The more a soldier thinks of the false steps of those that are gone before, the more likely he is to avoid them.'[38]

That winter, as Wolfe's melancholy returned, so his family correspondence grew ever longer and more reflective. In a rambling letter to his mother of 6 November 1751, he confessed himself reconciled to the soldier's lot: for all its hardships, the military life was much to his liking. Yet he was drawn to his vocation by something more than the surface 'glare and blaze' of an officer's scarlet and gold. He wrote, 'there is an object much beyond it that attracts my eye; and it is with some concern that I see those that direct us often miss the proper mark, and set us, their servants, upon wrong pursuits'. This growing sense that destiny had marked him down for greater things than patrolling the

Highlands fed into an intense patriotism that Wolfe was itching to harness before it was too late: 'while I have vigour, if the country wants a man of good intentions, they'll always find me ready – devoted, I might say – to their service'.[39]

In a pattern already seen at Glasgow and elsewhere, Wolfe slowly began to warm towards his new Highland neighbours, making the most of such entertainment as Inverness could offer. Every fortnight there was an assembly patronized by British officers. The fiddles and bagpipes, firelight and reels, proved irresistible to the local gentlewomen, even though they hailed from such staunchly Jacobite clans as the Frasers, MacDonalds, and McIntoshes. As wild as their own hills, these 'female rebels', as Wolfe dubbed them, were only too willing to set aside their political scruples for an evening of 'sound and movement'. In a symbolic act of reconciliation, Wolfe had claimed the honour of partnering the daughter of Alexander MacDonald of Keppoch, a valiant old chieftain slain leading his clan in a futile charge at Culloden.[40]

Despite such welcome distractions, the long winter took its toll upon Wolfe's spirits. On 22 December 1751 – his twenty-fifth birthday according to the calendar then in use – he picked up his pen to write to his mother and to take stock of himself. This significant anniversary found him in an unusually sombre and philosophical mood. The winter was wearing away, he began, and with it life itself. It was the dead of night, and all was quiet and peaceful – 'one of those intervals wherein men think of what they really are, and what they really should be; how much is expected, and how little performed'. The letter, which was so long that it encompassed several instalments, addressed themes that had troubled Wolfe since his first arrival in Scotland. Lengthy stints with the regiment raised the possibility that he would imbibe 'the tyrannical principles of an absolute commander', becoming 'proud, insolent, and intolerable'. Only regular leave would allow him to mingle with his social superiors, and thereby remind him of his own 'true condition'. Time away from the regiment would also permit Wolfe to enjoy the company of women and their softening influence; but his recent disappointment in love had left him wary. He was determined that this last refinement should never be bought at the price of 'loss of reason'. He added bitterly: 'Better to be a savage of some use than a gentle, amorous puppy, obnoxious to all the world.'[41]

The winter of 1751–52 was harsh. That Christmas, as the temperature plummeted ever lower, the 20th's officers built up their fires and resignedly munched upon 'exceeding bad mince-pies' that the wife of the regiment's sutler forced upon them. Despite this unappetizing fare, as Wolfe told his father, it had been 'a merry Christmas indeed', with no shortage of 'mirth and pastime' or 'good fellowship'. Wolfe's efforts to improve relations with the local population were now paying off. Unlike most of their quarters, where they had been shunned as 'no better than the sons of darkness, and given up unto Satan', in Inverness – thanks to conspicuous weekly attendance at the Kirk – their reputations were 'as white as the snow' that blanketed the surrounding hills.

Of course, there were always exceptions. Wolfe's friend and major, Arthur Loftus, was unable to curb his lusts. Wolfe added: 'I'm afraid that Loftus will everywhere be the same man, equally abandon'd to the fury of his wild passions, to the great havock and spoil of Scotch chastity.' But the major's carnal pleasures came at a price. He claimed to suffer from a 'rheumatick scurvy' similar to Wolfe's. As mercury worked wonders for *his* 'disorder', Loftus had urged Wolfe to use it too. Mercury was the era's standard, and only, treatment for syphilis, a fact of which Wolfe was only too well aware. 'Sure, if I was to follow his council', he joked, 'we should misapply that noble specifick.'

Wolfe's persistent 'gravel' was, however, no laughing matter, although he was optimistic that the drastic treatment he had embarked upon to ease it would ultimately prove effective. Using language that suggests an unusual acquaintance with the inner workings of his body, he explained:

> I have begun to use soap to cleanse the passages in the kidneys and all the urinary channels, which are at present a little clogg'd. This, with the aid of some very good Rhenish wine from Aberdeen, must infallibly set everything to rights, and relieve me from the apprehensions of future lacerations and incisions.

The brother of Wolfe's landlady had died two days before of the same distemper. 'I was glad to find', he quipped blackly, 'that there's some distant hopes of a cure, when matters are even at the worst.'[42]

Christmas cheer had buoyed up Wolfe's spirits into the New Year, but they soon dropped once more. Until the spring thaw there was little chance of straying beyond Inverness, and Wolfe found his 'long confinement' more irksome than ever. Once again, the necessity of leading by example placed him under immense strain. As he told his father, he could not drink or gamble for fear that his officers, who were 'already but too much inclined to that ruinous and disastrous vice', would follow suit. In May, Lord Bury was expected to venture north to review his regiment. Wolfe had long since lost respect for his colonel; but, as Bury enjoyed shooting, his arrival would at least give him a chance to indulge in his own favourite pastime as they embarked upon a rambling tour of inspection from one remote outpost to another.[43]

Bury, who finally arrived in Inverness on 13 April 1752, lost no time in souring relations with the locals. Keen to demonstrate their loyalty to the Hanoverians, the town's magistrates had greeted Bury with an invitation to an entertainment to be held two days later, on the Duke of Cumberland's birthday. Bury responded by tactlessly suggesting that the party should be postponed until the following day, 16 April – the sixth anniversary of Cumberland's victory at nearby Culloden. Taken aback at this boorish request, which reopened the very wounds they had been hoping to heal, the magistrates maintained that it was now too late to change their arrangements. That was indeed regrettable, his Lordship replied, as he had already mentioned the matter to his men, and dreaded to think what outrages they might commit upon the town in their disappointment. Bury's bullying achieved its object, and the magistrates of Inverness were grudgingly obliged to celebrate the bloody rout of the Jacobite army.[44]

Wolfe must have attended Bury's provocative party, although he failed to mention it in any of his letters. His own opinion of his colonel had not improved with close acquaintance. Writing to his father on 23 April, he complained that Bury was full of 'fair words and promises'; although agreeing that Wolfe's 'long confinement' should come to an end, it was far from certain that Cumberland would grant the extended leave that he still craved. And, in Wolfe's scornful opinion, hide-bound soldiers like Bury lacked vision: they believed that 'a stupid kind of obedience and conformity to their will supplies the want of military virtue and ability'.[45]

In mid May, with Bury still at his side, Wolfe and the 20th Foot left Inverness for new quarters at Fort Augustus, following the remarkable road that General Wade had cut and blasted along the south-west side of Loch Ness. Fort Augustus was the centremost of three strong points dominating the Great Glen fault line that slashed diagonally through the Northern Highlands; anchoring the chain were Fort George, still under construction northeast of Inverness, and to the south-west, at the head of Loch Linnhe, the old Fort William.[46]

Since its construction a decade earlier, Fort Augustus had provided a base for patrols into the surrounding countryside. Whilst Wolfe made his headquarters there with a garrison of eighty recruits, the seasoned bulk of the battalion was soon dispersed in penny packets on the onerous 'Highland duty'. Wolfe was scarcely surprised when Lord Bury speedily decamped for Fort William, ready for his return to England. Wolfe intended to visit his outposts, and perhaps accept an invitation from the Laird of Macleod to view the clan's fortress of Dunvegan Castle on the Isle of Skye.[47]

The times remained turbulent. Within weeks of his arrival at Fort Augustus, Wolfe reported a murder that created a sensation at the time, and which later featured in Robert Louis Stevenson's great adventure novel *Kidnapped*. According to Wolfe's information, the 'bloody deed' had been committed by two Highlanders at the instigation of the wife of a banished rebel, Charles Stewart. The victim was Colin Campbell, who had been appointed 'factor', or overseer, to Stewart's forfeited estate; the alleged motive for the murder was Campbell's intention to uproot the old tenants and replace them with others. The suspected assassin, Allan Breck Stewart, was never brought to justice, although James Stewart, the brother of Charles, was convicted of the crime and hanged in chains near the remote spot where Campbell had been shot down.[48]

At Fort Augustus Wolfe was involved in another episode that highlighted the troubled state of the Highlands in the wake of rebellion, and which could likewise have been plucked directly from the pages of Scott or Stevenson. When Prince Charles Edward Stuart fled Scotland for France in 1746, he had left behind a cache of gold – the so-called Loch Arkaig treasure – against the day when he would return to raise the Stuart banner once more. This Jacobite war chest was entrusted to the keeping of Ewen Macpherson of Cluny: he had led his clan throughout the '45, and in September 1746, when Charles Edward was a hunted fugitive in the heather, sheltered him in his own bolt-hole, a man-made cave complex on Ben Alder nicknamed 'Cluny's Cage'.[49]

Prince Charlie never came back again, but six years later Cluny remained at large, his capture a prime objective for patrolling redcoats. Wolfe and his men searched for him in vain. According to one near-contemporary story, Wolfe offered 'Macpherson of Phonas' no less than £5000 to betray Cluny's 'lurking place' – an offer that Phonas spurned, 'from his attachment to his chief'. Impressed by this tribal loyalty, Wolfe was thereafter 'most attentive' to Phonas, which given that clans-man's 'character and manners, surprised every person'.[50]

Wolfe also developed a healthy respect for the elusive Cluny and his kinfolk, although this did not stop him from scheming to slaughter them. In a candid letter written several years later to Captain Rickson – now returned from Nova Scotia and himself posted to Fort Augustus – Wolfe offered the following advice:

> Mr McPherson should have a couple of hundred men in his neighbourhood, with orders to massacre the whole clan if they show the least symptom of rebellion. They are a war-like tribe, and he is a cunning, resolute fellow himself. They should be narrowly watched; and the party there should be well commanded.

Wolfe revealed that he had himself tried to eliminate Cluny and his clan through a plan of breathtaking ruthlessness. A small sergeant's detachment was sent out to capture Cluny; if they succeeded, and the Macphersons attempted to rescue their chief, the sergeant had orders to kill him instantly. That, Wolfe calculated, would have led to the destruction of his detachment, so providing him with an excuse to march immediately into the Macphersons' territory with fire and sword. The plan came to nothing, although there is little doubt that Wolfe wanted to implement it. He asked Rickson: 'Would you believe that I am so bloody? It was my real intention, and I hope such execution will be done upon the first that revolt, to teach them their duty and keep the Highlands in awe. They are a people better governed by fear than favour.'[51]

Wolfe was, therefore, not above sacrificing a patrol of his own men in hopes of instigating a bloodbath to rival the infamous massacre of the Glencoe MacDonalds in 1692. The scheme reveals an unscrupulous

streak that has left even his most ardent admirers shocked, disap-
proving, and seeking an explanation in the brutalizing influence of
the Highlands. But for Wolfe the professional soldier, the ends clearly
justified the means.[52]

Despite Wolfe's scepticism about his prospects of leave, Cumberland
was eventually persuaded that Lord Bury's diligent lieutenant-colonel
deserved a furlough. On 11 June 1752, General Churchill informed Wolfe
that both he and Captain William Howe of his regiment had permission
to absent themselves from duty for ten months to settle their 'private
affairs in England'. There was no mention of Wolfe's longed-for foreign
leave, but it was a start.[53]

Wolfe's furlough was to begin immediately, and he lost no time
in taking it. Quitting Fort Augustus in mid-June, he inspected the
regiment's detachment ensconced in the fortified barracks at Ruthven,
before moving on to Perth, where he stayed with his old friend, Major
Arthur Loftus. Wolfe planned to start his furlough by visiting his
favourite Uncle Walter in Dublin, and at the end of the month sailed
from Portpatrick, near Glasgow, for Ireland. The exact details of Wolfe's
Irish itinerary are obscure, but he travelled first through the north of
the country, probably visiting Belfast and Londonderry, before making
a special pilgrimage to the site of the Battle of the Boyne. If proof is
required of Wolfe's Protestant ancestry, it is surely his emotional reaction to the ground where King William had triumphed over 'Popery'
back in 1690: 'I had more satisfaction in looking at this spot than in all
the variety I have met with,' he assured his father.

Wolfe arrived in Dublin looking tanned and fit – 'leaner than can be
described, and burnt to a chip', as he put it. Uncle Walter, by contrast,
was in a sorry state, swathed in flannel against the rheumatism or gout;
his doctors were unsure which was to blame for the pain that racked the
old soldier's frame. Despite his complaints, Major Wolfe was as cheerful
and chatty as ever, and his nephew found Dublin and its inhabitants
equally lively and to his taste; although already a 'prodigious city', it
was still expanding. Georgian Dublin's streets bustled with a robust
population. The women in particular caught Wolfe's eye, being 'very
handsome', with 'clearer skins and fairer complexions' than their rivals
across the Irish Sea. Neither were they shy about displaying their

charms. Wolfe's glowing tribute to the beauty of Ireland's daughters was heartfelt: quite 'by accident', whilst travelling through the country, he had met 'the widow of a poor officer who was killed at Fontenoy'. Whether this chance encounter led to a love affair is impossible to establish, although there are hints that the relationship involved more than mere friendship. Three years later, a letter to Wolfe from the same widow arrived at his parents' home, obliging him to explain who she was; and after Wolfe's death a satirical sketch depicted a naked and voluptuous 'Irish Venus' performing an energetic mourning dance and prostrating herself before his monument.[54]

Sometime in August, Wolfe crossed over to Bristol, travelling on to his parents' new house at Blackheath, on Croom's Hill and within Greenwich Park. The Wolfes' neighbours included Philip, Lord Chesterfield, the driving force behind Britain's belated switch from the 'old style' to 'new style' calendar. In reckoning dates, Britain had previously lagged eleven days behind the rest of Europe, but on 3 September 1752, finally fell into step. It is unknown whether James Wolfe woke on the morning of what was now officially 14 September bemoaning the loss of a week and a half's worth of precious leave; elsewhere, his resentful countrymen rioted to the cry of 'Give us back our eleven days!'[55]

Now, at long last, Wolfe received permission to travel beyond Great Britain. It is likely that his father had lobbied Cumberland on his behalf. James vowed never to forget the general's 'generous proceeding' – a term suggesting something more than yet another donation from the parental coffers. Wolfe left Blackheath on 2 October, and two days later boarded the packet ship that plied between Dover and Calais during those intervals when Britain and France were at peace. The crossing lasted just three and a half hours, but the Channel proved choppy enough to turn Wolfe's queasy stomach: 'I never suffered so much in so short a time at sea,' he groaned.

Within days, Wolfe was in Paris. His first impressions, as reported to his father soon after, were mixed. The houses of the nobility were 'very magnificent, far surpassing any we have in London'. But the famous Tuileries Gardens were a great disappointment – 'as disagreeable a sandy walk as one would wish' – and far inferior to the Mall or Greenwich Park. As for the Parisians themselves, they were sprightly enough, although obsessed with appearances. Wolfe was eager to engage a master to teach him French, and would soon be taking lessons in horsemanship, fencing and dancing. Wolfe's arrival had coincided with a widespread mood of relief and celebration for the recovery of King Louis XV's heir, the Dauphin, who had been dangerously ill with small-pox. A fortnight earlier, the Duc d'Orléans had provided a magnificent fête at the Château of Saint-Cloud, complete with spectacular fireworks and a lavish masked ball for 4000 members of elite society. Wolfe learned that the entertainment had been 'in the highest taste', although the expense was 'prodigious'. His comments reflected the ambivalence with which Englishmen of his class viewed their old enemies. Whilst scoffing at the foppish superficiality of the French, they nonetheless acknowledged the superior sophistication of their culture – and flocked to Paris in hopes that some of that polish would rub off on *them*.[56]

Wolfe lost no time in paying his respects to Britain's ambassador in Paris, William Anne Keppel, Earl of Albemarle. The father of Wolfe's colonel, Lord Bury, in 1746 Albemarle had reluctantly assumed the mantle of commander-in-chief in Scotland after Cumberland returned in triumph to London. It was a frustrating and thankless task, but Albemarle had done a conscientious job, earning his reward of a prime diplomatic posting. A stocky Dutchman in his forties, Albemarle was a Francophile; he was on friendly terms with both King Louis and his mistress, the remarkable Jeanne Poisson, Madame de Pompadour. Bury had paved Wolfe's way to France with a letter of introduction to his father. Its effect was gratifying, as Albemarle had treated Wolfe with 'excessive politeness'. Whatever Wolfe's gripes about Bury's lackadaisical approach to military matters, he now lost no time in acknowledging his sincere appreciation for this crucial patronage.

Albemarle spared no pains in taking Wolfe under his wing. Whenever the ambassador came to Paris from his country residence at Fontainebleau, he invited Wolfe to his home just outside the city, and immediately put him at his ease there. Many other British visitors to Paris enjoyed Albemarle's hospitality, and Wolfe was able to widen his circle of acquaintances. They included the eighteen-year-old Charles Lennox, Duke of Richmond, a promising soldier with whom Wolfe struck up a lasting friendship. Richmond, who was soon after appointed to a captaincy in the 20th Regiment, wanted a knowledgeable companion to accompany him on a tour of the fortresses of Flanders and Lorraine.

Wolfe recommended his soldier friend Guy Carleton for a job that was likely to generate both pension and patronage, and Cumberland approved the appointment. Another of Wolfe's Paris acquaintances, Lady Archibald Hamilton, died of a fever on 3 December; her son, William, aged twenty-one, was an ensign in the Third Foot, or 'Buffs', and a 'friend and companion' for whom Wolfe hoped to do his best. As the future Sir William Hamilton, whose wife Emma became the mistress of Horatio Nelson, he was destined to provide yet another link between Wolfe and the legendary sailor who would seek to emulate him.[57]

Through Albemarle's influence, Wolfe soon gained a privileged insight into the very heart of the French court. On New Year's Day 1753 he received his first taste of Versailles. Writing to his mother next day, Wolfe pictured himself 'a cold spectator of what we commonly call splendour and magnificence'. He had travelled out to the vast palace in Richmond's coach, and at Albemarle's invitation waited upon him as he passed through the various apartments to be received by the Queen, her children, the Secretary-of-State, and finally, by the real power behind the throne, Madame de Pompadour, who made a point of greeting the British ambassador with special 'civilities and courtesy'. Wolfe's visit coincided with an installation of a Knight of the Order of the Holy Ghost, and he had a fine view of the ceremony in the King's chapel. But Wolfe refused to be dazzled by the glitter of Versailles. He was repelled by the fawning rituals of the court, as a 'multitude of men and women were assembled to bow and pay their compliments in the most submissive manner to a creature of their own species'.[58]

For all his disdain for such bowing and scraping, Wolfe was soon back inside Versailles, this time bending his own knee before the King himself. On 9 January, Wolfe and his cousin John Whetham were amongst a select handful of Britons presented, at Albemarle's proposal, to the French royal family. Last, but not least, they were brought before Madame de Pompadour, who received them whilst at her toilette. Wolfe was impressed. As he told his father the following day:

> We found her curling her hair. She is extremely handsome, and, by her conversation with the Ambassador and others that were present, I judge she must have a great deal of wit and understanding.[59]

As Wolfe readily detected, 'la Pompadour' was not just a pretty face.

There was much more to the famous royal mistress than the peachy complexion and extravagantly frilled silk dresses captured in the lush canvases of François Boucher. Her friends and admirers included Voltaire, that acerbic flag-bearer of the Enlightenment, and Etienne-François de Stainville – like Wolfe, a veteran of Dettingen and Lauffeldt – who, as the Duc de Choiseul, would become one of France's finest Foreign Ministers. Perhaps the most striking evidence of the breadth of the Pompadour's interests was her extensive personal library: these 3525 volumes ranged from poetry and novels – including translations of *Moll Flanders*, *Robinson Crusoe* and *Tom Jones* – to history, biography and philosophy.[60] When Wolfe met her, Madame de Pompadour was at the height of her powers, wielding immense influence over appointments and policy. She was not to know that the gauche young British officer she had conquered so easily would soon play a crucial role in dismantling France's American empire.

Although he seldom dined without enjoying the company of some of the prettiest belles in Paris, Wolfe remained immune to their charms. As he explained to his mother, the wound left by his failed courtship of Elizabeth Lawson was still too raw. Whilst now largely recovered from the 'disorder' into which his 'extravagant love' had plunged him, he could 'never hear her name mentioned without a twitch, or hardly ever think of her with indifference'. But even heartbreak had its uses, as Wolfe explained:

> It has defended me against other women, introduced a great deal of philosophy and tranquillity as to all objects of our strongest affections, and something softened the disposition to severity and rigour that I had contracted in the camp, trained up as I was from my infancy to the conclusion of the Peace, in war and tumult.

Meanwhile, Wolfe's determination to hone his social skills was yielding dividends. His French had improved, although with so many English-speaking friends progress was slower than anticipated; and whilst Wolfe's dancing master believed that time was too short for him to perfect the intricate moves of the minuet, he had learned enough 'to dance not to be laughed at'. Each daybreak Wolfe was out riding. With the natural advantage of long legs, he hoped soon to manage 'a horse at a hand-gallop'. Wolfe's lanky physique stood him in equally good stead in the fencing class, where his master declared him to have 'no inconsiderable lunge'. All this tuition cost money – as did food, servants and lodgings, suits of clothes, and the ruffles that Wolfe was obliged to wear on his shirts when mixing in polite society. He was soon asking his long-suffering father, the general, for fresh funds, swearing upon his honour that his outlay on gambling and women combined had 'not amounted to twenty Louis-d'ors'.[61]

By the beginning of March 1753 Wolfe was tiring of Paris and its superficialities. In addition, as he told his mother, the French could not help looking upon the English as their enemies – and rightly so. Wolfe's thoughts were now returning to professional matters. Lord Albemarle had mentioned that Louis XV planned to hold a military encampment in the early summer, and felt that Wolfe would make an ideal observer. Wolfe lost no time in writing to Lord Bury to propose himself for the job, particularly as it seemed likely that the Prussians and Austrians would also send troops.[62]

Wolfe doubted that Cumberland would approve his request, and with good reason; in fact, the Duke responded by ordering him home immediately, even though his leave of absence was not over. The scattered companies of the 20th Regiment were due to assemble in Glasgow by the end of the month, and Cumberland expected its errant lieutenant-colonel to join them. Frustrated at a lost opportunity to view 'half the armies in Europe', Wolfe had no option but to obey rather than risk the royal wrath.[63]

It was soon clear that Wolfe's presence was badly needed. Following a brief stay with his parents in Blackheath, and a jolting journey northward by post-chaise and on horseback, he arrived in Glasgow to find his battalion in a sorry state. Perhaps unsurprisingly given his compulsive philandering, Major Loftus had died of apoplexy, leaving a tearful widow and daughter behind him. One ensign had been struck speechless with palsy, whilst another collapsed in convulsions after supper on the very night that Wolfe rejoined the regiment, a sight that had shocked everyone present. And if that was not enough, if Wolfe's colourful letter is to be credited, some of the subalterns were spitting blood, and others wanted to sell their commissions and quit the regiment before they were utterly ruined.[64]

Despite these 'melancholy circumstances', Wolfe himself was in unusually high spirits. That summer, the regiment marched back into the Highlands, a rugged region that he had grown to love. Long before the cult of the 'picturesque' and 'romantic' landscape, Wolfe could characterize the western side of Loch Lomond, where he accompanied five companies of the regiment on road-building duty, as 'beautifully rough and wild'. Wolfe's relish for Highland fishing and shooting – those twin passions of the Victorian gentleman – was equally precocious. Writing to his mother from the lochside camp of Inverdouglas that June, he reported that a man might find much entertainment thereabouts, 'provided he has strength to climb up the mountains, and has keenness to pursue the game they produce'. Wolfe clearly anticipated good sport. Always fond of dogs, he was delighted that his cousin Edward Goldsmith had sent him 'the finest young pointer that ever was seen', plus a fishing rod and reel. With a salmon rod donated by Uncle Walter in Dublin, flies from his father and his own guns, Wolfe was well appointed to massacre the local wildlife.[65]

The summer of 1753 was Wolfe's last in Scotland. In September the 20th Regiment quit Glasgow for new quarters in England, marching south in fine weather, its officers and men sunburned darker than the battalion from Minorca that replaced them. The regiment was due to be inspected *en route* by Cumberland himself. Despite great efforts to restore order since his return from France, Wolfe feared that his men would make a 'very indifferent appearance' under the critical royal eye. Their uniforms were old and shabby from work on the Highland roads, and their drill distinctly shaky. This resulted from the interference of Lord Bury, who wanted to alter the exercise pace from quick to slow, with the result that the men were 'between the two' and could perform neither properly.[66]

Prior to its inspection, the regiment halted at Warwick, where Bury intended to hold a preliminary review of his own. It was assumed that Cumberland would inspect the 20th at Reading; but, when they arrived there, the review was postponed owing to the Duke's illness. On 30 October 1753, the regiment was inspected instead by Lieutenant-General James Campbell. Despite Wolfe's fears, Campbell was impressed, noting the 20th's 'utmost good descipline' and the excellence of its NCOs. For all his growing corpulence, Cumberland was far from lethargic. He remained keen to see the regiment for himself, so Wolfe's men drilled in the cold for four or five hours a day in readiness for his recovery. This relentless square-bashing paid off. When Cumberland finally saw the 20th Regiment in early November, he was pleased to approve of their marching and manoeuvring 'and in particular of the silence and obedience he observed, and ready compliance with orders, without the confusion sometimes perceived in the execution of things that seem new'. *However*, Cumberland had also remarked that another unit, Henry Pulteney's 13th Foot, fired its muskets faster than the 20th – an observation that rankled with the competitive Lord Bury. As he was 'very desirous that no regiment should exceed his own' in *any* way, he directed that the 20th should henceforth imitate the 13th's platoon exercise.[67]

Wolfe's long march south ended at Dover Castle, where the bulk of the 20th went into garrison for the winter. Set high upon the White Cliffs, the decaying medieval fortress was a bleak billet, reputedly haunted by the restless spirits of Anglo-Saxons. The grim and windswept setting helped kindle a spirit of discontent amongst Wolfe's men. They also consorted with prostitutes, a commerce that Wolfe denounced in his orders as 'the last and most dangerous degree of brutality, ignominy and vice'– outspoken language that suggests guilt-ridden memories of his own spree in London, but which also highlights the very real drain that venereal diseases could exact upon regimental manpower.[68]

Dover's close links with France brought further problems. The port was suspected of being a transit point for British-born recruits for the French Army, including deserters. Wolfe was ready to reward soldiers prepared to detect those engaged in this treasonable traffic. Himself fiercely patriotic, he had a blunt message for any man contemplating service under the lilies of King Louis:

> he sets no sort of value or estimation upon them, and that he had much rather they were in the Irish brigades than in the army of Great Britain; but if ever he hears that any deserter shall dare hereafter to threaten to desert, he'll be immediately whipped out of the regiment, with every mark of infamy, contempt and disgrace, as unworthy to continue in it, and as a fit recruit for the rebel battalions, hired by the French to serve against their country.[69]

In February, Wolfe received official notice that his stint at cheerless

THE SEAT OF WAR IN NORTH AMERICA, 1754 – 1760

N

CANADA

Q

Trois Rivières

NEW FRANCE

MONTREAL

Richelieu R.

Lake Huron

La Gallette

Isle-aux-Noix

Fort St Frédéric
(Crown Point)

Lake
Champlain

Lake Ontario

Lake
George

Fort Carill
(Ticonderc

Fort Niagara

Fort
Oswego

Fort William Henry

Mohawk R.

New York

Albany

Lake Erie

Appalachian Mountains

Fort Duquesne
(Pittsburgh)

Pennsylvania

NEW
YORK

Ohio R.

Monongahela R.

Appalachian

BRI

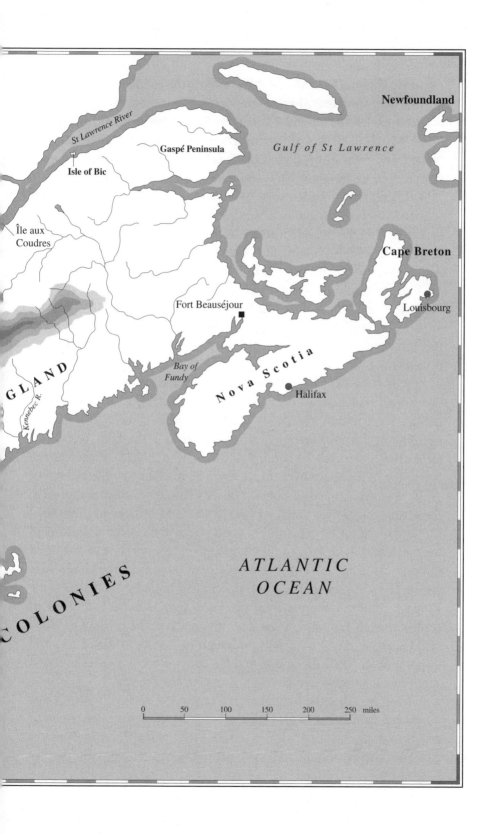

Newfoundland

St Lawrence River

Gaspé Peninsula

Gulf of St Lawrence

Isle of Bic

Île aux
Coudres

Cape Breton

Fort Beauséjour

Louisbourg

G L A N D

Bay of
Fundy

N o v a   S c o t i a

Halifax

Kennebec R.

C O L O N I E S

ATLANTIC
OCEAN

0   50   100   150   200   250   miles

Dover would soon be at an end. Next month, the 20th Regiment marched for the West Country, where its ten companies were to be split equally between Exeter and Bristol. Writing to his mother from Sittingbourne on 24 March, his relief at leaving Dover was undisguised: 'I am sure there is not in the king's dominions a more melancholy dreadful winter station than we have just left ... So much for the vile dungeon!'[70]

As his regiment headed west, Wolfe secured leave that enabled him to spend several spring and summer months with his parents at Blackheath. In July, he accepted an invitation to stay with his old friend, General Sir John Mordaunt, at his house at Freefolk, near Whitchurch. Although charmed by the rolling Hampshire countryside, Wolfe was disconcerted to find a portrait of the general's niece, Elizabeth Lawson, hanging in the dining room. As he told his mother, the sight of his old 'mistress' robbed him of his appetite for two or three days, 'but time, the never failing aid to distressed lovers', eventually made her image 'a pleasing, but not a dangerous object'.[71]

Wolfe's leave expired at the end of September. By early October, he had joined that half of the regiment posted to Exeter, setting up his headquarters within the ruddy sandstone walls of the city's ancient Rougemont Castle. Exeter had a reputation as a southern bastion of Jacobitism, populated by confirmed Tories who looked askance at the prevailing Whig establishment. It was a potentially volatile billet, but Wolfe was determined to defuse tensions through a tactful approach. Repeating the tactics that had helped to build bridges in Inverness, Wolfe 'danced the officers into the good graces of the Jacobite women' of the neighbourhood. Wolfe himself maximized the social skills acquired in Paris, assuring his mother that he danced more than any Devonshire squire. On 30 October 1754, the regiment had hosted a ball to mark the King's birthday. The females of the local Tory families had attended readily enough, but not a single man would accept the invitation. Wolfe could scarcely credit such folly, although he was determined to avoid disputes at all costs. As he had told his father some days previously, 'It is not in our interest to quarrel with any but the French.'[72]

A clear sign that the long-expected renewal of war with France was imminent came that same month, when Wolfe's battalion received orders to draft one hundred men to reinforce Colonel Thomas Dunbar's 48th Foot, which was bound for North America, along with another redcoat regiment, the 44th Foot.[73] This deployment marked a response to news from across the Atlantic, where the ongoing rivalry between the British and French colonies had provoked bloody skirmishing in the Ohio Valley. That July, a young Virginian officer of militia named George Washington, who had been sent to uphold his colony's interests in that coveted region, was himself obliged to surrender to a superior enemy force and sent packing from his makeshift stronghold at Fort Necessity. An escalation was only a matter of time, but aside from a scattering of undermanned and superannuated independent companies, based in the colonies of New York and South Carolina, Britain's regular troops on the continent were concentrated in Nova Scotia, where they were needed to keep watch upon the Acadians.

Under an ambitious plan of operations drawn up by the Duke of Cumberland, the 44th and 48th Foot would form the disciplined backbone of a force headed by Major-General Edward Braddock. Appointed commander-in-chief in North America, Braddock was to preside over a strategy intended to eliminate four key French fortresses. Braddock himself was to bolster his regulars with American recruits, then, in conjunction with locally raised 'provincial' units, push through the Pennsylvanian wilderness to capture Fort Duquesne at the Forks of the Ohio River. Meanwhile, orders had been issued for another two regular regiments to begin recruiting within New England. Under the command of William Shirley, the lieutenant-governor of Massachusetts, they would strike at Fort Niagara. If all went well, and Braddock achieved his first objective, his troops would march to swell Shirley's army. A third expedition, composed of New York provincials and led by Britain's superintendent to the northern Indian tribes, Colonel William Johnson, was ordered against Fort St Frédéric at Crown Point. Lastly, the continuing threat to Nova Scotia was to be countered by a strike at Fort Beauséjour, in the Bay of Fundy.[74]

The 20th Regiment's draft for Braddock's force was taken from the five companies based at Bristol. Its order book reported that the men selected had behaved themselves 'with all the steadiness, chearfulness, and obedience that may be expected from brave men and good subjects, not a man declined the service, and all marched off with a resolution never to dishonour the corps they served in, and to do their utmost for his Majesty's service and the good of their country'.[75]

Such stoicism reflected well upon the *esprit de corps* that Wolfe had inculcated within his battalion. Had these same men known what awaited them in the backwoods of Pennsylvania, their reaction might have been very different.

5

Waiting in the Wings

De English I'm certain be no politicians,
To squander deir money like prodigal elves,
Since for half de expenses of deir expeditions,
We'd do to old France twice de mischief ourselves.

John Mason, 'Monsieur's Touch of the Times', *c.* 1758

James Wolfe spent the Christmas of 1754 on leave with his parents at fashionable Bath. By then that city had acquired much of the character that would remain integral to so many of the Georgian era's most popular and enduring novels and plays. The elegant neoclassical buildings around which its social life revolved – the Assembly Rooms, Queen Square, the Playhouse and the Pump Room – were already in place. This imposing physical landscape was the work of the postmaster and quarry owner Ralph Allen, 'the man of Bath', and a father and son partnership of architects, John Wood senior and junior. No less solid was the social code that ruled the lives of the city's well-heeled visitors. This elaborate etiquette was the creation of Bath's veteran master of ceremonies and uncrowned king, Richard 'Beau' Nash. During the second quarter of the eighteenth century, Allen, Nash and the Woods together transformed Bath from a sleepy provincial city into a Mecca to which families like the Wolfes flocked annually to mingle with others of their kind. By 1750, the tally of seasonal visitors had already reached 12,000. Although some came to drink the spa's famous waters for the benefit of their health, many others were lured by livelier attractions. Bath functioned as a purpose-built centre for dancing, gambling, gossip and flirtation; it was a rarefied world in which fortunes might be lost and marriages made.[1]

Whilst staying at Bath, Wolfe learned that Lord Albemarle, his benefactor in Paris, had died. As Albemarle's son Lord Bury would now succeed to the earldom, he was expected to relinquish his colonelcy of the 20th and lend his illustrious name to a more prestigious regiment. For Wolfe – Bury's diligent lieutenant-colonel for the past five years – this development raised hopes that he might at last be promoted to fill the vacancy.

By January 1755 Wolfe was back with his unit in Exeter, but he soon travelled up to Bristol, where he was obliged to serve upon a general court martial assembled to try defendants for their lives. This grim duty, and the bitterness of the winter weather, brought on yet another of Wolfe's periodic bouts of gloomy reflection analysed, as usual, in a letter to his mother. Unlike his parents, who had kept their 'good looks', Wolfe moaned, *he* already cut a 'meagre, consumptive, decaying figure'. He blamed his gaunt appearance upon more than a decade of hard soldiering:

> The campaigns of 1743, '4, '5, '6, and '7 stripped me of my bloom, and the winters in Scotland and Dover have brought me almost to old age and infirmity, and this without any remarkable intemperance. A few years, more or less, are of very little consequence to the common run of men, and therefore I need not lament that I am perhaps somewhat nearer my end than others of my time.[2]

This letter is interesting for several reasons: it is the first to suggest that, alongside his other assorted ailments, Wolfe was suffering from one of the killer diseases of the age – consumption – and that he was already reconciled to the prospect of an early death. The image of a pale, cough-racked Wolfe, seeking a glorious and merciful bullet in preference to a lingering death from pulmonary tuberculosis, is a plausible one, and has become enshrined in the revisionist treatments of his career. But if Wolfe really *was* afflicted with such a debilitating 'wasting' illness, it is difficult to comprehend how he could have continued with his arduous regimental duties, let alone embarked upon active service; likewise, Wolfe's fatalistic acceptance that his life was unlikely to be long should not be taken as evidence that he was utterly heedless of it – still less that he harboured a 'death wish'. Wolfe's statements could just as easily be seen as nothing more than the melancholy musings of a chronic hypochondriac much given to mood swings.

Whatever the reality behind Wolfe's words, back at his Exeter head-quarters he resorted to his customary cure for depression – immersion in the routine of soldiering. On the last day of January 1755, the growing likelihood of war with France led to a barrage of orders calculated to prepare the 20th Regiment, and especially its raw young recruits, for what lay ahead. In the future, Wolfe announced, deserters would be regarded as cowards and traitors, and could expect no mercy. But he hoped that his men would instead seize the opportunity to demonstrate their courage and fidelity. Indeed, Wolfe did not doubt that the battalion would confirm the good opinion that the Duke of Cumberland himself had already expressed of it.

In the wake of this uncompromising opening edict came a detailed catalogue of instructions intended to maximize the 20th's fighting efficiency. Once again, the emphasis was upon integrating the recruits: the officers were to spare no pains over their training and welfare, supervising their target practice and bayonet drill, their diet, and even the company that they kept. With time all too short, Wolfe also advocated a realistic approach to the crucial question of how his battalion should deliver its firepower. Under the regulation system used since Marlborough's day, a British regiment was split up into eighteen fire units, or 'platoons'. Each of these was numbered and grouped into one of three larger 'firings'. In action, the platoons fired in various convoluted patterns, all intended to ensure that no significant section of the line was left unloaded and vulnerable to attack. Such was the drill-book and parade-ground theory, but amidst the bloody mayhem of battle the system invariably broke down into an undisciplined free for all: an appalled Wolfe had seen this for himself during his first fight at Dettingen in 1743. Alongside its sheer complexity, another major drawback of the regulation platoon firing was the fact that it paid no heed to the battalion's underlying company structure: soldiers found themselves commanded by strangers rather than their own familiar officers and sergeants – a factor that only contributed to rapid collapse of control.

Wolfe instead ordered his regiment to adopt another unofficial, but far more practical, system of musketry. This so-called 'alternate fire', which was already used in the formidable Prussian army of Frederick the Great, employed a simplified tactical system, firmly grounded upon the administrative company itself. Each of the ten companies now constituted a fire unit in its own right; if required, these 'sub-divisions' could be readily split into two platoons, or doubled up into powerful 'grand-divisions' capable of truly punching their weight. As the alternate fire was 'the most simple, plain, and easy, and used by the best-disciplined troops in Europe', Wolfe ordered, 'we are at all times to imitate them in that respect'. Yet, for all their obvious utility, Wolfe's regimental methods remained unorthodox and likely to irritate the conventional drillmasters at the Horse Guards. In all other respects, therefore, his men were to conform to the established discipline, performing *exactly* what was required of them at official reviews.[3]

In March 1755, the 20th Foot took up new quarters in Winchester. Soon after, in early April, Wolfe learned that the vacant colonelcy of the regiment was to be filled by Lieutenant-Colonel Philip Honeywood. Wolfe was mortified. Although pessimistic about his prospects of promotion, he had assumed that the post would at least go to a senior officer, not a man of his own rank. After all his efforts to turn the 20th into an elite unit, Honeywood's appointment was a slap in the face. As Wolfe told his father, if the 'like civilities' were observed in the future, the regiment would need a new lieutenant-colonel; he had informed the new Lord Albemarle that he would rather starve than 'serve one moment longer than I can do it with honour'.[4]

For all his wounded pride, Wolfe had no cause to fear that he'd forfeited the favour of powerful men. Lieutenant-General Sir John Mordaunt remained a close friend and, whilst based at Winchester, Wolfe was his regular guest at nearby Freefolk. That spring, Mordaunt was kept busy inspecting units, including Honeywood's 20th Foot. The review was a great success, and Wolfe conveyed his high delight via his regimental orders, thanking the officers and soldiers alike for their 'extreme handsome appearance under arms'. Mordaunt had 'expressed his satisfaction in the strongest terms' and would report as much to Cumberland and the King.[5]

Soon afterwards, Wolfe received welcome confirmation that he remained in the good graces of Cumberland, who, as the British Army's Captain-General, was a potential fount of patronage. On 2 July, the Duke was guest of honour at Portsmouth, where a mighty fleet lay anchored at Spithead to await news of French intentions. After first sounding out Cumberland's confidant Albemarle, Wolfe and several of his officers travelled down to the coast to witness the 'magnificent military scene' for themselves. Cumberland was greeted by Portsmouth's governor, his crusty old comrade 'Hangman' Hawley, and was delighted with the enthusiastic reception he received from the port's inhabitants. He was also pleased to see Wolfe. James reported to his father that the Duke's 'civilities to me were sufficient proofs, that he did not dislike our coming'. Wolfe's jaunt had been gratifying for another reason. Britain's leading sailor, Lord George Anson, whose epic circumnavigation in the *Centurion* between 1740 and 1744 had made him a popular hero, and who was now First Lord of the Admiralty, had been no less obliging towards him. Anson invited Wolfe to a great dinner he hosted for the officers of the fleet, and showed him 'all sort of politeness'. If Wolfe remained piqued at Honeywood's promotion, this recognition from the heads of Britain's land and sea services – powerful men who both enjoyed access to the highest levels of government – should have gone far to mollify him.[6]

That summer, the 20th Regiment stayed quartered in Hampshire, split between Winchester and the port of Southampton. Its future deployment remained uncertain, although it seemed clearer than ever that a formal declaration of war with France was only a matter of time. In June, a confused and indecisive naval engagement had been fought in the rolling fog off Cape Breton, after a British squadron encountered a French convoy carrying reinforcements for Canada. As Wolfe wrote to his old friend Rickson on 19 July, if the French chose to resent that 'affront', the war would 'come on hot and sudden'. The pride of the Royal Navy – the 'finest fleet', in Wolfe's words, that Britain had ever put to sea – still lay at Spithead, in hourly expectation of orders to sail. It was commanded by Vice-Admiral Sir Edward Hawke, an officer whose aggression matched his surname, and the public expectation of spectacular naval victories ran high.[7]

With his headquarters now at Southampton, Wolfe took the opportunity to pay a social call upon his father's sister, Anne Burcher, who lived some ten miles away at Lyndhurst, in the New Forest. He found his aunt to be 'a very surprising old gentlewoman', who in looks, manner and speech bore a striking resemblance to her brother, 'Uncle Wat' of Dublin. Mrs Burcher and her husband inhabited 'a lonely miserable mansion' in the very depths of the forest, then a wild and remote backwater. Unused to company, and themselves fallen upon hard times, they were 'a good deal affected' to receive a visit from their rising relative.[8]

The Burchers' gangling soldier nephew must have made an arresting sight, not least because that summer Wolfe had abandoned the wig customary for men of his class and had taken to wearing his own red hair cropped short. Reporting this transformation to his mother, he wrote: 'I'm sure you would smile now if you saw me as I am with the covering that nature has given me.' Wolfe no doubt hoped that this description would help to raise his mother's spirits, which had been brought low by a protracted bout of the gout. James, meanwhile, continued to suffer from the gravel. At Southampton he had at least found a remedy that eased his pain, and one that was far more palatable than the liquid soap he'd imbibed in desperation in the Highlands. This called for an ounce of oil of sweet almonds and an ounce of syrup of marshmallows, all served up in a large glass of the familiar 'Rhenish'.[9]

But it took more than the Rhineland's wines to fortify Wolfe against the dire news that now came from across the Atlantic. On 9 July, as it neared its objective of Fort Duquesne at the Forks of the Ohio, General Braddock's formidable army of regulars and provincials had been cut to pieces by the French and their Indian allies. Two thirds of Braddock's force was killed or wounded, shot down by expert and ruthless guerrilla fighters who were barely glimpsed as they flitted through the surrounding forest. Losses amongst the officers had been especially heavy, and the general himself had died of his injuries. The first newspaper reports blamed the disaster upon the cowardice of the humble redcoats: abandoning all vestiges of discipline, they had succumbed to panic, even shooting their own gallant officers. Wolfe was at first inclined to accept these assessments, telling his father that he had 'but a very mean opinion' of the infantry's courage, and lamenting the dire effects of 'Geneva and pox' upon them. In fact, Braddock's regulars – who included the one hundred men recently drafted from Wolfe's own battalion – had stood their ground for several hours before breaking. Pitted against an unfamiliar and merciless enemy in a bewildering wooded wilderness, the real wonder is that they did not run sooner.[10]

For all his ranting against the hapless rank and file, Wolfe was too professional a soldier not to probe more deeply into the underlying causes of the débâcle. Writing soon after to his Uncle Walter, he identified inadequate training – and the sheer novelty of North American forest warfare – as the problem. Wolfe wrote:

> You know how readily the infantry under the present method of training are put into disorder even on the battlefield of Europe. How much more then when they are led on to encounter a horde of savages ambush'd behind timber in an unknown trackless country! Some day we will learn the lesson; meanwhile we can only look on and marvel at the insensate stupidity which tollerates this laxity in our affairs.[11]

As conflict escalated in America, Wolfe and his battalion continued to brace themselves for the inevitable test of strength with France. By early October the 20th was again concentrated at Winchester, preparing for yet another inspection, but eager for real action. As Wolfe grumbled, their 'whole military business' was 'confined to reviews'. That autumn, there were growing fears that the French would invade south-east England. Wolfe doubted the viability of such a venture. After all, as he told his friend the Duke of Richmond, then a captain in the 20th Foot, the enemy had to overcome both the unpredictable Channel weather and the Royal Navy before even getting ashore; and if they did manage to land, they would encounter 'the old hereditary hatred that this nation bears to that in its full vigour'.[12]

Although there had still been no formal declaration of war, the government took the invasion threat seriously. The 20th Foot was ordered to Canterbury to reinforce that sector, brigaded with another battalion of infantry and a regiment of dragoons. 'Hangman' Hawley was to command the district, although Wolfe could not think of a worse choice to meet an invasion should it ever come. The troops feared and hated him, and had nothing but contempt for his military knowledge. And in Wolfe's opinion, it was not only Hawley who lacked professional competency; indeed, the army's officer corps in general was equally ignorant and apathetic. Amongst so much mediocrity, Wolfe explained to his mother, it was hardly surprising that *he* – a man of 'but a very modest capacity, and some degree of diligence a little above the ordinary run' – should be generally considered one of the best officers of his rank in the army. Wolfe was at pains to emphasize that this evaluation – which

has since drawn accusations of false modesty and unbridled egotism
– was scarcely flattering:

> I am not at all vain of the distinction. The comparison would do a man of
> genius very little honour, and does not illustrate [distinguish] me, by any
> means; and the consequence will be very fatal to me in the end, for as I rise
> in rank people will expect some considerable performances, and I shall be
> induced, in support of an ill-got reputation, to be lavish of my life, and shall
> probably meet that fate which is the ordinary effect of such conduct.[13]

Wolfe's frank assessment of himself against the yardstick of his
lackadaisical peers was borne out at Canterbury. It was there, on 15
December 1755, that he issued a series of regimental orders that would
become celebrated after the death in battle that he had prophesied. As
a 'man of Kent', Wolfe was now quite literally defending his homeland.
He was determined that his own native orchards and hop fields would
witness no repetition of the shameful misconduct widely believed to be
responsible for Braddock's defeat.[14]

The instructions that Wolfe issued to his men breathed a Churchillian
spirit of defiance: 'every inch of ground' capable of defence was to be
'disputed with the enemy'. *Any* soldier – regardless of rank – who threw
away his weapon in the heat of action, could expect to face a court martial. *Any* sergeant who quit his post, or who failed to take the place of
his fallen officer, would be tried for his life. *No* man, whether officer, sergeant or common soldier, should abandon his colours unless seriously
wounded: 'while a man is able to do his duty, and can stand and hold
his arms, it is infamous to retire,' Wolfe pronounced. Indeed, if a man
fell out of the ranks, or turned tail, he would be instantly put to death
by his officer or sergeant, because 'a soldier does not deserve to live who
won't fight for his king and country'. The same penalty would befall
any soldier who dared to open fire without orders, as 'the cowardice or
irregular proceedings of one man is not to put the whole in danger'.

Alongside these dire threats came a good deal of practical advice
intended to inspire confidence. In any struggle for Kent's enclosed
landscape, determination and discipline would provide the keys to victory. For example, Wolfe stated, 'a cool well levelled fire, with the pieces
carefully loaded', was far deadlier than 'the quickest fire in confusion'.
When defending earthworks, the men were to open fire when the enemy

came within effective range – about 200 yards – and to keep it up until they were very close. If the attackers actually reached the parapet, his men were to fix bayonets and 'make a bloody resistance'. Wolfe's orders for tackling an enemy battalion out in the open were equally to the point: 'after firing a few rounds', they would probably be commanded 'to charge them with their bayonets'.

There were also simple instructions for dealing with an assault by column against the centre of the line. Whilst the wings angled their fire obliquely, that section of the battalion destined actually to meet the attack must reserve its fire. Ideally, the men should load their muskets with one or two extra balls. Such a double, or even triple, dose of lead would deliver a bruising jolt to the firer's shoulder; it was a drastic – and highly unusual – tactic, but one that was to become something of a Wolfe speciality.[15] Finally, when the enemy were just *twenty* yards away, they were to 'fire with a good aim'. This heavy, close-range volley would, Wolfe believed, 'necessarily stop them a little' – something of an understatement for a gambit that would surely have blasted the enemy's front ranks into bloody oblivion. Once again, if the issue remained undecided, it was to be clinched with the bayonet. Throughout, the essence of Wolfe's tactical creed was controlled aggression: in 1755, he was already recommending the fusion of fire and steel that was destined to be used so effectively by the British Army against the French in the Iberian Peninsula more than half a century later.

Throughout the winter of 1755–56, Wolfe and his well-honed battalion remained at Canterbury, ready to repel the anticipated invasion. But as Wolfe had long suspected, the French were chary of mounting a hazardous cross-Channel operation. Yet, given their conspicuous preparations, and Britain's vulnerability both at home and in the Americas, it was obvious that the enemy would strike *somewhere*. Wolfe did not doubt that their first attack would be both 'vigorous and successful'.[16]

This prediction was all too accurate, but the blow, when it finally fell, was more devastating than even Wolfe had feared. Bustling French activity at Dunkirk, which had heightened concerns for the security of Kent and Sussex, was merely a smokescreen. The real target lay far to the south. On 8 April 1756, a French flotilla commanded by Vice-Admiral Roland-Michel Barrin, Marquis de La Galissonnière left Toulon, ferrying a formidable strike force of 15,000 troops under Marshal Louis-François-Armand Vignerot du Plessis, Duc de Richelieu. Ten days later, they made an unopposed landing upon the Balearic island of Minorca.

Since its capture by British forces in 1708 during the War of the Spanish Succession, Minorca had become a prized base for the Royal Navy, well sited for monitoring the activities of France's Mediterranean fleet and protecting Britain's lucrative trade with the Levant. Its land defences hinged upon the impressive bastions of Fort St Philip, a strongpoint guarding the vital harbour of Port Mahon. In 1756, these were defended by four redcoat battalions, under the command of the venerable Lieutenant-General William Blakeney. Aged eighty-four, he was an extreme example of George II's preference for long-service officers of his own generation. Ten years before, when already an old man, Blakeney had won fame for his determined defence of Stirling Castle against the Young Pretender's forces. Now he faced a far more professional enemy, equipped with an extensive siege train of cannon and mortars capable of pounding his defences into rubble.

In any case, Minorca's real bulwark was not some static fortification but the roving warships of the Royal Navy. By dispersing La Galissonnière's fleet, they could sever the besiegers' logistical lifeline, so turning the tables and obliging *them* to surrender. Unfortunately, the protracted invasion scare of the previous winter had persuaded Lord Anson to concentrate upon home defence, so the squadron eventually sent out to the Mediterranean under Vice-Admiral John Byng was badly under strength, and after a winter's battering in the stormy Channel, in sore need of refit.

Byng also knew that ship for ship the enemy enjoyed the advantage of heavier armament. For all the jingoism of his countrymen – who assumed that brave British tars could cheerfully outfight anyone afloat whatever the odds against them – the French were not to be underrated at sea. Despite his misgivings, on 20 May Byng attacked La Galissonnière off Minorca. The rival fleets were fairly evenly matched, but neither came to close quarters and the encounter was indecisive. Summoning a council of war, Byng decided to withdraw to Gibraltar and repair his ships rather than make another attempt to relieve the island. This was a fatal misjudgement. With the British naval threat now lifted, Richelieu's men were at liberty to push forward their siege of Fort St Philip without interruption. The outnumbered garrison fought back bravely, but with no hope of relief, surrendered on 28 June. In recognition of their stubborn resistance, Blakeney and his men were granted the 'honours of war'. They marched out of the shot-scarred fortress with drums beating and regimental colours flying in the breeze, and were evacuated to Gibraltar rather than impounded as prisoners of war. Admiral Byng was less fortunate. The loss of Minorca was a national humiliation – far more stinging than Braddock's defeat in the remote North American forests. News of the island's fall reached England on 14 July, generating a wave of rage and shame. If the shaky Newcastle–Fox administration was to weather this storm, a scapegoat was required. Although the ultimate responsibility for the disaster rested with the ministry itself, the unfortunate Byng was replaced by Hawke and recalled in disgrace to stand trial for his life.[17]

That spring, like many of his countrymen, Wolfe had followed this unfolding drama with mounting consternation. On 19 May 1756 – the day after Britain finally declared war on France – the 20th Regiment marched to new quarters at Devizes in Wiltshire. Wolfe reacted to each depressing bulletin from the Mediterranean as his battalion pursued a sluggish progress westward, bringing ruin to the public houses of those villages that lay in its path, and which were obliged to provide billets. By 7 June, when Wolfe had reached Bristol, he already accepted that Minorca was doomed, although he felt sure that its 'poor little abandoned garrison' would fight with courage, if nothing else. Writing with bitter sarcasm from his headquarters at Devizes on 27 June, Wolfe wished his father 'joy of Admiral Byng's escape, and of the safe arrival of our fleet at Gibraltar' – a move that had left old Blakeney in 'an ugly scrape'. Wolfe himself felt the humiliation keenly. His father, who was now too infirm for active campaigning, was fortunate that he at least could escape service in such 'dishonourable times'. When Minorca's loss was confirmed, Wolfe delivered a damning verdict upon the whole sorry affair, concluding that his countrymen were 'the most egregious blunderers in war that ever took the hatchet in hand'. In coming weeks, Wolfe wasted no sympathy upon the hapless Byng – particularly as he believed the admiral could have retrieved his own and his country's honour by intercepting Richelieu as he returned to Toulon with the bulk of his victorious troops. Wolfe suspected that Byng was a 'dog'; and if he had lost a single day lingering at Gibraltar, then he would be what was much worse, 'the most damnable of traitors'.[18]

That spring the 20th Regiment gained a new colonel, although this time the incumbent gave Wolfe no cause for complaint. William Kingsley, who succeeded Honeywood on 22 May 1756, was, as Wolfe reported to his mother, 'a sensible man, and very sociable and polite'.[19] He was also a conscientious professional soldier, fully capable of inspiring the men of his regiment: it was as 'Kingsley's' that the 20th Foot would soon acquire a glorious reputation on the battlefield.

With Britain now officially at war, the summer of 1756 found Wolfe and his battalion keyed up and awaiting orders for active service. In August, they marched to Shroton, near Blandford in Dorset, where another five battalions of infantry, six squadrons of cavalry and two troops of light horse were encamped on a breezy heath. At Devizes Wolfe had been laid low by 'a damm'd boil' for nearly three weeks, but life under canvas suited him better. A general review of the troops on Blandford Downs delighted civilian spectators, although the hypercriti-cal Wolfe felt that their applause – and that of some of the army officers present – was undeserved. There was still much to learn, and without some improvement, he warned his father, they were 'in imminent danger of being cut to pieces' as soon as they met the enemy.[20]

The British Army's woeful lack of professionalism was a Wolfe hobby-horse, but that summer at least, his criticisms were justified. Conflict with France had required a rapid expansion of the military establish-ment. Beginning with relatively modest augmentations of existing units, the recruitment drive swiftly gathered momentum. By the autumn of 1755 those Chelsea Pensioners who were still hale enough to shoulder a musket had been recalled to the colours for static garrison duty, so releasing other more robust troops for active service in the field; that December, ten new regiments of infantry were created; and in the fol-lowing March, during the continuing invasion scare, a Press Act was implemented to conscript the unemployed poor for wartime service. Such measures meant that many units were now struggling to absorb large batches of inexperienced officers and unseasoned men.[21]

Under these desperate circumstances, and at Newcastle's urging,

George II had taken the deeply unpopular step of calling upon foreign troops to shore up the defences of his beleaguered kingdom. Many patriotic Englishmen – notably the fiery William Pitt – resented their monarch's resort to mercenaries, preferring the concept of a home-grown, if amateur, militia to an influx of 15,000 Hessians and Hanoverians. But Wolfe saw things very differently: here was a rare chance for the British to learn from professional soldiers trained in the methods of the era's leading commander, Frederick the Great. Wolfe explained his stance to the Duke of Richmond:

> Altho' I think it reflects no honour upon the British Nation to call for foreign aid, yet for reasons that are obvious to your Grace and myself, I am glad the Hanovers are to come; new officers, and new battalions unaccustom'd to movements, untrain'd and undisciplin'd are not wholly to be depended upon in a war of this sort; natural courage seldom prevails against experience and military knowledge.[22]

Whilst serving in the 20th Foot, Richmond had been allowed to come and go much as he pleased, with Wolfe sparing no pains to oblige him. To modern eyes, Wolfe's accommodation of his aristocratic subordinate smacks of sycophancy, but this was an age of deference, and Richmond held one of the most prestigious titles in the land. And, as far as the regiment was concerned, the appearance of the Duke's impressive name on its designated page in the annual *Army List* lent lustre to the corps: his physical presence with his company was a bonus. Given his social rank, Richmond was also a man of immense influence, and Wolfe did not doubt that he could deploy this for the public good in more useful ways than by commanding a company of infantry.

Indeed, Wolfe had swiftly identified the powerful Richmond as a channel for propagating his *own* notions of military discipline throughout the British Army. That summer, Wolfe watched the blue-coated Hessian infantry and artillery at exercise, and was impressed by their discipline. Writing to Richmond, who had now been promoted to lieutenant-colonel of the 33rd Foot, he reported that 'their steadyness under arms, and strict attention' was 'worthy of imitation', as was the 'exact knowledge' that every officer had of his own duties. In fact, their drill was 'neither intricate nor difficult' and therefore 'calculated for the genius and temper of the people'. Wolfe now looked to Richmond, a leader by birth, to provide an example by which a similarly 'solid and substantial degree of discipline' could be introduced into the British infantry. Unlike Wolfe, who'd been denied his wish to see the troops of France, Prussia and Austria back in 1753, Richmond *had* witnessed the pre-war manoeuvres of Europe's armies. This was a circumstance that Wolfe did not hesitate to recall and exploit. He wrote: 'as your Grace has seen and brought away many excellent things from the armies upon the Continent, they may, by your help, become general among our troops, and improve them'.[23]

Wolfe soon had another opportunity to see the efficient German soldiers at close quarters. In early September, he accepted Richmond's invitation to accompany him and his illustrious guest, the Prince of Nassau, on an excursion to watch Hessian infantry and artillery demonstrate 'the Prussian discipline' near Winchester. This display was to be followed by breakfast with the Hessians' general, the Comte d'Isembourg, and dinner amongst the splendour of Richmond's family seat at Goodwood, high on the South Downs. As Wolfe told his father, there was 'too much pleasure and too much honour' in the Duke's offer to spurn it.[24] Once again, Wolfe's reputation for consummate professionalism was forging links with powerful patrons.

One inevitable consequence of the official outbreak of war that May was a dislocation of international trade, bringing with it a steep rise in the cost of bread. This crisis was exacerbated when steady rain ruined the harvest. From late summer, the resulting hardship caused widespread discontent and rioting. In a century noted for endemic disorder, 1756 would rank as one of the worst years of all, rumour blaming Jacobite sympathizers for helping to foment the trouble. Even though the menace of a French invasion had by no means receded, thousands of regular troops were sent to overawe the mobs.[25]

Unrest was initially concentrated in the midlands, but by the autumn, serious rioting had spread to the cloth-manufacturing district of Gloucestershire. On 19 October, Wolfe received orders to break up his Dorset camp, to take three companies of his own battalion and another three from Howard's 3rd Foot and then march for the trouble zone, there 'to assist the civil power in suppressing riots, etc'.[26] By 24 October Wolfe's command had reached Chipping-Sodbury. The next day, as he

sardonically informed his mother, he would enter 'the enemy's country'. Wolfe did not anticipate much trouble, as he had enough men 'to
beat the mob of all England collected'. In fact, the mission promised to
'turn out a good recruiting party', as the Gloucestershire weavers were
so poor and wretched that they might 'hazard a knock on the pate for
bread and clothes, and turn soldiers through sheer necessity'.[27]

Wolfe's arrival in the Cotswolds coincided with a crisis for the
region's staple industry – the production of stout woollen cloth. The
wool textile trade had been crucial to England's economy since the
middle ages; in the eighteenth century it remained the major manufacturing industry, second only to agriculture as an employer. Woollen
cloth was produced throughout Great Britain, but by 1750 the industry
had become concentrated in two regions, the west of England – including Gloucestershire, Wiltshire and Somerset – and the West Riding of
Yorkshire. At the century's start the west of England, which specialized
in a finer quality product, had predominated; but in coming decades
Yorkshire gradually gained the upper hand. This changing balance
between the two regions stemmed from fundamental differences in
their industrial organization and structure. Yorkshire was home to
innumerable 'master manufacturers', men of modest means but with
sufficient capital to buy wool from the dealers and process it themselves.
In the West Country by contrast, as the economist Josiah Tucker noted
in 1757, the industry was dominated by 'clothiers' who bought the
wool and then paid for its processing by hundreds of outworkers; the
clothier was, in short, 'master of the whole manufacture from first to
last'. The yawning gulf between wealthy clothier paymaster and humble
– but fiercely independent – artisan made for acrimonious industrial
relations. In 1756 this background of mutual hostility between masters
and workers, intensified by unusual dearth, sparked the outbreak that
Wolfe was sent to quell.[28]

At the request of the local magistrates, who hoped to arrest the rioters' ringleaders, Wolfe deployed his half dozen companies throughout
the district. It was, as Wolfe told his mother, 'an extraordinary country'
of hills, woods, cornfields and rivulets, with 'innumerable little white
houses in all the vales, so that there is vast variety' – each mile bringing
'a new and pleasant prospect'. But, that winter, this seemingly idyllic
pastoral landscape was the backdrop to a grim little drama of misery

and want. Reporting to the new Secretary at War, William Wildman, Lord Barrington, Wolfe left no doubt where his own sympathies lay: the weavers were 'a good deal oppress'd by their masters', who had cut wages so low that they could no longer live by their labour; with provisions so costly, many of them were 'extreamly wretched and miserable, tho' they are of the greatest use to the publick'. Those weavers with the harshest masters had obliged others to down tools, seizing their shuttles and smashing their looms. The clothiers spoke of negotiating with those 'unhappy men', but Wolfe doubted whether talking would solve the problem, as there was not enough work for them all. Coming weeks brought little sign of improvement. Although twelve clothiers agreed to raise wages, the 'seeds of discontent' remained on both sides. In the present state of affairs, Wolfe warned Barrington, without troops 'it wou'd be difficult to preserve the publick peace'. Wolfe was surprised by the weavers' obstinacy, although, as he told his mother, their complaint was a just one. They were now so desperate that violence appeared inevitable. Wolfe wrote: 'I am afraid they will proceed to some extravagancies, and force the magistrates to use our weapons against them, which would give me a great deal of concern'.[29]

As the dispute dragged on, the remaining seven companies of the 20th were ordered up from Plymouth and the three of the Buffs sent back there. In December 1756, Wolfe shifted his headquarters eastwards to Cirencester, where he spent Christmas. He reckoned that service against such 'poor devils' as the half-starved weavers was rather a dishonour to the corps than a chance of acquiring glory. But any military operation – however inglorious – warranted professionalism and care, and Wolfe's deployments demonstrated both, with a central reserve poised to support his scattered detachments should they require assistance.

In January 1757 the disturbances spilled over the River Severn to the Forest of Dean, so posing an interesting strategic conundrum. Mobs had begun intercepting provision barges on the river. Fearing that their blockaded city would starve, Bristol's magistrates appealed for military aid. Wolfe responded on 19 January by sending a company of men into the Forest, commanded by one of his most vigorous officers, Captain William De Laune. He was to cross the Severn at a point where the rioters were known to congregate. It was anticipated that the malcontents would strive to seize the necessary boats, so the wily Wolfe had 'recommended stratagems, and surprises' to distract them. Although the rioters possessed firearms, De Laune had strict instructions to ignore all provocation. Instead, his men were 'to receive the insults of the rabble with a soldierlike contempt' – unless, that was, a magistrate gave them positive orders to open fire. From Wolfe's experience, such decisiveness was unlikely. As he complained to Richmond, the spineless magistrates were themselves part of the problem. Wolfe warned: 'they will pay for their neglects, some time hence, when the troops are withdrawn'.[30]

Wolfe's tactful handling of a tense situation earned the approval of Barrington, a man who did not suffer fools lightly. In late February, rather than having to await further instructions from the War Office, Wolfe was authorized to use his own discretion when dealing with the rioters. By then, however, the situation in Gloucestershire had momentarily calmed and Wolfe was able to focus once again upon his own career prospects.

Whilst James Wolfe was contemplating the unruly weavers of Gloucestershire, Britain's continuing military misfortunes had opened up another potential path towards the promotion he craved. As 1756 drew to its end, public anger over the loss of Minorca showed no sign of abating; whipped up by the press, this bolstered opposition to the foundering Newcastle–Fox administration. Unwilling to assume sole blame for the disaster, Fox resigned in October. When Pitt refused to fill the gap by serving alongside Newcastle, the Duke likewise declined to carry on. In mid November, the King grudgingly agreed to a new ministry, fronted by the colourless William Cavendish, Duke of Devonshire, but with Pitt as Secretary of State for the Southern Department – a brief that embraced responsibility for North America – as its real leader. Pitt's influence was swiftly apparent in the prompt return of the Hessians and Hanoverians. In theory at least, their place would be taken by a 30,000-strong militia, reformed along lines proposed by Pitt's staunch supporter, Lieutenant-Colonel George Townshend.

Like its predecessor, the Devonshire–Pitt coalition rested upon unstable foundations. These became shakier still as the lingering shame of Minorca's loss was compounded by news of fresh disasters from further afield. In India, British prestige plummeted after tension between the East India Company and the native ruler of Bengal ended in violence. When Calcutta fell to the forces of Siraj-ud-Daula, Company employees were jammed into a tiny cell – the notorious 'Black Hole of Calcutta' – and some fifty of them suffocated during a single, stifling night. From North America, where Britain's colonies struggled impotently to present a united front against New France, the tidings were equally depressing. That summer, the arrival of reinforcements under a new commander-in-chief, John Campbell, Earl of Loudoun, came too late to prevent the loss of the important outpost of Oswego on Lake Ontario. Besieged by the French during August, Oswego's dispirited garrison made only a feeble resistance before striking their colours. The commander of the French regular troops in North America, the veteran Louis-Joseph, Marquis de Montcalm, deemed them unworthy of the honourable terms granted to the defenders of Minorca; instead, they were disarmed and chivvied off as prisoners of war, although not before scores of their sick and wounded had been butchered by Canada's Indian allies – indispensable, but independent tribal warriors over whom Montcalm and his officers could exert only limited control.

European developments also gave grave cause for concern. In what historians have characterized as a 'Diplomatic Revolution', 1756 saw a reversal in the long-established system of alliances. This upheaval resulted in part from Newcastle's policy of paying subsidies to guarantee the security of George II's valued but vulnerable Electorate of Hanover. Fearful of Russian advances into Germany, Prussia – which had sided with France during the War of the Austrian Succession – now succumbed to British diplomatic approaches, and in January signed the Treaty of Westminster, by which both powers and Hanover agreed to aid each other if war erupted. Chagrined at Prussia's defection, Bourbon France promptly retaliated by allying herself with Habsburg Austria; Russia soon joined them. It was a dramatic turnaround: Austria – Britain's traditional continental counterbalance against French ambitions – was now in league with the arch-enemy; and, in a development that injected a surface element of religious rivalry, the swingeing realignment ranged Catholic against Protestant. European hostilities soon followed. They began in September, when the ever-belligerent Frederick the Great invaded Saxony, so exposing Hanover to a counter-strike from France and her allies.

The Devonshire–Pitt ministry therefore inherited an unenviable situation, not least because the 'patriot programme' espoused by Pitt when he was in opposition had offered no middle way between an all-out European war and – what he believed to be Britain's true calling – a 'blue-water' colonial conflict decided by sea-power. Now in office himself, Pitt had little option but to change tack: at the reopening of Parliament in early December 1756, he not only promised reinforcements for America but also pledged assistance to Britain's beleaguered European confederates.[31]

With these growing commitments, Britain needed ever more military manpower, not merely to defend itself but to prop up distant battlefronts. Despite the army's expansion during the previous year, the situation remained so critical that the new ministry took the drastic step of launching a major recruitment drive within the recently rebellious Scottish Highlands. Two full battalions composed entirely of Highlanders – a total of more than 2000 officers and men – were to be raised for American service. Wolfe, who knew the Highlands and their inhabitants, was keen to command them. He told Richmond of his hopes for promotion to full colonel, 'with the direction and supervision of the two Highland Battalions'. This was, he added, 'no great favour to ask, and a very dangerous honour to obtain'. Wolfe felt that his flaming red hair would work in his favour: 'I have very much the look of a *Highlander*; in that respect, [I] shou'd be acceptable to the corps,' he wrote.[32]

The Highlands' potential as a martial reservoir had long been recognized by British officers, not least those who had recently fought the Jacobites. In 1749, the Duke of Cumberland himself was enthusiastic about a proposal to send Highlanders to defend the frontier colony of Nova Scotia. Tough and expendable, the clansmen were considered well suited to that rugged environment. As James Wolfe put it to Rickson in 1751:

> I should imagine that two or three independent Highland companies might be of use; they are hardy, intrepid, accustomed to a rough country, and no great mischief if they fall. How can you better employ a secret enemy than by making his end conducive to the common good?[33]

By 1757 the British Army already fielded many hundreds of High-landers. The famous Black Watch regiment, formed from Highland Independent Companies back in 1739, had served with distinction at Fontenoy in 1745; as the 42nd Foot, it was amongst the first wave of regular reinforcements to disembark at New York during the summer of 1756. More generally, the poor but overcrowded Highlands had a long tradition of exporting soldiers. The armies of Sweden, France and Holland had all welcomed their talents, and many British regiments – even those with no nominal territorial connection to Scotland – included clusters of Highlanders on their muster rolls.

Despite these precedents, the authorization of the two new battalions in early 1757 was a significant innovation, marking the onset of a deliberate policy of large-scale recruitment in the Highlands. Coming just a decade after the close shave administered by Bonnie Prince Charlie's army, this was viewed with understandable nervousness by some Whig politicians, who believed it amounted to little more than the rearming of flagrant rebels. Indeed, one of the proposed battalion commanders, Simon Fraser, the Master of Lovat, had been 'out' for Prince Charles Edward, leading his clan at the battle of Falkirk; his father, the fat and foxy old Lord Lovat, was beheaded in 1747 for his role in the rebellion. But desperate times required equally desperate measures, and with Cumberland's backing, Pitt persuaded a sceptical George II to approve the initiative.[34]

The experiment was remarkably successful. Both Fraser's battalion, and its counterpart commanded by Archibald Montgomery, were soon recruited to above their full strength. Enlistment was driven by the enthusiastic cooperation of chieftains keen to disassociate themselves from Jacobitism and to demonstrate unswerving loyalty to the victorious Hanoverian regime. Like the British Army in general, coercion and hardship helped to fill the ranks, but many recruits were volunteers. Powerful ties of clanship enabled the Highland gentry to mobilize their kinsmen; and serving King George was the only means by which Highlanders could openly wear the tartan of their forefathers and flaunt their traditional broadswords and dirks.

The systematic recruitment of Highlanders that began in 1757 saw the real establishment of kilted regiments as a fixture within the British Army. It was likewise the beginning of a remarkable process by which the Gaelic-speaking Highlander, hitherto despised by his wary Lowland neighbours as a thieving and vermin-ridden barbarian, would come to symbolize Scottish heroism, and ultimately – as a perusal of shop-windows along Edinburgh's Royal Mile confirms – to dominate Scotland's image of itself.[35]

Wolfe's admirers have suggested that *he* inspired Pitt's decision to harness Highland manpower. As Lord Albemarle – Wolfe's former colonel – had passed Pitt a paper from Cumberland urging that course, they have detected a logical link.[36] Although there is no hard evidence to support this theory, and Albemarle's position as Cumberland's *aide-de-camp* readily explains *his* involvement, Wolfe's letter to Richmond shows that he was certainly enthusiastic about the scheme. And whilst Wolfe was not granted his wish of commanding the new Highland battalions, events would soon demonstrate that his affinity with them was real enough. Indeed, the emergence of the Scottish Highlander as quintessential warrior of empire would be inextricably bound up with that of James Wolfe himself.

During that same winter of 1756–57, men of influence worked to bring about Wolfe's promotion to full colonel. His staunch friend Sir John Mordaunt had taken it upon himself to recommend Wolfe to the King. Although grateful for this unsolicited patronage, Wolfe doubted whether the old monarch, who held notoriously rigid views on seniority, could be swayed in favour of such a young officer. 'I don't expect it will produce much', he wrote to his mother on Boxing Day 1756, 'because, by the King's rule, my turn is not yet come.'[37]

Some weeks later, whilst still based at Cirencester, Wolfe received a letter that proposed another possible way forward. It came from the Duke of Bedford, who, as the Lord Lieutenant of Ireland, wielded patronage over Britain's strategic reserve of troops on the separate Irish establishment. Two lucrative Irish offices – barrackmaster-general and quartermaster-general – had recently become vacant. On 6 February 1757, Wolfe received a letter from Bedford's secretary offering him both appointments. Bedford, who was a long-standing friend of Wolfe's father, did not doubt that the King would also endorse the rank of colonel that traditionally went with them. Wolfe lost no time in writing to thank the Duke for his intervention: he would follow his commands

exactly. As Wolfe emphasized to his father, however, if the Irish posting – which he now understood to be limited to quartermaster-general
alone – failed to deliver the rank of colonel, he would relinquish it
immediately and return to his battalion. After all, Wolfe was a soldier,
not some paper-shuffling administrator. He added: 'I had rather see
the King of Prussia's operations the next campaign than accept of this
appointment with all its advantages.'[38]

Bedford too urged George II to approve Wolfe's promotion to colonel.
But, as Wolfe had predicted, the King again demurred on the grounds
that he had not yet served for long enough in his existing rank. Despite
this setback, Wolfe decided to accept the proffered Irish appointment
regardless and, on 29 March 1757, he attended St James's to kiss the
King's hand in formal acceptance. Wolfe soon afterwards revealed to
Rickson that he remained lukewarm about an office that neither pleased
nor flattered him: had he known in good time that it would fail to
deliver his long-sought promotion, he'd have excused himself from 'a
very troublesome business'.[39]

Wolfe now hoped that growing concerns over the security of Hanover
might offer better prospects of action and advancement. By February
1757, the worsening continental situation made British involvement
there ever more likely. Even Pitt, who had vehemently opposed the
Treaty of Westminster with Prussia a year earlier, now asked Parliament
for funds to help pay for troops – the so-called 'Army of Observation'
– to defend the Electorate. In mid March, Wolfe was reporting rumours
that Cumberland was to command this foreign contingent; although
it was highly unlikely that any British regiments would go with him,
Wolfe had asked Albemarle to secure an interview with the Duke, in
hopes that he might join his staff.[40]

At the personal request of Frederick of Prussia, and the insistence of
his father, Cumberland eventually agreed to head the 'Army of Observation' – but only if the ministry he left behind him was overhauled.
In early April, both Pitt and his brother-in-law, Richard Grenville, Earl
Temple, who had served briefly as First Lord of the Admiralty, were
dismissed. By then, the King's patience with Pitt had long since run
out. His hostility was heightened by Pitt's efforts to win a reprieve for
Byng. After a lengthy trial, the admiral had been sentenced to death for
failing to do everything possible to save Minorca – albeit with a strong

recommendation for mercy. This clemency failed to reflect the national mood. Minorca's loss marked a miserable nadir of British prestige, and the clamour against the man held culpable was unprecedented in its intensity. The King himself was adamant that Byng should pay the ultimate penalty. His subjects too were baying for blood – and they got it: on 14 March 1757, the admiral was shot in Portsmouth harbour on the deck of his own flagship. Whatever else could be laid to Byng's account, he was clearly no coward; as witnesses reported, he faced the marine firing squad with superlative courage.

Cumberland sailed for Hanover in early April, accompanied by a staff of trusted British officers that included several close friends. Wolfe was not amongst them. Upon his arrival in Germany, it soon became clear that the Duke's reluctance to accept the command was well justified: he had been proffered a poisoned chalice. In a throwback to the dismal days of the 1740s, Cumberland was once again in nominal command of an army composed of disparate elements – Hanoverians, Hessians and Brunswickers, plus smaller contingents from other German territories. As before, he faced a French force that was not only homogeneous but also numerically superior; indeed, at roughly 100,000 men, it outnumbered his own by two to one. The French commander, Marshal le Comte D'Estrées, was no Saxe, but neither was Cumberland his young energetic and confident self. Now monstrously overweight, asthmatic and plagued by an old leg wound that obstinately refused to knit, he was in poor physical shape to take the field.

The ensuing campaign wrecked Cumberland's reputation as thoroughly as his health. At the outset, the King's instructions were scarcely encouraging – and dangerously ambiguous. They stipulated a defensive stance, with Cumberland ordered to *protect* Hanover and the territory of Britain's allies from foreign aggression; above all, he was to ensure that in dire necessity his army could retreat northwards to Stade, near the mouth of the River Elbe, and there maintain itself – a move that would, however, leave Hanover defenceless. Cumberland's problems were exacerbated by developments to the east. On 18 June 1757, the seemingly invincible Frederick the Great was roundly defeated by the Austrians at Kolin, near Prague. Cumberland could now expect no help from the Prussians. Under mounting pressure, and anxious to safeguard his communications, the Duke fell back before D'Estrées's swarming forces.[41]

As Cumberland desperately sought to stave off disaster in Germany, the chaotic British political scene finally achieved some degree of stability. The collapse of the flawed Devonshire–Pitt administration in April had left a vacuum that proved difficult to fill. Although Pitt and Newcastle despised each other, it was increasingly clear that the only workable solution was an administration that included them both and exploited their very different talents. Despite widespread doubts that they could ever work together, Pitt and Newcastle accepted office on 29 June. Pitt was again appointed Secretary of State for the Southern Department, whilst Newcastle became First Lord of the Treasury. With his flair for oratory, Pitt would provide charismatic war leadership. Meanwhile, Newcastle's financial acumen and voracious appetite for paperwork, allied to his broad base of parliamentary support, would contribute the ballast necessary to keep the administration on an even keel. Only time would tell whether this ill-matched pair could pull in harness.

When the Pitt–Newcastle coalition assumed power, the fate of Cumberland's hard-pressed 'Army of Observation' remained undecided. It was nonetheless clear that action was required – both to relieve pressure on the Duke and to answer Frederick the Great's cries for help. As Pitt's supporters opposed any large-scale commitment of British troops to Germany, the proposed solution to the problem – like the new administration itself – was a compromise. During the previous year, Frederick had mooted the possibility of a British amphibious expedition against the French coast. This scheme, which might be expected to prompt a substantial diversion of French manpower from Germany to counter the threat, would permit the Royal Navy to operate close to home waters; and, as it envisaged a hit-and-run raid rather than a full-fledged campaign, only a relatively modest taskforce of redcoats would be needed.

With no time to lose, the basic strategy was quickly agreed. It remained to select a specific target. Sir John Ligonier, who was now Lieutenant-General of the Ordnance, had received intelligence suggesting that the western naval base of Rochefort in the Bay of Biscay was vulnerable to a surprise attack. This information came from Captain Robert Clerk, an engineer who had visited the port three years earlier, noting that the defences amounted to nothing more formidable than a single unfinished rampart and a dry ditch. Such paltry fortifications could be swiftly stormed by troops using scaling ladders, without a formal siege. The King responded to Ligonier's proposal with enthusiasm, and the scheme received outline approval at a ministerial meeting in mid July. It would involve 8000 troops, transported by a powerful naval squadron under Hawke. The King's choice as commander of the land forces was Wolfe's friend and patron Lieutenant-General Sir John Mordaunt; he was backed by major-generals Henry Seymour Conway and Edward Cornwallis, Wolfe's former colonel.[42]

Within a week, Wolfe had been summoned to London and informed that he was to join the expedition. Units allocated to the force included the first battalion of Kingsley's Regiment; as its lieutenant-colonel, Wolfe would naturally go too. But in a development that reflected Wolfe's growing reputation – and which surely owed something to Mordaunt – he also received the crucial staff appointment of quartermaster-general to the expedition. Secrecy surrounded the whole operation. Wolfe remained in the dark about its destination, but whatever the objective, he held small hopes of success. As he told his 'honest little friend' Rickson, the British Army's lamentable leadership, discipline, and engineers were all 'great and insurmountable obstructions' to *that*. Wolfe subsequently wrote to Richmond in an equally pessimistic vein: the Duke, who would not be accompanying the expedition, was well out of it, as the most that could be expected was 'some flashes of courage', accompanied by disorder and confusion.[43]

By 10 August all the troops had assembled on the Isle of Wight and were ready to embark. They included Lieutenant-Colonel the Honourable James Murray of the 15th Foot, a combative Scot whose future career was destined to be interwoven with Wolfe's. Writing to his colonel, Jeffery Amherst, Murray too was innocent of the expedition's destination, although he hoped they would at least find the enemy unprepared, so 'that we may do something for the honour of our poor country'. Murray was confident that Amherst's regiment would play its part well, as officers and men alike were in high spirits. The troops had been awaiting their transports for the past fortnight, although Murray, an experienced soldier and 'old expeditioner', was unsurprised at the delay – indeed, he had never known the shipping to be ready in time.[44]

Whilst Hawke's formidable fleet awaited a favourable wind, Wolfe stayed in the same dreary farmhouse that had lodged General Wentworth before the ill-fated expedition to Cartagena seventeen years earlier. This was hardly an auspicious omen, but Wolfe was too busy to dwell on the past. The thousands of redcoats concentrated around Newport drew plenty of company: there were balls, concerts, a theatre – in short, as he told his mother, 'all the camp amusements'.[45] Alongside the frivolity there was much serious soldiering as the ten battalions were put through their paces. The Duke of Richmond, who crossed the Solent to watch them at exercise, was surprised – and impressed. Writing to his brother Lord George Lennox, who was serving with Cumberland, Richmond was delighted that Mordaunt had 'dared to follow common sense and to put into execution what everybody had long since thought right'. Instead of employing the intricate new regulation drill imposed by Adjutant-General Robert Napier, which had puzzled the entire army, Mordaunt ordered his regiments to adopt the simplified system long since used by the 20th Foot. In keeping with Wolfe's regimental orders of 1755, rather than splitting into platoons, the battalions were drawn up in companies, with the men under their own officers; they practised nothing but the Prussian-style 'alternate fire', and performed the same essential drill movements as the 20th, without wasting time on 'such absurdities' as forming square. 'This is truly great', Richmond enthused, 'and you have no idea how much it has improved the other regiments.' Although Mordaunt had acted upon his own initiative, and in defiance of Cumberland's regulations, Richmond felt sure that the Duke would approve.[46]

Richmond could not have been more wrong. Upon hearing of Mordaunt's innovations, Cumberland immediately fired off a strongly worded directive to Secretary at War Barrington from his headquarters in Germany. The Duke was surprised to hear that his orders, approved by the King himself, should be 'changed according to the whim and supposed improvements of every fertile genius'. For the future, *all* general officers – not excepting Mordaunt – were to conform *exactly* to Standing Orders.[47]

Cumberland could be forgiven his bad-tempered outburst; when he wrote, on 28 August, he was mired in negotiations to salvage Hanover and its defenders. During previous weeks, Cumberland's fortunes had dwindled as his motley army was pushed steadily northwards by overwhelming French forces. The Duke finally turned at bay on 24 July, at Hastenbeck, near Hameln on the River Weser. For three days, sporadic fighting sprawled across a scrappy battlefield of wooded hills and marshland until Cumberland was forced to break off the combat and withdraw towards Stade, thereby abandoning Hanover to its fate. While D'Estrées's replacement, Minorca's conqueror, the Duc de Richelieu, paused to plunder the helpless Electorate, King George authorized Cumberland to negotiate a peace. At all costs, he must preserve Hanover and its army. On 8 September, Cumberland and Richelieu signed the Convention of Klosterzeven. Although the units of the 'Army of Observation' were allowed to disperse unmolested, the Hanoverian contingent was obliged to retire across the Elbe into Denmark, leaving the Electorate defenceless.

King George was livid at this 'betrayal'. Convinced that Cumberland had sacrificed Hanover at the stroke of a pen, he recalled him in disgrace. Spurned by the father he loved, the humiliated and heartsick Duke swiftly resigned all his military commissions. The erstwhile 'hero of Culloden' now retired into private life, seeking solace in his passion for horseracing.[48]

When Cumberland put his signature to the Convention of Klosterzeven, the Rochefort flotilla was already under way. It had finally weighed anchor on 7 September – nearly a month behind schedule – and even then continued to be dogged by delays. What should have been a short four-day passage to the Bay of Biscay was tripled by adverse weather. Always a lamentable sailor, Wolfe was prostrated by seasickness long before the fleet entered its churning waters. The expedition finally neared its destination at noon on the 20th, but, owing to fog and unfavourable winds, another three days passed before the first objective – the fortifications upon the Isle of Aix that covered both Rochefort and La Rochelle – could be attacked.[49]

Guided by a Huguenot pilot, Joseph Thierry, two British warships sailed close enough to the fort on Aix to pound it with their broadsides; the fire of the *Magnanime*, boldly commanded by Captain Richard Howe, was especially hot, and within two hours the island was in British hands. Whilst the fighting was still under way, Wolfe obtained

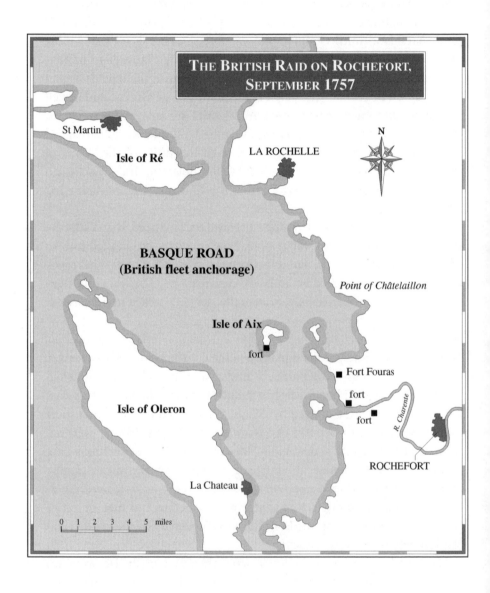

THE BRITISH RAID ON ROCHEFORT,
SEPTEMBER 1757

St Martin

Isle of Ré

LA ROCHELLE

N

BASQUE ROAD
(British fleet anchorage)

Point of Châtelaillon

Isle of Aix

fort

Fort Fouras

fort

Isle of Oleron

fort

R. Charente

ROCHEFORT

La Chateau

0 1 2 3 4 5 miles

Mordaunt's leave to go ashore to reconnoitre. Landing soon after the fort had hauled down its colours, he scrambled over the battered ramparts and trained his telescope upon the mainland. Back aboard the *Ramillies*, he reported what he had seen to Mordaunt and Hawke. From Wolfe's observations, it was proposed to attack another battery, Fort Fouras, next morning. Its capture would not only permit a landing, and further assaults upon the fortifications guarding the mouth of the River Charente that snaked inland to Rochefort, but also safeguard any re-embarkation. According to Wolfe, Hawke approved the plan 'with a great deal of warmth'; encouraged by this, Wolfe hinted that 'it might not be amiss to cause some diversion' towards La Rochelle by sending the fleet's bomb-ketches to draw the enemy's attention that way.

In the event, the attack on Fort Fouras was abandoned because shallow water prevented Hawke's ships from approaching within effective range. In addition, fresh intelligence revealed the presence of defences at the very spot picked for the disembarkation of the troops. Meanwhile, naval reconnaissance of the coastline stretching northwards towards La Rochelle had identified an alternative landing-zone, embracing the sandy bays either side of the headland at Châtelaillon. But here too there were problems. As before, the warships were unable to get close enough inshore to cover a landing with their guns, and the beaches were backed by dunes that made it impossible to assess the strength of any defending force that might be lurking behind them.

Mordaunt was a brave and experienced soldier who had commanded brigades at Culloden and Lauffeldt. But at sixty he was now well past his prime and prone to bouts of nervousness – a poor choice to head an expedition demanding resolution and decisiveness. Hesitant from the outset, Mordaunt rapidly lost the initiative and allowed the operation to stall. Faced with a succession of conflicting reports, he proved reluctant to land. Instead, on 25 September, Mordaunt sought the advice of a council of war. For a full day senior army and naval officers debated the viability of landing – and what could be achieved if they actually got ashore. It rapidly became clear that they were particularly receptive to negative arguments, drawing the most pessimistic conclusions from the available evidence. Rather than accept engineer Clerk's verdict on the vulnerability of Rochefort's defences, the council members preferred to credit the contradictory testimony of two prisoners who maintained that the port's ditch could be flooded – so ruling out a surprise assault using scaling ladders. On the basis of this uncorroborated evidence, the council lamely concluded that an attack upon Rochefort was 'neither advisable nor practicable'.

Although the primary target of the raid was thereby abandoned, it remained possible to harass the enemy in other ways. After all, a formidable armament had been assembled at great public expense, and given Byng's recent fate, it was perhaps wise to do at least *something* with it. Various options were considered and rejected before Conway convinced Mordaunt to reconsider an attack upon Fort Fouras. True to form, on 28 September the commander-in-chief called *another* council of war to assess the risks. Wolfe again counselled action: he believed the post to be weakly fortified and open to assault from the rear. When a French prisoner confirmed that there was no landward ditch to thwart such an attack, the council approved a landing at Châtelaillon that very night. Early next morning the first wave of troops were in their longboats and ready to go when a strong wind blew up from the land. Under such conditions, it would be daylight by the time they got ashore, and several hours before a second wave could follow. The landing was promptly cancelled.

A further reconnaissance of the Bay of Châtelaillon was ordered that morning, 29 September. Wolfe again went along, this time accompanied by Colonel George Howard and Lieutenant-Colonel Murray. He returned convinced that an assault was still possible. Indeed, they had 'not seen any entrenchments, redoubts, batteries, or troops to prevent their landing', although, he felt obliged to add, there was no way of knowing *exactly* what lay behind the masking dunes. But this information came too late to influence events. Exasperated by landlubberly dithering, Hawke had already delivered a letter bluntly informing Mordaunt and Conway that, if they'd nothing better in mind, he intended to return with his squadron to England. Uncertain about the enemy's strength, and now presented with the admiral's ultimatum, the generals grasped the opportunity to terminate the operation, justifying their decision by observing that French fleets were expected from North America and the West Indies, and that Hawke's first duty was to be ready to meet them.

So the formidable armada sailed for home without landing a single redcoat on the soil of mainland France. The abject failure of the enterprise seemingly confirmed the depressing lesson of Cartagena – that Britain's soldiers and sailors were incapable of co-operation. After landing at Portsmouth Wolfe headed straight for the seclusion of his parents' house at Blackheath, both for the fresh air and exercise, and to avoid being pestered with questions about the expedition. As he told his mother, the whole affair had been managed so badly, and with such lack of zeal and regard for the country's honour, that he was 'ashamed to have been of the party'. Writing to his Uncle Walter, Wolfe said the capture of Aix had marked the high point in the campaign, but, although the enemy were thereby thrown into 'confusion and consternation', the British commanders had allowed this 'lucky moment' to slip through their hands. Amongst the ensuing debates and councils, it was never regained. Wolfe still seethed at the memory of their muddling and prevarication. If they had only blundered on and fought a little, they could have at least compensated with courage for their lack of skill. But such excessive caution – or whatever other named it deserved – created a bad impression amongst the troops, who, to do them justice, had showed 'all the signs of spirit and goodwill'.[50]

Wolfe's bitter words reflected the frustrations of the rank and file. The regiments trained up at Newport camp had been spoiling for a fight, only to be denied any opportunity to prove their mettle. For Private James Miller of the 15th Foot – whose boy-hood dreams of martial glory had recently led him to enlist 'at a very tender age' – the Rochefort expedition was a rude awakening. He recalled: 'we certainly cut but a poor figure on our return, and were frequently insulted in our quarters by the vulgar, as if soldiers were answerable for the conduct of their superiors. I was now pretty well cured of the romantic notions imbibed in youth'.[51]

As the mortified Miller discovered, the Rochefort fiasco dragged the prestige of the redcoats to a new low. The expedition's disappointing outcome only fuelled a mood of national crisis. At home, that summer saw extensive rioting against the new Militia Bill, which, after much debate and amendment in both Houses of Parliament, had finally received the royal assent on 28 June; ironically, a measure intended to ease the burden on Britain's regular army only exacerbated the manpower shortfall as troops were required to tackle the anti-militia mobs.

And from across the Atlantic came yet more bad news. A vast force under Lord Loudoun had assembled at Halifax, Nova Scotia, destined to assault Louisbourg. But by the time all was ready the French had concentrated a superior defensive fleet and nothing could be done. Worse still, in Loudoun's absence Montcalm swooped down upon the vulnerable New York frontier, burned Fort William Henry and captured its garrison; once again, his Indian allies could not be prevented from massacring scores of prisoners. Lurid accounts of the carnage – such 'cruelty and barbarity' as was scarce to be believed – received prominent press coverage, stoking calls for retribution.[52]

Amongst all the gloom and recriminations, Wolfe's own stock continued to rise. His conspicuous zeal at Rochefort had not gone unnoticed. Admiral Hawke reported favourably to Lord Anson, who relayed this praise to King George himself. The result, as Wolfe reported to his father on 21 October, was the promotion he had craved for so long. He was given the brevet – or temporary – rank of colonel of the 20th's 2nd Battalion; ordered as part of the ongoing drive to increase army manpower, it had begun drumming up recruits during the previous September, when Wolfe was on riot control duties in the Cotswolds. This long awaited recognition was all the more welcome, Wolfe believed, because it reflected favourably upon his conduct during the expedition.[53]

But the performance of Wolfe's superiors at Rochefort met with a very different response. Public outrage at this latest humiliation to befall Britain's armed forces provoked a dense barrage of pamphlets and newspaper editorials, and an official inquiry was ordered to establish just what had gone wrong. It opened on 12 November and ran for more than a week. As commander-in-chief of the land forces, Mordaunt faced intensive questioning; his evidence, presented as a written statement, amounted to little more than a long list of excuses for doing nothing. Wolfe was amongst those called to testify, but he carefully avoided open criticism of his old friend and patron. What Wolfe *did* say, however, made it clear that he at least had favoured a landing – despite the risks. Along with the gallant Captain Howe, he was one of the few officers to emerge from the affair with any credit. As Horace Walpole observed, this fiery pair 'soon contracted a friendship like the union of a cannon and gunpowder'. In his personal correspondence, Wolfe lavished praise upon the dark and silent Howe. His evaluation of 'Black Dick' would be vindicated by an illustrious career extending far into the era of warfare with Revolutionary France.[54]

The Rochefort inquiry's verdict, delivered on the 21 November, was uncompromising. The expedition had foundered from the moment that 'the great object of it' was laid aside at the first, fateful, council of war. The board members could find no evidence that the shore defences were formidable enough to prevent a disembarkation, or that Rochefort was a tougher proposition than the engineer Clerk had originally indicated; and if a landing could be contemplated as late as 28 September, they wondered, then why not days earlier when the British still enjoyed the advantage of surprise?[55]

Given these damning conclusions, Mordaunt was brought before a court martial, charged with disobeying his orders. The trial began on 14 December, and over the next six days the same sorry story unfolded. But, despite the evidence piling up against him, Mordaunt had no doubt that he would be acquitted. His confidence was well placed: as his orders had allowed him scope for discretion, a count of disobedience was difficult to sustain. George II was unsatisfied with the resulting 'not guilty' verdict. His disgust was clear when he snubbed Mordaunt at court, and dropped him – along with Conway and Cornwallis – from his personal staff.

Once again, Wolfe was called as a witness; and once again, he pulled his punches. In his private correspondence Wolfe showed no such restraint. Never before, he told Rickson, had there been such a collection of people so unfit for the service they were sent upon: they were 'dilatory, ignorant, irresolute', with 'some grains of a very unmanly quality, and very unsoldier-like or unsailor-like'. But despite its outcome, Wolfe had no regrets about joining the expedition, reckoning that it was always possible to 'pick up something useful from amongst the most fatal errors'. Indeed, Wolfe had learned some fundamental lessons of amphibious warfare – above all, the importance of careful organization, swift reconnaissance and vigorous action. An admiral should seek to 'run into an enemy's port immediately after he appears before it', landing the troops as soon as possible; and at all costs, no time should be lost 'in idle debate and consultations when the sword should be drawn'.

What Wolfe witnessed off Rochefort also helped to define his own attitude as a soldier. At its heart lay a readiness to risk failure and death in the determined pursuit of victory – and glory. As he explained to Rickson,

> nothing is to be reckoned an obstacle to your undertaking which is not found really so upon trial; that in war something must be allowed to chance and fortune, seeing it is in its nature hazardous, and an option of difficulties; that the greatness of an object should come under consideration, opposed to the impediments that lie in the way; that the honour of one's country is to have some weight; and that, in particular circumstances and times, the loss of a thousand men is rather an advantage to a nation than otherwise, seeing that gallant attempts raise its reputation and make it respectable; whereas the contrary appearances sink the credit of a country, ruin the troops, and create infinite uneasiness and discontent at home.[56]

Wolfe had been given precious little chance to distinguish himself at Rochefort, but his consistent advocacy of action – a stance duly noted in press coverage of the official inquiry – undoubtedly enhanced his professional reputation.[57] That December he was invited to meet the Prince of Wales – the future George III – to explain the system of discipline used in the 20th Foot. Reporting their conversation to one of his captains, Henry Parr, Wolfe recalled how he had told the Prince of the corps' obedience, 'high spirit of service and love of duty', with which 'he appeared to be greatly pleased, knowing well that from good indications, joined with order and discipline, great military performances usually spring'.[58]

Wolfe spent Christmas 1757 with his parents at Bath. Three years had passed since the family last gathered there, and much had happened in the interim. For Britain and its empire, there had been an almost unalleviated chain of disasters: Braddock's defeat; the loss of Minorca; Cumberland's humiliation at Klosterzeven; the infamous 'massacre' at Fort William Henry; and now, to compound all, the dispiriting outcome of the attempt against Rochefort.

But the tide was finally about to turn. At long last, James Wolfe would have an opportunity to put his own creed of soldiering to the test.

6

Louisbourg

A nobler emulation ne'er was known,
Nor British valour ever better shown,
'Till forc'd by Fate, the Gallic bands retreat,
'Twas Britons only, could have urg'd the feat.

John Maylem, 'The Conquest of Louisbourg', Boston 1758

For Britain, 1757 had brought nothing but defeat, and from nowhere had the tidings proved grimmer than North America. It was plain to all that drastic action was required if Britain's beleaguered American colonies were to confront and overthrow New France. As the dreary year drew to a close the ministry dominated by William Pitt resolved to reverse the inglorious trend. During the last days of December, a steady stream of orders from Whitehall crossed the Atlantic. Pitt's clean sweep brushed aside Lord Loudoun, a conscientious but conspicuously unlucky soldier who had presided over an era of defeat. Pitt had turned against him in mid December, resolving upon his recall and replacement by his erstwhile brigadier, James Abercomby. The latest commander-in-chief in North America was charged with implementing an ambitious new offensive, and Britain's colonies were invited to join an all-out struggle against the common foe. Lieutenant governors from Massachusetts Bay to Pennsylvania received detailed instructions calculated to harness their resources more effectively than ever before. These mingled appeals to patriotism with handsome promises to reimburse the costs involved in fielding hefty contingents of provincial troops. Pitt's pragmatic new approach proved irresistible. Colonial assemblies that had offered only half-hearted cooperation to Loudoun's directives now responded with enthusiasm.

Pitt's policies were instrumental in rallying the colonies behind the mother country, but his wider role in overhauling the Anglo-American war effort should not be exaggerated. Although he had held a cornet's commission as a youngster, Pitt was no soldier. It was Cumberland's replacement as commander-in-chief, Sir John Ligonier, who transformed Pitt's plans for America into a coherent strategy. Now raised to the rank of field-marshal, he produced two successive drafts, then thrashed out the final version with Pitt over Christmas. Instead of staging just one major strike, like that mustered against Louisbourg under Loudoun, the new strategy called for simultaneous attacks on several fronts. There would be another attempt at Louisbourg, but this time the crucial naval component was to remain on station in North America to give the earliest possible start to the campaign. A second expedition was to advance overland against Canada via Lake Champlain. In addition, a third force would seek to wipe away the stain of Braddock's defeat by capturing Fort Duquesne at the Forks of the Ohio. Taken together, these three fronts involved the deployment of more than 20,000 regular troops, matched by as many provincials.[1]

By New Year, London was buzzing with talk of this ambitious strategy. Within army circles an even greater stir was caused by news of those men who had been picked to implement it. James Abercromby's elevation scarcely marked a break with tradition. In his early fifties but prematurely aged, he was a stolid and unimaginative officer of whom little more could be said save that he had reached senior rank without either disgrace or distinction. But elsewhere there were dramatic changes to the traditional command structure. Recent defeats gave weight to those who believed that the time was ripe to replace superannuated and lacklustre generals with others who compensated in ability for what they lacked in seniority. Promising young officers of proven merit would now get their chance.

Credit for this revolution has traditionally been accorded to Pitt; but, once again, it belonged primarily to Ligonier. Ironically, the instigator of the new military meritocracy was himself one of the oldest soldiers in the army. Although now in his late seventies, Ligonier remained both mentally and physically vigorous. A confirmed bachelor, he nonetheless continued to take pleasure in the company of young actresses and singers. If gossip was to be credited, the venerable field-marshal simultaneously maintained four mistresses with a combined age of just fifty-eight.

Ligonier also enjoyed the favour of George II. He had earned it in a glittering fighting career that had begun under Marlborough and had only ended with the celebrated cavalry charge that saved Cumberland's bloodied army at Lauffeldt. But there were limits to what even Ligonier could achieve; the plodding Abercromby's appointment was proof of that. Given his monarch's notorious conservatism in these matters, Ligonier faced a daunting task. Yet he was instrumental in persuading the King to accept a quartet of promising soldiers for the coming campaign in North America. Forty-two-year-old Jeffery Amherst, who had served as Ligonier's *aide-de-camp* during the War of the Austrian Succession, and who had recently accompanied Cumberland's army in Germany with responsibility for the Hessian contingent, was leapfrogged from colonel to major-general in command of the troops destined for the fresh assault on Louisbourg. This was a remarkable jump – particularly as Amherst was a staff officer who had never before held a combat command; but he and Ligonier were close, and the field-marshal's influence was clearly decisive.[2] Three other colonels were appointed brigadier-generals. John Forbes – another Ligonier protégé – would take command of the expedition to Fort Duquesne. The personable, vigorous and charismatic George Augustus, Lord Howe, who was already serving with his regiment in America, would act as second-in-command to Abercromby; aged thirty-four, he was elder brother to Captain Richard Howe of the *Magnanime*. And James Wolfe – at thirty-one the youngest of them all – was assigned to Amherst's Louisbourg operation. Writing to his brother Lord George Lennox, Wolfe's friend Richmond believed that these 'extraordinary rises' were 'for the good of the service'. They would enable 'people of merit' to exercise command whilst they were 'in the prime of their age'. He added: 'We have seen the contrary too much by the list of our decrepit old generals.'[3]

The precise circumstances of Wolfe's promotion are unclear, although the reputation he had so recently made at Rochefort must have stood him in good stead. Whatever the reasoning behind his selection, by Christmas Day 1757 the well-informed army agent John Calcraft was already reporting the news that Wolfe was amongst those officers bound for America, although in 'what shape' he did not yet know.[4]

Whilst Ligonier, Pitt and the more conscientious of their Cabinet colleagues were hammering out the finer details of the coming American campaigns, and selecting the men who would execute them, Wolfe, as already noted, was celebrating Christmas at Bath in company with his parents. By 7 January 1758, following an uncomfortable journey by jarring coach and lumbering post horse, he was back with his battalion at Exeter. That morning he opened a letter from London that galvanized him into action. The departure of the reinforcements for North America was imminent, and Wolfe, who clearly hoped to secure a key command across the Atlantic, had no intention of missing the boat. Although still saddle-sore from his recent ride, he set off for London late that same afternoon. Night found the colonel and his trusty servant François crossing the bleak and featureless expanse of Salisbury Plain; the darkness was so intense that when their candle spluttered and failed a halt seemed inevitable. Luckily, the ever-resourceful François produced a tinderbox to strike a light; their lantern rekindled, the journey resumed. Wolfe reached London by 1.00 p.m. on the 8th, having covered 170 miles in some twenty hours.

Over bad roads in the very depth of winter, this was breakneck pace indeed. It leaves no doubt that Wolfe remained hungry for action – wherever he could find it. As he explained to Rickson on 12 January: 'Being of the profession of arms, I would seek all occasions to serve, and therefore have thrown myself in the way of the American war.' Wolfe pictured himself as ignorant of public affairs and political intrigue, content instead to be carried along 'with the current unheeding'. Unheeding or not, Wolfe's growing fame swiftly secured him the command he craved. Writing to his uncle Walter from Blackheath on 21 January he revealed: 'The King has honoured me with the rank of Brigadier in America, which I cannot but consider as a peculiar mark of his Majesty's favour and confidence.' He would do his best to deserve it.[5]

That same day Richmond observed that Wolfe's appointment was now common knowledge in the capital, although both he and Colonel Guy Carleton, who was rumoured to be going with Amherst as quartermaster-general, made 'a great secret of it and are mighty discreet'. In fact, George II was adamant that Carleton, who had once cast a slur upon his monarch's beloved Hanoverian troops, should *not* go to America. Henry Fox reported that 'The King was in a passion on Carleton's being named to him, and has refused it I hear absolutely.'[6]

Of the various offensives to be mounted in North America, Amherst's strike against Louisbourg was the most important – and the riskiest. Unlike Abercromby's advance down the Champlain Valley, it involved a combined operation, requiring close cooperation between the army and navy. As Cartagena and Rochefort had shown, the inter-service harmony crucial for the success of such expeditions could by no means be taken for granted, although in Vice-Admiral Edward Boscawen it was hoped that Amherst would find a willing and competent colleague. Nicknamed 'Wry-Necked Dick' from his habit of cocking his head to one side, Boscawen came from a venerable Cornish family and boasted a formidable fighting reputation, as his alternative moniker, 'Old Dread-nought', testified. He'd served with distinction at Cartagena, and had been wounded during the victorious clash with the French off Cape Finisterre in 1747. Most significantly for the coming campaign, Bos-cawen had a creditable track record of conducting difficult combined operations, having commanded an expedition sent to India to besiege the French post of Pondicherry in 1748.[7]

In recognition of the high priority given to the Cape Breton campaign, Amherst was allocated the lion's share of the redcoats earmarked for the American theatre of operations – no less than fourteen battalions. Unlike Abercromby, whose force included thousands of short-service provincials, his troops were all professionals. To help direct his sub-stantial army, Amherst was given three brigadiers. Besides Wolfe, there were Charles Lawrence and Edward Whitmore, both of whom were his seniors in age and service.

For Wolfe, promotion to brigadier-general in America brought with it the dread prospect of an Atlantic crossing. In the event, Boscawen's departure from Portsmouth was delayed by contrary winds. Wolfe vented his impatience and trepidation with some choice observations upon the 'hellish' port's garrison and inhabitants. The former were 'vagabonds that stroll about in dirty red clothes from one gin-shop to another'; as for Pompey's 'diabolical citizens', he doubted whether there was 'such another collection of demons upon the whole earth'.[8]

The fleet finally set sail from St Helen's, off the Isle of Wight, on 19 February. For Wolfe, aboard the *Princess Amelia*, the crossing was even more protracted than he had feared. Once safely back on dry land, he recalled the ordeal with his customary hyperbole. 'From Christopher Columbus's time to our days there perhaps has never been a more extraordinary voyage,' he complained to Lord George Sackville. Dogged by 'contrary winds, calms, or currents', the passage had consumed eleven valuable weeks.[9]

It was only on 9 May 1758 that Boscawen's fleet reached Halifax, Nova Scotia. This was scarcely an auspicious opening to the campaign. The projected strategy had envisaged the earliest possible start date for the assault upon Louisbourg, so leaving good time to undertake such 'ulterior operations' as Amherst and Boscawen considered 'most practicable and expedient'. Their instructions allowed for pushing onwards against Quebec, provided, of course, that the remaining troops were equal to 'so great and arduous an enterprize'. Other possibilities included strikes against the French settlements in the Gulf of St Lawrence or, more ambitiously, Louisiana.[10]

The main campaign was now already a month behind schedule and some of the troops converging upon Halifax from Ireland, New York and Boston had yet to arrive; and of the redcoats' commander, Major-General Amherst, there was still no sign. This enforced delay was put to valuable use. Each day saw training operations calculated 'to accustom the troops to what they were soon to encounter'. Not only were the men taken into the woods and exercised in the kind of bush fighting they could expect to wage if they made it ashore on Cape Breton, but they were also 'frequently landed in the boats of the transports'. Such efforts to familiarize the redcoats with the techniques of amphibious warfare were not only unprecedented but also desperately needed. The Louisbourg task force lacked purpose-built landing craft. Instead, it was obliged to rely upon an odd assortment of vessels: men-of-war's boats, flat-bottomed bateaux from New England, and whaleboats requisitioned from the Greenland fisheries.

The landing drills evolved during those hectic weeks became standard practice for decades to come. For example, orders issued on 21 May warned that any firing of muskets from the boats was strictly forbidden; to avoid accidents, bayonets must only be fixed once the men were ashore; immediately the troops quit their craft they were to 'form and march directly forwards to clear the beach and charge whatever is before them'; they should resist the temptation to pursue too far, and instead secure the beachhead for the comrades who followed. Wolfe, the supreme trainer of troops, was now in his element. One observer noted: 'In all these operations you may imagine that General Wolfe was remarkable active. The scene afforded scope for his military genius.'[11]

Alongside the military preparations, the great gathering of army and naval officers provided opportunities for carousing. Here, too, Wolfe played his part. On 24 May, the brigadier hosted a lavish dinner at Halifax's Great Pontac coffee house, picking up a bill for £98 12s. 6d. The reckoning covered food for the forty-seven diners, the hire of ten musicians and fifteen waiters – and drinks. The tally of bottles consumed – seventy of Madeira, fifty of claret, twenty-five of brandy – suggests that it must have been quite a night, with many patriotic toasts to the success of British arms. This convivial scenario is hard to reconcile with modern characterizations of Wolfe as an aloof and awkward loner, ill at ease with his fellows. Instead, it meshes with the memory of Lieutenant Henry Hamilton of Amherst's 15th Foot, to whom Wolfe appeared anything but stiff, formal and unapproachable. Indeed, his 'action' was free, 'his gestures open as those of an actor who feels no constraint'. And, despite Wolfe's admittedly curious 'assemblage of feature', there was 'a certain animation in the countenance and spirit in his manner that solicited attention and interested most people in his favour'.[12]

Before leaving England, Boscawen had received instructions that in the event of unforeseen delays with the arrival of the various contingents, the expedition should get under way immediately that the number of troops concentrated at Halifax – ultimately expected to total more than 13,000 men – reached 8000. With Amherst still absent, command of the land forces fell to Brigadier Lawrence, an officer familiar with Cape Breton. Towards the end of May, Boscawen, Lawrence and Wolfe prepared a preliminary plan of action. This was influenced by information that their most obvious landing zone, embraced within the great sweep of Gabarus Bay, now bristled with formidable defences. It was therefore thought best to strike where the enemy was less ready to receive them. According to Wolfe, 3000 men were to land at Miré – some ten miles north of the fortress itself – and then march overland towards Gabarus Bay. At the same time, attacks would be made against Lorembec and La Baleine to the east of Louisbourg; in addition, a small diversionary force would strike Gabarus Bay, whilst Boscawen menaced the harbour mouth. If that plan foundered another must be tried, Wolfe insisted, 'for we must get on shoar or perish altogether in the attempt'. He added that nothing could be finalized until they actually *saw* their objective; and it was still possible that Amherst might arrive in good time to propose something better.[13]

But where *was* Amherst? Like Wolfe, he'd undergone a frustratingly convoluted Atlantic passage. Recalled unexpectedly from Germany, he had only set sail from Portsmouth on 16 March. Amherst berthed aboard the *Dublin*, a seventy-four-gun man-of-war captained by George Brydges Rodney. They had been under way for just four days when Rodney revealed the craving for prize money that would characterize his long career at sea. A French East Indiaman bound for Brest with a valuable cargo of coffee and redwood proved too tempting for him to resist. As this catch was valued at £30,000, Rodney made a detour to the neutral Spanish port of Vigo; from there the prize could be convoyed safely back to England. Amherst, who was increasingly anxious to continue on his way, refused to go ashore 'that it may never be said that I was diverting myself at Vigo'. It was 1 April before they were once more under way. Thereafter, adverse winds, impenetrable coastal fogs and the *Dublin*'s 'very ignorant' pilot all conspired to ensure that they only sighted Halifax harbour at 8.00 a.m. on 28 May. By a happy coincidence, at that very moment, Boscawen's fleet was emerging. At noon, Amherst boarded the *Namur*, meeting Brigadiers Lawrence and Wolfe.[14]

In coming days the dank and stormy Nova Scotian climate continued to hamper operations. On 30 May the fleet was dispersed by a gale. Next day the scattered warships and transports hove in sight of Louisbourg. At last the fog lifted for long enough to reveal their objective. The dour grey fortress occupied a peninsula on the south-west side of a large and sheltered kidney-shaped harbour. The town's grid-like complex of streets was enclosed within defences that reflected the latest principles of military architecture. Attackers from the land were confronted by a line of squat and powerful-looking bastions, which were themselves protected by a smooth man-made slope or 'glacis', and beyond that, extensive swamps. The seaward defences looked equally formidable: the anchorage itself was guarded by gun batteries, one of them sited on an island within the very mouth of the harbour. Louisbourg held a garrison of some 3500 troops, of whom one battalion had slipped in just hours ahead of Boscawen's fleet. These regulars could be reinforced with militia, and about 3800 sailors from the eleven warships sheltering within the harbour. Direction of the defence was entrusted to the governor of Isle Royale, Augustin de Boschenry de Drucour. An experienced naval officer with almost three decades of service behind him, Drucour knew only too well that Louisbourg was much weaker than appearances suggested. The landward fortifications were poorly sited, leaving them vulnerable to enfilade fire from flanking batteries; and some of the damage inflicted during the siege of 1745 still remained unrepaired. Worst of all, the island's all-pervading damp had seeped into the very mortar of the walls, leaving them liable to crumble like mouldy cheese under sustained bombardment.[15]

But for all their flaws, Louisbourg's defences would only be tested if a besieging force managed to claw itself ashore. The fate of fortress and garrison alike therefore hinged upon the success or failure of the British amphibious assault that was now imminent.

As if to compensate for his tardy appearance, Jeffery Amherst lost no time in rejecting the contingency plan agreed in his absence. He possibly reasoned that the ten miles of rugged and unfamiliar terrain stretching between Miré and the fortress itself would prove too irksome to negotiate. Despite its recently upgraded defences, Amherst instead focused his attention upon Gabarus Bay. On 1 June a trusted officer, Major James Robertson of the Royal American Regiment, was sent there to investigate. Next day, after the fleet began to drop anchor in the bay, Amherst, Lawrence and Wolfe transferred to a sloop and reconnoitred the shoreline for themselves. The thorough Boscawen had already despatched decoy boats to draw the defenders' fire and pinpoint the location of their gun batteries.[16]

On the basis of these observations a descent was planned for daybreak on 3 June; its execution would depend upon the prompt arrival of the remaining troops. Three assaults were projected, each of them to be led by one of the brigadiers; Edward Whitmore would hopefully arrive in time to play his part in the plan. Amherst reckoned that this triple onslaught would maximize the chances of success: 'by dividing their force we may be sure to succeed somewhere,' he announced. Once ashore, and confronted by the enemy's regular troops, Amherst's redcoats were to adopt the simple and aggressive tactics previously advocated by Wolfe: 'they are to march up close to them, discharge their pieces loaded with two bullets, and then rush upon them with their bayonets'.[17] The army's right wing, under Whitmore, would seek to land at Pointe Blanche. Lawrence would head for a brace of bays further to the left. Wolfe, to the westward of all, was ordered to make for Anse de la Cormorandière – the Cove of the Cormorant.

Wolfe's objective was the most heavily defended sector, and with good reason: a successful landing there could overrun the defenders' flank and rear, severing their line of retreat to Louisbourg. But this first plan was never implemented. Though Whitmore and most of the missing troops duly arrived, bringing Amherst's army to its full strength of about 13,000, the surf was still too violent. The continuing delay prompted another important change to the dispositions. In place of the three-pronged assault, there would now be just *one* genuine attack. Orders issued on 4 June disclosed that Wolfe was to lead it. His objective remained the Anse de la Cormorandière; it was chosen in the belief that the surf there was less wild than elsewhere, and that the warships would be able to approach close enough inshore to cover a landing with their broadsides. The divisions of Lawrence and Whitmore were to make diversionary feints against Pointe Blanche and Pointe Platte and be ready to support the real assault.

In keeping with its hazardous task, Wolfe's spearhead division of more than 3000 men mustered the toughest soldiers of Amherst's force. There were twelve companies of grenadiers – traditionally the most aggressive men in each regiment. In addition, it included a freshly raised corps of light infantry. Selected from nimble and resourceful marksmen, they were the first representatives of a British Army tradition that would become legendary during Wellington's Peninsular campaigns. They were joined by the entire complement of Fraser's Highlanders – a hardy and well-disciplined battalion that had already earned Wolfe's ungrudging praise. This force of shock-troops was completed by several companies of the New England irregulars known as 'rangers'. Brigadier Lawrence had deplored the conduct of these unruly and hard-drinking Yankees when he saw them on their home turf in Boston. At Halifax, Wolfe too was unimpressed; he chose one of his favourite epithets to dismiss them as '*canaille*'; another eyewitness noted their 'cut-throat, savage appearance'. But, as events would soon demonstrate, for all their rough edges, the rum-swilling rangers deserved their place in that elite fraternity.[18]

With the campaign already lagging badly behind schedule, Amherst was anxious to attack as soon as possible. But poor weather continued to thwart his plans and kept the infantry cooped up aboard the rolling transport ships. Early on the 6th conditions cleared and Boscawen signalled to prepare to land. The troops actually entered their boats and were rowing towards the designated rendezvous when heavy rain and thick fog again put a damper on proceedings. The men were ordered back aboard their ships. On the evening of 7 June the wind and swell at last abated. Boscawen believed something could be done next morning. At midnight the long-suffering troops once more clambered down into their boats. This time there was no cancellation.

At 4.00 a.m. on the 8th, the bomb ketch *Halifax* and frigate *Kennington* opened fire upon the shore defences at la Cormorandière. Other vessels directed their guns against different sectors. With the same objective of deflecting attention from the real attack, the 28th Foot, which had arrived too late to participate in the Halifax landing drills, was convoyed eastwards towards Lorembec, taking good care to show itself to Louisbourg's garrison as it passed the harbour mouth.

The coastal bombardment lasted for some fifteen minutes before Wolfe's boats rowed briskly in for the shore. The designated landing zone presented a daunting prospect. Ahead loomed a rocky coast, fringed by pounding surf that proved 'greater than was imagined'. Such natural obstacles alone were formidable enough for men in flimsy open boats, but they were bolstered with extensive man-made defences. The cove was flanked by gun batteries calculated to deliver a murderous crossfire. Beyond the shoreline were entrenchments manned by musketeers and mounting 'swivels' – light cannon that functioned like monstrous shotguns. The beaches themselves were screened by a mass of felled trees, their tangled branches presenting a formidable barrier to sea-borne assault.[19]

Propelled by straining Royal Navy oarsmen, the bucketing boatloads of redcoats moved ever onwards into the cove. The shoreline remained ominously silent – but not for long. Private James Miller of the 15th Foot now received the baptism of fire that he had been denied at Rochefort.

As he recalled, the hidden defenders 'preserved their fire, until our boats got near the shore, when such a tremendous one commenced from their great guns, and small arms, as I have never since beheld!' Grapeshot and musket balls flayed the waves. To Major Alexander Murray of the grenadiers, it was as if handfuls of shot were being flung into the water. Wolfe was in the thick of things. His cutter flew a red ensign to mark the division's centre, but its flagstaff was soon severed by gunfire. The heavy swell only contributed to the confusion. A boat carrying part of the grenadier company of Miller's regiment was swamped and overset; the heavily laden occupants all drowned, save for a few who could swim, and the drummer, who was found 'bouy'd up' (sic) by his instrument.

Convinced that a landing in the cove was impossible, Wolfe waved his hat as a signal for the division to withdraw and try its luck elsewhere. As one journalist observed, 'the fate of the expedition seemed to depend upon this moment and the most sanguine almost despaired of setting foot on shore'. But the situation suddenly changed. Several boatloads of light infantry, led by a trio of bold young subalterns, had meanwhile reached a narrow strand concealed within a craggy spur to the right of the cove. Scaling the slippery rocks above, the drenched handful maintained a precarious toehold until their battalion commander, Major George Scott, reinforced them. Spotting this encouraging development, Wolfe hastened to support Scott's men. Plunging into the sea, he landed amongst the foremost, facing 'the hottest fire with only his cane in his hand'; their muskets soaked and useless, the grenadiers and Highlanders who followed him put their faith in bayonets and broadswords. As ever more redcoats and rangers dragged themselves dripping and battered from the pulverizing surf, so the British bridgehead expanded.

It had been a close-run affair, clinched only by the leadership of the officers and the courage of their men. In the opinion of Captain George Fletcher of the 35th Foot, 'there never was a greater spirit shewn in British Troops, than that on the eighth of June'. According to Major Murray, Wolfe was so pleased that he promptly presented guineas to two of the men who had come ashore with him. Wolfe also lavished praise upon the three light infantry officers – lieutenants Browne of the 35th and Hopkins of the 48th, and Ensign Grant of the 3/60th – whose daring and initiative had first shown the way to victory, declaring that the credit for 'the landing of the troops, and the honour of the day', was entirely theirs.

Fearing for their line of retreat, most of the defenders now quit their posts in blind panic. The few who refused to flee included an unusually stout Indian chief, who was killed and scalped by Lieutenant Hopkins. His body bore many old scars and a 'medal of distinction from the French king'. This curiosity, which carried a design in the antique style, was plucked from around his neck and presented to Admiral Boscawen as a keepsake. As the French scampered for the refuge of Louisbourg, the back-up divisions of Whitmore and Lawrence landed with no more opposition than the crashing surf. Once ashore, the redcoats pursued as fast as the boggy and rock-strewn terrain permitted until they were halted by gunfire from the fortress walls. As a satisfied Amherst observed, this bombardment pinpointed the range of the defenders' artillery, showing exactly where the besiegers might form their camp in safety.[20]

Both Amherst and Drucour knew that the boldly executed amphibious assault was the decisive moment of the campaign. Prisoners taken that morning assured the British that 'the greatest part of our business was done in the landing of our troops'. The French engineers had been confident that such an outcome was impossible 'for almost any number of men'; indeed, 'none but madmen would have attempted it, where the English did'. Revisiting these dramatic events in his personal correspondence, Wolfe felt inclined to agree. He told his uncle Walter that the attempt to land was 'rash and ill-advised', only succeeding 'by the greatest of good fortune imaginable'. Writing to Sackville, he considered that the landing was 'next to miraculous', adding dryly, 'I wouldn't recommend the Bay of Gabarus for a descent, especially as we managed it'.[21]

Wolfe was reticent about his own role, but others did not doubt that his swift reinforcement of Scott's precarious foothold was crucial. Had the Red division sustained a bloody check, Amherst's army might never have floundered ashore. According to one sober and detailed eyewitness journal, although Wolfe had 'opposed this attack in council', he nonetheless proved the most vigorous to promote it. The same account left no doubt that Brigadier Wolfe had begun the campaign as he meant to go on. As the more orthodox siege operations unfolded, the whole army would discover his 'bravery, activity and judgement'.[22]

With a British army now established upon Cape Breton, Louisbourg's fall was only a question of time. But there remained much to play for. If Amherst was to push onwards to Quebec, Louisbourg must be subdued without delay. Each day that Amherst remained outside its walls diminished his prospects of reaching the St Lawrence that summer. Drucour, who knew this only too well, resolved to hold the British at bay for as long as possible. In this task he was aided by the island's climate. The same surf that had bludgeoned Wolfe's assault troops now hampered the landing of the besiegers' supplies and cannon. Several valuable days were lost before the weather relented and Boscawen's exhausted crews could ferry the crucial gear ashore. Meanwhile, outposts and redoubts were established to defend the British camp from sudden sorties by the garrison and the attentions of its prowling Indian allies.

On 12 June, the French abandoned their outlying posts. All of their resources would now be concentrated upon the defence of the fortress itself. Wolfe was placed in command of a 1220-strong detachment of picked men and sent on a looping march around the harbour to secure Lighthouse Point, a vital position that overlooked the harbour mouth and the Island Battery that shielded it from attack by sea. Work began immediately on the construction of gun positions.

On the barren rocky terrain it was impossible to raise the customary earth defences against enemy fire; instead, batteries were laboriously constructed from bundles of brushwood, or 'fascines', and 'gabions' – soil-filled wicker cylinders. After yet more backbreaking toil, artillery pieces were hauled into position. By the 19th Wolfe was ready to retaliate with cannon and howitzers against the half-dozen French men-of-war that harassed the besiegers with their broadsides. When the warships shifted beyond the range of his guns, Wolfe's men laboured night and day to prepare another position capable of tackling the Island Battery. It commenced firing on 25 June and swiftly silenced the opposition.

Taking some 400 men, Wolfe now marched westwards to the head of the harbour in dogged pursuit of the French flotilla. Alive to the danger, the warships' gun crews unleashed a hot fire upon Wolfe's detachment as they struggled to erect fresh batteries. Occasional skirmishes enlivened

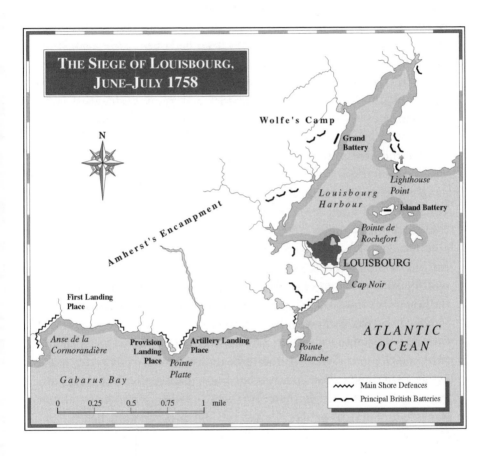

THE SIEGE OF LOUISBOURG,
JUNE–JULY 1758

N

Wolfe's Camp

Grand
Battery

Lighthouse
Point

Louisbourg   Island Battery
Harbour

Pointe de
Rochefort

LOUISBOURG

Cap Noir

Amherst's Encampment

First Landing
Place

ATLANTIC
OCEAN

Anse de la
Cormorandière

Provision
Landing
Place

Artillery Landing
Place

Pointe
Blanche

Gabarus Bay

Pointe
Platte

0   0.25   0.5   0.75   1   mile

⌇⌇⌇ Main Shore Defences

⌒⌒ Principal British Batteries

the laborious pick and shovel work. At 6.00 a.m. on 1 July about 300 of the garrison sallied forth but were rebuffed by the light infantry. Wolfe's reputation as a fire-eater was growing by the day. As Lieutenant William Gordon of the 40th Foot noted in his journal, 'General Wolfe was in this skirmish and as usual in the most danger.' [23]

That evening, the brigadier seized high ground facing the West Gate of the fortress. Within two days, this too had been secured with a redoubt. A nearby battery now lobbed shells directly upon the town, whilst Wolfe's gun positions at the harbour's head had opened fire against the increasingly desperate French ships. Hemmed within their shattered ramparts, Drucour's garrison grew ever more disconsolate. One of his battalions, the *Voluntaires Etranger*, included many disgruntled Swiss and Germans. As early as 13 June, as Captain Philip Townsend of the 22nd Foot noted in his diary, a sergeant and four men deserted, claiming that their entire regiment was of the same mind. Ruthless measures were taken to curb this drain upon manpower: bodies were soon seen dangling from gibbets mounted on the walls.[24]

Each day, in a bid to boost the defenders' morale, Drucour's plucky wife fired three cannon from the ramparts. But even the spirited Madame Drucour was not without her softer side. According to a letter printed in the *Boston Gazette*, she took advantage of a flag of truce to send Wolfe a 'pyramid of sweetmeats'. Touched by this unexpected gift, the brigadier reciprocated 'with a pineapple, which he happened to have'. Exactly how Wolfe came to be in possession of this exotic fruit whilst investing a far-flung northern fortress was not explained. Neither did Madame Drucour neglect Amherst: he received some fresh butter, made by her own hands. The *Gazette*'s hard-nosed correspondent was, however, unimpressed. Surely such courtesies were inappropriate to a bitter struggle for survival between 'inveterate enemies', he grouched.[25]

All was back to normal by 9 July. Early that morning a thousand of the garrison mounted a determined sally that caught the British pickets napping. Lord William Dundonald, captain of the 17th Regiment's grenadier company, was surprised and killed along with several of his men. Others were captured. But the interlopers were themselves taken off-guard by a sudden counter-attack. They were busy demolishing Dundonald's defences when the tireless Major Murray and his grenadiers tumbled them out again at bayonet point. According to Captain

William Amherst, the general's younger brother and *aide-de-camp*, these Frenchmen were scarcely capable of defending themselves, having been made 'beastly drunk' before they attacked. Dundonald's fate excited little sympathy. He had 'suffered for his want of vigilance'.[26]

Thereafter the siege ground on towards its inevitable conclusion. On 16 July Wolfe took possession of heights directly in front of the fortress. The parapet itself was now brought under musket fire. British casualties remained surprisingly light, although each day brought episodes such as that noted by Captain Townsend on 19 July, when Ensign Godfrey Rowe of the 48th Foot was 'killed by a cannon ball which knocked his head off as he looked over ye breast work out of curiosity not duty'. Next day, Townsend recorded, another deserter came into camp claiming that the garrison had plenty of powder but little ball; they were instead reduced to firing such motley projectiles as broken bottles, bolts, scrap iron and old nails. To this, the besiegers responded with a steady barrage of more conventional shot and shell. Louisbourg's citadel was soon ablaze. Amherst believed that such drastic measures were justified by circumstances: 'Burning the town is spoiling our own nests but it will probably be the shortest way of taking it,' he noted.[27]

On the 21st, one of Wolfe's batteries scored a bull's-eye on the *Entrepreneur* man-of-war. Captain Townsend witnessed the spectacular consequences:

> I was this day in ye trenches when a lucky ball from Mr Wolf by some accident set fire to a parcel of cartridges on board one of ye ships which caused a great explosion and soon after we saw ye ship in flames and she set fire to two more ...

Townsend was clearly cock-a-hoop that Britain's much-maligned redcoats were now showing the Royal Navy just how things should be done. He added that the destruction of three warships was a 'great grief' to Admiral Boscawen, who had promised 'great matters' when they sailed from Halifax but had so far done nothing. In fact, Townsend continued, the army had no need of Boscawen's assistance, although to be fair some of his sailors *had* hauled cannon up for Brigadier Wolfe. Of Wolfe himself Townsend could not speak too highly: he was 'ye most indefatigable active man I have ever heard of, and to him very much is owing our success hitherto and forwardness in ye seige'.[28]

The climax of the campaign was fast approaching. By 25 July Wolfe had completed a battery capable of smashing a breach in one of Louisbourg's great landward bastions. It would soon be viable to attempt storming the defences. William Amherst, who was in the trenches at daybreak, reported that Wolfe was 'in a great hurry to have the scaling ladders ready'. Anticipating action, Wolfe sent his commander a curt note: 'you will be pleas'd to indulge me with *six* hours' rest, that I may come in the trenches at night'.[29]

That same night, the Royal Navy, which, for all of Captain Townsend's claims to the contrary, had played a crucial supporting role throughout the siege, took a more direct hand in events. Boatloads of British seamen armed with cutlasses, pistols and boarding axes rowed stealthily into the harbour under cover of darkness and fog. In a classic 'cutting out' operation they swarmed aboard the two remaining French warships and swiftly overpowered their crews. *Bienfaisant* was sailed clear of the harbour by huzzaing tars; the *Prudent* ran aground, stuck fast and was torched where she lay.

For Governor Drucour this latest setback was the final straw. Next day, the 26 July, he approached Amherst with an offer to capitulate on the same terms granted to the British garrison of Minorca two years earlier. These would have allowed his men to march out to fight another day with the full 'honours of war' – their muskets smartly shouldered, drums beating and regimental standards snapping bravely in the breeze. But Amherst had no intention of relaxing his grip. Drucour's conditions were rejected outright and he was given just one hour to consider surrendering at discretion. The alternative was to face attack by land and sea. Amherst was not bluffing. A surviving plan shows that Wolfe had been selected to command the projected assault upon the breaches; these were to be assailed by two columns of picked troops, each headed by a daredevil forlorn hope consisting of a sergeant and twelve grenadiers.[30]

All was now set for a general assault upon the garrison. As Wolfe later wrote to Sackville, 'the men were animated with perfect rage against them, and asked impatiently when we were to storm the town'. The temper of the entire army was running high. After three years of warfare in North America, during which the Anglo-Americans had been on the receiving end of treatment that flouted the accepted

European laws of war, there were scores to be settled. As Wolfe had noticed at Halifax, the troops were 'irritated against the enemy', and had 'a quarrel of their own to decide besides the public cause'.[31]

Of the battalions now filing into the trenches before Louisbourg, the 48th Foot had been at Braddock's defeat in 1755, an encounter which none of the British wounded left on the battlefield were known to have survived. The 35th Foot likewise included men present during the previous year's notorious events at Fort William Henry; there, Montcalm's failure to prevent his Indian allies from murdering scores of the garrison was perceived by the British as an unforgivable war crime. Many other redcoats had seen the scalped and mutilated bodies of their comrades, or at least listened to lurid campfire tales of torture at the hands of the 'savages'. All such episodes stimulated a desire for revenge from which Wolfe was not immune. Early in the siege he had voiced his views in a note to Amherst:

> When the French are in a scrape they are ready to cry out in behalf of the human species, when fortune favours them – none more bloody, more inhuman; Moncalm [sic] has chang'd the very nature of war, and has forced us in some measure, to a deterring, and dreadfull vengeance.[32]

But Louisbourg's garrison was not obliged to face such awful retribution. Although the stalwart Drucour and many of his battalion officers were ready for whatever Amherst might throw at them, civilians trapped within the fortress felt differently. They rightly feared a bloodbath if the redcoats were obliged to clamber forwards over the bodies of their comrades. Instead, it was agreed that the garrison should surrender unconditionally. There would be no 'honours of war' for them; they would be shipped off to Britain as prisoners of war.

On 27 July the British took formal possession of the fortress's gates. At noon, the garrison lay down their arms. Onlookers included Wolfe's good friend, Lieutenant-Colonel Ralph Burton of the 48th Foot. For that veteran of Braddock's disastrous campaign, Louisbourg's fall was truly a moment to savour: 'I had the pleasure of seeing 2000 French troops ground their arms, pull off their accoutrements and go to the right about,' he wrote. Another officer was 'agreeably entertain'd' by the sound of the 'Grenadiers' March' played by the fifes and drums of the redcoats who entered the battered walls; it was, he crowed, a fine tune that the French had not danced to for some time. Private Miller likewise expressed satisfaction at the outcome: 'Thus with much perseverence, loss and fatigue,' he recalled, 'we had taken the strongest garrison in North America, and opened the road to Canada.'[33]

As Miller observed, Louisbourg's fall cleared the way for future operations against the very heart of New France. Whilst Drucour's stubborn defence had helped to ensure that British troops would not reach Quebec that year, the capture of the 'Dunkirk of America' remained an event of immense significance. The first clear-cut Anglo-American victory of the war, it marked the turn of what had previously seemed like an unstoppable tide of defeat and disaster. Louisbourg's capture gave a badly needed boost to the morale of Britons on both sides of the Atlantic. From New York to London, from Boston to Bristol, news of the victory sparked celebratory bonfires and much quaffing of strong beer. Throughout Massachusetts, for example, 'such demonstrations of joy among His Majesty's loyal subjects were scarcely ever exceeded'. William Amherst, who delivered his brother's victory despatches to Pitt in person on 18 August, was embraced and assured he 'was the most welcome messenger to arrive in this kingdom for years'. Newcastle was still more ecstatic, constantly repeating that he had given 'orders for two corporations to be made drunk' in celebration of the great news. Indeed, the captain noted, the joy occasioned by Louisbourg's capture was universal, with 'all ranks of people doing their utmost to express it'.[34]

    This deeply gratifying outcome resulted from a combination of interlocking factors. First, the untried Jeffery Amherst had vindicated Ligonier's faith in his abilities, carrying through a difficult task with unswerving professionalism. Secondly, the rank and file had demonstrated an admirable zeal for the service; as Wolfe observed, they worked 'with the utmost cheerfulness', and even the soldiers' women had volunteered to help drag cannon to the batteries. But a third, and even more significant, circumstance underpinned the spectacular success. Britain's land and sea services had at last forgotten their traditional rivalries and instead cooperated wholeheartedly. Writing to Richmond on 28 July, Wolfe emphasized the importance of this development:

For the first time, the fleet and army have agreed to work together. The Admiral has given us all possible aid of marines, sailors, boats, cannon, ammunition, and every thing that was ask'd or requir'd: and I do believe that if the enterprise had been four times as difficult, our union would have carried it thro.[35]

In a letter to Sackville, Wolfe was equally unstinting in his praise of the Royal Navy. The cutting-out operation of 25 July had demonstrated 'incredible audace [audacity] and conduct'; the naval officers in general, and Rear-Admiral Sir Charles Hardy in particular, had cheerfully given the army their utmost assistance, riding out 'some very hard gales of wind, rather than leave an opening for the French to escape'. As for Admiral Boscawen, he had 'given all and even more' that they could have asked of him. Besides furnishing 'arms and ammunition, pioneers, sappers, miners, gunners, carpenters, boats', he was, Wolfe confessed, 'no bad *fantassin* [foot-soldier] himself, and an excellent back-hand at a siege'.[36]

Events at Louisbourg had offered a striking contrast to the squabbling, indecision and inaction at Cartagena, Rochefort and elsewhere – and it was not only high-ranking officers who recognized that fact. To Lieutenant Thomas Webb of the 48th Foot, the siege's outcome was 'a singular proof of the extensive good arising from a mutual harmony and agreement between the two fighting bodies of this kingdom, who, with united heads and hearts, effected, what nothing else could do, the reduction of that valuable fortress'. Webb believed that the auspicious occasion should be marked by the striking of a commemorative medal, whilst the officers present ought to be distinguished with 'a cross half red and half blue, representing the union of the fleet and army; to be neatly embroidered and worn on the left side of the coat, near the breast'.[37]

Boscawen, like Amherst, won acclaim for his sterling performance at Cape Breton. But the popular hero of the campaign was undoubtedly the fiery and tireless Brigadier Wolfe. One young officer who was well placed to assess his contribution was Lieutenant Thomas Bell of the marines. Men from Bell's unit had been sent across the Atlantic to serve aboard Boscawen's fleet, but he obtained the admiral's permission to go ashore in the capacity of volunteer and Wolfe's *aide-de-camp*. What Bell witnessed during the ensuing weeks made an indelible

impression upon him. Not content with commanding the vital amphibious landing, Bell reported, Wolfe and his detached corps had hounded
the French fleet

> round the harbour for four miles, built fresh batterys every day as they
> moved from his fire, and with his small corps came and took post within
> 200 yards of the town, while the engineers were still bouggering [about] at
> 600 yards distance. He open'd the trenches, called in the army, and pushed
> them within forty yards of the glacis and in short took the place without
> the assistance of any one regular bred fumbler. He has been general, soldier,
> and engineer. He commanded, fought and built batterys and I need not add
> has acquir'd all the glory of our expedition.[38]

Bell's breathless tribute smacks of hero worship, yet it reflects opinions that were widely held within the Louisbourg expeditionary force.
Wolfe's energy and aggression impressed officers and men reconciled to
the familiar litany of bungling, delay and demoralizing defeat. Glowing
reports of his conduct were swiftly disseminated throughout Britain's
North American army as veterans of the siege wrote to friends posted
elsewhere on the continent. For example, Lieutenant John Knox of the
43rd Foot, which remained exiled in Nova Scotia, received a detailed
journal of the siege that lauded Amherst and all of his brigadiers, but
singled out Wolfe for special praise: 'Mr Wolfe being the youngest in
rank, the most active part of the service fell to his lot; he is an excellent
officer, of great valour, which has conspicuously appeared in the whole
course of this undertaking'.[39]

Wolfe's performance at Louisbourg also consolidated his growing reputation amongst the army's rank and file. According to James
Thompson, a grenadier sergeant in Fraser's Highlanders, Wolfe – who
was 'tall, and as straight as a rush' – was a familiar and popular figure
throughout the siege, and enjoyed a special rapport with the Highlanders. Back at Halifax, Wolfe had praised Fraser's battalion as composed
of 'very useful serviceable soldiers, and commanded by the most manly
corps of officers I ever saw' – an assessment that surely puts paid to
modern claims that he 'hated' Scots.[40] According to Thompson, Wolfe
visited Fraser's regiment frequently. At his approach, the men turned
out with 'the greatest alacrity', passing the word in Gaelic, 'here comes
the red-headed corporal' – a reference to the brigadier's tawny hair
and the fact that he sported an aiguillette, or shoulder knot, similar

to the worsted badge of office then worn by corporals. In a remarkable testimony to Wolfe's paternalism, Thompson maintained that the
general acted like a 'father' to him, and customarily addressed the men
as 'Brother Soldier'. Thompson added: 'Oh, he was a noble fellow! And
he was so kind and attentive to the men, that they would have gone
through fire and water to have served him.'[41]

Common knowledge within the army itself, Wolfe's fame spread far
beyond its ranks after Amherst's despatches to Pitt were not only published in the official *London Gazette*, but also appeared in two popular
monthly periodicals, the *Gentleman's Magazine* and the *London Magazine*.[42] In addition, private letters containing eyewitness accounts of the
siege surfaced within many other newspapers and pamphlets on both
sides of the Atlantic. By the mid eighteenth century, Britain *and* her
North American colonies already enjoyed a long-established tradition
of newspaper journalism. During the 1750s, the industry was undergo-
ing a spurt of growth, encouraged by the steady demand for news of the
escalating global conflict with France. As newspapers did not employ
special correspondents, first-hand reports from the war's front lines
were eagerly seized upon; and owing to the prevalence of shameless
plagiarism, the choicest anecdotes achieved wide circulation.

In 1758 this dynamic press was instrumental in propelling James
Wolfe to hero status throughout the British Empire. Two examples
from many illustrate this phenomenon. In its August issue, the Edin-
burgh-based *Scots Magazine* carried a 'private letter' from Louisbourg,
describing the amphibious assault in which Wolfe had distinguished
himself. This was, enthused the writer, 'one of the boldest attempts
that ever was made'; indeed, 'nothing could stop the impetuosity of
our troops, headed by such a general'. Meanwhile, several Boston and
New York newspapers carried a detailed letter that emphasized Wolfe's
prominent role throughout the siege and which ended in a veritable
paean: 'Brigadier General *Wolfe* has acquired no small reputation by his
conduct, and bravery on this expedition, and merits no small share in
the reduction of *Louisbourg*.'[43]

Such fulsome press coverage underlay Wolfe's swift elevation to a
household name in Britain and North America alike. It is possible to
argue that this publicity bequeathed him a unique role as the first truly
transatlantic hero. The latest round of strife with France had already

thrown up other contenders for that honour. In 1754, twenty-two-year-old Virginian Major George Washington had enjoyed a brief blaze of international celebrity following the widespread publication of a journal recounting his perilous mission into the contested Ohio country. In the following year, the Irish-born Indian trader William Johnson earned a reputation – and a knighthood – after notching up an unexpected victory over the French and Indians at Lake George. And ever since, a tough Massachusetts ranger named Robert Rogers had been making a name for himself in a series of daring and bloody frontier raids and skirmishes. But for Washington and Johnson, fame had been fleeting, whilst Rogers's exploits, whilst undoubtedly colourful and newsworthy, exerted little influence upon the broad course of the war. Wolfe by contrast, achieved prominence through his pivotal role in that rarest of all occurrences – the authentic historical turning point. Allied with the fortuitous rise of the press, and its timely hunger for heroes, this placed him in an altogether different league of celebrity from his potential rivals.[44]

During the late summer of 1758, the Anglo-American cause remained in dire need of such heroic models. Indeed, in the North American colonies, the victorious Louisbourg bulletins had been seized upon with such rampant relief and enthusiasm in part because they arrived in the wake of very different tidings from the New York frontier. There, the vast army laboriously assembled under the commander-in-chief, Major-General Abercromby, had experienced catastrophic defeat at the hands of the Marquis de Montcalm.[45]

Disturbing hints of these dismal developments far to the south had reached Amherst's command on the very day that it took possession of the shattered walls of Louisbourg. Initial reports claimed that Lord Howe, the driving force behind Abercromby's campaign, had been killed in action. Although Howe's known boldness gave credence to the rumours, Wolfe could only hope that they were false. 'If this last circumstance be true', he wrote, 'there is an end of the expedition, for he was the spirit of that army, and the very best officer in the King's service.' Indeed, Wolfe added, such a loss would be one of the greatest that could befall the nation.[46]

Three days later, as he penned a long letter to Sackville, Wolfe learned that Howe's death had been confirmed: he was the first to fall during a skirmish on 6 July as Abercromby's unwieldy army groped its way through dense forest towards the outer defences of Ticonderoga. It was there, at the point where the waters of Lake George flowed into Lake Champlain, that Montcalm had decided to make his stand.

Just as Wolfe had predicted, Howe's death knocked the wind out of Abercromby's sails. During the months before his army's advance, Howe had stamped his personality upon it. Like Wolfe, he excelled in training and motivating men. He too led by personal example; and in contrast to his outspoken fellow brigadier, Howe was noted for his tact towards all and sundry – not excepting the inhabitants of His Majesty's North American colonies. In a war where relations between the King's soldiers and the colonials they had been sent to defend had frequently resulted in tension, Howe possessed the happy knack of charming Britons and Americans alike. The brigadier's open and unpretentious manner had endeared him to many colonists, and his tragic death caused a genuine outpouring of grief. The *Boston News-Letter* reported the 'utmost concern' at the loss of an 'excellent young nobleman', who, 'at an age when others go to learn the art of war, at once appeared a finish'd statesman, and general; sober, temperate, modest and active, and did his business without noise'. The soldiers of Massachusetts Bay held Howe in such high esteem that their province's notoriously tight-fisted assembly later voted a handsome sum for the erection of a monument to his memory in Westminster Abbey. Had he lived, it is possible that Howe would have rivalled, or even eclipsed, Wolfe as the hero of the Anglo-American war effort. Instead, the obituaries and poetic tributes prompted by his death offered a modest blueprint for the outpourings of both that would soon greet that of Wolfe himself.[47]

In a doleful despatch to William Pitt, Abercromby conceded that as Howe was 'universally beloved and respected throughout the whole army', his 'untimely fall' had produced both 'grief and consternation'. Robbed of his right-hand man, the commander-in-chief soon blundered to disaster. Montcalm had less than 4000 men with which to bar the path of Abercromby's 15,000. But almost all of them were trained professionals, and they enjoyed the advantage of fighting from behind the cover of a stout breastwork of loop-holed logs. This wooden wall was further protected by a forbidding abatis, formed from the tangled

and sharpened branches of countless felled trees. Convinced that reinforcements were hurrying to Montcalm's aid, on 8 July Abercromby
nonetheless authorized a frontal assault upon the Marquis's formidable
position. His men marched forward without so much as a preliminary artillery bombardment to cover them. Waves of infantry were
mown down in a futile attempt to break through. The British regulars
shouldered the brunt of the fighting and suffered terrible losses.[48]

The provincial troops that composed more than half of Abercromby's army remained relatively unscathed, and theoretically available for
fresh operations. But Wolfe, that arch-professional, placed little faith in
the services of amateurs. In a much-quoted tirade he observed:

> the Americans are in general the dirtiest most contemptible cowardly dogs
> that you can conceive. There is no depending upon them in action. They
> fall down dead in their own dirt and desert by battalions, officers and all.
> Such rascals as those are rather an encumbrance than any real strength to
> an army.[49]

Wolfe's characteristically intemperate language was less than fair. By no
means all of the provincial units conformed to this unflattering picture,
but enough of them *did* to shake British confidence in their motivation
and effectiveness. That August, the lamentable performance of Connecticut and New Hampshire provincials in two separate skirmishes on
the New York frontier had only reinforced such prejudices.[50]

What was needed to shore up the bloodied Lake George army were
veteran redcoats – like the victorious regiments now lying idle at Louisbourg. As Wolfe informed Amherst in a hectoring tone, Abercromby's
army was 'cut deep'. If Boscawen was unable to carry the army to
Quebec as originally hoped, then no time must be lost in sending
reinforcements to the continent instead. Wolfe himself was chafing to
embark with four or five battalions 'to the assistance of our countrymen'. He ended his letter with a comment that teetered upon the brink
of insubordination: 'I beg pardon for this freedom, but I cannot look
coolly upon the bloody inroads of those hell-hounds the Canadians;
and if nothing further is to be done, I must desire leave to quit the
army.'[51]

Amherst had little need of Wolfe's advice. He had heard of Abercromby's defeat on the night of 31 July, and on the following day

consulted Boscawen. Amherst wanted to get the French prisoners shipped off as soon as possible and, if at all practicable, to forge onwards against Quebec. If that scheme was not realistic, then he did not doubt that Abercromby would appreciate reinforcements. Amherst intended to send him five or six of his battalions; the remainder would garrison Louisbourg for the winter and make diversions up the St Lawrence and to St John's River in the Bay of Fundy. By 3 August, Boscawen was convinced that an advance to Quebec was out of the question. He said the same on the 5th, and, when Amherst pressed him again on the following day, maintained his position.[52] When he received Wolfe's letter on the 8th, the frustrated Amherst could therefore be forgiven for revealing some exasperation. Yet his response showed remarkable restraint. He concluded:

> Whatever schemes you may have, or information that you can give, to quicken our motions, your communicating of them would be very acceptable, and will be of much more service than your thoughts of quitting the army; which I can by no means agree to, as all my thoughts and wishes are confined at present to pursuing our operations for the good of His Majesty's service; and I know nothing that can tend more to it than your assisting in it.[53]

Meanwhile, the logistical challenge of organizing transatlantic transport for thousands of French prisoners led to frustration and frayed tempers. Some believed that the 'polite treatment' afforded to the vanquished garrison had made them 'extremely impudent' towards the victors. If rumour was to be believed, one French officer was brazen enough to thrust his hand under a Highlander's plaid, 'in an improper place'. Whether motivated by lechery, mischievousness or simple curiosity to establish exactly what, if anything, a Scotsman wore beneath his kilt, the intrusion did not go unresented. As one New England newspaper noted with approval, the aggrieved Highlander promptly avenged the insult by unsheathing his broadsword and lopping off the offending hand, along with the arm attached to it. When the maimed Frenchman gamely attempted to draw his own blade, the Scot settled matters by splitting his head to the shoulders.[54]

The French garrison was finally dispatched to England on 15 August. During the enforced hiatus in operations, Wolfe, who had long taken a close interest in Britain's North American colonies, pondered their future, expressing his thoughts in a remarkable letter to his mother. Although the colonies were tinged with 'the vices and bad qualities of the mother country' – not least because Britain continued to dump its convicts upon them – they would, Wolfe predicted, 'some time hence, be a vast empire, the seat of power and learning'. The cornerstone of the structure could have been laid that very year if only Abercromby had acted with 'half as much caution and prudence' as Amherst, and if that 'great man' Lord Howe – whom Wolfe would 'ever lament' – had been spared. But even now all was not lost. If the government prosecuted the American war with necessary vigour, Wolfe did not doubt that the French would soon be rooted out from the continent, leaving the British to share it with the Spaniards.[55] Of course, Wolfe's vision of the future naturally assumed that his transplanted countrymen would wish to remain loyal subjects of King George.

On 21 August, Wolfe received Amherst's orders to embark with three battalions, the 15th, 28th and 58th. Bound for the Bay of Gaspé in the Gulf of St Lawrence, the troops were to be convoyed by a powerful fleet of seven ships of the line and three frigates, commanded by Rear-Admiral Hardy. Their objective was to spread panic throughout the region and to destroy its fishing industry. Another two battalions, under Robert Monckton, the colonel of the 2/60th and lieutenant-governor of Nova Scotia, were sent to uproot French settlements along the St John's River. Wolfe accepted his own inglorious mission without enthusiasm, writing that same day to his father in sarcastic vein: 'Sir Charles Hardy and I are preparing to rob the fishermen of their nets, and to burn their huts.' When that 'great exploit' was over, Wolfe added, he would return to Louisbourg and, if no orders arrived to detain him further, take passage from there to England.[56]

Delayed by adverse winds, Hardy's fleet only sailed on 28 August. Thomas Bell, Wolfe's devoted *aide-de-camp*, accompanied him on the expedition, keeping a detailed journal of proceedings. Young Bell was a wide-eyed observer of the curious islands and wildlife encountered during the voyage. The Rochers aux Oiseaux were 'wholly inhabited by birds, many of whom came into the ship, some with red heads, others with red and yellow rings round their necks, all extremely small';

1. *George II at the Battle of Dettingen, 1743 (detail)*. John Wootton's painting (*c.* 1743) shows the last occasion on which a British monarch led his troops into action. On the King's right is his favourite son, the Duke of Cumberland, who served as a Major-General and was wounded in the leg. In the background, Wootton shows the British infantry repulsing the cavalry of the French *Maison du Roi* (National Army Museum, Chelsea, Neg. 7685).

2. *William Augustus, Duke of Cumberland, 1750.* The Swiss artist David Morier painted Cumberland when he was still celebrated as the victor of Culloden in 1746. The backdrop to the portrait depicts the rout of the Jacobite army (National Army Museum, Chelsea, Neg. 46193).

3. *Louis XV.* The official portrait of the French monarch during the era of the Seven Years' War, from the studio of Louis-Michel Van Loo (Library and Archives Canada, C–000604).

4. *James Wolfe, c. 1749.* Attributed to Joseph Highmore, this portrait in oils was possibly painted in London to mark Wolfe's promotion to major of the 20ᵗʰ Foot (Library and Archives Canada, C–003916).

5. *The Siege of Louisbourg, 1758*. Based upon an eyewitness sketch by Captain Charles Ince of the 35th Foot, engraved by Pierre Charles Canot in 1762, this views the fortress from the Lighthouse Battery established by Wolfe (New Brunswick Museum, Saint John, Acc. No. W908).

6. *Major-General James Wolfe, 1759*. A vivid watercolour portrait by Brigadier-General George Townshend (McCord Museum of Canadian History, Montreal, Acc. No. M245).

7. *Brigadier-General James Wolfe, c. 1758*. This striking oil painting by an anonymous artist was acquired in 1924 by the prominent Canadian collector and Wolfe scholar John Clarence Webster. As Wolfe only held the rank of brigadier for the Louisbourg expedition, Webster conjectured that the portrait was commissioned to commemorate his triumphant return from Cape Breton, and possibly painted at Bath in late 1758 (New Brunswick Museum, Saint John, Acc. No. W1841).

8. *Louis-Joseph, Marquis de Montcalm.* The veteran commander of Canada's field forces from 1756 until his death in 1759, shown here in a painting by an anonymous artist, probably copied in the late nineteenth or early twentieth century from a portrait in the possession of the Montcalm family (Library and Archives Canada, C–027665).

9. *Pierre de Rigaud, Marquis de Vaudreuil,* c. 1755. This portrait by an unknown artist shows Vaudreuil at around the time he was appointed Governor-General of New France, a post he held until the colony's conquest in 1760 (Library and Archives Canada, C–147538).

Major General James Wolfe.
Commander in Chief of his Majestys forces on the Expedition against Quebec.

10. *Major-General James Wolfe*. An engraving by Richard Houston, c. 1766, from a painting by J. S. C. Schaak, itself apparently based upon a drawing by the prolific Captain Hervey Smyth. Although the precise origin of the design is unclear, the fact that a simple line version appeared in the *Grand Magazine* of 1760, and that Wolfe is depicted in the plain uniform he is known to have favoured throughout the Quebec campaign, suggests that it was based upon the work of an eyewitness, rather than a London-based artist. Prior to the publication of the engraving of Benjamin West's 'Death of Wolfe', this full-length profile was the best-known public image of Wolfe. It was widely disseminated, appearing, for example, on the sign of Israel Putnam's General Wolfe tavern, opened in Pomfret, Connecticut in 1768. (New Brunswick Museum, Saint John, Acc. No. W1862).

the Iles de la Madeleine boasted a score of inhabitants, fishermen who hunted 'sea cows [walruses] ... who for horrid ugliness may vie with any other creatures whatever'; on nearing Gaspé they passed the headland of Percee, so named from its 'extremly singular' outlying island pierced by three natural arches.[57]

The flotilla dropped anchor in the extensive Bay of Gaspé on 5 September 1758. As Wolfe later reported to Pitt, some of the inhabitants were already gone, whilst others surrendered, or were surprised and captured in the woods. Then the methodical work of destruction began. By 11 September, everything of value at Gaspé – the buildings, boats, nets and stocks of dried fish – had been torched. Wolfe's prisoners provided pilots for raiding parties sent against secondary objectives. Lieutenant-Colonel James Murray and Captain Paulus Aemilius Irving of the 15th Foot dropped down the coast to attack Miramichi and the settlements at Pas-Beau and La Grande Rivière, whilst Major John Dalling of the 28th Foot moved north against Mount Louis. Like embers from a bonfire, they fell upon these outlying communities to kindle fresh conflagrations.

Wolfe's modern critics have condemned these events as mere mindless brutality, claiming that they amounted to a 'bloody rampage' – a vindictive series of 'ill-disguised atrocities' that gave free rein to his 'violent nature'.[58] Such emotive verdicts, which seek to cast Wolfe as a vicious disciple of 'Butcher' Cumberland, and a ruthless soldier who revelled in the sufferings of civilians, are unsupported by the facts. Although the raids undoubtedly left the region's inhabitants 'wretched and miserable', there is nothing to suggest that Wolfe derived any personal satisfaction from them. On the contrary, as he informed Amherst, they had 'done a great deal of mischief', spreading 'the terror of His Majesty's arms through the whole gulf' – but added 'nothing to the reputation of them'. And despite the bloody precedents of North American frontier warfare, where women and children, white and Indian alike, had all too often suffered by accident or design, here at least fire did not march hand in hand with the sword. Although obliged by his orders to lay waste the inhabitants' livelihoods, Wolfe took considerable pains to preserve their lives. According to Bell, Wolfe feared that the villagers of La Grande Rivière, who had scattered into the woods at his redcoats' approach, would starve during the coming winter. He therefore sent a boat with a message to their seigneur offering more craft to bring them all safely in; if they 'preferred liberty', they could keep the boat for their own use. Even the enemy recognized the raiders' restraint. Reporting the thoroughness of Wolfe's expedition in burning and carrying off everything of value, New France's Governor-General, Pierre de Rigaud, Marquis de Vaudreuil, nonetheless felt obliged to concede that the British had treated their prisoners 'very well'.[59]

Neither was the expedition pointless in strategic terms. First, it sought to divert French attention from Abercromby's dispirited army on Lake George. Secondly, and more importantly, it destroyed food stocks that were crucial for Quebec's survival. Indeed, Bell reported, just a week before Wolfe's command reached Gaspé, no less than twenty-six shallops had sailed for Quebec, all of them laden with fish. The Gulf settlements were therefore a legitimate target; and, as Wolfe reported to Pitt, 'a material article of subsistence to the Canadians' was now 'in a great measure, ruined'. The significance of this blow was underlined by the crew of a French sloop captured by Dalling's men. They already told of 'great scarcity of provisions, and great distress at Quebec', with troops and inhabitants alike reduced to a winter diet of horsemeat; the colony would be starved into submission – *unless* it received 'very early and very powerfull assistance'. With Gaspé's fisheries gutted by Wolfe's men, Quebec's resistance would now depend more than ever upon such aid from across the Atlantic.

Although it undermined the precarious economy of New France, Wolfe's fiery Gaspé foray also revealed worrying signs of continuing tensions between Britain's soldiers and sailors. As already emphasized, at Louisbourg Wolfe had nothing but praise for Boscawen and his colleagues, not excepting Sir Charles Hardy. Yet Wolfe returned from the Gulf of St Lawrence with serious misgivings about the determination of Hardy and some of his subordinates. Wolfe hinted at these in his despatches to Amherst and Pitt. In general, his orders were executed 'as far as troops who were limited in their operations by other powers, could carry them'; more specifically, Captain Jacobs of the *Kennington* frigate, who had ferried Irving's detachment, 'did not think it safe to remain upon the coast' long enough for the soldiers to do their work thoroughly. As a result, Irving had no alternative but to leave most of the inhabitants behind in the woods contrary to his instructions. In Wolfe's opinion, the naval dereliction did not end there. When the detachments were sent out from Gaspé, he had conferred with Hardy about furthering operations in the St Lawrence River 'to distress or alarm the enemy, and cause some diversion in favour of General Abercromby'; the rear admiral, however, 'did not think it proper at that season to carry the squadron as high as the Isle Bic'. Off the river's south bank, and within 175 miles of Quebec, this marked the point at which the St Lawrence narrowed sufficiently to give a blockading squadron a fair chance of intercepting enemy shipping.

Wolfe's public criticisms stopped there, but Bell's private journal went much further. Jacobs was guilty of 'scandalous timidity', he wrote, and Hardy was scarcely bolder. When Wolfe 'found what a small game he had to play', and wanted to push onwards into the St Lawrence, Bell claimed, the admiral had 'urged many reasons and difficulties' against such a move. And that was not all. Bell also alleged that Hardy failed to act upon intelligence, gathered by Major Dalling's party, to engage a French fleet that had recently sailed from below Quebec, bound for Brest. Justified or not, such strident opinions boded ill for future inter-service cooperation.

On 30 August, whilst Wolfe was *en route* to Gaspé, Jeffery Amherst finally embarked for Boston at the head of five battalions, intended to reinforce Abercromby's bloodied Lake George army. Meanwhile, the shot-pocked ruins of Louisbourg were entrusted for safe keeping to the elderly Brigadier Whitmore, with a garrison of four battalions. Hardy's squadron arrived back there on 29 September, although Wolfe had no intention of wintering in dreary Nova Scotia. When, just days later, Admiral Boscawen and his fleet made sail for England, Wolfe went too, as a passenger aboard the *Namur*.

Amherst had already written to inform Pitt that Wolfe considered himself authorized by his original letter of service to return to Britain once the siege of Louisbourg was over. Indeed, the general himself had been told of this arrangement before he left England. However, as Secretary at War Lord Barrington pointed out in a brusque letter to Wolfe, Pitt was 'a stranger to any such power', and feared that the brigadier's premature return would result in the 'greatest prejudice to the king's service'. Barrington himself was 'much surprised' that Wolfe could have placed any such interpretation upon his instructions, and, for the record, stated categorically the King's pleasure that he 'should *not* stir from America, without further orders from His Majesty, or his superior officers there'. Writing to Pitt, the exasperated Barrington doubted whether Wolfe could be stopped if he was already coming over, but he would send the letter anyway for form's sake. It was indeed too late. Barrington's rebuke left the War Office on 2 October 1758 – the day after Wolfe sailed for home.[60]

Wolfe only read Barrington's reprimand six months later, when he found it waiting for him upon his return to Louisbourg. In an equally forthright reply, Wolfe maintained that the commander-in-chief, Sir John Ligonier, had approved his actions, and as the alternative was to spend a winter languishing at Halifax under the command of an officer only recently promoted over his head, he'd thought it 'much better to get into the way of service, and out of the way of being insulted'. The officer in question was Charles Lawrence, who had been 'younger' to Wolfe in terms of seniority, but was created colonel and brigadier in America shortly before him. Lawrence, as Wolfe readily conceded, was 'a very worthy man', but, under the circumstances, he preferred to resign his commission than take his orders. And as the style of Barrington's letter was 'pretty strong', Wolfe, who clearly had no reservations about crossing swords with a member of the Cabinet, took the liberty to point out that he would willingly have joined Amherst on the Lake George front, and had actually offered to head reinforcements to Abercromby. He ended this blistering epistle with a blunt statement of his code as an officer. As he never asked or expected any favour, so he never intended to submit to any ill usage whatsoever. It is almost possible to hear the satisfied thump of Wolfe's crested seal on the molten wax.[61]

When Boscawen's fleet arrived at Spithead on 1 November 1758, Wolfe remained blissfully unaware of the feathers he had ruffled in Whitehall and promptly penned Pitt his detailed report of the Gaspé expedition. Three days later, in a letter suggesting that he really *was* oblivious of any wrongdoing, but which must have caused Barrington's blood to boil, he blithely informed him of his return to England. In a characteristic act of paternalism, Wolfe begged the Secretary at War to intervene on behalf of seventy-two invalids from the victorious Cape Breton force, who had been sent home in the captured *Bienfaisant*. These 'poor creatures' were put ashore without so much as a sergeant to arrange billets for them, and Wolfe feared they would 'suffer every kind of distress' from the winter weather; he had already taken it upon himself to arrange shelter for the veterans in the garrison barracks. It was this kind of direct, practical care for the humble rank and file that won James Wolfe the devotion of the hard-bitten redcoats.[62]

Upon his landfall, Wolfe lost no time in establishing contact with Sir John Ligonier, sending off two letters to the old cavalryman. These have not come to light, but from Ligonier's response it is clear that Wolfe had mooted the possibility of serving with the British contingent that was now operating alongside the Hanoverians, Hessians, Brunswickers and other assorted Germans against the French forces menacing the Rhine frontier. Candid letters to his friends likewise indicate that Wolfe's personal inclinations drew him strongly towards European, rather than American, service. Wolfe was a long-standing admirer of Frederick the Great, 'the first soldier of this age and our master in the art of war', and had made no secret of his hankering for the grand-style manoeuvring of conventional continental warfare. The Allied army in Germany was now under the direction of Frederick's brother-in-law, Prince Ferdinand of Brunswick – himself 'a great and able prince'.[63] In addition, Wolfe's patron Lord George Sackville was second-in-command of the British contingent, which included his former regiment, Kingsley's 20th Foot. The prospect of campaigning amongst old friends, and under such an illustrious and gifted general as Ferdinand, was an alluring one.

Germany held powerful attractions for Wolfe, but in the event, it was never an option. As Ligonier pointed out, there were no suitable vacancies there, and volunteers were unacceptable as the King would 'not give leave for anyone to serve in Germany without an employment'.[64] Although obliged to reject Wolfe's offer, Ligonier had left him in no doubt that he continued to enjoy his confidence – and favour. Whilst at Louisbourg, Wolfe learned that he had finally achieved the rank of full – rather than brevet – colonel of the 2nd Battalion of the 20th Foot. This promotion was announced in the *London Gazette* on 21 April 1758. Some weeks later, his unit was designated a separate regiment, the 67th Foot.[65] After he had seen his own regiment, the field-marshal wrote, Colonel Wolfe was welcome to come to London, where, amongst the rest of his friends, no one would be more pleased to see him. This cordial invitation from Britain's senior soldier gave a strong hint that Wolfe's recent services had not gone unheeded, and that a fresh command was in the offing.

Denied his first choice of military theatre in Europe, Wolfe remained ambitious for active service – *wherever* he could find it. North America offered the obvious field of opportunity. It was there that Wolfe had made his name, and upon his return to England his recent exploits continued to garner him laurels. That November and December, the *London Magazine* published substantial extracts from a lively account of the siege of Louisbourg by a naval officer, which once again sang his praises.[66] And for all the glory lately harvested on Cape Breton, the conquest of Canada remained unfinished business. On returning from Gaspé, and before sailing with Boscawen, Wolfe had assured Amherst of his willingness to complete the job: 'If you will attempt to cut up New France by the roots,' he pledged, 'I will come back with pleasure to assist.'[67]

Three weeks after his arrival in England, on 22 November, Wolfe wrote to Pitt from London, leaving no doubt of his readiness to do just that. After first seeking to explain the circumstances under which he had returned from America, despite – as he had since been told – the minister's intentions to keep him there, Wolfe added:

> I take the freedom to acquaint you, that I have no objection to serving in America, and particularly in the river St Lawrence, if any operations are to be carried on there. The favour I ask is only to be allowed a sufficient time to repair the injury done to my constitution by the long confinement at sea, that I may be better able to go through the business of the next summer ...[68]

Whilst in the capital, Wolfe accepted Ligonier's invitation to call upon him. According to the version of events that he subsequently reported to Amherst, Wolfe had assured the field-marshal that he was ready to return to America 'upon the first order'. Their discussion had then turned to the navigation of the St Lawrence River, and the 'project of besieging Quebec'. Wolfe now learned that it was 'a settled plan' to attack Canada on two fronts – via the St Lawrence and by way of Lake George. Once again, Wolfe had emphasized his 'desire to go up the River' – albeit with a significant proviso: he wished 'to be excused from taking the *chief direction* of such a weighty enterprise'.[69]

In coming days, Wolfe maintained the pressure on Pitt, emphasizing his willingness to serve *anywhere* the minister wished to send him. Writing to Rickson from Salisbury on 1 December, he explained: 'I have this day signified to Mr Pitt that he may dispose of my slight carcass as he pleases, and that I am ready for any undertaking within the reach and compass of my skill and cunning.' Here Wolfe might have added '... and *health*': long years of campaigning in all weathers had now added the persistent ache of rheumatism to the stabbing agony of the gravel. Despite his 'very bad condition', Wolfe remained driven by a desire to fight for his country, assuring Rickson that he 'would rather die than decline any kind of service that offers'. Although his inclinations drew him to Germany, and his temperament to the cavalry, it was not for Wolfe to choose his fate. As a professional soldier, his job was to obey orders. In his opinion, these now seemed destined to take him once more to America.[70]

7

To Quebec

Come each death-doing dog who dares venture his neck,
Come follow the hero that goes to Quebec.
Jump aboard of the transports and loose every sail,
Pay your debts at the tavern by giving leg-bail.
And ye that love fighting shall soon have enough,
Wolfe commands us my boys, we shall give them hot stuff!

Sergeant Ned Botwood, 'Hot Stuff', 1759

On 7 December 1758, James Wolfe took lodgings in Queen Square, Bath, hoping to recuperate for the anticipated campaign across the Atlantic. Twelve months had passed since he had last visited the teeming spa in the aftermath of the Rochefort débâcle, and what a year it had been. Wolfe was now the much-lauded hero of Britain's first major victory in the gruelling war with France. With his recent exploits still highlighted in the public journals, the gaunt young officer must have aroused considerable interest amongst the fashionable folk who thronged the city. It was probably whilst at Bath that he posed for a portrait, dressed in a powdered wig and civilian clothes, but clutching a symbol of his new martial fame – an unfurled plan depicting the siege of Louisbourg.[1]

That month, Wolfe's persistent lobbying of William Pitt for a fresh military posting bore fruit, although the yield was weightier than he had anticipated. Reporting events to Amherst – who had now replaced the demoralized Abercromby as commander-in-chief in North America – Wolfe told him how he had been at Bath for barely a week before being summoned back to London 'to be present at a meeting of some of the principal officers of state'. It there emerged that Pitt had put his name forward to the King for *command* of the Quebec expedition. At this, Wolfe informed Ligonier that, unless he was given the privilege of picking his own officers, the field-marshal 'wou'd do me a great kindness to appoint some other person to the chief direction and permit me to serve under him'. This stipulation, Wolfe confided to Amherst, was not understood in the way intended. Wolfe's meaning here is unclear: was his firm stance seen as unwarranted highhandedness, or misinterpreted by Ligonier and his Cabinet colleagues, and taken as a conditional acceptance of the proffered Quebec command? Whatever the precise tone of the meeting, Wolfe agreed to take on the job; but he did so with genuine reservations, and only then because of his strong sense of professional and patriotic duty. He added: 'In short, they have put this heavy task upon my shoulders, and I find nothing encouraging in the undertaking, but the warmest and most earnest desire to discharge so great a trust to your satisfaction as my general, and to His Majesty and the publick.'[2]

Wolfe's resigned and fatalistic attitude is at odds with claims that his prompt return from Nova Scotia that winter was a deliberate gambit to ensure that he, and not Amherst, would head the prestigious St Lawrence expedition; he has been accused of acting with breathtaking ruthlessness, and of spouting 'pure humbug' in asking to be excused the chief command.[3] On the spot in London, rather than thousands of miles away in Halifax, James Wolfe was certainly well placed to attract notice and advancement; but, as already seen, whilst undoubtedly ambitious and hungry for active service, he hoped to find it in Germany, not America.

At Louisbourg, the methodical Amherst had handled planning and logistics, leaving Wolfe free to make a name for himself as a dashing and carefree brigadier. There he had revelled in the role of zealous subordinate, but the Quebec campaign promised to be very different, bringing heavy responsibilities. As the draft 'proposals' for the expedition made clear, although Amherst, as commander-in-chief upon the North American continent, would 'direct all operations', the substantial detachment made from his army 'for the reduction of Quebeck' would be a distinct, self-contained force. Its commander, Colonel Wolfe, would enjoy the temporary rank of major-general during the expedition; once it was over, he would revert to brigadier acting under Amherst's orders.[4] But whilst at the head of his own independent army, Wolfe, the master tactician, would also be obliged – for the first time in his career – to assume responsibility for the more cerebral business of strategy.

The pessimism of Wolfe's letters at this period supports the hypothesis that the Quebec command was more than he had bargained for, and that he believed himself promoted beyond his talents. Wolfe soon expressed his misgivings to his Uncle Walter:

> I am to act a greater part in this business than I wished or desired. The backwardness of some of the older officers has in some measure forced the Government to come down so low. I shall do my best, and leave the rest to fortune, as perforce we must when there are not the most commanding abilities.[5]

For all his nagging doubts, once he had accepted the command, Wolfe swiftly rose to Pitt's challenge. By 20 December he was already wielding his new patronage to select his own officers, seeking to entice his old Westerham friend Lieutenant-Colonel George Warde upon 'distant, difficult, and disagreeable service, such as requires all your spirit and abilities'; as yet, he remained unable to disclose the objective of what promised to be a 'very hazardous enterprise'. Four days later, on Christmas Eve, Wolfe wrote to Pitt from Bath, stressing the importance of the earliest possible naval presence in the St Lawrence River for the success of the coming campaign, and enclosing supporting letters from two trusted subordinates in garrison at Louisbourg.[6]

In a repetition of the previous year's timetable, detailed planning for the forthcoming North American campaigns absorbed the festive season. By 29 December 1758, voluminous instructions had been prepared for Major-General Amherst. These sought to improve upon the advantages recently gained at Louisbourg and elsewhere – and to repair the crushing disappointment suffered at Ticonderoga – 'by the most vigorous and decisive efforts, to establish, by the blessing of God on his arms, His Majesty's just and indubitable rights, and to avert all future dangers to His Majesty's subjects in North America'.[7]

Amherst's orders emphasized the paramount importance of the St Lawrence expedition. He must spare no effort to ensure that the necessary troops, supplies and transport ships were all concentrated at the designated departure point of Louisbourg in good time for the projected start date, 7 May. According to the original plan, Wolfe's army was to consist of 12,000 men. He was allocated ten redcoat battalions – on paper at least, some 11,000 bayonets – plus a powerful 'train' of

siege and field artillery manned by 300 blue-coated gunners of the
Royal Artillery. All of these regulars were already serving in North
America; they were to be joined by 600 rangers from New England and
Nova Scotia.

Besides preparing the essential groundwork for Wolfe's strike at
Quebec, Amherst was to orchestrate his own 'irruption into Canada'
via Crown Point, at the foot of Lake Champlain, or La Galette, on the
St Lawrence facing Lake Ontario – or by *both* routes if practicable.
Amherst should attack Montreal or Quebec, 'or both of the said places
successively', either in one body or by dividing his forces. As second-
ary objectives, Amherst was to re-establish Oswego, destroyed by the
French back in 1756, and, if possible, to push operations as far west as
Niagara; the capture of that fort would not only win mastery of Lake
Ontario, but also sever communications between Canada and Louisiana. In total, Amherst would command about 14,000 men, but, unlike
Wolfe, his redcoats would serve alongside thousands of provincial
troops. He therefore faced the formidable task of corresponding with
the governors of the various colonies involved, in hopes of getting their
quotas into the field on schedule. Amherst was urged to start his own
campaign by 1 May, as nothing was so crucial for the various operations
in North America – particularly that against Quebec – 'as putting the
forces early in motion, on the other frontiers of Canada, and thereby
distracting the enemy, and obliging them to divide their strength'.

Although the armies involved would initially be far-flung, independent commands, they formed part of an interlocking strategy calculated
to exert a vice-like pressure: if all went to plan, Canada would face
simultaneous assault on at least two fronts. Co-ordination and co-operation, as Wolfe fully appreciated, were the keys to victory. On the same
day that Pitt despatched his instructions, Wolfe also wrote to Amherst.
He couldn't guarantee to capture Quebec, because he knew neither the
place nor its defenders, but what he *could* promise – provided of course
that the fleet carried them up the St Lawrence – was to 'find employment
for a good part of the force of Canada', so easing Amherst's progress
towards Montreal; indeed, unless the enemy could manage 'to throw
in early and powerful succours', Wolfe could see no reason why he and
Amherst might not 'meet and unite for their destruction'. Ligonier hammered home the same point in a personal letter to Amherst, hoping that

the projected operations would be 'so concerted as to take place at the same time as near as the nature of the thing will permit, which cannot fail of creating a diversion equally advantageous to both'.[8]

In accepting the Quebec command, Wolfe had insisted upon choosing his own staff officers. He was now able to secure the services of Colonel Guy Carleton as quartermaster-general, even though the King himself had previously blocked his participation in the Louisbourg campaign. The post of adjutant-general, along with the brevet rank of major, went to a deserving but poorly connected officer, Isaac Barré, who had served as a brigade-major under Wolfe at Louisbourg.[9] In return, Wolfe expected Barré's 'utmost assistance', so that he might prove himself 'no bad judge of merit'. This was a crucial promotion that Barré, who for 'want of friends' had long languished as a subaltern, never forgot; as he later told Pitt, Wolfe had 'rescued' him from obscurity.[10] For his *aides-de-camp*, Wolfe retained the services of the devoted Thomas Bell, adding another youngster who had distinguished himself on Cape Breton, Captain Hervey Smyth – 'little Smith' – of the 15th Foot. Elsewhere, he found room for tried and trusted subordinates. Captain William De Laune was seconded from Wolfe's own 67th Foot to lead a company of light infantry in Canada; there, he could expect to encounter more formidable foes than the rioting West Country weavers he had faced in 1756. Such conscientious efforts to further the careers of men who had earned his patronage won Wolfe his lasting reputation as the 'officer's friend'.[11]

Crucial for the success of Wolfe's campaign were his three brigadiers: more than anyone, it was to them that he would turn for advice and support. But, here at least, he did not get entirely his own way. In the original 'proposals' for the expedition, the brigadiers were listed as Robert Monckton, James Murray and Ralph Burton – all of them currently in America with the rank of brevet or full colonel.[12] Monckton was duly appointed as senior brigadier – Wolfe's second-in-command. The second son of John, 1st Viscount Galway, and some six months older than Wolfe, Monckton had fought in Flanders during the 1740s, but it was after transferring to Nova Scotia in 1752 that he had made his name. In 1755 – the year of Braddock's massacre – Monckton gave a valuable fillip to Anglo-American morale by capturing Fort Beauséjour in the Bay of Fundy. Since then, he had held important appointments in that troubled province, helping to round up and remove the Acadians, and in the autumn of 1758, heading the expedition to destroy French settlements on the St John's River. Monckton was reputedly a competent and experienced officer, and Wolfe's delight at his appointment was heartfelt. He wrote:

> I cou'dnt wish to be better supported, your spirit and zeal for the service will help me thro all difficulties – I flatter myself that we set out with mutual good inclinations towards each other, and favourable opinions. I on my side shall endeavour to deserve your esteem and friendship.[13]

Wolfe was no less content with the second name on the list. Like Monckton, James Murray was both an aristocrat and a career officer. The youngest son of Alexander Lord Elibank, the thirty-seven-year-old Murray was unquestionably an experienced soldier, with more than two decades of service behind him. As a teenager – like many of his countrymen – he had served as a 'cadet' in the famous Scots Brigade maintained by the Dutch. In 1740, Murray was commissioned second-lieutenant in one of the marine battalions raised for the Spanish war. Unlike the sickly Wolfe, he participated in the costly expedition to Cartagena, returning two years later as a captain in the 15th Foot. During the War of the Austrian Succession, Murray was badly wounded at the siege of Ostend in 1745. In the following year, when a British expedition was sent to raid the French East India Company's depot at Port L'Orient, Brittany, only to be bushwhacked by local militia, Murray distinguished himself at the head of his regiment's grenadier company. Since then, he had served alongside Wolfe at Rochefort and under him at Louisbourg. Wolfe rated Murray highly, gladly reporting the 'infinite spirit' he had shown on Cape Breton, and recommending him for promotion. But despite his impressive service record, Murray's rank had remained pegged at lieutenant-colonel of the 15th Foot since 1751: to his intense chagrin, his promotion was stalled because his elder brother Alexander was a notorious Jacobite and, even now, remained a close associate of the Young Pretender in France.[14]

The coming campaign offered fresh prospects of advancement, although Murray hoped to find it under the aegis of Jeffery Amherst, who was not only commander-in-chief, but also colonel of the 15th Foot.

That spring, whilst still unaware of his appointment to Wolfe's command, Murray begged Amherst to take his battalion into his own army. Whatever road the general took to Quebec, Murray wrote, he hoped that the 15th would go with him; if Amherst had decided otherwise, he added, the 'mortification' would be 'inexpressible'. Even after learning of his Quebec posting, Murray remained an embittered man, bristling at Lord George Sackville's sincere observation that this new chance for distinction would overcome all 'difficulties'. What 'difficulties' were these, Murray wondered? He knew of none arising from any shortcomings of himself as either an officer or a Briton; if they arose from objections to his Jacobite kinsmen, he told Amherst, then they must be permanent, and it was the 'height of folly' for him to endeavour to overcome them.[15]

Innocent of Murray's craving to serve under Amherst, Wolfe wrote him a warm welcome to his command. Ligonier and Sackville had been pushing for Murray's promotion to colonel, Wolfe reported, and he had himself expressed the opinion that nobody deserved it better. In words which must later have returned to haunt him, he added:

> In the mean time you are commissioned as a general officer in America only, of which I wish myself joy, because we are to serve together and as I know we think very well of each other, I persuade myself we shall serve heartily, cordially and zealously.[16]

The third brigadier listed in the original draft, Ralph Burton, was lieutenant-colonel of the 48th Foot. A veteran of the Monongahela and Louisbourg, he was one of the most seasoned officers in America and a close friend of Wolfe. Despite these recommendations, Burton was not destined to complete the trio of brigadiers: that honour went instead to a very different candidate, the thirty-four-year-old George Townshend.

Like Monckton and Murray, Townshend came from aristocratic stock, but there the similarities ended; although present at the bloody battlefields of Dettingen, Fontenoy, Culloden and Lauffeldt, he had only ever served on the staff, never commanding so much as a company in action. Once an *aide-de-camp* to Cumberland, Townshend subsequently alienated the Duke by publishing an acerbic account of his Flanders campaigns. In 1748 he was commissioned a captain in the prestigious First Foot Guards – a rank equivalent to lieutenant-colonel in the army

– only to resign two years later. Despite his flirtation with soldiering, Townshend was essentially a political animal. Along with his brother Charles – whose reputation as the original 'Champagne Charlie' did nothing to blur his head for high finance – by 1755 he had hitched himself to the rising star of William Pitt. At loggerheads with Cumberland's professional army, Townshend lost no opportunity to promote its amateur counterpart, the militia; this was a stance that many saw as a deliberate goading of the captain-general.

George Townshend had another potent weapon in his arsenal – what Horace Walpole characterized as a 'talent of buffoonery in black lead'. He delighted in lambasting his political opponents with cartoons doodled on table napkins, and which sometimes emerged as satirical prints; a gifted artist, he was certainly capable of producing vivid and spontaneous sketches that captured in a few economical lines the jutting nose and jaw of George II, or the gross bulk of Cumberland. Townshend's predilection for heaping ridicule upon others said much about his own character: in the opinion of the historian Sir Lewis Namier, it was 'the resort of the intelligent under oppression'. Namier identified other traits that should be borne in mind. Although 'warm-hearted and sensitive', Townshend was nonetheless 'unsteady and odd'; he was also 'intermittently ambitious', 'quarrelsome', 'lacking in judgement' and 'antagonistic to his superiors'.[17]

Following Cumberland's fall, Townshend returned to the army and in 1758 gained the rank of colonel. That summer, he badgered Pitt to send him on active service, offering to accompany a new expedition to the French coast. The request came to nothing, but Pitt soon succumbed to the demands of his loyal supporter. On 21 December, Townshend was summoned to London and told of his appointment as brigadier on the Quebec expedition. As the cynical Walpole observed, he had 'thrust himself again into the service' and, 'as far as wrong-headedness will go', was 'very proper for a hero'.[18]

If Wolfe felt disappointment that his own favoured candidate had been shunted aside to make way for Pitt's placeman, he chose to conceal it. Instead, he penned another letter of welcome; indeed, when Townshend's name was proposed by Ligonier, he had not doubted that such an example from a man of his rank and character would have the 'best effects upon the troops'. Wolfe had also taken the liberty of telling the field-marshal that what Townshend 'might be wanting in experience was amply made up, in an extent of capacity and activity of mind, that would find nothing difficult in our business'. These words have been interpreted as a deliberate slight, intended to put Townshend, the highborn military dilettante, firmly in his place.[19] If this was so, then Wolfe was guilty of tactlessness, but nothing more: by his own stringent standards, Townshend – who would rank as second brigadier, and therefore senior to the battle-hardened Murray – *was* inexperienced. It would be unwise to cite the letter as evidence of some deeper dislike; indeed, Wolfe went on to express the belief that he and Townshend would 'concur heartily for the public service'.

As he faced the most challenging assignment of his career, James Wolfe had no obvious reason to doubt the ability or loyalty of any of his subordinates. Writing to his Uncle Walter, he declared himself satisfied with his brigadiers, who were 'all men of great spirit'.[20]

But it was not just red-coated colleagues that Wolfe now had to work with. Like that sent against Louisbourg, the Quebec expedition would be a combined operation, with the land forces escorted and supported by a powerful fleet. Wolfe's ability to co-operate effectively with the Royal Navy, as Amherst had worked with Boscawen on Cape Breton, was essential for its success. His secret instructions from the King, issued on 5 February 1759, urged him to maintain a good understanding with his naval counterparts, as their assistance was of the utmost importance.[21]

The Quebec fleet was commanded by Vice-Admiral Charles Saunders, backed by two rear-admirals, Philip Durell (who had remained in charge of the North American squadron at Halifax) and Charles Holmes. In the modest but capable Saunders, Wolfe could not have asked for a better partner. One of that elite band of officers who had survived Anson's epic circumnavigation in the *Centurion*, Saunders had acquitted himself well during the War of the Austrian Succession. His subsequent promotions owed much to the patronage wielded by Anson as First Lord of the Admiralty, although there is no suggestion that this favour was misplaced. Saunders enjoyed a reputation for bravery and professionalism that even Horace Walpole felt obliged to acknowledge, observing that, 'No man said less, or deserved more.'[22]

From Wolfe's perspective, Saunders's second-in-command was a very different proposition. Philip Durell had extensive experience of American waters, first serving there as a teenaged able seaman, and his local knowledge contributed to the success of both the 1745 and 1758 Louisbourg expeditions. But Wolfe doubted Durell's determination. His misgivings fed into wider concerns, first raised during the Gaspé raid, that the North American squadron was reluctant to risk the navigation of the St Lawrence. On Christmas Eve, Wolfe had communicated his disquiet directly to Pitt, bluntly stating his opinion that Durell was 'vastly unequal to the weight of business'. Wolfe was worried because it was vital to send a squadron to the Isle of Bic, directly the weather permitted, to prevent the French from pushing essential supplies and reinforcements through to Quebec. Pitt took no action to replace Durell, although he urged him to ready his squadron for immediate service and to reach Bic 'as soon as ever the navigation of the Gulph and River St Lawrence shall be practicable'; Saunders too was enjoined to reiterate Durell's orders to blockade the St Lawrence 'in the strongest manner'.[23]

The naval force allocated to the St Lawrence operation gave impressive evidence of the ministry's determination to take Quebec. Unlike Wolfe's army, which was already in North America, much of the shipping would have to be sent from Britain. A great flotilla of merchant vessels, amounting to 20,000 tons, was to be assembled. It would be convoyed across the Atlantic by no fewer than fourteen ships of the line, six frigates, three bomb-vessels and three fire-ships. These would join the ten line of battle ships and four frigates of Durell's Halifax squadron, and another six thousand tons of merchant shipping that Amherst was assembling locally. With the problems caused by delays to previous expeditions fresh in mind, no effort was spared to gather the transports and ready the fleet for service. Despite some minor hitches, by the end of January Saunders was able to report that virtually his entire force was assembled at Spithead.[24]

According to an anecdote that had gained currency by the mid nineteenth century, on the eve of Wolfe's departure for Spithead he dined with Pitt and his brother-in-law, Richard Grenville, Earl Temple. After dinner, so the story goes, the young major-general grew increasingly animated, boasting of the great deeds he would soon perform across the Atlantic, even rapping his sword hilt upon the table and flourishing the blade above his head. Pitt and Temple looked on aghast at this unexpected and embarrassing display. When Wolfe's carriage had drawn away, Pitt turned to his relative in horror: how could he have entrusted the crucial Quebec expedition to such a posturing braggart?[25]

This belligerent image, which curiously enough mirrors the sword-waving stance of Wolfe's statue on the Green at Westerham, was promoted in Philip Henry Stanhope's popular *History of England*. In deference to that author's rank and reputation as 'an elegant and impartial historian', Wolfe's first serious biographer, Robert Wright, felt obliged to give the story at least some credence. Perhaps indignation at the cruelties perpetrated by the French and their Indian allies at Fort William Henry and elsewhere led Wolfe to momentarily lose his self-control, and express himself with unusual violence? As Wright pointed out, however, the story 'was related to Earl Stanhope by his friend Mr Grenville, who had it from the lips of Lord Temple'; in this process of transmission it was liable to undergo distortion and exaggeration; and, as another Wolfe biographer has noted, Temple was himself an 'accomplished and malicious liar'.[26] No mention of any such meeting survives in Wolfe's correspondence, although this does not mean that it never occurred. But whilst Wolfe's fiery temper certainly left him all too prone to express himself forcefully, the outrageous behaviour reported by Temple fails to ring true; in particular, it is difficult to reconcile it with the sombre mood in which he accepted the St Lawrence command – a mixture of resignation and grim determination, without so much as a hint of bravado.

As he prepared to sail for America, Wolfe's thoughts were not entirely dominated by affairs of war and state. Whilst at Bath, he had taken the opportunity to court the twenty-five-year-old Katherine Lowther, who was staying at the spa with her mother, the widow of Robert Lowther, a former governor of Barbados. Wolfe's progress was remarkably rapid, although it is possible that he was consolidating groundwork first laid down nearly two years before. In January 1757, he had told the Duke of Richmond of 'a little amour' that was providing the 'most pleasing remedy imaginable' for his impetuous temper. There is a further hint of burgeoning romance late that same year, when Wolfe spent Christmas with his parents at Bath; after rising early to rejoin his regiment, he had asked his mother to apologize to her 'pretty neighbours' – who included the Lowthers – for any disturbance to their sleep.[27]

Whatever its origins, in December 1758 Wolfe's courtship of Katherine Lowther was both swift and effective. Although no correspondence between them is known to have survived, a wide range of contemporary evidence leaves little doubt that they were engaged to marry upon James's return from America. Two remarkable relics also testify to their relationship. The first is a fine miniature of Katherine Lowther by Richard Cosway that she gave to Wolfe as a keepsake and which he carried across the Atlantic; in the event of his death, the first clause of his will stipulated, 'Miss Lowther's picture' was to be 'set in jewels to the amount of five hundred guineas, and return'd to her'.[28] The second – and even more extraordinary – survival is a copy of Thomas Gray's *Elegy Written in a Country Churchyard*; this too was presented to Wolfe by his fiancée before he sailed for America.[29] First published in 1751, Gray's *Elegy* is one of the few poems of the era to have enjoyed lasting popularity. Its melancholy themes clearly moved Wolfe, who scribbled several marginal notes on his copy. One verse struck a particular chord, prompting him to underscore the last, prescient line:

> The boast of heraldry, the pomp of power,
> And all that beauty, all that wealth e'er gave,
> Awaits alike the inevitable hour.
> The paths of glory lead but to the grave.

Like Elizabeth Lawson before her, Katherine Lowther unwittingly caused a rift between James Wolfe and his protective parents. Ten years earlier, following his failed romance with Miss Lawson, Wolfe had dutifully knuckled under, acknowledging the wisdom of his parents' opposition to the match and ruefully conceding his own youthful folly. But in early 1759, as he prepared to lead an army to Quebec, things were very different. Wolfe was now a mature thirty-two-year-old, a national hero celebrated in the newspapers and consulted by the foremost soldiers and statesmen in the land. This time he refused to back down, and the ensuing rupture was irreparable. In mid February, when the time approached to leave London for Portsmouth, Wolfe – once the very image of filial obedience – could not bring himself to make the short trip to Blackheath to say his farewells in person. Instead, he sent a brief note to his mother, tendering his 'good wishes and duty' to her and his father, the old general.[30] They would never meet again.

On Valentine's Day 1759, Rear-Admiral Holmes's squadron sailed from Portsmouth, bound first for New York to collect troops and supplies, and then on northwards to the expedition's rendezvous at Louisbourg. Three days later, Saunders, with the remainder of the fleet, left port, making directly for Cape Breton.

Wolfe sailed with the vice-admiral aboard the stately ninety-gun *Neptune*. It was a rough and tedious voyage, and the queasy Wolfe suffered accordingly. Writing to Amherst from mid Atlantic, he confessed: 'your servant as usual has been very sensible of the ship's motions'. When not prostrated by seasickness, or contemplating his copy of Gray's *Elegy*, Wolfe mulled over the coming campaign. His despatch to Amherst, which sprawled across eight closely written pages, addressed likely problems. The most pressing was a drastic shortfall in the number of his troops: Ligonier's figure of 12,000 men was based upon an optimistic assumption that the North American battalions would receive a timely influx of recruits from units recently sent to the Caribbean. But the West Indies, with its lethal diseases, was a notorious graveyard for Europeans, and Wolfe feared, with good reason, that most of the anticipated replacements would have been 'scorched long since'. At most, he reckoned upon an army of just 9,000 – few enough to *besiege* a force that was unlikely to number any less.[31]

Wolfe's misgivings were understandable; after all, the Louisbourg command had totalled more than 13,000 men, and there was nothing to suggest that Quebec would be an easier nut to crack. With all due respect to the expedition's planners, he felt that Amherst should have been sent there at the head of a more formidable concentration of fifteen or sixteen battalions, with the residue of the regulars, plus the provincials, creating a diversion on the Lake Champlain front.

Although his own task was daunting enough, Wolfe knew that the obstacles facing the commander-in-chief should not be underrated: as the French already had a small fleet on Lake Champlain, he must build a flotilla capable of blasting it out of the water. Wolfe hoped, however, that his St Lawrence campaign would at least allow Amherst to get off to a flying start. As New France's governor-general, the Marquis de Vaudreuil, realized the importance of Quebec, he would surely gather the bulk of his forces there. Wolfe predicted that Amherst's initial objectives – the forts at Ticonderoga and Crown Point – could therefore be expected to make only a feeble resistance.

On 21 April, after some nine weeks at sea, Saunders was within striking distance of Louisbourg, only to be baffled by an impenetrable rim of ice. For more than a week, in the teeth of heavy snow and hard frost, he endeavoured to find a way through. Reckoning that it would take at least another ten days to get into Louisbourg, the admiral resolved to head for Halifax instead. Anchoring there on 30 April, he found Rear-Admiral Durell still in port with his squadron of fourteen vessels; all were unmoored and ready to sail with the first favourable wind, but for many amongst the newcomers their presence was disquieting. Saunders's despatch to Pitt registered no surprise that Durell remained at Halifax, even though the latter had been repeatedly urged to lose no time in pushing up into the St Lawrence. In his report to the Secretary of State, Wolfe too avoided open criticism of the rear-admiral, contenting himself with the comment that they had 'imagined' he would already have been at sea. But a letter written to Amherst that same day revealed his exasperation: 'We were astonished to find Mr Durell at anchor', he wrote. Wolfe no longer doubted that the French would get vital supplies into Quebec before Durell could intercept them.[32]

This unexpected scenario seemed to confirm Wolfe's warnings that Durell lacked backbone. The general's scornful reaction was shared by other soldiers, including one member of his close-knit 'family' of junior staff; the identity of this officer remains a mystery, but there is no doubt about the value of his vivid, detailed and highly opinionated journal of the Quebec campaign. At Halifax, he noted sarcastically how 'much time according to custom was spent in deliberation', before Durell and his officers finally 'determin'd that it wou'd be more agreeable to sail up the River when the spring was well advanc'd, than during so cold a season'.[33] Modern commentators are divided over whether Durell deserves such opprobrium, but the fact remains that, whilst he waited at Halifax in hopes of a thaw, more than a score of French frigates and merchantmen were picking their way through the maze-like pattern of cracks in the ice that packed the Gulf of St Lawrence. They brought news of British designs against Quebec, and, as Wolfe had feared, the provisions and ammunition essential for the city to withstand a siege.[34]

Durell's squadron finally sailed on 3 May, but owing to contrary winds only cleared harbour on the 5th; it carried a detachment of 650 soldiers under Colonel Carleton, to act as an advance guard for the main army. At Halifax, Saunders's battered fleet underwent a badly needed refit. The four redcoat battalions in garrison there also readied themselves for active service. Seriously under-strength, they had endured a harsh winter in their isolated posting, and would have lost heavily to the scourge of scurvy but for the foresight of their commanding officers, who swapped their salt rations for fresh beef, and kept them supplied with spruce beer: brewed from molasses and spruce tips, this mildly alcoholic beverage was a sovereign anti-scorbutic, and a life-saver for men denied access to fresh fruit and vegetables.[35] The arrival of Wolfe and Saunders administered a tonic of another kind. As Lieutenant John Brown of the Royal Americans wrote on 13 May: 'Now we begin to be alive again ... everything is getting ready for our expedition, so that once more I hope to have the pleasure of attending a conquering army.'[36]

That same day, as Wolfe recorded in the first entry of his personal journal of the Quebec campaign, Saunders's squadron sailed from Halifax.[37] On 15 May they anchored in Louisbourg harbour. Over the ensuing fortnight, stray ships and troops gradually came in, although dense ice and thick fogs continued to delay the concentration of the task force. As late as 27 May, Saunders noted, the harbour was 'so intirely filled up with ice, that for several days it was not practicable for boats to pass'. As a horrified Lieutenant John Knox of the 43rd Foot recorded in his diary, this failed to stop daredevil sailors crossing from shore to ship by leaping from one ice floe to another, 'with boat-hooks, or setting-poles, in their hands'. Knox could scarcely look for fear that these 'foolhardy seamen' would slip and perish in the freezing water.[38]

Wolfe now learned of the death of his father, who, despite his assorted illnesses, had reached the age of seventy-four. The news came as no surprise: as Wolfe told his Uncle Walter, he had left the old general in 'so weak a condition' that he never expected to see him again. As a mark of respect, he tied a black mourning scarf around his left arm.[39]

At Louisbourg, as at Halifax, the quartet of battalions left in garrison had endured a cruel winter. According to Private Richard Humphrys of the 28th Foot, the shattered fortress furnished indifferent winter quarters, and he and his comrades were 'greatly fatigued in repairing the breaches we had made with our cannon and bombs'. On 14 October a great 'hurricane' wrought havoc amongst the shipping and stirred up a ghastly wrack of bodies 'that had been lying in the harbour from the time of the siege'. Wolfe's arrival led to a flurry of activity as the Quebec army was formally organized. Besides the ten battalions, there would be another small unit formed from the grenadiers of the three regiments to remain in garrison; these 'Louisbourg Grenadiers' were placed under the command of Lieutenant-Colonel Alexander Murray, another veteran who owed his latest promotion to Wolfe. Each battalion already fielded its own company of light infantry, but Wolfe now ordered the formation of a further three-company-strong unit of these useful specialists, to be headed by Major John Dalling.[40]

Wolfe lost no time in stamping his mark upon his army. This is clear from an incident noted by the inquisitive Lieutenant Knox, who had hoped to witness the general's review of the garrison's grenadiers. The performance was over before Knox arrived, although he heard that the grenadiers had demonstrated 'great exactness and spirit, according to a new system of discipline', and that Wolfe was highly pleased with them. When some other commanding officers, who also expected to be reviewed, apologized that their men had not yet had an opportunity to master the latest drills, Wolfe had answered: 'Poh! poh! – new exercise – new fiddlestick; if they are otherwise well disciplined and will fight, that's all I shall require of them.'[41]

Although dangerously small for the task required of it, Wolfe acknowledged his army to be a fine one. He told Pitt that the troops were not only 'very good', but also 'very well disposed'. Their high morale reflected confidence in Wolfe's leadership. With the exception of the 43rd Foot, all of the battalions bound for Quebec had served with him at Louisbourg and knew his boldness at first hand. Wolfe's popularity amongst the rank and file was emphasized in a belligerent ballad, significantly entitled 'Hot Stuff', composed that spring by grenadier sergeant Ned Botwood of Lascelles's 47th Foot. Botwood's regiment had recently been issued with uniforms originally destined for William

Shirley's 50th Foot, captured at Oswego three years earlier; but Botwood left no doubt that it would be dangerous to confuse him and his mates with that disgraced unit:

> When the Forty-seventh Regiment is dashing ashore.
> When bullets are whistling and cannon do roar,
> Says Montcalm, 'Those are Shirley's, I know their lapels'.
> 'You, lie', says Ned Botwood, 'We are of Lascelles!
> Though our clothing is changed, yet we scorn a powder-puff;
> So at you, ye bitches, here's give you Hot Stuff.'[42]

That spring, a kindred *esprit de corps* prevailed throughout Wolfe's army. By 1759, the shared experience of waging war under the unusually punishing and ruthless conditions encountered in North America had gradually transformed a motley collection of raw and demoralized units into a formidable force of veterans, with a distinctive group identity. This 'American Army', as Wolfe and other officers called it, was not only skilled in the conventional tactics of Europe, but had also acquired considerable competency in the skirmishing characteristic of the wooded American wilderness. In addition, it was uniquely experienced in conducting amphibious operations. Such flexibility would prove crucial in coming months.[43]

Wolfe's men were recruited from throughout the British Isles, with a further smattering drummed up in the colonies themselves. In Ned Botwood's own 47th Foot, for example, no less than twelve per cent of the rank and file had been born in America; the same was true of the 48th, which had required a hefty transfusion of local manpower after its blooding at the Monongahela. The redcoats were a mixture of volunteers, motivated by economic hardship or a craving for change and adventure, and conscripts swept up by Britain's emergency wartime Press Acts. A random sampling of one of Wolfe's battalions, the 58th Foot, gives some idea of their varied civilian backgrounds. Like many of his comrades, William Bunney, from the remote Orkneys, was a 'husbandman', or agricultural labourer; another common occupation was represented by the Antrim-born weaver, John Bell. Others reflected a surprisingly wide range of trades: Thomas Clyma was a tin miner from Truro in Cornwall; James Baker, a harpsichord maker born in St James's, London; while Corporal John Johnson, of Huntington, Cambridgeshire, described himself as a 'writing master' – a skill he would draw upon to compile a vivid and valuable memoir of the Quebec campaign.[44]

Whilst his army coalesced at Louisbourg, Wolfe pondered the strategy he would adopt against Quebec; as usual, he set out his thoughts in a letter to his Uncle Walter. This leaves no doubt that, from the very outset, Wolfe recognized the vulnerability of Quebec's supply line with Montreal. To sever this, it was necessary to bring his army to the narrow plateau above the city, with its right on the St Lawrence River and its left against the River St Charles. The problem of course, was how to get it there. Wolfe believed it was the Royal Navy's business 'to be masters of the river, both above and below the town'. Although it *might* be possible for Saunders's ships to 'steal a detachment up the river St Lawrence' and disembark them some three or more miles above Quebec, Wolfe clearly expected to land upon the Beauport shoreline that stretched below the city, and then reach his favoured position to the west by crossing the St Charles – a manoeuvre that was likely to bring on 'a smart action' at that river.[45]

In formulating this strategy, Wolfe drew upon a detailed memorandum, prepared by his chief engineer, Major Patrick Mackellar, and originally presented to the Ordnance Office in July 1757.[46] Mackellar had been captured at Oswego in 1756, and was held at both Montreal and Quebec before being exchanged. As a soldier, Mackellar's access to Quebec's defences was naturally restricted, so his knowledge of them was patchy. The map that accompanied his memorandum was based upon a French plan published in 1744, and depicted the incomplete hotchpotch of fortifications constructed since the 1690s. It totally omitted a new wall, studded with bastions, built between 1745 and 1749. Yet this oversight was less significant than might be thought. Even the upgraded defences were inadequate by the standards of contemporary military engineering, lacking the outlying works essential to shield them from direct bombardment. They were reckoned incapable of offering serious opposition to a besieging force that managed to establish itself upon the dominating heights to the west – where Wolfe aimed to place his troops.

For all its flaws, Mackellar's report conveyed valuable information and advice. Whilst it would be advantageous to land the troops on the 'town', or north, side of the river, Mackellar wrote, he doubted whether such an operation, 'within a proper distance of the place', could be covered by the warships because the river was too shallow for 'a good way out'. Instead, Mackellar suggested landing initially on the Isle of Orleans, below Quebec, and making that a base from which subsequent moves could be made. As Wolfe told his uncle, he would know better how to play his hand once he had assessed the defenders' dispositions for himself. The letter also leaves no doubt that Wolfe still viewed his own campaign as part of a broader effort, and that no opportunity would be neglected to help Amherst's army to the south. He explained:

> If I find the enemy is strong, audacious, and well commanded, I shall proceed with the utmost caution and circumspection, giving Mr Amherst time to use his superiority. If they are timid, weak, and ignorant, we shall push them with the more vivacity, that we may be able before the summer is gone to assist the Commander-in-Chief.

On 10 May, the first of the French ships to give Durell the slip, the frigate *Chezine*, reached Quebec. Ten days later, another twenty-three craft, mostly merchantmen, came safely in. They arrived in the nick of time. On 23 May, signal beacons warned that British men-of-war were approaching the Isle of Bic. There could no longer be any doubt that Wolfe's formidable force was on its way.[47]

This alarming news found Canada rent by internal rivalries. Vaudreuil, who as governor-general was also overall commander of the colony's forces, was on poor terms with Montcalm, who commanded the regular troops sent over from France; temperamentally opposed, they had long since clashed over the strategy most likely to preserve New France from the coming Anglo-American onslaught. The Canadian-born Vaudreuil wanted to maintain frontier outposts that would oblige the British to spread their forces, and fight in the forests where the country's militia and Indian allies could practise their favoured mode of bush-fighting. By contrast, Montcalm, the professional soldier from Old France, preferred to abandon the far-flung forts, instead concentrating upon defending the core of the colony in the St Lawrence Valley. In the autumn of 1758, before ice sealed the St Lawrence, both men had sent 'ambassadors' to Versailles in hopes of winning approval for their own pet schemes.

Montcalm's arguments proved the more persuasive. He still enjoyed immense prestige as the victor of Ticonderoga, and his cause was championed at court by his remarkable young *aide-de-camp*, Louis Antoine de Bougainville. A gifted mathematician who would later enjoy a distinguished career exploring the Pacific, Bougainville's precocious talents had won him the friendship and favour of Madame de Pompadour – the royal mistress whose looks and intelligence had charmed James Wolfe in 1752. Although no longer King Louis's lover, her influence was undiminished, and she played a key role in directing French foreign policy. Such patronage counted: when Bougainville arrived back in Quebec aboard the *Chezine*, he brought orders announcing that Montcalm, and not Vaudreuil, would now exercise supreme military command. But besides the vital supplies – sufficient to feed the army for eighty days – and four hundred recruits for the regular battalions in Canada, there was precious little else to show for his efforts. The King and his advisers were too preoccupied with the European war on their doorstep to worry overmuch about distant New France. As the Minister of Marine, Pierre de Berryer had put it to Bougainville, 'one did not try to save the stables when the house was on fire'.[48]

Versailles nonetheless expected that Canada's defenders would lose no time in preparing to meet the impending British assault upon Quebec. Making a surface show of unity, Montcalm and Vaudreuil now worked together to organize a vigorous resistance. They concentrated upon fortifying the Beauport shoreline, stretching east of the city from the St Charles to the Falls of the Montmorency River; it was there that a force of New Englanders commanded by Sir William Phips had established itself in 1690, before making a futile attempt to assault the city; and it was there that Wolfe too hoped to gain a foothold. In addition to this long chain of trenches and redoubts, a bridge of boats was thrown across the St Charles, with its head defended by earthworks; the river's mouth was blocked by a boom, itself protected by two beached hulks mounting cannon. Small gunboats were also under construction – each capable of carrying a twelve- or fourteen-pounder cannon – along with floating batteries that could mount a dozen more. Eight of the recently arrived vessels were converted into fire-ships; the others were sent some sixty miles up the St Lawrence to Batiscan, to function as a supply depot; of their sailors, all save skeleton crews were sent downriver to help man Quebec's gun batteries.[49]

Despite this frantic activity, there remained chinks in Quebec's armour. During his mission to France, Bougainville had urged the construction of gun batteries to contest a British fleet's passage of the St Lawrence, both far off, in the lower river, and close to Quebec itself. Above all, it was vital to secure the Lévis heights on the south side of the St Lawrence and directly opposite Quebec. Strong artillery fortifications there would not only deny invaders a prime position from which to bombard the city, but also prevent their shipping from passing above Quebec and menacing its vulnerable landward defences. None of these projects was undertaken – not least because of a deep-rooted belief that Quebec's best defence lay in the dangerous waters of the St Lawrence River itself. Advocates of this stance could point to the dismal fate of a major British amphibious expedition, under Rear-Admiral Sir Hovenden Walker and Brigadier-General John Hill, back in 1711. Unlike Phips, they had failed to get anywhere near their objective, instead turning back after several ships foundered upon Egg Island, nearly 300 miles down river. Two points much closer to Quebec were deemed especially hazardous to shipping. The first was at Île aux Coudres, some fifty miles from the city, where the main channel followed a constricted course north of the island; the second was the 'Traverse' – the tricky zigzag approach to the Isle of Orleans, within striking distance of Quebec itself. Both chokepoints could have been made far more perilous by the construction of gun batteries. Once again complacency prevailed, and action was limited to the removal of the Traverse's marker-buoys. Scant attention was given to Quebec's western approaches. For miles above the city the shoreline was backed by daunting cliffs; such natural defences could be relied upon to deter any landing there; and, after all, there was surely little prospect that British warships would even penetrate to the upper river.[50]

Whatever the deficiencies of its defences, Quebec would not lack defenders. A powerful force was swiftly concentrated there. Its back-bone consisted of five battalions of regular troops, well-trained veterans with a track record of victory at Oswego, Fort William Henry and Ticonderoga. Reckoned at about 1600 men, these professionals of the Troupes de Terre were joined by another 600 of the colony's own resident regulars, the Compagnies Franches de la Marine. From a very different martial tradition, but equally formidable under the right conditions, was a contingent of more than 900 Indians. These tribal warriors were of 'different nations'. Conspicuous amongst them were the Ottawa – 'pagans' from beyond the Great Lakes with a fearsome reputation for cannibalism – and the 'domesticated' Abenaki of the St Lawrence Valley's Jesuit mission villages. Despite such glaring cultural disparities, these 'savages' were all expert guerrilla fighters. But by far the largest segment in the army – about 10,000 strong – were local militia. This turnout was greater than expected, as both old men and boys, who could have claimed exemption on grounds of age, came forward to fight. Alongside this fierce determination to defend their country, the militia possessed other qualities that offset their status as part-time, amateur soldiers. Hardened to campaigning in all weathers, they were excellent woodsmen and marksmen, and whilst lacking the training and discipline to face British redcoats on the open battlefield, were well-suited to defending fortifications. All in all, including the naval gunners, Montcalm commanded little short of 14,000 fighting men.[51]

If it reached Quebec, Wolfe's under-strength army would have a hard fight on its hands. Alone of all the many British expeditions mounted during the American campaigns of the Seven Years' War, it was *outnumbered* by the enemy.[52]

On 4 June 1759, despite foul and foggy weather, Saunders's fleet weighed anchor and began to work its way out of Louisbourg harbour. By 10.00 a.m. on the 6th, the whole flotilla – twenty-two warships plus 119 transports, ordnance and supply vessels – had joined and made sail for the eastward. It was an awesome sight: Lieutenant Knox could scarcely imagine a 'more eligible prospect'. For all the difficulties and dangers ahead, morale was high amongst soldiers and sailors alike. As Knox noted: 'The prevailing sentimental toast among the officers is – British colours on every French fort, port, and garrison in America.'[53]

Wolfe too was now in confident mood. Although the embarkation returns totalled just 8535 redcoats, gunners, and rangers fit for duty – even less than he had counted upon – they were eager to tackle Quebec's defenders. Wolfe reported to Pitt: 'Whatever the event is, I persuade myself that His Majesty will not be dissatisfied with the behaviour of the troops.'[54] In addition to the land forces, Saunders's great fleet may have carried as many as 13,500 sailors and marines. Although the seamen's priority was the laborious business of crewing their vessels, and the marines were chiefly responsible for shipboard security, both offered potential reservoirs of manpower.[55]

Aided by favourable north-easterly winds, the expeditionary force made good progress. Once within the St Lawrence, its members marvelled at the region's majestic scenery and curious wildlife. Knox reported 'an immense number of sea-cows' rolling about his ship, all 'as white as snow'. For diversion, he and his fellows fired muskets at them, and were amazed to see their shot glance off the unheeding beasts as if from a rock.[56] By the evening of 18 June, the fleet dropped anchor near the Isle of Bic. It was now confirmed that Durell had indeed missed the French supply squadron, which had anchored there on 9 May. As if to make amends, Durell's advance squadron had forged onwards to take possession of Île aux Coudres, then pushed four warships and some troop transports still further upriver. Indeed, since leaving Halifax, Durell had shown commendable zeal, making short work of negotiating the notoriously hazardous waters of the St Lawrence.[57]

This achievement rested upon foundations for which Durell could also claim some credit. During the winter of 1758–59 considerable strides were made in charting the St Lawrence. Much of this progress stemmed from the chance collaboration of two gifted young surveyors: James Cook, destined, like Bougainville, for future fame as an explorer of the Pacific, but then master of the sixty-gun *Pembroke*; and a Dutch engineer officer, Samuel Holland of the Royal American Regiment. Both men had served at the siege of Louisbourg, where Holland's spirit had led Wolfe to praise him as 'a brave active fellow', and they first met on the day after the fortress's surrender. Wandering along the Cape Breton coastline, the Yorkshire seaman had been intrigued to find Holland drawing a chart with the aid of the instrument known as a 'plane table'. Cook was keen to improve his own knowledge of navigation and surveying, and the pair swiftly struck up a friendship. The *Pembroke*'s captain, John Simcoe, who was himself deeply interested in navigation, invited Holland onboard to demonstrate the use of his table.

As Holland later recalled in a letter to Simcoe's son, this encouragement had momentous consequences:

> Under Captain Simcoe's eye, Mr Cook and myself compiled materials for a chart of the Gulf and River St Lawrence ... Another chart of the River, including Chaleur and Gaspe Bays, mostly taken from plans in Admiral Durell's possession, was compiled and drawn under your father's inspection, and sent by him for immediate publication ... These charts were of much use, as some copies came out prior to our sailing from Halifax to Quebec in 1759.[58]

The *Pembroke*, under a new captain, John Wheelock, but with James Cook remaining as master, was amongst the vessels that Durell sent ahead from Île aux Coudres. On 8 June, they encountered the treacherous Traverse, and two days were spent sounding the passage. In his log for 10 June Cook tersely noted the outcome: 'Ret[ire]d satisfied with being aquanted with ye channel.' Thanks to the combined efforts of Cook and his fellow masters, the lead division sailed safely through; on 25 June, with ships' boats serving as buoys, the main fleet under Saunders followed. To the consternation of the French – particularly the blushing seamen who 'had always represented the navigation of the river to be extremely difficult' – not a single vessel foundered. Quebec's first line of defence had been punctured with almost contemptuous ease.[59]

The fleet defiled into the deep-water channel south of the long, leaf-shaped Isle of Orleans, and by 27 June thirty-eight transport ships had assembled off St Laurent d'Orléans. That morning, the army's First Brigade made an unopposed landing on the island. It was, noted Lieutenant Knox, 'a most delightful spot'. Through his telescope he saw fine country 'on every side', studded with windmills, churches and sturdy stone-built farmhouses, and well cultivated with wheat, flax, barley and peas. Others, who had clearly expected to find Canada a barren wilderness, agreed: it was, one officer reported, as fertile a country 'as any in America'. Indeed, the Isle of Orleans looked 'like a garden, from one end to the other'.[60] But the charming landscape was eerily empty: every male capable of carrying a musket was with Montcalm's army at Quebec; whilst by Vaudreuil's order, upon the first approach of the British, the women and children had been forcibly evacuated from their homes and compelled to seek refuge in the woods.[61]

Impatient to reconnoitre his objective at long last, Wolfe immediately gathered a company of rangers and walked to the island's West Point. From there, his curiosity was finally satisfied: some four miles off, across the river's extensive Basin, was Quebec. It crowned Cape Diamond, a dark mass of rock that jutted like a whale's head. The prize stood plain enough, the problem was how to grasp it. From the outset, it was obvious that Wolfe would have to rethink his plan of landing upon the Beauport shore. One of the officers with Wolfe's reconnaissance party explained why: the enemy already occupied six miles of shoreline, from the Falls of Montmorency to close by the River St Charles. Over the four-mile stretch from Montmorency to Beauport the river banks were 'very high and steep'; from Beauport to the St Charles, by contrast, they were 'low and level', curving 'in the form of an amphitheatre': the entire frontage was deeply entrenched, and generously supplied with gun batteries. After surveying the scene, the same eyewitness noted, Wolfe had observed that his first move would be to occupy Point Lévis opposite Quebec, 'as he cou'd bombard the town from that side, and the fleet cou'd not lay in the Basin shou'd it remain in the hands of the enemy'. In his own journal, Wolfe also recorded his intention to land below the Falls of Montmorency.[62]

That afternoon, a violent storm blew up. Seven transports lost their anchors and were driven ashore or fouled each other, and several flat-bottomed boats were smashed into driftwood; the destruction of these purpose-built landing craft, which had recently been evolved by the Admiralty, was especially worrying and would hamper the coming operations. As if to capitalize upon this elemental assault, late on the night of 28 June the French unleashed five fire-ships and two rafts on the rapid ebb tide in a bid to burn the fleet. The British knew of their coming. At noon, Private Humphrys reported, two former members of Shirley's Regiment, who had been captured at Oswego and since obliged to enlist with the French, came in with a warning that the enemy were busy preparing 'fire floats in order to send down amongst our shipping'. That night, the *Sutherland* man-of-war, which was anchored to the west of the fleet, saw the fire-ships coming, and her brisk cannonade panicked their crews into lighting their fuses too soon. For all that, the blazing vessels, which bristled with gun barrels packed with round and grape shot, terrified the sentries posted upon the island's western tip, who fell back to Wolfe's camp and spread alarm. Lieutenant Knox was made of sterner stuff, although he conceded that nothing could be more formidable than those 'infernal engines'. Knox added: 'They were certainly the grandest fire-works ... that can possibly be conceived, every circumstance having contributed to their awful, yet beautiful, appearance.' Some of these 'dreadful messengers' ran aground, the rest were coolly towed out of harm's way by Saunders's tars, who went to windward of the flames and snagged the craft with grappling hooks. Wolfe, who had recently grumbled about the 'strange neglect' of the men-of-war's crews during the gale, now praised their 'vigilance and dexterity'. For Quebec's defenders, the fire-ships' failure was a bitter disappointment. Humphrys crowed: 'how foolish they look'd when they found their only scheme miscarried'.[63]

Admiral Saunders shared Wolfe's views on the importance of seizing Point Lévis without delay. On the night of 29 June, Brigadier Monckton, with four battalions and some light troops, crossed from the Isle of Orleans, landed at Beaumont, and marched for the point. There was no opposition save for the harassing fire of militiamen and Indians, but when Monckton reached his objective, he displayed unexpected indecision. According to one account, 'a kind of counsel was held' to decide 'whether the post was tenable'. Wolfe was 'amaz'd' at this hesitation, as he had issued positive orders to occupy ground 'which he knew would be highly essential in his future operations'.[64]

Point Lévis was duly occupied, but soon after another incident only increased concerns that Wolfe's second-in-command lacked nerve and judgement. On 1 July, when the French sent gunboats and rafts to bombard Monckton's camp, the brigadier responded by arraying his entire command on the beach, with regimental colours unfurled. Presented with this tempting target, the French gun crews – who lay beyond range of the redcoats' muskets – had a field day. During the ensuing cannonade, Ensign Malcolm Fraser of the 78th Highlanders recalled, four of his regiment were killed and another eight wounded, whilst another nine men of the 15th Foot were felled by just one ball. Fraser was not the only soldier to register concern at such needless casualties. Sergeant James Thompson of the Highlanders was likewise scathing of Monckton's ineptitude: they were only lucky that the French gunners had resorted to round shot rather than canister, which would have mowed them down 'like grass'. That day, Wolfe's *aide-de-camp* Thomas Bell reported affairs at Point Lévis to be 'in an odd state': how could they have been 'so simple' as to turn out the whole detachment, he wondered? Upon arriving at the scene, Wolfe too was astonished to see the men 'expos'd to the artillery of four contemptible boats', apparently because of far-fetched rumours that the Indians intended to land. Surprised at the 'ignorance' shown in the construction of the redoubts there, Wolfe supervised fresh fortifications before returning to the Point of Orleans.[65]

Next day, detachments were pushed out from Point Lévis. They soon encountered grim signs that the coming campaign would be waged with all the customary ferocity of North American wilderness warfare. Ensign Fraser saw the bodies of several British grenadiers on the road near the camp, 'all scalped and mangled in a shocking manner'. The sight caused him to reflect that 'no human creature but an Indian or Canadian could be guilty of such inhumanity as to insult a dead body'. He would know better before the summer was through.[66]

Reconnoitring upriver from Monckton's position, Wolfe gained a closer view of Quebec. From Pointe aux Pères the lower town was just a mile away, within easy range of bombardment. But the destruction of Quebec meant little unless Wolfe could also confront, and eliminate, the flesh and blood army mustered to defend it. The problem of exactly how to grapple the wily Montcalm would dominate his thoughts for the rest of his life. Wolfe's powers of concentration were not helped by his deteriorating health: that evening, as he studied his plans by lamplight, he suffered a severe attack of the gravel. His journal noted the return of the old enemy in staccato style: 'Bladder painful. A good deal racked.' John Warde, the brother of Wolfe's childhood friend George, later heard that when he landed at Quebec 'poor Wolfe was seized with a fit of the stone' and 'made bloody water'. Before Wolfe turned in for the night, the faithful Bell read to him. Whether the captain chose to revisit Gray's *Elegy*, or selected a cheerier text, his ailing commander did not specify.[67]

Having gauged the daunting scale of the problem before him, Wolfe lost no time in seeking to solve it. In truth, there was none to spare,

with three months at most before the onset of autumn and the promise
of ice obliged Saunders to withdraw his ships whilst he still could. On
3 July, Wolfe consulted the admiral about strategy. 'Our notions agreeing to get ashore if possible above the town', he noted in his journal, 'we
determin'd to attempt it.' Over coming days the plan developed. The
assault would commence with a 'warm bombardment' from Pointe aux
Pères, whilst Townshend's brigade made a diversionary strike below the
Montmorency Falls. Brigadier Murray, meanwhile, had sent a detachment along the south bank of the St Lawrence to the Chaudière River, to
identify possible landing sites across the St Lawrence. On 5 July Murray
reported back: he was satisfied an attempt could be made at St Michel,
three miles above Quebec. General orders issued that day suggested that
a landing was indeed imminent. The troops were to be kept on a tight
rein: no buildings of any kind were to be burned without orders; non-
combatants who stayed in their homes were to be treated with humanity;
and anyone offering violence to a woman would face death.[68]

But the St Michel plan was shelved. A letter Wolfe wrote to Murray
later that month reveals that he was troubled by uncertainties regarding
the enemy's dispositions, his own communications, the utility of the
unwieldy rafts – or *radeaux* – intended to ferry the troops across the
river in lieu of the handier flat-bottomed boats, which were still below
Quebec, and not least, the level of naval support for the operation. These
doubts ultimately undermined his readiness to risk a potentially disastrous assault without at least considering the alternatives. As Wolfe put
it: 'I chose to look about me a little before we undertook.'[69]

Stymied at St Michel, Wolfe searched for other landing zones. On
6 July, according to Bell, he ventured into the Basin, to examine the
enemy's Beauport entrenchments. During these hectic and stressful
days Wolfe's health continued to deteriorate: on 4 July he suffered what
he described as a 'sad attack of dysentery'. Soon after Wolfe endured
another, very different, indignity. In his journal for 7 July, he reported:
'Some difference of opinion upon a point termed slight and insignificant and the Commander in Chief is threatened with parliamentary
inquiry into his conduct for not consulting an inferior officer and seem-
ing to disregard his sentiment!' Wolfe did not name his insubordinate
antagonist, although George Townshend's rank, character and political
connections must make him the prime suspect.

Despite such distractions, Wolfe continued to seek a way forward, and ordered a dramatic redeployment of the troops remaining on the Isle of Orleans. In the early hours of 9 July, he landed with ten companies of grenadiers on the north shore, to the right of the Montmorency Falls, and was swiftly reinforced by Townshend's brigade. The move took the French completely by surprise and was unopposed; they had given little thought to Montmorency, but soon regretted this 'false security' upon realizing that Wolfe's new position 'commanded most advantageously' the entire left of their camp.[70] Two days later, despite appalling weather, Wolfe's new base was consolidated by the arrival of Brigadier Murray at the head of two more battalions.

Only the narrow Montmorency River now separated Wolfe from the enemy that he yearned to encounter. But the river flowed swiftly down to its roaring falls. Its banks were steep, particularly on the French-held western side, which was further bolstered by breastworks; although fordable some three miles up, that crossing was closely guarded by Montcalm's men.[71] The Montmorency therefore posed a formidable obstacle to large troop movements – but not to raiding parties: Wolfe's new camp soon acquired a reputation as a hot spot. The morning after the first landing brought a taste of things to come. A large band of Indians crossed the river and overran Captain Benoni Danks's company of rangers, who were posted in woods to cover a working party. Caught off guard, fourteen rangers were killed and scalped before grenadiers drove the Indians back, just in time to save the wounded from a similar fate. The withdrawal of the tribal warriors was skilfully executed: Wolfe himself felt obliged to acknowledge the 'admirable management of those savages in their retreat', which was made under the covering fire of their colleagues from the far bank of the Montmorency.[72]

In coming weeks, the adjoining woodland often became the venue for vicious clashes, as parties of Indians and Canadians ambushed redcoats sent to cut fascines for the camp's defences. Corporal John Johnson of the 58th Foot recalled that whilst the service at Quebec that summer was always hard and hazardous, 'it was generally reckoned by all, that the duty at Montmorenci far exceeded all the rest, both for difficulty and danger', with frequent 'sharp skirmishes'.[73] One of the Louisbourg Grenadiers described a typical encounter:

On the 17th [July] we went out a fascining, and to make oars, with a small

N

0   1   2   3   4   5   miles

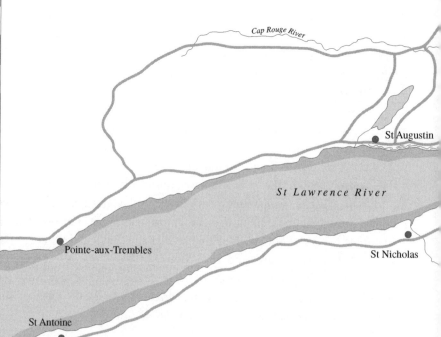

Ancienne Lo

Cap Rouge River

St Augustin

St Lawrence River

Pointe-aux-Trembles

St Nicholas

St Antoine

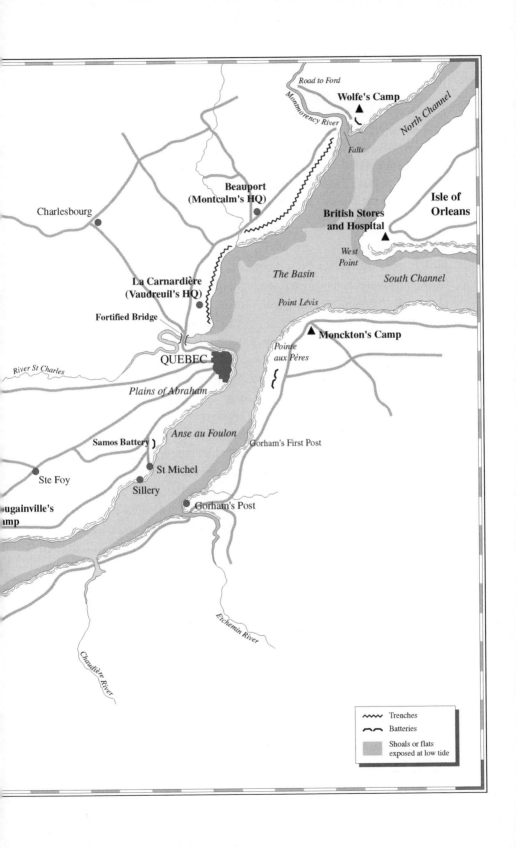

party to cover us; five were kill'd of which four were scalp'd, and we was
oblig'd to quit the wood directly; the Indians came up very close, and kill'd
and scalp'd one man close by us; the grenadiers of the 45th Regiment fir'd
upon them, and I saw one drop; but the Indians took him off in a minute . . .
our people returning upon them, made them fly so fast, that they were
oblig'd to leave their blankets and match-coats, with several others things,
behind them; but we could not get one of them prisoners . . .[74]

The vulnerable Montmorency camp was soon fortified, but in the
process relations between Wolfe and Townshend suffered a serious
breach; although never even mentioned by Wolfe, his brigadier recorded
their confrontations in painstaking detail. When Townshend first
arrived at the Montmorency headquarters, so his journal reports, Wolfe
hinted that he had been tardy in shifting his brigade. Smarting from this
rebuke, Townshend was further piqued when his efforts to secure the
camp by constructing a 'very good parapet' drew a sarcastic response
from Wolfe, who accused him of making 'a fortress'; in his opinion,
compact redoubts were more readily defended than such extensive
lines. In coming days, Townshend's grievances mounted: Wolfe made
light of his reports that French officers were reconnoitring the camp
from across the river, so raising fears – as it transpired, well-founded
– that they intended to establish a battery there; three days later, after
Townshend heard that Wolfe was leaving for the Point of Orleans, and
dashed down to the waterside to confirm the orders to be followed in
his absence, the general received him 'in a very stately manner', without
'advancing five steps'. Townshend noted Wolfe's words: "'Sir", says he
very dryly. "The adjutant general has my orders, permit me Sir to ask
are ye troops to encamp now on their new ground or not to do it until
ye enemies battery begins to play?"'[75]

Townshend does not paint a pretty picture. But if, as seems highly
likely, *he* was the officer who had threatened Wolfe with an official
inquiry just days before, then a certain coolness in his commander
is understandable. Wolfe was plainly irritated by Townshend – the
part-time soldier and political hack he had never asked for – and
had difficulty hiding his feelings. The antipathy was clearly mutual.
Although it is unlikely that such frictions weighed overly upon Wolfe's
mind, they did nothing to ease the burden of responsibility that he
already shouldered.

Wolfe's move to Montmorency had been a bold manoeuvre, implemented without a hitch under the enemy's very noses. Yet it brought
him no closer to solving the enduring conundrum: how to tempt Montcalm into a battlefield confrontation. And whilst the plan brought the
bulk of his troops within musket shot of the enemy, Wolfe's own army
was now split by a five-mile stretch of the St Lawrence. True, the depot
and hospital facilities on the Isle of Orleans remained as an intermedi-
ate staging post, secured by marines spared from the fleet, but with a
full brigade of infantry at Point Lévis, Wolfe's ability to concentrate his
available manpower would depend more than ever upon meticulous
planning, and upon ungrudging co-operation between the army and
navy.

Whilst Wolfe shifted position, his batteries opposite Quebec were nearing completion, with mortars and heavy guns being manhandled into
place. The town's defenders sought to hamper this ominous work but,
although hot, their fire was ineffectual. Wolfe was also accumulating
artillery at Montmorency, as he told Monckton on 12 July, with the aim
of establishing 'such a tremendous fire, that no human head can venture
to peep up' under it. He was now contemplating a major assault on the
Beauport position, drawing upon all three of his brigades: to that end,
Monckton was to press ahead with the construction of floating batteries and rafts. Once the Montmorency camp was properly fortified, and
the artillery ready, Wolfe pledged, 'wind and tide permitting we will
attack them'.[76]
    That evening, mortars at Pointe aux Pères began shelling Quebec.
Their effect was soon apparent: the incendiary devices, or 'carcasses',
that streaked across the river like comets were especially devastating,
kindling several serious blazes. Three more British batteries subsequently opened fire, ultimately wreaking widespread devastation. As
one artillery officer gleefully reported some weeks later, 'we have
been so successful as scarce to leave a house in the place that is not
battered down by our guns, or burnt to ashes by our mortars'.[77] By
bombarding Quebec in this fashion, Wolfe has drawn accusations of
unleashing 'terror' against helpless civilians, revealing a ruthlessness
rivalling that shown against German cities by Air-Marshal Sir Arthur
'Bomber' Harris during the Second World War. Such comparisons are

inappropriate: under the era's laws of war, the fortified city of Quebec – like Louisbourg – was a legitimate target; and as most of its inhabitants had long since been evacuated, with 'all persons who could be of no service in the siege, such as ladies and others ... desired to withdraw from the city', and the remainder promptly fleeing into the countryside directly the bombardment began, the charge of 'war crimes' lacks substance.[78]

The shot and shell that rained down upon Quebec boosted the morale of Wolfe's men, and cheered newspaper readers in Boston and New York, but the city's destruction was of limited value in military terms. Wolfe had already urged Monckton to 'be very sparing' of his heaviest thirty-two-pound cannon balls. It was, he added, of little purpose to demolish houses with shot that could be better employed against other targets: instead, the enemy's boats and 'every swimming thing must be shatter'd'. Such gunnery would help to clear a path towards Wolfe's primary goal – a full-scale clash with Montcalm. On 13 July, his journal records, he visited Saunders 'to adjust matters with him and prepare to attack the French army'. Three days later, they held another conference 'concerning the projected descent'. By now, the army's elite grenadier companies had assembled upon the Isle of Orleans, ready for 'a particular purpose'. As Wolfe explained to Monckton, the plan would involve assaults on both flanks of the French camp at Beauport. Using either rafts or the warships' longboats, Monckton was to ferry troops from Point Lévis against the right of Montcalm's encampment. This waterborne assault was to coincide with 'a prodigious fire' against the French left from Wolfe's massed artillery at Montmorency, and an attack across that river. Wolfe only awaited the 'naval preparations' to begin.[79]

Meanwhile, a squadron consisting of Captain John Rous's fifty-gun *Sutherland* and three smaller vessels was ordered to pass above the town that night, 16 July, to deflect the enemy's attention from where the blow was actually intended. The move was not executed. A derisive Thomas Bell heard that Rous blamed this inactivity upon insufficient wind, even though 'it positively blew a hott gale'. In fact, it was the *Sutherland*'s pilot who vetoed the move upriver. There was no such hesitation two days later, on the night of 18–19 July, when the *Sutherland*, accompanied by the *Squirrel* frigate, two armed sloops and two transports, passed Quebec to enter the upper river; three companies of grenadiers and a battalion of the Royal Americans went with them. The fire from Quebec's batteries was heavy but inaccurate, and the squadron's only casualty was the frigate *Diana*, which ran aground on the south shore, although luckily beyond reach of the French gunners.[80]

Whilst Wolfe had always appreciated the importance of striking above Quebec, and had already considered landing at St Michel, such a move depended upon the navy's ability to penetrate the upper river. As one well-informed officer observed:

> Mr Wolfe had long wish'd to see some of our ships of war above the town, in order to make himself acquainted with the coasts of the river and to satisfy himself if any attempt cou'd be made on that side, and at any rate to divide the enemy's force, and lead their attention that way.[81]

With these options now apparently opening before him, Wolfe temporarily abandoned the projected Beauport assault and once again turned his attention upriver. On the 19 July, he reconnoitred the 'country immediately above Quebeck'. In his journal, Wolfe now confided his belief that if 'the stroke that was first intended' (the landing at St Michel) had actually been implemented, it would 'probably have succeeded'. But there remained at least some doubt: 'probably' is substituted for the crossed-out 'infallibly'. Next day, according to Captain Bell, Wolfe went up the south bank of the St Lawrence as far as the Chaudière River. Wolfe clearly liked what he saw: 'General chearful', Bell noted.

Captain-Lieutenant Samuel Holland – the same young engineer who had befriended James Cook at Louisbourg – was amongst the officers who accompanied Wolfe on this scout, and like Bell, he was impressed by his buoyant mood. Many years later, Holland recalled that when they came to the Etchemin River, nearly opposite to the small cove known as the Anse au Foulon, the general expressed curiosity about an encampment of Indians and Canadians on the hill above it; through Holland's spy-glass, he watched them paddling their canoes and washing in the river. Holland was told to keep the spot under close observation, and when he reported that no formal guard was maintained there, Wolfe 'seemed much pleased'. Back at Monckton's camp at Point Lévis, and after careful thought, he had exclaimed: 'There, my dear Holland. That will be my last resort.' Such a course would only be followed, Wolfe explained, if his other plans were tested, and failed. Meanwhile,

Holland was to conceal Wolfe's intentions from 'each and everyone', and to spread the belief that a landing at the Foulon was impossible.[82]

If Holland's memory can be trusted, and there seems no good reason to doubt it, by mid July Wolfe had already identified the Foulon, less than two miles from Quebec, as the location for a last-ditch landing – one to be implemented only if less hazardous alternatives foundered. It was a spot that would become better known as 'Wolfe's Cove'.

The *immediate* result of Wolfe's reconnaissance was a fresh plan to land a detachment on the north shore, almost certainly near St Michel. On 20 July, he ordered Monckton to be ready to embark part of his brigade in sixteen or more of the flat-bottomed boats; propelled by twenty oarsmen, each was capable of carrying sixty redcoats, giving an initial assault force of about 1000 men. Under cover of darkness they were to row along the south shore until they saw three lanterns hanging abreast on the *Sutherland*. More troops would push ashore as Monckton's boats came up, to attack any houses or other enemy posts. It was, Wolfe observed, essential to reach 'a rising ground over the village', where the road to Quebec ran, and then to lose no time in cutting timber to construct a defensive abatis. The rest of Monckton's brigade was to lie concealed in the brush on the south shore, ready to embark and reinforce the first wave once it had dug in. Wolfe added: 'If we can take four or five good posts, and keep 'em till our friends, arrive, it may bring on a very decisive affair.'[83]

Wolfe was clearly in earnest. That same day Saunders sent Brigadier Townshend three longboats to collect artillery for the general, who intended to 'make his attack above the town'. But within hours, Monckton was ordered to postpone the assault for 'a day or two'.[84] Wolfe blamed the halt upon 'particular circumstances'. These emerge from an exchange of letters between Wolfe and Brigadier Murray, two days later, on 22 July. Murray, who remained at Montmorency, was convinced that an attack at St Michel – the very scheme that he'd but recently urged upon Wolfe – could still succeed. Now, the brigadier was seething with frustration at missing a chance to share in the glory of the impending assault. His letter failed to mask his disappointment. He wrote:

> be assured I as ardently wish you success, as if you had done me the honor
> to employ me in procuring it. I am too much a Britain [sic] to be insincear

in this respect, and am too much a soldier to grumble that I am left here inactive with one of the regiments of my brigade when the other two are gathering laurels in the bussy part of your army.[85]

Wolfe replied in conciliatory vein. Murray would get his chance soon enough: indeed, he was to lead the grenadiers, light infantry and other troops intended for the landing, supported by Monckton's brigade. However – and here is surely one reason for the postponement of the plan – Saunders did not believe that all of the flat-bottomed boats required for the operation could get past Quebec 'without danger, and difficulty'; instead, they would have to manage with those that were already above the town, and hope to assemble more warships there. Wolfe remained optimistic of getting ashore; and once they were 'safe landed', he did not doubt that the admiral would give his best support.[86]

Attempts to reinforce the squadron in the upper river were baffled by adverse weather. In the early hours of 23 July, two more warships, the *Lowestoft* frigate and *Hunter* sloop, attempted to pass the town, but, as Captain Bell reported, 'the wind failed them just abreast of it'. By now, the revived St Michel plan had likewise lost momentum; within days, it too had been discarded. In the lengthy despatch that he later wrote to Pitt, Wolfe explained that it was abandoned because the enemy were 'jealous' of his intentions and had taken measures to repel them.[87]

According to French sources, this increased vigilance and defensive activity was itself a response to the arrival of British ships in the upper river. After the first vessels passed Quebec there 'was not a doubt, but they intended either to cut off our supplies ... or to attempt a landing' near Sillery – half a mile upstream from St Michel. Without delay, a mortar and two cannon were positioned nearby, at Samos. The gunners there knew their business, as Wolfe himself could testify: on 21 July they severed the mast of the barge in which he was reconnoitring the shoreline, and the accuracy of their fire quickly obliged Rous to shift his little squadron upriver and out of range. Jean-Daniel Dumas, a tough and experienced captain in the colony regulars who had orchestrated the massacre of Braddock's command on the Monongahela, was sent with 600 men, and some of the 'savages', to shadow the ships' movements.[88]

Provided the enemy stayed alert, the mere presence of a handful of British warships above Quebec offered no immediate solution to Wolfe's problem. The arrival of the *Sutherland* and her consorts certainly gave hope for greater things to come; but it did *not*, as naval historians have claimed, instantly transform the strategic situation by granting the British control of the St Lawrence River.[89] To achieve such dominance, more warships – and a significant number of transports and landing craft – would need to follow the *Sutherland*'s lead and push into the upper river. Only a substantial squadron, with the ability to carry and disembark thousands of men, could give Wolfe's army a fighting chance of getting ashore in strength and armed with the crucial weapon of surprise; without it, the latest plan, like the others before it, was too hazardous to implement. Wolfe's old quandary remained: how to concentrate his redcoats at any given point before the French could react, assemble overwhelming forces, and shoot them down as they floundered ashore.

On 20 July, whilst reconnoitring the north shore, Wolfe had sent a detachment under Guy Carleton upriver to gather intelligence. Landing next day at the village of Pointe-aux-Trembles, about twenty miles above Quebec, Colonel Carleton's grenadiers and Royal Americans skirmished with Indians and militia before taking more than a hundred prisoners – women, children and a Jesuit priest. These civilians were returned to Quebec under a flag of truce: all of the women, regardless of their social rank, 'spoke equally well of the treatment they had received from the English officers'. Several were invited to dine with Wolfe himself and were 'greatly charmed' by his politeness, although it is unlikely that they can have been won over by his looks. Madame Saint-Villemin, who was captured when the British intercepted a French sloop at the Isle of Bic in late May and brought to the Isle of Orleans on 3 July, described Wolfe as 'a young man of approximately thirty years, tall, extremely thin, red-haired, and very ugly'.[90]

Amongst all the gallantry and badinage with the female 'guests' delivered into camp by Carleton, Wolfe had joked about the 'circumspection' of the French generals; he had offered them fine opportunities to attack him, and was surprised that they had not obliged. By then, remarkably similar sentiments had surfaced within Montcalm's army. Rather than exploiting his superior numbers to harass Wolfe's isolated camps, it was murmured, the Marquis preferred to sit inactive behind his Beauport entrenchments, waiting for the enemy to come to him; although undoubtedly brave, he was 'in no wise enterprising'.[91] Montcalm's modern critics have gone further, branding him a 'chronic defeatist' who had convinced himself that he was 'engaged in a lost cause'. This attitude, it is argued, was engendered during a career in which, despite exemplary gallantry, Montcalm had too often found himself on the losing side. In consequence, he was more concerned with maintaining his honourable name than with beating the enemy.[92]

Such overwhelmingly negative verdicts give a lopsided impression of Wolfe's opponent, and must be balanced here. Dark-eyed and stocky, Montcalm offered a marked physical contrast to Wolfe. In other respects, however, the two soldiers had much in common, sharing a strong sense of duty and an unswerving devotion to their chosen profession. Montcalm's determination to uphold his personal reputation was scarcely unusual: a similar obsession with honour united the international brotherhood of the blade that officered Europe's armies and navies. It is also misleading to suggest that Montcalm's previous career had conditioned him to accept the inevitability of defeat. Aged forty-seven in 1759, and therefore Wolfe's senior by fifteen years, Montcalm could boast some three decades of service, much of it in the field. His campaigns in Bohemia and Italy during the War of the Austrian Succession had indeed been characterized by setbacks, wounds and captivity, but this was just one side of the coin. Since coming to Canada in 1756 the Marquis had known only victory.

For all the mutterings that it stirred amongst his subordinates, there was also ample justification for Montcalm's defensive strategy at Quebec. Barely a year had passed since a similar stance had yielded the stunning triumph at Ticonderoga. By keeping within his Beauport entrenchments the Marquis could deny Wolfe what he most desired – a stand-up fight in which his redcoats would enjoy an advantage over the Canadian militiamen who composed most of the Quebec army. In addition, Montcalm's confidence in his militia's ability to undertake *offensive* operations had been badly dented by a farcical episode on the night of 12 July, when a cross-river raid was mounted by 1600 men – chiefly Canadians, but including Indians and volunteers from the regular battalions – under the command of the veteran Captain Dumas. This expedition was intended to eradicate the British batteries preparing to bombard Quebec from Pointe aux Pères, but far from surprising the enemy, it swiftly degenerated into a panicked rout after jittery militiamen and soldiers opened fire upon each other in the darkness.[93]

By the summer of 1759, Montcalm was homesick, hankering for the wife and children he had left behind at the family château at Candiac, in Languedoc. But whilst lacking Governor-General Vaudreuil's highly personal stake in the fate of New France, the Marquis was not indifferent to the outcome of the campaign, nor oblivious of his professional duty to thwart King Louis's enemies. If not an aggressive, or inspired, general, he was far from being an incompetent one. With a substantial army, trusted subordinates and a strong position to hold, Montcalm had little reason to doubt that a careful defensive campaign would frustrate the best efforts of his younger opponent, and add another victory to the list of those that had already won him promotion and glory.

Of course, Wolfe's assessment of Montcalm's strategy invites an evaluation of his own. If his critics – both at the time and since – are correct, the charge of excessive caution that he levelled against his rival is ironic: since arriving before Quebec, they argue, Wolfe's own strategy had been characterized by indecision, hesitation and a marked reluctance to test the enemy's defences. In his grumbling letter to Wolfe of 22 July, Brigadier Murray maintained that a decisive blow could have been struck at St Michel when it was first considered, particularly given 'the enemy's inattention to every thing above the town' at that time. A more damning assessment of Wolfe's generalship was offered by James Gibson, apparently a naval officer, in a letter to Governor Lawrence in Halifax. Commenting upon the events of 20 July, when Wolfe resurrected his earlier plan of attacking at St Michel, Gibson wrote:

> Within the space of five hours we rec[eived]d at the generals request, three different orders of consequence, which were contradicted immediately after their reception; which indeed has been the constant practice of the gen[eral] ever since we have been here to the no small amazement of everyone who has the liberty of thinking. Every step he takes is wholly his own; I'm told he asks no one's opinion, and wants no advice.[94]

Wolfe's modern critics have been equally unforgiving of his reluctance to implement an upriver landing in July: after all, this was the very man who had recently castigated Sir John Mordaunt and his colleagues for their indecision before Rochefort. Yet, when given the opportunity to do so, Wolfe had failed to practise the aggressive doctrine of amphibious warfare that he had preached so forcefully less than two years earlier – that nothing should be 'reckoned an obstacle ... which is not found really so upon trial'.[95]

But, as has been emphasized, the essential prerequisite for any such 'trial' was adequate naval support. Throughout July 1759 this was plainly lacking. The Royal Navy had been unable to shift enough ships, and the flat-bottomed boats essential for any major landing, past Quebec and into the upper river. Even below Quebec, it was struggling to establish ascendancy over the enemy's boldly handled gunboats and floating batteries. At first, Wolfe and his army colleagues blamed this situation upon timidity: on 6 July, Wolfe complained that the enemy were 'permitted to insult us with their paltry boats carrying cannon in their prows'; two days later, he noted that the British frigates and bomb ketches remained at a 'prodigious distance' from the French, and bemoaned such 'amazing backwardness in these matters on the side of the Fleet'. Bell was likewise surprised that the British shipping was 'insulted every day', and boats' crews taken prisoner, without anything being done to prevent it.[96]

In fact, as Wolfe ultimately recognized, the Royal Navy's embarrassments during the opening phase of the campaign largely resulted from environmental factors beyond its control. Deep within the St Lawrence, the British fleet lay at the mercy of the river's distinctive wind and tidal patterns. Both placed Saunders's ships at a crucial disadvantage when attempting to push beyond Quebec and into the upper river. With the strong ebb-tide running against him for almost eight hours *twice* a day, and the prevailing winds throughout the summer months blowing into his teeth from the west, the admiral had precious few opportunities to slip ships swiftly past Quebec's gun batteries. And in the Quebec Basin, his captains rapidly learned a lesson as old as the dawn of gunpowder warfare at sea: reliant upon the wind to manoeuvre, the mightiest man-of-war might find itself obliged to recoil from the puniest oar-powered galley.[97]

Geography likewise proscribed the navy's effectiveness: as Major Mackellar had warned, the entire Beauport shoreline was buffered by extensive mudflats, in places more than a mile wide, that prevented warships from supporting a landing with their broadsides; indeed, Admiral Saunders had swiftly concluded that none of his ships could be 'of the least use' there. Elsewhere, the enemy's positions lay above the maximum elevation of the men-of-war's guns. Owing to the 'nature of the river', Wolfe informed Pitt, 'the most formidable part' of the task force was 'deprived of the power of acting'.[98]

The navy's problems were clearly an important factor behind Wolfe's failure to risk a landing during his first weeks before Quebec. His hesitation to strike without a reasonable chance of success is understandable on other grounds. At the head of his first independent command, Wolfe was acutely aware of the hopes that rested upon him; his men were few enough, and a bloody repulse would have badly damaged – or even ended – his chances of taking Quebec that year. Alongside the burden of command, and perhaps because of it, Wolfe had been plagued by painful and debilitating illness, with both his bladder and bowels in a sorry state. But despite his problems, and for all his caution, Wolfe had not lacked moral courage. He refused to be browbeaten into attacking the enemy before the time was ripe, even though this incurred the resentment of Brigadier Murray. And whatever the gripes of his own subordinates, from his enemy's perspective, Wolfe had been far from idle. His activity was clear enough in the shot and shell that arched across the St Lawrence from Pointe aux Pères, the batteries and battalions now arrayed at Montmorency, and the disconcerting moves up river, like Carleton's raid upon Pointe-aux-Trembles, that had raised fears for Quebec's supply lines. Upon returning to her countrymen from captivity, Madame Saint-Villemin – who had testified so bluntly to Wolfe's ugliness – was no less sure of his determination: indeed, she maintained that he was 'in no mood' to withdraw 'his people' without doing *something*.[99]

Wolfe had not wasted his weeks on the St Lawrence, but the pressure upon him to strike a decisive blow was mounting by the day; few in either army now doubted that it must fall soon. The key question was *where*.

8

Deadlock on the St Lawrence

The French were landed on mountains high,
While we poor souls in the valleys did lie,
'Cheer up my lads', General Wolfe did say,
'Brave lads of honour, brave lads of honour,
Old England, she shall win the day'

Anon, 'Brave Wolfe'

On the afternoon of 23 July 1759, Wolfe and his brigadiers conferred with Admiral Saunders. It was nearly a month since they had arrived before Quebec. Bloody bickering between outposts was now a regular occurrence, and the city blazed periodically from the effects of the incendiary devices sent howling over from Pointe aux Pères; but as yet, there had been no significant clash between the rival forces. With the summer slipping by, Wolfe and his colleagues had pressing reasons to break the deadlock. The general recorded the outcome of their discussion in his journal, using the terse phrases typical of that intriguing but frustratingly sparse document: 'Resolution to attack the French army. Debate about the method.' It was the old story: Wolfe's objective – to engage and defeat Montcalm – was as clear as ever; but the problem remained how to get at him when he hoarded his troops behind entrenchments and refused all attempts to lure them out. As the frustrated Thomas Bell put it, the French were 'dirty fellows for not being troublesome', save by their cannon.[1]

Although various plans were plainly under consideration, Wolfe's own attention was now shifting away from the upper river – where the Royal Navy's presence was still limited to the fifty-gun *Sutherland*, the *Squirrel* frigate, and four armed sloops and transports – towards Montcalm's sprawling camp at Beauport; it lay tantalizingly close to his own largest troop concentration, yet with the fast-flowing Montmorency River between them this proximity was deceptive. On 26 July, Wolfe decided to probe the enemy's left flank by leading a reconnaissance to the up-river ford. Brigadier Murray, along with a strong escort composed of the 35th Foot, William Howe's light infantry and a company of rangers, went with him. As Wolfe reported to Monckton, the ford was certainly 'practicable', but for that very reason was heavily guarded by an entrenched detachment, which could be readily reinforced from Montcalm's main army. The densely wooded terrain also favoured the skulking tactics of Canada's Indian allies. At about 4.00 a.m., a small band of warriors waded across the ford to harass Wolfe's men but were soon rebuffed. After concealing his troops amongst the trees, Wolfe examined the ford as closely as the enemy's fire permitted. Around midday another, far more formidable, war party, which had crossed higher up the river and crept down undetected under cover of the east bank, surprised Wolfe's advanced posts. These fell back in confusion, spreading disorder as they went; as one junior staff officer reported, 'the scale of victory was doubtful for some time'. But Howe's light infantry, and two companies of the 35th regiment, held firm and riposted against the Indians' flanks; threatened with a pincer movement, they fell back across the water. The excited redcoats pursued too far and came under heavy fire from the French-held bank. Casualties included Thomas Bell, who was winged near Wolfe. His journal for the day concluded with the feisty memorandum: 'I got my arm broke by the rascals.' In all, the British suffered more than forty killed and wounded – enough to convince Wolfe that 'it was to no purpose to attempt a passage there'.[2]

As Wolfe considered alternative means of striking at Quebec, its defenders staged an offensive of their own. At midnight on 27 July a 'most formidable fire-raft', cobbled together from surplus shipping, was ignited and sent down river in another attempt to torch Saunders's fleet. This blazing behemoth was no more successful than the fire ships launched a month before. Once again, the cool courage of the British sailors baffled the effort. Lieutenant Knox, who witnessed the spectacle from Point Lévis, described how the boatloads of 'gallant seamen' swiftly grappled the raft and dragged its components to the shore, where they spluttered harmlessly. Struck by their 'singular uncouthness', Knox couldn't resist recording the words that one of the intrepid tars shouted to his shipmate: 'Dam-me Jack, did'st thee ever take hell in tow before?' The boatmen of the *Stirling Castle* earned a warming '½ pint of brandy each' for their services that night.[3]

Whilst the remains of the fire-raft smouldered at the riverside, Wolfe and his colleagues continued to weigh up potential plans. One possibility, a direct river-borne assault across the Basin upon the Lower Town itself, was swiftly discarded. The chief engineer Major Mackellar had long since cautioned against such a scheme. Even if the troops got ashore, there remained the difficulty of surmounting the daunting fortifications that blocked access to the Upper Town. Naval reconnaissance confirmed that Quebec was indeed 'formidably entrenched within': the assault would be not only costly, but also pointless.[4]

But Wolfe was now developing an ambitious plan intended to provoke Montcalm into a full-scale confrontation. It involved seizing the westernmost of two redoubts on the extreme right of the Beauport shoreline, close to the gaping 'jaws' of the Montmorency Falls and below the left flank of the enemy's encampment. On 28 July Wolfe jotted down the key elements in his journal: an assault force of grenadiers was to 'get footing', covered by the fire of one or two 'cats' – shallow-draft transport vessels armed with cannon – which could be run aground. The first landing force would consist of just four companies of grenadiers, equipped with large quantities of tools and no less than 10,000 musket cartridges. Their priority was to extend the redoubt, enabling them to defy any counter-attack. The operation was to be directed by Wolfe's trusted friend, Lieutenant-Colonel Ralph Burton, who would have more men should he want them. The plan's viability hinged upon two assumptions: that the target redoubt lay beyond musket shot of the entrenchments behind it; and that the supporting vessels could come close enough to provide effective covering fire. Wolfe himself was sure of the first point, whilst the *Pembroke*'s master, James Cook, had assured Saunders that a cat could approach within one hundred yards of the redoubt. On the basis of Cook's intelligence, Wolfe reckoned it would be a 'short affair' to capture the objective. The real 'business', he added grimly, would be to keep it.[5]

In the course of the next day, 29 July, the plan snowballed from an opportunistic landing by a few hundred men into a major operation involving most of the army. Wolfe scribbled fresh orders for diversions intended 'to give the enemy some jealousy above the town'. On the following morning – when the attack was scheduled to begin – Monckton was to send the 48th Foot upriver from Point Lévis towards the outpost established by ranger captain Joseph Gorham at the mouth of the Etchemin River; the remaining three battalions of his brigade were to be ready to embark in the men-of-war's boats if the first wave required reinforcement. Meanwhile, Rear-Admiral Holmes, who now commanded the little squadron in the upper river, was to drop down to St Michel, 'to cannonade them, and put on an appearance of landing'. Wolfe calculated that Montcalm would snap up his bait, and attempt to dislodge the grenadiers before they dug in. He promised Monckton: 'If the Marquis gives Burton and I only two hours we shall knock his batt[alio]ns about most furiously.'[6]

Subsequent orders increased the plan's scale and complexity. The initial attack would now involve all of the grenadiers, sustained by two hundred of the Royal Americans. Besides Monckton's troops from Point Lévis, further support would come from the two brigades at Montmorency: if required, Townshend and Murray were to cross another fording place *below* the Falls, which was only passable at low tide, and then march along the beach to reinforce the attack. In an attempt to wrongfoot the enemy, Colonel Howe, with his light infantry, the rangers and the 58th Foot, would march up the Montmorency River, as if to menace the ford where Wolfe had skirmished four days before. Once the main attack was well under way, he was to abandon his feint and return. When the time was right, the massed field-pieces and howitzers at Montmorency were to open fire upon the French camp. At long last, a major assault seemed imminent. That same day, Wolfe added a codicil to his will.[7]

But Tuesday 30 July was sultry and still. This dead calm obliged Wolfe to postpone the attack for a day. During the lull, several redcoats went over to the enemy. Desertion was the bane of all eighteenth-century armies and, for obvious reasons, was particularly common on the eve of major offensives. Having already issued his detailed orders for the attack, Wolfe grew apprehensive that they would now be disclosed to the enemy; as French reports reveal, these fears were justified. There was another cause for concern – the 'Dislike of the gen[era]l officers and others to this business', although, as Wolfe noted sourly, *they* had nothing better to propose.[8]

Oblivious to the doubts and dissensions of their commanders, Wolfe's men remained in high spirits. After all of the false starts and frustrations of the past month, they were itching for action. Now, at long last, they would get their chance. Wednesday 31 July proved hot, but with breeze enough for the attack to proceed.[9] At about 8.00 a.m., the grenadiers and Royal Americans from the Isle of Orleans, and the 15th and 78th Foot from Point Lévis, began boarding their flat-bottomed boats and were rowed to the rendezvous points. Some two hours later, at high tide, the armed transports the *Russell* and the *Three Sisters* ran aground and began a 'smart fire' upon the French redoubts and batteries. But the operation had barely begun before it struck problems: the water was far shallower than expected, and the cats grounded beyond effective range of their targets. A member of Wolfe's 'family' complained: ''Twas said that at the top of the tide they cou'd get within fifty yards, instead of which their distance was six hundred.' The attack was backed by the fifty-gun *Centurion*, Anson's flagship during his celebrated circumnavigation, but her greater draught obliged her to keep still further off, in mid-channel. As a result, the naval firepower intended to pave the way for the landing did little more than 'annoy' the enemy.

It was not only James Cook who had miscalculated. Reconnoitring the shore from the *Russell*, Wolfe swiftly saw that his chosen objective was far closer to the French entrenchments than he had believed, and within easy musket range: it would swiftly become a slaughter pen for the men sent to seize it. If his troops were to land beyond musket shot of the enemy, he must wait for the tide to fall. In any event, Townshend's troops from Montmorency could only support him once the ford below the Falls was shallow enough for them to cross. It was also clear to Wolfe that the cats were struggling to suppress the enemy's fire; aboard the *Russell*, he was repeatedly struck with splinters and had his cane knocked out of his hand by a cannon ball. Saunders too had a close shave, one shell 'falling so near his boat as to damage some of the oars and half fill her with water', raising fears that the fleet would lose 'a gallant commander'. Meanwhile, the waiting troops rowed back and forth in their open boats, exposed to both enemy shellfire and a broiling sun.

Despite these discouraging developments, Wolfe resolved to stage a full-scale assault upon the enemy's entrenchments. In his journal, which was written up piecemeal as the day unfolded, he observed: 'Their confusion and disorder inclines me to attack them.' Monckton and Townshend were ordered to prepare for action. By now, however, the French had ample warning of exactly where the blow would fall. They could be seen manning their trenches and massing formidable forces behind them. The threatened sector was commanded by Montcalm's capable second-in-command, Major-General François-Gaston, Duc de Lévis. His unconcern for the shot and shell that rained down from the batteries at Montmorency helped to embolden the Montreal militiamen who awaited the British onslaught.

It was nearly 4.00 p.m. before the tide had ebbed sufficiently for the British to attack. But now, as they pulled for the shore, the landing craft hit a fresh problem, grounding on a previously unsuspected spit. Valuable time was lost, and Wolfe's *aide-de-camp*, Hervey Smyth, was sent to halt Townshend's march. The water between the bank and the beach was sounded, to discover whether the troops could wade ashore without soaking their ammunition; it was five feet deep in places, so, in company with Captain James Chads of the *Vesuvius* fire-ship, Wolfe took his boat close inshore to find a better spot for a second attempt. Striking midway between the stranded transports, the first wave eventually landed at about 5.30 p.m. With the water up to their waist-belts, they formed as best they could.

For all the day's delays and dangers, and the daunting defences ahead of them, the morale of Wolfe's men was still surprisingly high. One eye-witness noted that 'the greatest spirit and chearfulness was discernable through our whole army, and all waited with the utmost impatience for the moment of attack'. This hunger to meet the enemy led swiftly to disaster. Instead of waiting for their supports, the spearhead units attacked alone. 'As soon as we landed', recalled one sergeant-major, 'we fixed our bayonets and beat our Grenadier's March, and so advanced on.' Wolfe was exasperated by the grenadiers' 'strange behaviour', which had transformed his co-ordinated attack into a disorderly stampede. Exactly what triggered it remains a mystery, but a likely answer lies in the personal rivalry between two officers of the Royal Americans. On the previous day, Captain David Ochterlony, 'a North Briton', had fought a duel with a 'German' colleague. Both men were wounded, Ochterlony so badly that his friends begged him not to join the coming assault. But the Scot declared 'that it should never be said that a scratch, received in a private rencounter, had prevented him from doing his duty'. At the landing, Ochterlony and his men were ranged alongside the grenadier company of Gustavus Wetterstrom, who was probably the officer with whom he had recently crossed swords. Ochterlony called over to Wetterstrom that, although *they* were not grenadiers, his men would be the first into the redoubt. With the grenadiers 'taking fire' at this challenge, the whole command bolted towards the enemy. The redoubt had been abandoned, but in the packed trenches topping the steep grassy bank behind it, the Canadian militiamen coolly held their fire until certain of their targets. Then, as the bold sergeant-major testified, they 'pour'd their small-shot like showers of hail, which caus'd our brave grenadiers to fall very fast'. Breathless from their sprint, and suffering heavy casualties at point-blank range, the grenadiers milled about in confusion. At that very moment, the storm that had threatened for some time finally broke, unleashing what the log of the *Lowestoft* described as 'a vilent squall of wind, atended with thunder, lightning, and havey rain'. The downpour snuffed out the murderous French fusillade. But whilst granting the hard-pressed grenadiers a timely reprieve, it left the slope too slick and slippery for them to even contemplate scaling.

By now Monckton's men were landed and drawn up on the beach in good order. Townshend too was across the ford and marching to join the attack. But as a fresh assault promised prohibitive casualties with little prospect of success, and the turning tide threatened to cut off retreat by way of the ford, Wolfe decided to call off the attack and retire whilst he still could. Unlike the impetuous advance of the grenadiers, the withdrawal was conducted with impressive discipline. After the wounded were placed in the boats, Monckton re-embarked the 15th, most of the 78th, and what remained of the bloodied grenadiers and Royal Americans. The rest of Fraser's battalion joined Townshend's men as they retraced their steps along the strand. Wolfe went with them. The sullen redcoats were 'saluted all the time by the infernal clamours of the Indians and the *vive le roy* of the French'. They still hoped that Montcalm's jubilant troops might be tempted to quit their breastworks and fight them in the open, 'though', as one officer derisively reported, 'the poltroons, who were twice our numbers, dared not come down to us, though often invited by the hats waved at them from our general officers and troops'.

The rapidly rising tide made Townshend's retreat a tense business. It became even more so after the two companies of Fraser's Highlanders who were with him absolutely refused to recross the ford until certain that some of their comrades, who had been left aboard one of the stranded cats, had all re-embarked safely. The brigadier's agitation is clear from his notes, which describe how he waited for the stubborn Celts 'until ye tide of flood was so high that the regiments could scarcely wade over ye ford and the enemy had time to bring their guns to rake them in their retreat'.

As the cats could not be refloated, Saunders ordered them burned. The smoke wafted over the beach, which was now empty save for a sprinkling of red-coated bodies, and the Canadians and Indians who had ventured down to plunder and scalp them. In all, the attack had cost the British some 440 casualties, including forty-seven killed. Amongst the slain was Sergeant Ned Botwood, the bellicose balladeer of the 47th Foot. Not surprisingly, French losses were far lighter, with sixty killed and wounded, chiefly by the brisk cannonade from across the Montmorency.[10]

In his journal, Wolfe summed up the affair as a 'foolish business'. Next day, in official orders, he castigated the grenadiers for their 'impetuous, irregular and unsoldierlike' behaviour, contrasting it with the formidable coolness and discipline of Amherst's and Fraser's battalions.[11] Unbridled grenadier aggression had certainly contributed to the reverse, but, as Wolfe readily acknowledged, it was only part of the story of 'that unlucky day'. Besides the various 'accidents' that could not be foreseen, he told Saunders, his plan had suffered from flaws for which he was prepared to take the blame. His worst mistake had been to put too many of the troops into boats instead of adopting the safer course of landing them at Montmorency and then marching them over the ford.[12] As Corporal John Johnson of the 58th Foot pointed out, however, in an analysis since echoed by Wolfe's modern critics, the plan was compromised by a more fundamental weakness: even if the redcoats had scaled the Beauport heights, and driven the defenders from their breastworks at bayonet point, the bulk of Montcalm's forces would still have remained between them and the River St Charles, ready to renew the fight from behind that formidable barrier. Put simply, Wolfe had attacked the 'wrong end' of Montcalm's position.[13] Wolfe himself was well aware of the disadvantages of striking where he did, but attacked nonetheless: as he explained in his despatch to Pitt, there he could employ the massed artillery at Montmorency and, if necessary, concentrate his whole army – advantages not to be found anywhere else. But, above all, Wolfe added, 'the desire to act in conformity to the King's intentions, induced me to make this trial, persuaded that a victorious army finds no difficulties'.

The total failure of Wolfe's 'first push' prompted much rejoicing amongst Quebec's defenders. The white flag of the Bourbons fluttered above their entrenchments in defiant triumph, whilst the sterling performance of the Canadian militiamen earned the ungrudging approval of French regular officers who had previously doubted their reliability under fire.[14]

Wolfe determined to put the setback behind him. On 1 August he wrote confidently to Monckton: 'This check must not discourage us. The loss is not great.' The brigadier was enjoined to keep his men at 'gentle exercise' and to prepare for another – and hopefully happier – 'attempt'. Neither did the repulse dent the morale of Wolfe's battalion officers and their men. After all, the troops concerned had acquitted themselves bravely, and if British grenadiers could be excused anything surely it was boldness. Their commander, Lieutenant-Colonel Alexander Murray, who had returned unscathed, although with his uniform shot through in four places, assured his wife, 'I think nothing on earth could behave better than we did.'[15]

But the defeat at Montmorency provided ready ammunition for Wolfe's critics amongst the expedition's senior officers, who now became more vocal in their attacks upon him. Reporting the situation when he left Quebec for Boston on 11 August, Captain Alexander Schomberg of the damaged *Diana* frigate noted that Wolfe's 'enemies and rivals' were now bemoaning his 'impetuosity'. According to James Gibson, who was himself hostile to Wolfe, some of the 'general officers' had scarcely hesitated to state that the Montmorency attack was 'impracticable'. Indeed, he added: 'One of them of knowledge, fortune and interest I have heard has declar'd the attack *then* and *there*, was contrary to the advice and opinion of every officer.' From the qualities listed, it is probable that the 'general officer' in question was George Townshend, MP, who had already clashed with Wolfe, and whose grumbling was loud enough to become common knowledge. Writing to his wife a week after the failed attack, Lieutenant-Colonel Murray observed: 'Townshend is well, but a malecontent.'[16]

One of the most celebrated stories to emerge from the Quebec campaign maintains that Townshend was not content to disparage Wolfe verbally: he also drew upon his celebrated artistic skills to ridicule his commander – whose distinctive physique and physiognomy left him an all too easy target – circulating disrespectful caricatures amongst his brother officers. No less than eight cartoons of Wolfe, reputedly those created by Townshend that summer, are now in Montreal's McCord Museum. Although Townshend certainly took his paints, pens and brushes to Quebec, executing a fine watercolour portrait of Wolfe and producing some striking sketches of Montcalm's Indian allies, the authenticity of most of the cartoons attributed to him is questionable.[17] Despite such doubts, and the absence of any mention of the drawings in eyewitness journals, there is at least some support for the tale. Horace Walpole *may* have been referring to the episode when he observed that 'Wolfe was not a man to waive his eminence from fear of caricatures', whilst an early collection of military anecdotes relates how Townshend produced a scurrilous sketch of Wolfe planning fortifications around 'a disreputable building'; when the officers assembled at mess the cartoon passed from hand to hand, eventually reaching Wolfe himself, who calmly pocketed it, saying: 'If we live, this shall be inquired into; but we must first beat the enemy.'[18]

If Townshend – the army's third in command – really did squander his precious time in such a childish, disloyal and irresponsible fashion, then Wolfe was right to distrust him. Indeed, although it has become customary to blame the harmful wrangling within the higher echelons of the Quebec army upon Wolfe's own 'prickly' personality, convincing contemporary evidence suggests that the characters of his subordinates were equally significant. The journal kept by a member of Wolfe's immediate military 'family' is especially revealing on this point. Whilst highly partisan, it deserves careful consideration, not least because its strident judgements were destined to be borne out by subsequent events.[19]

In the opinion of the journal's author, Townshend was temperamentally unfitted for high command. His 'fickle inconstant mind' made him 'exceedingly subject to very high and very low spirits'; and as his patronage was not motivated by merit, he was invariably 'surrounded by the most indifferent subjects in an army'. Townshend's bawdy humour made him 'an excellent tavern acquaintance', but when it came to 'the movements and conduct of an army' he was 'without a scale', or – as a later age would put it – clueless.

But Townshend was not the only – nor the most malignant – 'evil spirit' to emerge in the wake of the 'miscarriage' at Montmorency. Wolfe's junior brigadier, James Murray, also sought to recruit supporters from amongst those who had 'undergone censure during the campaign', and who now believed that defeat was inevitable. These pessimists 'lookt on the whole affair as over, and that no future attempt would be made'. The same commentator maintained that Murray, not Townshend, was the real ringleader of the opposition to Wolfe: he was 'the deadly nightshade, the poison of a camp'; alongside *him*, Townshend appeared more mischievous than malicious. Murray was crippled by jealousy of his younger commander's 'high reputation'. He owed his rank to Wolfe, but was immune to all feelings of gratitude or honour, instead repaying this trust by becoming 'the very bellows of sedition', adept at fomenting discord and persuading others that their merits were not properly rewarded; and, whilst courageous enough in action, Murray's bravery stemmed from ambition, not zeal. Although a 'tolerable good commander of a brigade', anything more was 'too extensive for him'. Murray was not content to foster opposition to Wolfe amongst the army's officers; he had also propagated his prejudices throughout the navy, even seeking to convince Admiral Saunders that Wolfe 'was a madman who would lead him into scrapes'.

Instead of being seduced by Murray and Townshend's scheming, the journal's author claimed, most officers 'took offence at it, so gross were their reflections, and so well establish'd the character of Mr Wolfe'. This offered a striking contrast to that of his opponents:

> Mr Wolfe had a very peculiar turn for war. Personal bravery to excess – an exceeding contempt of money – firmly attach'd to officers who distinguish'd themselves in military exploit. He received with great coolness any person of any rank whatever that wanted a large share of zeal for the service. Thus

a friend of the brave, an enemy to the base, he work'd up courage to such a pitch in his little army that it became necessary often to desire the soldiers not to expose themselves without a necessity for it.

Most subalterns apparently remained oblivious to the dissensions in the Montmorency camp. For example, John Knox makes no mention of them in his exceptionally detailed daily journal of the siege. Other more senior officers, like Alexander Murray of the Louisbourg Grenadiers, were well aware of the factionalism but preferred to keep aloof and 'meddle with no politicks or party'.[20]

Faced with the unexpected enemy within, Wolfe outwardly responded to his detractors with disdain. He 'held their cabal very cheap', the anonymous staff officer reported, and paid little heed to 'ill grounded opinions'. But for all of Wolfe's efforts to make light of the sniping against him, the knowledge that two of his three brigadiers were openly critical of his actions, and actively seeking to undermine his authority throughout the task force, only added another burden to those he already carried. As if the physical and mental strains of the campaign were not enough, he was now obliged to take measures to vindicate his own actions and to guard against the machinations of those very men who had been appointed to assist him. According to Captain Bell, the section of Wolfe's journal that the general deliberately destroyed during the last days of his life 'contained a careful account of the officers' ignoble conduct towards him in case of a Parliamentary enquiry'.[21]

One of Bell's brother officers heard Wolfe declare that, when Townshend and Murray were separated, Townshend was 'innocent'; he even maintained that a desire to split up the conniving pair lay behind Wolfe's selection of Murray to command his next gambit – the despatch of a substantial force far up the St Lawrence. As Wolfe later explained to Pitt, the brigadier was sent to aid Holmes in destroying the enemy's shipping, 'in order to open a communication with General Amherst'. In his orders to Murray, Wolfe was more expansive: the brigadier's objectives would also include the magazines and stores at Deschambault, nearly forty miles above Quebec. In addition, Murray was to fight any of the enemy's detachments – provided he was not heavily outnumbered – and was empowered to burn houses or take women prisoners, both in an effort to provoke such a clash. Lastly, Wolfe wrote, 'You may land

and do what mischief you can on the south shore and at last oblige the enemy to divide his force and carry his attention to the upper river.'[22]

Murray marched at midnight on Sunday 5 August, taking Dalling's Light Infantry, his own 15th Foot and 200 marines from Monckton's camp at Point Lévis. All lay concealed near Gorham's Post until the following afternoon, when they embarked aboard the twenty flat-bottomed boats that were to ferry them upriver to join Holmes's squadron. These crucial craft had slipped past Quebec that night, under cover of a masking mist; Montcalm's sentries heard their oars stroking upon the river, and the drummers beat to arms, but it was too late to stop them.[23] On their passage, Murray's boats feinted towards St Michel, finding its defenders now well entrenched and alert. The enemy had also established a post at Cap Rouge, some eight miles above Quebec. Murray's troops reached Holmes at about 6.00 p.m. Besides the *Sutherland*, the *Squirrel* and the other vessels, the rear-admiral now commanded a pair of the floating batteries that had proved so useful to the enemy; his squadron already carried the third battalion of the Royal Americans, so giving Murray a landing force of about 1200 redcoats.[24]

As the British flotilla moved slowly up river, it was shadowed by enemy forces marching along the north shore. From his own 'ocular' observation, and the intelligence of prisoners, Murray reckoned them to be 4000 strong. In fact, their commander, Colonel Bougainville, initially had just 1000 men to guard Quebec's lines of communication. Although modest for this vital task, his force included the cream of Montcalm's regulars and militia, and a volunteer corps of hard-riding cavalry. Commanded by Monsieur de La Roche-Beaucour, in coming weeks these blue-coated troopers would become an increasingly familiar sight to the British.[25]

By 7 August, the British squadron lay off St Antoine, on the south shore about twenty miles from Quebec. On the following morning, Murray noticed three of the enemy's floating batteries across the river at Pointe-aux-Trembles, where Carleton had landed successfully on 21 July. He resolved to attack them, hoping that the French would be tempted to fight in their defence. Holmes agreed that it was 'very practicable to cut them off and drive them on shore', and deployed the two sloops and his own floating batteries for the operation.[26] The three companies of Dalling's Light Infantry were to head the amphibious assault at low tide, supported by both battalions. Murray signalled the attack with a wave of his hat, but Dalling's men rapidly ran into problems. Here – as at Montmorency – the landing zone was shielded by a hidden 'reef of rocks', and several boats promptly grounded upon it. The company of Highlanders led by Captain Simon Fraser eventually found a way through, only to be pinned down on the beach by heavy defensive fire. Murray himself now landed, furious that Dalling's two remaining companies were still offshore. As one of Fraser's men noted, the brigadier 'unfairly attributed the cause to shyness, when in reality it was owing to two boats running on the reef'. As soon as these craft could be refloated, Captain De Laune pushed in to Fraser's support and their men together maintained a brisk fire from behind sheltering rocks. With the rising tide, most of them were soon up to their waists in water, and much of their ammunition was soaked and useless. Because the boats carrying the support battalions were struggling to make headway against the flood tide, and French reinforcements could be seen converging upon the spot, Murray ordered a retreat. This encouraged the enemy to pursue, and the re-embarkation became a close-run affair. Private Richard Humphrys of De Laune's company reported that the naval oarsmen were disinclined to wait for them, 'but [by] threatening to fire at the boats if they did not instantly return and take us in, [we] soon made them return back', he wrote. Just the same, some of Dalling's men were 'obliged to swim for it'. The light infantry had suffered heavily, but 'as for the enemy's loss', Humphrys grumbled, 'we could not be a judge of, they being in the bush, and we never having the satisfaction to get on the sod'.

After the last dry cartridges were distributed amongst the survivors, the light infantry returned to the attack, this time at high tide. By now, the enemy had concentrated in more formidable numbers; they were concealed amongst trees and behind buildings, whilst a mounted officer could be seen galloping back and forth to direct operations. This was Bougainville, whose horse had been hit during the first attack, and who now mustered some 300 men – Indians, regulars, Canadian militia and the ubiquitous cavalrymen – to meet the renewed British assault.

Nothing daunted, Major Dalling and his long-suffering men once again headed for the shore; but, when they came within musket shot, the enemy unleashed such a heavy fire that the sailors were unable to man their oars. Many of them were killed or wounded, which obliged most of the boats to back off, or lie immobile and helpless. Under the circumstances, a landing was clearly impossible and Murray ordered the retreat to beat. As Humphrys gloomily noted, 'every thing went against us for this day'. That evening they returned to their ships 'in a most forlorn condition'. All night, and for much of the next day, the surgeons attended the injured, including Captain De Laune, who had suffered a 'flesh wound' to the shoulder.

Delighted with his victory, Bougainville believed he had inflicted losses of 300 killed and wounded. This was an exaggeration, as British accounts tally the toll at less than half of his claim, but there was no doubt that they had been decisively rebuffed. Although scarcely mentioned in most accounts of the Quebec campaign, Murray's bloody attempt to get ashore at Pointe-aux-Trembles was a significant episode that taught clear lessons: the upper St Lawrence river – where the northern shoreline was lower, more lightly defended and theoretically more accessible than either the rugged cliffs directly above Quebec or the heavily manned Beauport sector – offered no easy option for a landing force. A combination of navigational conditions, particularly the strength of the tides and the presence of offshore shoals, proscribed naval operations there as elsewhere; and, without the crucial element of surprise, even the most determined attack by troops in open boats could be repelled with ease by a few hundred well-led defenders. The point was not lost on Wolfe: he believed that Murray must now be convinced 'of the difficulties that presents themselves above as well as below' Quebec.[27]

Despite this setback, Murray was determined to try again. Next day he wrote to Wolfe in confident mood. The French might well sing the *Te Deum* in celebration of their latest deliverance, but the tune would soon be his. He added: 'I am sure of a stroke in a few days.'[28] Meanwhile, on 10 August, he brushed aside feeble opposition to land upon the south shore at St Antoine. Encamping his troops there, Murray sent Dalling out reconnoitring. When the major's command came under sniping fire from militiamen, Murray retaliated by burning all the houses in the neighbouring parish of St Croix. A manifesto was nailed to the church door, warning that, if the harassment continued, the inhabitants could expect no quarter. After several straggling marines were slain, and their butchered bodies left on the beach, Murray marched at the head of the 15th and 3/60th and torched the buildings of St Nicholas in retribution. After this uncompromising response, Murray's manifesto swiftly took effect and the attacks petered out.

Leaving his marines to hold the camp, on 18 August Murray embarked the rest of the troops under cover of darkness. At daybreak on the 19th they made an unopposed landing on the north shore near Portneuf, then marched rapidly up to Deschambault, where a large house stored the spare clothing and equipment of the French regular troops and the personal baggage of Montcalm and Lévis.[29] Everything was burned, the conflagration being kindled with the officers' silk stockings and waistcoats. The blaze triggered a series of explosions: it was conjectured that casks cached in the storehouse cellar had contained gunpowder or cartridges. The raiders spent the rest of the day wrecking anything of value, and skirmishing with the enemy's Indians and some dragoons who had spurred to the scene, each with an infantryman riding pillion; they kept their distance, owing, Murray believed, 'to the dread they had of the English musket' – interesting testimony to the superior range and hitting power of 'Brown Bess'. When all was in ashes, Murray's men re-embarked at low tide. They carried off some sheep and shot a hundred cattle, leaving the carcasses strewn across the beach. Bougainville, whose upriver command had now been reinforced to 1600 men, was twenty-one miles away when Murray struck and arrived too late to intercept him. This tip-and-run raid caused considerable alarm in the French camp. Fearing that the British planned to dig in across his line of communications, Montcalm immediately gathered his crack grenadiers and had force-marched them as far as Pointe-aux-Trembles before learning that Murray was already gone.[30]

Well planned and executed, the Deschambault strike underscored the importance of surprise for any landing on the north shore. But the magazine there was no more than a secondary objective of the expedition. As Murray had emphasized to Holmes, their 'principal bussiness' was the elimination of the enemy's shipping – the warships and transports that had entered the St Lawrence ahead of Durell, and which furnished the food that kept Montcalm's army from starvation. Murray's men had seen the frigates 'very plain', but they remained beyond reach. Aided by a north wind, and lightened by temporarily removing their guns, they had recently shifted from their anchorage at Batiscan and ascended the Richelieu Rapids to Trois Rivières. Deep within hostile territory, Holmes was unable to follow suit, and the raiders were obliged to content themselves with capturing and burning a brigantine that lay midway between the rival flotillas.[31]

During Murray's absence, Wolfe continued to pursue his objective of bringing Montcalm to a major confrontation. By creating a diversion, he hoped that the brigadier's raid would deflect the Marquis's attention, so leaving his Beauport army weakened and more vulnerable to attack. As Montcalm's reaction to the landing at Deschambault and the steady expansion of Bougainville's far-flung command both demonstrated, this strategy was at least partially successful. But it failed to deliver the decisive engagement that Wolfe craved.

Throughout early August, Wolfe drilled his men for another full-fledged assault upon Montcalm's army. His journal reports that large detachments of troops were out 'scouring' the woods; this would not only accustom them to the terrain, and oblige the enemy to keep their distance, but also prepare them 'for a decisive action'.[32] By seeking to cause maximum disruption upriver, Murray's raid naturally played an important role in Wolfe's plan, but it was a potentially disastrous one. The brigadier had been ordered to spend no longer away from the army than was absolutely necessary: both he and his men were essential for the anticipated engagement. As the days passed, Wolfe grew increasingly impatient for Murray's return. Writing to him on 11 August, he declared: 'I mean to attack the French Army, but wish to have you and Carleton and the light infantry to assist.' Lieutenant-Colonel Young, with his Royal Americans, had enough men to hold the enemy's attention in the upper river, but Wolfe wanted Murray's own 15th Foot back with him, 'for the decisive blow'. Two days later he drummed home the point: when Murray had done his best, he was to return, concealing his movements as much as possible. Young was to 'make what parade he can' and threaten descents upon both shores. Wolfe added a note leaving no doubt where his own interests now lay: 'it's enough that I let you know, how much it imports us to keep their attention fixed above.' On 15 August, Wolfe wrote Murray a third letter that conveyed the growing urgency of the situation. The brigadier and his men were now 'much wanted'; if Murray had 'no very great stroke in view', Wolfe would be glad to have him back. The following day, in the last surviving entry in his journal, he noted Murray's continuing silence.[33]

By this time, alongside a battlefield confrontation with Montcalm, Wolfe was considering another option – 'a general assault' against Quebec itself. To this end, he told Murray, 'a numerous artillery' had been prepared at Pointe aux Pères to silence the 'barbet battery' defending the quayside of the Lower Town. Wolfe likewise informed Monckton that the campaign would 'probably conclude with an assault upon the town'. This plan, which would involve storming ashore from the river, was a sign of Wolfe's growing desperation. It resurrected the proposal that had been briefly considered in late July, only to be discarded as extremely risky and ultimately futile. In the opinion of Major Mackellar, the revived version offered no better prospects, particularly as the warships' guns lacked the elevation to bombard the Upper Town. It was likewise jettisoned. By 21 August, Knox reported, 'the enterprise of storming Quebec' had been abandoned 'as too desperate to hope for success'.[34]

As the siege dragged on, Wolfe reluctantly acknowledged the possibility of failure. Reporting the deadlock to Brigadier Whitmore at Louisbourg on 11 August, he conceded that the enemy's numbers, and the strength of their defences, meant that 'the event of an attack upon them' was now 'very uncertain'. Although determined as ever to seek 'a battle when occasion offers', he was also contemplating a fallback position at Île aux Coudres, fifty miles below Quebec: a large body of troops based there during the coming winter would at least provide some 'check' upon the enemy, capable of 'distressing them in the most essential manner'. Whitmore was urged to assemble the materials to build barracks for Wolfe's men and to forward them without delay. This 'strong fortress', as Knox described it, was to be garrisoned by three thousand men. Before the end of August, that project too had been set aside. As Wolfe told Pitt, 'it was too late in the season, to collect materials sufficient for covering so large a body'.[35]

More than ever, Wolfe's hopes now hung upon a decisive clash with

Montcalm; and for that he required the redcoats and boats of Murray's roving command. But it was not only by depleting the army's resources that the brigadier's prolonged raid exacerbated Wolfe's problems. It also created fresh tensions within the troubled command of the Quebec task force. By taking troops from Point Lévis, the upriver expedition had weakened Robert Monckton's position there. Wolfe himself did not consider that a cause for concern. On the contrary, he wrote to Monckton: 'I have thought of your situation when Murray is detached, and heartily wish you may be attacked – you have more than enough to beat the whole French army.'[36] But if the sometimes acerbic author of the Wolfe 'family' journal is to be believed, it is highly unlikely that Monckton – whom he dismissed as 'timid', 'of a poor capacity', and 'fat-headed' – shared his general's undisguised enthusiasm at the prospect of a full-scale assault upon his isolated camp.[37] This is a harsh assessment of the expedition's second-in-command, but other evidence suggests that Monckton was growing increasingly nervous about the security of his position. Such fears can scarcely have been soothed when, just a day after Murray marched, Wolfe cheerfully raised the possibility of reinforcing him with men drawn from one of the remaining battalions of Monckton's dwindling brigade – 'that excellent regim[ent]t', Fraser's Highlanders; after all, Wolfe assured him, he would still have Kennedy's 43rd and Webb's 48th Foot 'entire'.[38] Soon after, Monckton received a request to detach 200 men of the 43rd to join Murray's command. That, along with an order to transfer some of the Highlanders over to the Isle of Orleans, and other alterations to the manning of his posts, was apparently the final straw, prompting Monckton to take umbrage and voice his disquiet to Wolfe's adjutant-general, Isaac Barré.

Having already fallen out with Townshend and Murray, Wolfe had no intention of souring relations with his senior brigadier. He dashed off two letters in as many days, offering his 'hearty excuses' for any offence that he might unintentionally have caused. 'You may be quite assur'd that I have all possible regard and esteem for you,' he wrote. Wolfe added: 'I am too well convinc'd of your upright sentiments, and zeal for the publick service, not to set the highest value upon your friendship.' Besides leaving Monckton in no doubt that he was a prized subordinate, Wolfe also sought to calm his fears for Point Lévis: if the enemy attacked anywhere, he assured him, it would be *his* camp at

Montmorency; to get at Monckton, by contrast, they must first cross the St Lawrence – under the guns of two naval squadrons – and then attempt to land amongst strongly entrenched posts, heavily defended by artillery. Wolfe added:

> The least of your redoubts well mann'd would repulse an army so com- pounded as theirs is. I mention these things that you may not think I weaken you too much by the detachments that I am obliged to send or call away for the service.[39]

Wolfe's prompt and fulsome apologies pacified Monckton, and it seems that no more was said on the matter: a potentially disastrous rift had been avoided. But Wolfe was now increasingly troubled at the con- tinuing absence of the troops under Murray – along with so many of the flat-bottomed boats that were essential for any amphibious operations. His mounting frustration was evident when he wrote to Monckton on 19 August: 'I wish we had Murray's corps back, that we might be ready to decide it with them.' It was now clear that the diversionary strategy had backfired. Three days later Wolfe added: 'Murray, by his long stay above and by detaining all our boats, is actually master of the opera- tions – or rather puts an entire stop to them.'[40] The situation was only complicated by the fact that the Royal Navy was still struggling to gain control of the St Lawrence above Quebec. All communication with Murray had been severed by the French floating batteries, and the rein- forcements intended for him had been unable to get through.[41]

In a fresh effort to recall Murray, on 24 August Monckton was told to fire signal rockets from Gorham's Post: hopefully 'the people above' would 'take the hint' that something was wanted.[42] The next evening, after leaving Captain Rous upriver in the *Sutherland* in company with Colonel Young and his Royal Americans, and the 200 marines to guard the camp at St Antoine, Murray and Holmes finally returned to Point Lévis.

Besides a detailed account of his own protracted operations, Murray brought the first firm news of the substantial British forces that had been operating to the south, under the direction of the commander-in- chief, Jeffery Amherst. These had made remarkable progress. According to prisoners and intercepted letters alike, not only had Amherst himself captured both Ticonderoga and Crown Point, but his troops had secured another key objective of Pitt's offensive, Fort Niagara.[43]

For Wolfe and his army, this intelligence gave much-needed encouragement. Throughout August, as successive schemes were mooted, only to be discarded as impracticable, the Quebec task force had grown increasingly anxious for hard information of Amherst's progress. As envisaged by Ligonier, Pitt and their colleagues back in London, the success of the campaign in North America, of which Quebec was the primary objective, depended upon *co-operation* between the two main armies. Wolfe had repeatedly promised Amherst his unstinting support, and that offer had been reciprocated with equal enthusiasm and apparent sincerity. For example, on 6 May, Amherst had written from Albany: 'I will close in upon the enemy to the utmost I can at the time you are up the River'; until then, he would strive to cause 'jealousies in different corners at a greater distance', so distracting and dividing the opposition.[44]

Faced with the rump of Canada's defenders, who were both more numerous and in a far stronger position than anticipated by the campaign's planners, as the siege wore on Wolfe and his men counted upon Amherst to make good his pledge and push vigorously for the St Lawrence. In mid July, prisoners plucked from Wolfe's camp at Montmorency had claimed how 'it was generally reported in their army that the General was not sanguine about taking Quebec until he would be joined by General Amherst, whom he was expecting with the greatest impatience'.[45] Letters from Wolfe's army, which surfaced in the Boston and New York newspapers, conveyed a similar message. One sent from Point Lévis on 29 July ended with the plea: 'We earnestly want to hear from General Amherst'; others written some two weeks later expressed the prevailing view that it would require another campaign to take Quebec – *unless* Amherst joined them. If that junction occurred in good time, the British would soon hold all Canada. To help Wolfe, it was not even necessary for Amherst to reach Quebec. As John Knox observed in early August, merely by advancing into French territory he would exert pressure, so compelling Montcalm 'to draw off some of his forces hence to the side of Montreal', and thereby enabling Wolfe's troops 'to give a satisfactory account of the capital of Canada'.[46]

When he wrote to Brigadier Whitmore on 11 August, Wolfe confessed that he knew absolutely nothing of Amherst's campaign. Given, however, the weakness of the forces defending the Lake Champlain front under Brigadier-General François-Charles de Bourlamaque – no more than 3000 regulars, militia and Indians – it was assumed that he must by then have taken both Ticonderoga and Crown Point. Army gossip supported that interpretation but, as Wolfe told Murray two days later, he needed hard news, not 'soldiers gazitt'.

Murray's return confirmed the campfire rumours. Although the problem of mustering the provincial contingents had delayed the onset of his campaign by nearly two months, Amherst ultimately assembled an imposing force of 16,000 regulars and provincials; of these, 5000 were allotted to Brigadier-General John Prideaux for the westward thrust against Oswego and Niagara. Amherst began moving down Lake George on 21 July, and next day landed near Ticonderoga. Following instructions, Bourlamaque contented himself with a token resistance, evacuating most of his troops and leaving just 400 men to slow Amherst's advance as best they could. Fort Carillon and its outlying breastworks – the objective against which Abercromby's fine army had foundered so bloodily just a year before – was now taken in exchange for a handful of dead and wounded. On 26 July, Ticonderoga's garrison retreated by water, blowing up the fort as they went. Twenty miles to the north, Fort St Frédéric at Crown Point fell without even demanding the barest formalities of a siege, as Bourlamaque withdrew to a stronger defensive position at Isle-aux-Noix, set in the Richelieu River close to its junction with Lake Champlain.

The commander-in-chief reached the ruins of Crown Point on 4 August. He had made rapid progress, but his drive towards Montreal soon lost momentum – and then ground to a complete halt. As expected, a miniature French fleet controlled the lake, and it was of course necessary for Amherst to build his own ships to counter it. But whilst these vital vessels were under construction, Amherst made no other move to forward elements of his own 'Grand Army' against Bourlamaque's new position; instead, he set his men to building an impressive – but totally unnecessary – new fort at Crown Point.

Amherst now pinned all his hopes upon the western wing of his army. On 28 July, after learning that Prideaux had been killed whilst besieging

Niagara, he had sent Brigadier-General Thomas Gage to replace him. Gage arrived at the re-established base of Oswego on 16 August, to find that Niagara had already fallen to the Anglo-Americans on 25 July. This was a devastating blow to the French, who now feared that the British would lose no time in exploiting their success to cross Lake Ontario and descend the St Lawrence to Montreal. Upon learning the news on 8 August, Montcalm had immediately detached some 900 men from his Quebec army, and sent them under the Chevalier de Lévis to shore up that front. Ligonier's divide-and-conquer strategy was beginning to deliver dividends. New France's embattled defenders now dreaded 'that the fatal moment was fast approaching, when the whole colony would pass under the yoke of the English'. But the western arm of Amherst's army, like his own force on Lake Champlain, promptly halted. On 17 August, five Canadians arrived at Quebec bearing news that the victorious Anglo-Americans showed no signs of advancing from Oswego. From this, it was inferred that the threat to Montreal from that quarter had receded. Although Amherst was confident that Gage would lose no time in taking the feeble post of La Galette, and then forging ahead to Montreal, the brigadier's assumption of command failed to restart the stalled campaign.[47]

Scarcely more than a week after learning that the Lake Ontario front had stabilized, Quebec's defenders received an even greater boost to their morale. They were now assured, from impeccable sources, that Amherst *himself* had no intention of advancing further into New France until he was certain that Wolfe would capture Quebec. This damaging revelation resulted from Amherst's own efforts to get word of Wolfe. By early August he had heard nothing concrete from the Quebec army. The rumours that periodically rippled through the sprawling Crown Point encampment were contradictory and far from optimistic. In hopes of filling the intelligence void, on 7 and 8 August Amherst sent out two scouting parties with despatches for Wolfe. Each was to take a different route across country to Quebec. As Amherst told Gage: 'I doubt not but I shall by one avenue or the other, succeed in acquainting Mr Wolfe of the operations on this side, and that I may soon get information of his progress, from which my motions here must be guided.'[48] The first party eventually reached Wolfe – albeit only after a tortuous trek through the Maine wilderness. But on 24 August the second was intercepted *en route* by Abenaki Indians from the notorious mission village of St Francis, south of the St Lawrence and some twenty miles from Trois Rivières. Amherst's despatches for Wolfe were swallowed before their contents could be ascertained, but the Abenaki recovered tin canisters containing a cache of personal letters from officers at Crown Point to their friends in Wolfe's army. These divulged that 'Mr Amherst's operations were, henceforward, to depend on the success Mr Wolf should meet with before Quebec'; days later, deserters from Crown Point also claimed that Amherst now intended to confine his campaign to repairing forts Carillon and St Frédéric.[49]

Amherst was wary of advancing further into the enemy's territory until he knew of Wolfe's fate. If Quebec's attackers had been rebuffed, he could expect to encounter not Bourlamaque's puny corps but the united force of Canada. Whilst awaiting the clarification he needed, Amherst preferred to stay put at Crown Point, building his fort and ships – but doing absolutely nothing to maintain pressure upon the enemy. Amherst's reluctance to risk what he had already won was understandable, but his passivity failed utterly to reflect the spirit of his original orders from Pitt, which had urged him to *attack* Montreal or Quebec; nor did it honour his own repeated promises to Wolfe.

Amherst's inactivity is all the harder to excuse because it was obvious that his own swift advance had resulted from Wolfe's efforts at Quebec. This point was not lost upon his men. Writing on 6 August, one officer in the Black Watch – a regiment that had suffered fifty per cent casualties during its furious assault upon Ticonderoga in July 1758 – attributed the painless conquest of both that fortress and Crown Point to 'Mr Wolfe for the diversion he makes'; without him, 'there would have been a tough piece of work of it'. The army surgeon Richard Huck likewise believed that the French only withdrew from Ticonderoga because they were 'hard pushed at Quebec'. Indeed, Amherst's New York provincials were now beginning to murmur that if Wolfe failed, it would be the fault of their army. Even Amherst's own *aide-de-camp*, Captain James Abercrombie, was scathing of his chief's defensive mentality, which appeared to broadcast that he was ready to dig in for the winter. Should Bourlamaque grasp that fact, he could release troops capable of tipping the balance against Wolfe. If no new effort was made to pin down Canada's forces, Abercrombie warned, and so 'prevent the whole from opposing the main object', then Wolfe could justly claim that he had not received the support he was entitled to.[50]

During August, in a bid to break the continuing stalemate, Wolfe resorted to a strategy that he had long contemplated: the systematic devastation of the countryside around Quebec. This scorched earth policy was born of Wolfe's frustration at his own lack of headway, and his increasing anger at the enemy's failure to abide by what he regarded as acceptable codes of conduct.

Whilst still on passage to Nova Scotia from England, Wolfe had made Amherst a stern promise. If, despite his best efforts, Quebec refused to surrender, he proposed 'to set the town on fire with shells, to destroy the harvest, houses and cattle, both above and below, to send off as many Canadians as possible to Europe, and to leave famine and desolation behind' him.[51] Wolfe had lost little time in incinerating Quebec, but, as he explained to Pitt, the methodical ravaging of the countryside that began in August was a last resort – only implemented because milder measures had failed.

When he first arrived before Quebec, Wolfe had issued a proclamation, in French, which was nailed to the door of the church at Beaumont. Mingling dire threats with offers of fair treatment, this was an unsubtle attempt to persuade the Canadian *habitants* to remain neutral during the coming campaign. The 'unparalleled barbarities' visited by the French upon the frontiers of Britain's North American colonies gave ample justification to take the 'bitterest revenge', Wolfe pronounced. But, he added: 'Britons breathe higher sentiments of humanity, and listen to the merciful dictates of the Christian religion.' Provided the local populace took no part 'in the great contest' between Great Britain and France, they would be permitted to 'remain unmolested on their lands, inhabit their houses, and enjoy their religion in security'. If, however, through 'a vain obstinacy and misguided valour', they took up arms, then they must expect to see their homes, churches and harvest destroyed, with the inevitable consequence that their families would 'perish by the most dismal want and famine' during the coming winter.[52]

As Wolfe knew only too well, every adult male in Canada was obliged by law to perform militia service. Those who heeded his manifesto would inevitably incur the wrath of their own government. If Wolfe's proclamation was anything other than a wildly optimistic ploy, intended to strip Quebec of the bulk of its defenders without firing a shot, then it carried more than a whiff of hypocrisy. Had the French invaded his native soil, Wolfe would have expected his own countrymen – whether redcoats or rustics – to fight to the death. An assumption that the Canadians would prove any less determined in defence of their homeland was one example of Wolfe's unswerving belief in the superiority of all things British that, whilst common enough amongst Georgian males of his background, inevitably strikes modern readers as pompous and arrogant.

In the event, the proclamation had not the slightest effect. Militiamen of all ages rallied to the defence of Quebec, whilst, as ordered, their families abandoned their homes to seek refuge in the woods, taking their livestock with them. Since the start of the campaign, scouts of rangers and light infantry from Wolfe's army had scoured the countryside. Besides gathering intelligence and lying in wait for the enemy's irregulars, they had rounded up cattle, hogs and sheep to augment the army's salt rations, and searched out the local women and children from their bolt holes. These civilians became hostages to guarantee the good treatment of British prisoners, who, Wolfe 'had reason to think', the French 'did not use very well'.[53]

Given the notorious breaches of the laws of war by France's Indian allies, Wolfe had some grounds for his concerns. After all, his own army included men who could testify to such cruelties from personal experience. Describing the infamous massacre at Fort William Henry two years before, one private in the 35th Foot remembered how, 'after an honourable capitulation they kill'd, scalp'd and took prisoners a great number of our men, and robb'd and stripp'd all the rest'. That bloody day was seared upon the battalion's collective memory. During a fierce skirmish near Quebec in early August 1759, the 35th's officers and sergeant-major recalled it to rally their men, crying out, 'my good boys, don't forget Fort William Henry'.[54]

Wolfe raised the same 'infraction', and the resentments it had caused, when he reproached Vaudreuil for using Indians. If, as an intercepted letter suggested, three captured British grenadiers were to be 'burnt alive' by the 'savages', then the severest reprisals would follow. Frenchmen, Canadians and Indians alike, all would be treated as 'a cruel and barbarous mob, thirsting for human blood'. Vaudreuil refused to be intimidated. None of Wolfe's 'menaces, invectives and accusations' would turn them into 'either cowards or barbarians', he declared. As for the three grenadiers, they had fared like all other prisoners taken by the Indians, being ransomed from their captors 'at considerable expense'. Turning to the French army's resort to tribal warriors, the governor-general merely shrugged: throughout the conflict, *both* sides had employed such allies whenever they could recruit them, and Wolfe's army was unusual in having none. French soldiers accepted the cruelties that inevitably resulted from such practices as 'the fortunes of war'.[55]

Wolfe's own policy of hunting down the militiamen's families, and then impounding them on board the fleet's transports drew bitter criticisms from the enemy. On 25 July, after Major Dalling marched a hefty haul of prisoners into camp, the French protested. As Knox noted, 'The Town-Major of Quebec, who came down with the last flag of truce, took upon him to reflect on our conduct in making so many captives among the old men, women, and children of the country.' The dismal plight of these 'wretched families' moved Knox to pity. He wrote:

> Though these acts of hostility may be warrantable by the laws of nations and rules of war, yet, as humanity is far from being incompatible with the character of a soldier, any man, who is possessed of the least share of it, cannot help sympathising with, and being sincerely affected at, the miseries of his fellow-creatures, even though his enemies.[56]

Neither was Wolfe immune to his prisoners' sufferings, and he took measures to minimize them. Although commending the effectiveness of Dalling's dragnet, he also issued orders that any pregnant or sickly women, or those with infants, should be immediately freed, whilst cows were to be set aside to provide milk for the young children.[57] This compassionate directive is revealing. It provides a striking contrast to Wolfe's bloodthirsty threats, suggesting that here, as elsewhere, his bark could be considerably worse than his bite.

As his first proclamation had proved futile, on 25 July Wolfe ordered a second to be posted. This warned that, unless the 'barbarities' of the Canadians and Indians ceased, he would 'burn and lay waste the country', sparing only places of worship. As Wolfe informed Pitt, besides punishing the Canadians 'for many insults offer'd to our people', this escalation aimed to provoke Montcalm 'to try the event of a battle to prevent the ravage'. The deadline for compliance was 10 August.[58]

Wolfe cannot have believed that this latest proclamation would be any more effective than the first. It is clear that he envisaged an extensive programme of devastation in any event, and before the time was up it had already begun. On 6 August, Captain Gorham and a detachment of 250 rangers, regular volunteers and marines moved downriver to burn the parish of St Paul's Bay, on the north shore opposite to Île aux Coudres. The pretext was the inhabitants' 'presumption' in firing upon the British invasion flotilla when it first moved up the St Lawrence; since then, they had continued to 'distress the shipping', and just two days before, Canadian prisoners had been taken loaded with ammunition for them.[59] Following a skirmish on the morning of 11 August, Gorham landed and torched the village, consuming 'about fifty fine houses and barns'. The captain then swept down the north bank to Mal Baye; this 'very pretty parish' was burned in its turn, and the few remaining inhabitants and their livestock herded off. Gorham's men now switched to the south shore, cutting a swathe through the parishes of St Anne and St Roch. The captain reported that they contained 'the largest farms and produce the greatest quantity of grain I have seen'. Buildings and crops alike went up in flames.[60]

Justified as retribution, Joseph Gorham's raid set the pattern for the coming weeks. Noting that the enemy had been observed readying rafts and fire ships, Wolfe assured Monckton that if 'any more fire attempts' were made, he would retaliate by burning all the houses from St Joachim up to the Montmorency River; and if Gorham returned in good time, he was to torch 'every house and hutt' between the Chaudière and Etchemin Rivers. All the habitations and barns from Monckton's camp down to the church of Beaumont were also to be consumed. Nine days later, after Indians scalped four straggling sailors on the Isle of Orleans, Wolfe repeated his directive, adding: 'It is to very little purpose to withhold the rod, seeing they are incorrigible.'[61] These orders were implemented with thoroughness: on 19 August, a British deserter told how Wolfe was 'sending parties in all directions to burn all the buildings and lay waste the country'. August 21–24 were characterized by almost continual rain, but, as a French diarist recorded, this failed to stop the British burning everywhere.[62] Wolfe's scorched earth campaign reached a fiery climax at the end of the month when he despatched Major George Scott, with all the army's rangers, and several hundred redcoats, on a prolonged downriver foray 'to burn all the country from Camariska to the Point of Levy'. Scott's men embarked on 1 September. They were gone for more than two weeks, and in a fifty-mile sweep along the south shore burned 998 'good buildings'.[63]

In all, the New England newspapers estimated, Wolfe's raiders had destroyed 'upwards of 1400' farmhouses: it would take half a century for the ravaged region to recover. The 'great havock' wrought by the rangers was blamed upon the enemy's obstinacy in ignoring Wolfe's manifestos.[64] For the inhabitants of Britain's North American colonies, who were accustomed to lurid tales of French and Indian depredations upon their own frontier settlements, this was a just vengeance. Back in London, Wolfe's policy was viewed differently. When his despatch to Pitt was published in the London Gazette, the paragraph in which he explained his decision to lay waste the country was suppressed as unsuitable for public consumption.[65]

Wolfe's strategy continues to fuel accusations of unwarranted harshness, and his modern critics have been quick to detect a link between his 'campaign of terror' during the summer of 1759, and that inflicted upon the Scottish Highlands by his former commander 'Butcher' Cumberland. French-Canadian historians have been particularly unforgiving, accusing Wolfe of 'gratuitous' cruelty and comparing the devastation to that perpetrated in the Balkans during the 1990s.[66] Yet such emotive responses are misleading. As at Gaspé during the previous autumn, the systematic destruction of property was not accompanied by a wanton taking of life. Gorham's rangers were not the Waffen SS, and, for all the undoubted hardship and misery their activities caused, Wolfe's raiding parties left no Oradour-Sur-Glane in their wake. And although historians have not always done so, it is important to draw a distinction between that summer's undeniably vicious guerrilla warfare, which pitched British light infantry and American rangers against Canadian militia and Ottawa and Abenaki warriors, and Wolfe's treatment of the region's civilian population. Orders issued in late July repeated the earlier directive that women and children were 'not to be molested on any account whatsoever'; despite speculation to the contrary, there is no evidence that they were deliberately disregarded.[67]

Professional soldiers like Knox plainly found the consequences of Wolfe's methods hard to stomach, but nonetheless conceded that they abided by the contemporary laws of war. The recent history of Europe offered ample precedents. For example, during the winter of 1688–89, the armies of Louis XIV had brought desolation to the Rhineland, obliterating entire villages and towns. In 1704, after John Churchill, Duke of Marlborough and Prince Eugène of Savoy joined forces in Bavaria, they had begun to systematically plunder and burn the countryside: like Wolfe before Quebec, their object was to goad the enemy into a decisive battle.[68]

Marlborough and Eugène duly reaped a victory at Blenheim, but Wolfe's campaign of devastation was barren of results. The smoke that coiled balefully up from both banks of the St Lawrence, tainting the air with an acrid tang, failed to lure Montcalm from his entrenchments to halt the harrying. Neither did it achieve its object of curbing the savagery of the *petite guerre* that so enraged Wolfe. Scarcely a night passed without the Indians and Canadians lurking about his outposts, 'watching an opportunity to surprise and murder'. As Wolfe recognized, the ruthlessness was increasingly mutual, with 'very little quarter given on either side'.[69]

The frequent clashes between rival scouting parties and patrols followed the grim creed of American wilderness warfare. Inconvenient prisoners or wounded enemies risked being 'knocked on the head' with tomahawk or musket butt, and the lifting of scalps was commonplace. In his own official orders for 27 July, Wolfe had banned 'the inhuman practice of scalping' – except when the enemy were 'Indians, or Canadians dressed like Indians'. This last clause invited broad interpretation – not least because a subsequent order placed a tempting bounty of five guineas upon every 'Indian' scalp.[70] Captain Alexander Montgomery of the 43rd Foot invoked it to justify the cold-blooded killing and scalping of the priest of St Joachim and more than a score of his flock, after they were surrounded and persuaded to lay down their arms near St Anne on 23 August. This massacre was exceptional enough to be reported with disgust and indignation by young Ensign Malcolm Fraser, who had personally promised quarter to two of the captives and who could find 'no excuse for such an unparalleled piece of barbarity'. Indeed, it is tempting to dismiss Montgomery as the kind of brutal maverick to be found in any army, in any era. But although it exasperated Wolfe, Montgomery's mercilessness was not without motive. According to Sergeant Thompson of Fraser's Highlanders, the captain's brother had been killed by the Canadians and his body 'cruelly mangled by the savages'. Montgomery's 'resentment' found expression in his bloody act of vengeance.[71] Indeed, this single most notorious episode in the campaign's smouldering guerrilla conflict was just another testament to the brutalizing influence of North American wilderness warfare.

The methodical torching of the hamlets lining the banks of the St Lawrence was one consequence of Wolfe's inability to bring his enemy to battle; another was the collapse of his own precarious health. Since first arriving before Quebec, Wolfe had been plagued by painful and dispiriting ailments – the gravel, rheumatism and dysentery. They sapped his strength, and shortened his temper, but had not stopped him from performing his duties with energy and resolution. Wolfe had pushed himself hard, becoming a familiar figure throughout the army as he flitted between its far-flung camps. As Lieutenant Knox observed, no man could have displayed 'greater activity'.[72] His leadership was conspicuous, not only in combat situations but wherever his redcoats needed encouragement amidst the everyday dangers and hardships of the siege. Wolfe had repeatedly reconnoitred Montcalm's positions for a weak point, and, in hopes of extracting every last grain of intelligence, had even insisted upon interrogating all enemy deserters in person.[73] But in the last week of August the strain finally took its toll: Wolfe's health broke down totally and he was obliged to take to his bed.

Wolfe described his illness as a fever, attributing it to the 'extreme heat of the weather in August, and a good deal of fatigue'.[74] Early that month, Knox had noted that the troops were beginning to grow sickly, their 'fluxes and fevers' typical of the illnesses that inevitably afflicted soldiers in the field. It is possible that Wolfe fell victim to these prevailing distempers, but the timing of his physical collapse suggests that the campaign's mounting frustrations and anxieties – not least the likelihood of ignominious failure – also played their part. Whatever the precise cause, on 22 August, a doleful Knox reported the consequences:

It is with the greatest concern to the whole army, that we are now informed of our amiable General's being very ill of a slow fever: the soldiers lament him exceedingly, and seemed apprehensive of this event, before we were ascertained of it, by his not visiting this camp [Point Lévis] for several days past.

Two days later, when Knox crossed the St Lawrence to wait upon Wolfe at the small house that served for his headquarters, to receive orders for Monckton's brigade, 'the general was so ill above stairs as not to be able to come to dinner'. This was plainly the fever's crisis. Next day, 25 August, Knox noted that Wolfe was starting to recover, 'to the inconceivable joy of the whole army'.[75] Whilst now apparently out of immediate danger, Wolfe remained too weak to return to duty; deserters who arrived in Montcalm's camp on 29 August reported that he had been obliged to stay abed for the previous six days. It was the 31st before Wolfe was back on his feet, although even now he was still far from fit. Five days later, Admiral Saunders reported to Pitt that his young colleague remained 'greatly out of order'.[76]

Yet it was plain that the crisis of the campaign was fast approaching. Major-General James Wolfe would need all of his ebbing strength to surmount it.

9

The Heights of Abraham

Let loyal subjects fill their bowls,
And sing with me, I pray,
How General Wolfe at Quebec town,
The French did kill and slay

Anon, 'A Song on the Taking of Quebec'

Wolfe's fever marked the personal nadir of his campaign. Yet it was
to prove a turning point. On 27 August 1759, whilst still ill and 'indis-
posed', Wolfe sent his brigadiers a memorandum.[1] This requested them
to 'consult together for the publick utility and advantage; and to consider of the best method of attacking the enemy'. Wolfe included his
own opinion that any attack should focus upon the enemy's army, rather
than Quebec, and proposed three potential plans, all of them aimed at
Montcalm's sprawling Beauport position. Two of these were essentially
similar to that which had already misfired on 31 July; although differing
in detail, both proposed attacks across the ford below the Montmorency Falls, co-ordinated with landings from the St Lawrence River. The
other, which headed Wolfe's list of options, included a novel feature: a
large detachment would undertake a lengthy, looping approach march,
taking a day and a night. Crossing the Montmorency River at *another*
ford some nine miles up, the troops would aim to arrive at Beauport
before daylight and then fall upon the rear of the enemy's position. 'If
such a detach[men]t penetrates on their entrenchments', Wolfe wrote,
'and the rest of the troops are ready, the consequence is plain.'

On the morning of 28 August, Townshend and Murray joined
Monckton at Point Lévis, and all three met with Admiral Saunders
aboard the *Stirling Castle*. Next day, the brigadiers conferred again,
compiling and signing a joint response to Wolfe's memorandum. In

measured language, they unanimously rejected all of his proposals out-right.[2] Given the strength of the enemy's encampment ranged between the St Charles and Montmorency rivers, they argued, the success of any attack there was 'very doubtfull', whilst the difficulty of attacking via the ford below the Falls, and from boats lacking the close covering fire of warships, was all too clear from recent experience. As for Wolfe's proposal to march through the woods to the upper fording place, that was equally hazardous, being 'exposed to certain discovery, and to the disadvantage of a continual wood fight'. Above all, even if it *were* pos-sible to 'get footing' at Beauport, Montcalm would retain the option of falling back towards Quebec and disputing any attempt to cross the River St Charles.

Having dismissed Wolfe's plans, the brigadiers outlined their own:

> We therefore are of opinion that the most probable method of striking an effectual blow, is to bring the troops to the south shore, and to direct the operations above the town: when we establish ourselves on the north shore, the French general must fight us on our own terms. We shall be betwixt him and his provisions, and betwixt him and their army opposing General Amherst.

If Montcalm came out to fight, and was defeated in a pitched bat-tle, they added, then 'Quebec and probably all Canada' would fall – a far greater result than could be expected from another attack at Beauport. In addition, the inevitable weakening of the Beauport posi-tion, as Montcalm shifted forces to meet the upriver menace, could only enhance the prospects of a strike there. The brigadiers did not presume to advise whether their plan should be implemented immediately, or postponed to allow the continuing devastation of the colony and to favour the operations of Amherst's forces, which they now believed to be advancing 'into the heart of the country'. It was clear to them, however, that the commander-in-chief's progress would continue to 'depend upon the detention of the greatest part of the enemy's force on this side, for the defence of their capital'. Whatever Wolfe decided, they assured him, he would find them 'most hearty and zealous in the execution of his orders'.

Along with their reply, the brigadiers enclosed a suggested 'Plan of Operations'.[3] This advised that the camp at Montmorency should be evacuated without delay. Save for 1200 men to secure the bases on the

Isle of Orleans and at Point Lévis, and another 1000 for guarding the batteries at Pointe aux Pères, the rest of the army should shift to the south shore, above the Etchemin River. The brigadiers were confident that, under cover of darkness, an unopposed landing could be made anywhere within a twelve-mile zone stretching from 'the heights of St John' (possibly St John Baptiste), down to the Cap Rouge River. A 'proper place' for the enterprise, they advised, was 'half a league' above the Cap Rouge River. Under the brigadiers' plan, an initial landing force of between 2000 and 2500 men would disembark from the boats of the fleet, promptly backed by a second wave waiting aboard ships stationed nearby. In this way, they claimed, some 4000 troops could be landed during a single tide, all 'without the least jealousy given to the enemy'.

By 30 August Wolfe had received the brigadiers' answer. That day he wrote to Admiral Saunders: 'The generals seem to think alike as to the operations; I therefore join with them, and perhaps we may find some opportunity to strike a blow.' Although Wolfe fell into line with the brigadiers' recommendation, he did so with reluctance, and only acquiesced because his continuing ill health prevented him from executing his own favoured plan. As he told Saunders, this was 'of too desperate a nature to order others to execute'.[4]

Several of Wolfe's biographers have suggested that the 'desperate' plan in question involved nothing less than a landing at the Anse au Foulon, just one and a half miles from Quebec. It has even been argued that the proposals outlined in Wolfe's memorandum to his brigadiers were never intended to be taken seriously, but were put forward under the assumption that they would inevitably be rejected as unworkable, so obliging the brigadiers to advocate the only other option – a move upriver – and thereby implement the very strategy that Wolfe himself secretly preferred.[5]

It is certainly true that Wolfe had always appreciated the vulnerability of Quebec's logistical lifeline, and the desirability of landing on the north shore above the town. He had spent much of July searching for a foothold there, whilst Murray's August raid had tested its defences at length. And if Samuel Holland's memory was accurate, Wolfe had long since recognized the potential of the Foulon, keeping it in mind as a risky, last-ditch landing site if all else failed. But any large-scale

disembarkation upon the north shore demanded the element of surprise, and that depended upon naval control of the St Lawrence above
Quebec. When Wolfe drew up his memorandum, the Royal Navy had
not yet achieved such dominion. Indeed, so vulnerable was the small
British squadron left upriver after Murray's expedition, that Governor-
General Vaudreuil approved a scheme to reactivate the French frigates,
and descend the river to eliminate it in a surprise attack. Nearly five
hundred sailors were withdrawn from Quebec to crew their old vessels.
Braving the British batteries at Pointe aux Pères, and the guns of the
Sutherland off Pointe-aux-Trembles, on 27 August they finally reached
Cap Sante, above the Jacques Cartier River, where the frigates were
then moored.[6] That morning, the passage of some forty boats and nine
floating batteries, which were helped on their way by the flood tide and
a rare north-easterly wind, was noted with trepidation by Lieutenant-
Colonel Young, who had been left upriver aboard the *Sutherland* with
his Royal Americans. An edgy Young reported this ominous development to Murray: 'Captain Rous imagines they are gone up to assist the
enemy's ships in coming down,' he warned. Young planned to put his
men ashore, where they could better defend themselves; but, with provisions and ammunition running low, he feared for the fate of his isolated
command should Rous 'be obliged to run down the river' before the
French frigates. Having experienced the depredations of the Indians at
Fort William Henry, Young had some cause for nervousness.[7]

But the bold French plan was abandoned after the balance of naval
power in the upper river finally began to tilt in favour of the British.
On that same night of 27–28 August, five more of Saunders's ships
– the *Lowestoft* frigate and *Hunter* sloop, two armed transports and
another vessel – passed above Quebec despite the best efforts of the
town's batteries to stop them. As the admiral reported to Pitt, this was
their fourth attempt 'to gain their passage', and they only succeeded
now thanks to the same easterly winds that had sped the French naval
gunners up the river.[8]

When the brigadiers met with Saunders on 28 August therefore, the
strategic situation had just undergone a dramatic change; their proposal to transfer the operations upriver exploited this. But Wolfe wrote
his memorandum *before* this important development, when his gaze
remained focused upon the Beauport shore. Rather than the lunge at

the Foulon that his admirers have deduced, in reality Wolfe's 'own plan' was the first of those he had proposed to the brigadiers – the attempt to surprise the Beauport camp by an extensive approach march. Any doubt in the matter is removed by the detailed testimony contained in the journal kept by the anonymous staff officer.[9] He reported how Wolfe had explained his preferred plan to the brigadiers and proposed its execution to one of them. The scheme clearly rested upon careful reconnaissance and methodical planning. It may have originated in information supplied by a deserter – a Pennsylvanian captured at Fort Duquesne during the previous summer, and since obliged to enlist in the French forces – who arrived on 28 July with intelligence of alternative fords over the Montmorency. This was news, as Townshend had noted, that Wolfe 'seem'd to like much'.[10] The general had since sent a trusted ranger officer, Captain Moses Hazen, with a 'French' deserter (who may have been the Pennsylvanian) to scout the roads leading through the woods to the uppermost ford. Hazen found the passage unguarded and subsequently probed 'very near to Beauport'. Based upon this first-hand intelligence, Wolfe had 'form'd the design to fall on the back of the enemy's regular troops which were encamp'd there'. It involved two night marches to minimize the risk of detection, culminating in a surprise attack at dawn. The plan would have been implemented by a picked detachment: the Louisbourg Grenadiers, the light infantry companies of the battalions, the 28th and 58th Foot, three hundred of Fraser's Highlanders, plus all of the army's volunteers. This crack force had been rigorously trained by Wolfe himself, and 'constantly practic'd to move in the woods'. Given the extensive groundwork upon which his favoured plan rested, its blunt rejection by the brigadiers was mortifying. The same staff officer reported: 'I afterwards heard Mr Wolfe lament his want of health that he cou'd not execute his plan saying "twas the only project that had any pith and marrow in it".'

The disappointing outcome of his 'consultation' with the brigadiers left Wolfe dejected. Still convalescing from his illness, he was now more despondent than ever about the outcome of the campaign. When Saunders asked him to modify his despatches for Pitt, which the admiral felt placed undue blame for the failure of the Montmorency attack upon the difficulties encountered by the navy, Wolfe responded with weary resignation. 'I am sensible of my own errors in the course of the campaign; see clearly wherein I have been deficient; and think a little more or less blame, to a man that must necessarily be ruined, of little or no consequence,' he wrote.[11] Next day, when Wolfe sent a last letter to his mother, he was no more sanguine. 'The enemy puts nothing to risk, and I can't, in conscience, put the whole army to risk', he explained. 'My antagonist has wisely shut himself up in inaccessible entrenchments, so that I can't get at him without spilling a torrent of blood, and that per- haps to little purpose.'[12] Indeed, whilst he had accepted the brigadiers' plan, it is clear that Wolfe had no faith in its ability to deliver a decisive victory in the few weeks that remained before the army and fleet must decamp from Quebec.

But the easterlies still blew, and with them the strategic situation continued to swing in the invaders' favour: at midnight on 31 August, the *Seahorse* frigate, two armed sloops and a pair of provision-laden cats successfully passed into the upper river. Now at last, a naval volunteer aboard Saunders's flagship reported, there was a 'tolerable fleet above' Quebec.[13]

Now recovered sufficiently to resume formal command of his army, Wolfe lost no time in implementing the first phase of the brigadiers' plan of operations, the evacuation from Montmorency. As Wolfe's strength gradually returned, so did something of his old spirit. The withdrawal was an open admission of failure, but it might be turned to advantage nevertheless if that 'wary old fellow' Montcalm could be tempted to intervene. Most of the British artillery, the soldiers' wives, the sick, the wounded and the heavy baggage were evacuated by the morning of 1 September. The battalions remained behind in hopes of a final confrontation with their enemies across the Montmorency River. That night their tents were struck, creating the illusion that they too had stolen away with the dark. The troops meanwhile were ordered into the redoubts and houses, under strict instructions to lie low and keep silent. The men of Lascelles's 47th Foot were told to load their muskets with two balls, ready to rise up and unleash a double dose of lead against any of the enemy foolish enough to fall into the snare. But the canny Montcalm sniffed a trap and refused to snaffle up Wolfe's bait. The same ruse was repeated the following night, but with no more success. French reluctance to cross the Montmorency was only heightened by increased activity amongst Saunders's vessels, whilst the Royal Navy's ploy in anchoring half a dozen buoys off the Beauport shore, as if in preparation for another assault there, was taken seriously.[14]

On the morning of 3 September the final withdrawal began. At the official signal – the torching of the large barn in front of Brigadier Townshend's command post – the last four redcoat battalions filed out of their fortifications, set them ablaze, and marched down to the beach with drums beating in defiance. Embarkation under the very noses of the enemy is a notoriously tricky business, yet Wolfe was unconcerned: on the contrary, he continued to hope that the enemy would venture to attack him. Low tide had exposed a wide strand: this formed 'a very advantageous field for regular troops', commanded by the guns of the *Porcupine* sloop. The French wisely kept their distance; and, although their batteries cannonaded the British boats as they rowed the redcoats across to the points of Orleans and Lévis, not a man was lost.[15]

The withdrawal from Montmorency was a model operation of its kind, conducted with coolness, skill and professionalism. But for Wolfe, the loss of a position that had only been established by immense toil, and then maintained for eight weeks at a heavy toll in killed and wounded, was a bitter draught to swallow. Since arriving before Quebec, his army had suffered some 850 casualties. Reckoning every available 'fighting man', including the general officers' servants and 'persons attending the sick', the regulars and rangers were now just 7500 strong.[16]

Wolfe completed his celebrated despatch to William Pitt on the eve of the final evacuation of the Montmorency camp; unsurprisingly, its tone was far from buoyant. The lengthy report provided a detailed, frank and lucid account of the campaign, but it offered precious little hope of a victorious conclusion. Indeed, Wolfe faced 'such a choice of difficulties' that he found himself 'at a loss how to determine'. Having already failed in one set-piece attack upon the Beauport lines, he was reluctant to squander his soldiers' lives without at least some prospect of success. Whilst Wolfe acknowledged that his country's affairs deserved the most vigorous measures, he believed that the 'courage of a handful of brave men, should be exerted only, where there is some hope of a favourable event'. Wolfe's pessimism was, however, tempered by a stoic determination that was destined to strike a chord with newspaper readers already familiar with the deeds of Spartans, Thebans and Romans: despite all the discouragements, Wolfe assured Pitt that such of the campaign as remained would be employed, as far as his abilities allowed, 'for the honour of his majesty, and the interest of the nation'.

Wolfe now fixed his headquarters at Point Lévis. He had barely done so when an exhausted and bedraggled group of rangers arrived in camp bearing despatches from Amherst. Ensign Benjamin Hutchins and his three companions had followed a rough and roundabout route from Boston by way of the Kennebec River, reaching Wolfe's army on 4 September. For all their privations, Amherst's letter, which was dated at Crown Point on 7 August, did little more than confirm what Wolfe already knew – that Ticonderoga, Crown Point and Niagara were all in British hands. Amherst repeated his familiar pledge to do everything possible for 'effectually reducing Canada', but said nothing of how his own operations would achieve that objective. Yet his closing rallying cry – 'Now is the time!' – raised hopes that he must surely be on his way. According to one letter sent from Point Lévis that same day, it was widely credited that Amherst's army was now within just a week's march of Wolfe's, so spreading 'a universal joy throughout the whole camp'. Before the arrival of Hutchins and his haggard comrades there had been a growing recognition that Quebec's conquest might require a further campaign; but since their appearance, the same correspondent noted, scarcely anyone doubted that the 'finishing stroke' was imminent.[17]

Wolfe himself had no cause to suspect that Amherst was doing anything but his utmost to harass New France's defenders on the Lake Champlain front. It was as well that he did not know the truth. Far from advancing against Isle-aux-Noix, Amherst was still stalled at the southern end of Lake Champlain. As he awaited the completion of his freshwater fleet, the commander-in-chief increasingly looked to Brigadier Gage's western army to maintain pressure upon Canada. But, despite Amherst's express orders to advance against La Galette, Gage showed no sign of moving from Oswego. There, Sir William Johnson, Britain's superintendent of the Northern Indians, likewise urged him to attack, but the brigadier stayed put. Long since wary of 'running his head against a wall, or attempting impossibilities', by 6 September Gage was convinced that Amherst had now 'missed the opportunity of favouring General Wolfe', and would advance no further. Seeing no reason why his own, much smaller, army should behave any more aggressively, he contented himself with consolidating the forts at Oswego and Niagara.[18]

By early September 1759, therefore, Britain's original three-pronged offensive against Canada had dwindled to a single thrust: Wolfe alone was actively pushing home the attack. Growing disquiet that he was bearing a disproportionate share of the campaign's burden now surfaced openly in the colonial press. A letter from Crown Point, which reported the common view that any further advance by Amherst's 'grand army' would depend upon 'General Wolfe's success', prompted a critical editorial in several newspapers: in contrast to both Amherst and Gage, who faced little real opposition, Wolfe was grappling with fully three-quarters of 'the force of Canada', they emphasized. Surely, only a diversionary attack to split the enemy could give the young general a fighting chance of achieving his objective?[19]

Despite the ebullient tone of letters from the St Lawrence that appeared in New York and Boston newspapers, the 'joy' that followed the arrival of Amherst's despatches to Wolfe was not 'universal'. For Brigadier Townshend, the messengers brought bleak tidings. Although Ticonderoga had been taken in exchange for a scant handful of British slain, they numbered his younger brother Roger, who had been serving as Amherst's adjutant-general. George loved Roger dearly and the 'melancholy news' of his death threw him into black depression. The brigadier's mood had not lightened two days later, when he wrote to his wife, Charlotte.[20] For Townshend, the inglorious and indecisive campaign on the St Lawrence was distressingly different from those he had known as a young *aide-de-camp* in Flanders. Disillusioned and homesick, he now bitterly regretted his decision to lobby Pitt for an active service posting. Townshend was tired of being berated by the disgruntled Canadian women who continued to be brought captive into camp, and sickened by the campaign's spiralling brutality. As he put it: 'Our unequal force has reduced our operations to a sceene [sic] of skirmishing, cruelty and devastation. It is war of the worst shape.' The brigadier continued:

> Gen. Wolf's health is but very bad. His generalship in my poor opinion – is not a bit better, this only between us. He never consulted any of us until

the latter end of August, so that we have nothing to answer for I hope as to
the success of this Campaign ...

In his view, the expedition was now all but over. He thanked God that
another month must surely bring it to an end.

Townshend's impassioned letter is often cited as evidence for the
dismal depths to which his relations with Wolfe had sunk. Less emphasis has been placed upon what it reveals about his own state of mind.
Heartsick and apathetic, Townshend clearly expected the campaign to
end in failure. Intriguingly, there is nothing to suggest that he had the
slightest confidence in the plan that he had so recently formulated with
his fellow brigadiers. Rather than the dogged pursuit of victory to the
bitter end, Townshend's overriding concern was to return home to his
family – hopefully with his reputation intact. He drew some comfort
from the knowledge that the blame for the disaster that now seemed
inevitable must fall elsewhere, upon the sickly James Wolfe.

On the evening of 5 September, the British began their move upriver.
Brigadier Murray marched with four battalions from Point Lévis.
Between the Etchemin and Chaudière, they embarked aboard Rear-
Admiral Holmes's fleet. This was now formidable, consisting, in the
admiral's words, of 'five sail of men of war and about eleven transports';
it was sufficient to carry not merely a detachment of raiders, such as
Murray had led upriver during the previous month, but a powerful
landing force capable of meeting Montcalm's army. Next afternoon,
Monckton and Townshend embarked with another three battalions.
Wolfe joined them that evening, having left Guy Carleton with the
2/60th and some marines at the Point of Orleans, and Burton, at the
head of the 48th Foot, plus detachments from other battalions and more
marines, to secure the camp at Point Lévis and the batteries at Pointe
aux Pères. That night the ships were carried up on the flood tide and
anchored off Cap Rouge. Morale amongst the rank and file was high:
'The army in great spirits,' noted a volunteer in Captain Fraser's company of light infantry.[21]

As the British shifted upriver, the French adjusted their dispositions accordingly. No longer threatened from across the Montmorency,
Montcalm switched manpower from his left flank to his right. Bougainville's command was reinforced with more elite troops, and nearly all
of the remaining Indians. Including the guard posts strung out from

Sillery up to Trois Rivières, it now numbered perhaps 3000 men; of these, about half formed a mobile strike force.[22] With his own head-quarters fixed at Cap Rouge, Bougainville was well placed to counter any assault upon that sector. As Townshend noted on 7 September, although the bay there was 'a very good place for landing', the enemy had taken measures to safeguard it. Besides six or eight floating batter-ies clustered around the mouth of the Cap Rouge River, 'great numbers of Canadians and some regulars' were throwing up a breastwork; they were soon joined by La Roche-Beaucour's ubiquitous troopers. Lieuten-ant Knox observed that the defenders were not only 'numerous' but also 'very alert, parading and counter-marching on the heights in their rear, and their breast-works'.[23]

Undeterred by all this defensive activity, Wolfe and his brigadiers met aboard the *Sutherland*. The available battalions were reorganized into brigades and ordered to prepare for a landing that night. Fifteen hundred men were issued with provisions for two days and warned to make ready to enter the flat-bottomed boats. That afternoon, they climbed into their landing craft and Saunders ordered the *Seahorse* and *Lowestoft* into Cap Rouge Bay to engage the floating batteries and cannonade the enemy ashore. But the turning tide stymied the frigates' efforts to sail to close quarters and the landing was called off. For all the breezy confidence of the brigadiers' 'Plan of Operations', when put to the test, their own recommended landing zone offered no easy path ashore.[24]

It was necessary to try elsewhere. That evening, Wolfe and the brigadiers went further up river to reconnoitre the shoreline as far as Pointe-aux-Trembles, where Murray had been rebuffed a month before. Plans were laid for a mock attack there: the *Hunter* sloop, along with two transports full of Royal Americans and light infantry, was to move up with the flood tide on the evening of 8 September. They would make 'an appearance of intending to land', then drop down again with the ebb. Meanwhile, the real attack was to be launched, by 1500 men under Monckton and Murray, on the morning of 9 September. Once this first wave was ashore it would be reinforced by more troops, including those returning from the upriver diversion. Wolfe himself had 'fixed upon a place a little below Pointe-aux-Trembles' for the landing.[25] The location was not specified in the orders, but it was probably near St Augustin;

this fell within the geographic boundaries set out in the brigadiers' 'proposal', and there is nothing to suggest than any of them disapproved
of Wolfe's choice.

As it had now rained heavily for more than a day, however, the scheduled attack was cancelled. Crowded, sodden and miserable aboard their
transports, that evening half of the troops were landed on the south
shore at St Nicholas, to stretch their cramped limbs and dry out their
equipment. The dreary weather was not merely a source of discomfort
and potential illness amongst the redcoats. As Wolfe observed to the
Northern Secretary, Robert D'Arcy, Earl of Holderness, in a despatch
that reveals his awareness of the St Lawrence's hydrological eccentrici-
ties, the rain only exacerbated the violence of the ebb tide; the fact that
this could run for eight hours above the town lost 'an infinite deal of
time in every operation on the water'. Wolfe's own mood matched the
weather: although now sufficiently recovered from his illness 'to do
business', his constitution was 'entirely ruined, without the consolation
of having done any considerable service to the state, or without any
prospect of it.' [26]

That same day, 9 September, whilst the rain continued to put
a damper upon operations, Wolfe took a decision that would have
dramatic consequences. According to the junior staff officer whose
journal provides so many insights into the Quebec campaign, Wolfe
boarded a schooner and went reconnoitring downriver, keeping close
to the north shore. This little craft was named *The Terror of France*.
Three days earlier, under her master 'one Riddle', she had cheered the
entire British task force by braving the batteries of Quebec to pass the
town in broad daylight and in the teeth of the wind, before cheekily
firing her puny swivel guns in salute to Rear-Admiral Holmes.[27] It is
possible that the schooner's provocative name and recent antics both
appealed to Wolfe; it is beyond doubt that what he observed from her
deck during his downriver trip caused him to jettison the brigadiers'
favoured 'Plan of Operations' as decisively as they had spurned his
own memorandum to them. As Wolfe's chief engineer Major Mackellar reported, the general 'found another place more to his mind, and
laid aside all further thoughts of that at [near] Pointe-aux-Trembles'.[28]
Wolfe's health remained far from robust, but his old independence had
now re-asserted itself: there were to be no more 'consultations' with his

truculent subordinates. Wolfe had regained the initiative and, for what was left of his life, he would keep it.

On 10 September, the day after his lone reconnaissance, Wolfe returned downriver, this time accompanied by brigadiers Monckton and Townshend, Admiral Holmes, Major Mackellar, Colonel Howe and Captain Chads of the *Vesuvius*. Chads, who had worked closely with Wolfe during the attack of 31 July, was regulating officer for the landing craft; as such he was a crucial figure, and over the next few days would shoulder daunting responsibilities. According to Mackellar, the party reconnoitred the spot that Wolfe had now 'fixed upon'. This was none other than the Anse au Foulon. From their vantage point at Gorham's Post, just below the mouth of the Etchemin River, they focused their telescopes upon Wolfe's chosen objective. Mackellar, with his engineer's eye for ground, observed that the 'bank' – or cliff – above the Foulon was extremely steep and woody. Because of its natural strengths, only a single picket of about a hundred men guarded the narrow path running up from the shoreline, although as an added precaution, this had been broken up and barricaded. But, as Mackellar noted, about two hundred yards to the right 'there appeared to be a slope in the bank, which was thought might answer the purpose' and give access to the heights. Indeed, the major added: 'These circumstances and the distance of the place from succours seemed to promise a fair chance of success.'[29]

Not everyone on the reconnaissance agreed with this optimistic analysis. Admiral Holmes later noted sourly that Wolfe's 'alteration of the Plan of Operations was not, I believe approved of by many, beside himself'. Holmes pointed out that having rejected an attack upon that very sector 'when the first ships passed the town', and it was 'entirely defenceless and unguarded', Wolfe had revived the scheme at a time 'when it was highly improbable he should succeed'.[30]

Eminent historians have echoed Holmes's criticisms. Compared to a landing higher upriver, where the shoreline was more accessible, they argue, an attack at the cliff-backed Foulon introduced an unnecessary element of risk. Indeed, Wolfe's gambit rested upon two assumptions: that the Foulon would not be heavily defended; and that, once his troops were ashore, Montcalm would promptly pick up the gauntlet that he had thrown down, sallying out from his entrenchments to fight him. In addition, by seeking to place his army so close to Quebec's westward defences, Wolfe would fail to sever Montcalm's communications with Montreal completely. Besides the road that ran alongside the St Lawrence, there was another inland route; after leaving Quebec and crossing the River St Charles, this headed westward by way of Charlesbourg and Ancienne Lorette, keeping roughly parallel with the riverside route before intersecting with it some fifteen miles above Quebec. This not only provided a means of sidestepping any blocking force, it also gave Quebec's defenders an escape route in the event of defeat.[31]

Yet there were also cogent reasons in favour of Wolfe's plan. First, as recent events had demonstrated, given the vigilance and determination of Bougainville's men, the success of a British landing on the thickly wooded shoreline *above* Cap Rouge was by no means guaranteed. Secondly, with time running out, a decisive victory was needed – and without delay. Even the sceptical Holmes acknowledged this: 'the season was far spent, and it was necessary to strike some stroke, to ballance the campaign upon one side or another,' he conceded. Thirdly, by striking close to Quebec, Wolfe could concentrate *all* of his limited regular manpower, including the two full battalions of redcoats that had been left behind at the Isle of Orleans and Point Lévis after the bulk of the army moved upriver: this gave him another 1000 highly trained troops – no small consideration in a battlefield confrontation. Fourthly, unlike a landing above the Cap Rouge River, which would have allowed Bougainville and Montcalm to join forces unopposed, Wolfe's plan placed his army between them; of course, as his critics have noted, this risked a fight on two fronts. But if he had judged the situation correctly, it would provide an opportunity to destroy his opponents in detail, before they could unite against him. Lastly, and mostly crucially, Wolfe's chosen objective would finally allow him to strike where the enemy was not, so unleashing the most potent weapon of all – surprise. Writing to Lieutenant-Colonel Ralph Burton, Wolfe did not doubt that the Foulon scheme now offered the best chance of delivering what he had so long desired: a decisive clash with Montcalm. If the 'first business' succeeded, he added, it might bring on a general action – and *that* could yield 'the total conquest of Canada'.[32]

In selecting the Foulon for his 'stroke', it has been claimed that Wolfe acted upon the advice of Major Robert Stobo, a Scottish-born officer in the Virginia Regiment, who had learned much about Quebec during four years as a prisoner there. Handed over as a hostage following George Washington's surrender at Fort Necessity in July 1754, Stobo narrowly escaped execution on a charge of espionage. Undaunted by this close shave, he made two failed attempts to escape from Quebec before finally succeeding on 1 May 1759. After a perilous five-week voyage he arrived in Louisbourg. There his value was immediately recognized and he was despatched in the *Seahorse* to join Wolfe's expedition. As Colonel Andrew, Lord Rollo of the 22nd Foot explained to his friend Alexander Murray of the Louisbourg Grenadiers, Stobo's arrival was opportune, as he would be 'able to point out the avannues to the place which will greatly forward your approaches'.[33] Without doubt, Stobo was a remarkable individual, and his authenticated exploits require no exaggeration. His hard-earned local knowledge proved invaluable, underpinning Carleton's successful raid upon Pointe-aux-Trembles on 21 July. The claim that Stobo also alerted Wolfe to the path leading up from the Anse au Foulon surfaced in a published memoir of his life, although, as his biographer has emphasized, the evidence upon which it rests is 'intriguing but inconclusive'.[34] If Stobo did indeed point Wolfe in that direction, he must have done so before the general's solo reconnaissance mission on 9 September: the major had left Quebec two days before, accompanying Ensign Hutchins with Wolfe's response to Amherst's despatches. Whatever Stobo's precise role, according to Captain Holland, Wolfe had recognized the Foulon's potential for a surprise attack within weeks of arriving before Quebec. Since then he had kept it up his sleeve – an ace to be played should circumstances arise to balance the hazards of landing there.

By 10 September Wolfe was convinced that the right moment had come. That day, as Townshend recorded, the general had 'changed his mind as to the place he intended to land', owing to 'some intelligence' he had received. Deserters had divulged the detachment of the Chevalier de Lévis towards Montreal, 'with a large corps of chosen men'. Although Montcalm's second-in-command had marched west a month earlier, in response to the news of Niagara's fall, this was the first that Wolfe's army knew of it. The deserters maintained that Lévis had left with no fewer than 4000 troops. This was a wild exaggeration but, as Wolfe told Colonel Burton, it was 'likely enough' that Lévis *had* headed for Montreal, and his movement seemed to offer strong evidence that

Amherst was continuing to advance. In consequence, Wolfe added, there was all 'the more necessity for vigour on our side to second his endeavours'.[35]

For Wolfe, the deserters' 'intelligence' was a catalyst; acting upon it, he concerted his final plan. Its details were immediately revealed to Burton – Wolfe's trusted friend and his own choice for the brigadier's commission that had instead gone to the unstable Townshend.[36] The troops were to re-embark aboard the ships off St Nicholas next day, 11 September, and then sail slightly higher up the river, as if poised to land upon the north shore there. All the while, the fleet was to maintain a 'convenient distance', ready for the boats and warships to 'fall down to the Foulon'. If no 'accident' – from the weather or any other cause – intervened, they would 'make a powerful effort at that spot about four in the morning of the 13th'. The two battalions from the Isle of Orleans and Point Lévis were to assemble on the southern shore opposite the Foulon, at a spot known as 'Gorham's First Post', ready to cross over and reinforce the troops from upriver. Wolfe anticipated that the first wave would get into their boats between 10.00 p.m. and midnight on Wednesday 12 September, depending on circumstances. 'If we are forced to alter these measures', he added, 'you shall know it; if not, it stands fixed.'

Wolfe's strict schedule left precious little time to finalise the details of a complex amphibious operation. But having determined upon landing his army at the Foulon, Wolfe had pressing reasons for abiding by the precise timetable outlined to Burton: on the night of 12–13 September the onset of the ebb current, and the position of the moon, both offered optimum conditions for taking troops down river and landing them at their objective before daylight, undetected by the enemy. As already noted, Wolfe was now acutely aware of the influence of the tides upon his river-borne operations. It has been conjectured that Royal Navy navigators, including James Cook, gave him the benefit of their own direct observations of the St Lawrence's tidal patterns. Regardless of the origin of this data, Wolfe grasped its importance. He did not hesitate to exploit it to the full, choosing what one team of scientists and historians has described as 'the most auspicious date and time for his enterprise'.[37]

His mind made up, and with a viable plan before him, Wolfe was now in determined mood. All of the frustrations and doubts that had dogged him for the past two months were forgotten as he focused upon the task in hand. Closing his letter to Burton, he returned to a dominant theme in his personal creed as a professional soldier – one prepared to leave at least *something* to chance when the results justified the risks. He declared: 'in all cases it is our duty to try the most likely way, whatever may be the event'.

On 11 September, the troops ashore at St Nicholas were told that they would re-embark aboard their transports early next morning. They were to ready themselves to land and attack the enemy. After the bewildering feints and cancellations of recent days, it was clear that another major assault was in the offing, although as usual nothing was said of the objective.

Detailed instructions were now issued for the distribution and conduct of the troops in their landing craft.[38] They were to go into their boats at about 9.00 p.m. on 12 September, 'or when it is pretty near high water'. The first wave would be transported by the thirty remaining flat-bottomed boats – each carrying fifty men – plus the *Terror of France* schooner and another five long-boats and cutters. This force of about 1700 men, to be commanded by Monckton and Murray, would be immediately followed by a flotilla of frigates, sloops and transport ships, together carrying another 1900 redcoats, plus artillerymen. Wolfe himself had specified the order in which the troops should move off and land. William Howe would lead with 400 of his light infantry, the rest following in his wake according to regimental seniority.

Rear-Admiral Holmes held overall responsibility for landing the troops and supporting them with his ships. But, as regulating officer for the boats, Captain Chads was pivotal to the coming operation. Chads's word would be law, and no officer was to interfere with his 'particular province'; the likely consequences of such meddling – 'confusion and disorder' amongst the boats in the darkness – would scupper the attack before it had even begun. When they went into the boats the soldiers were to take nothing but their arms, ammunition and two days' rations. Their blankets, tents and other 'necessaries' would be brought up soon enough. As they could expect to spend hours in the open boats, they would receive an extra gill of rum: this must be mixed with the water in their canteens to make 'grog'. Success would depend upon planning, discipline and stealth. Above all, the troops must stay silent. Any sound could betray the enterprise. On no account, even when poised to jump ashore, were the men to fire their muskets from the boats.

The next day, Wednesday 12 September, the army embarked as ordered. When the troops were all on board, Wolfe issued his final instructions. These exploited 'agreeable intelligence', freshly delivered by another French deserter: he maintained that his commanders expected the British flotilla to move *higher* up the St Lawrence, to lay waste the country and eliminate the elusive shipping at Batiscan. For his part, Montcalm was staying put at Beauport, convinced that 'the flower' of Wolfe's army remained *below* Quebec.[39] The import was clear: Bougainville and Montcalm were pulling in different directions. By striking between them, at the point of least resistance, Wolfe would hit home with the force of a steel wedge hammered into a splitting log.

Through his orders, Wolfe also took pains to explain the timing of the attack. The enemy were now divided and low on provisions, there was a 'universal discontent' amongst the Canadians, and good reason to believe that General Amherst was advancing steadily. A vigorous blow now might 'determine the fate of Canada'. The orders likewise gave welcome reassurance to men who were wary of what the coming night and day might bring. As Corporal Johnson of the 58th Foot recalled, although none save the senior officers 'had the least intimation of the duty we were going upon ... everyone believed it to be some very hazardous undertaking'.[40] Now it was revealed that they would land where the enemy least expected. Their comrades at Point Lévis were ready to join them, along with artillery. Once the troops were ashore, a corps would be appointed to guard their landing place, whilst they marched on to seek battle with the French and Canadians. Finally, there came an appeal to the redcoats' patriotism and professional pride:

> The officers and men will remember what their country expects from them, and what a determined body of soldiers, inured to war, is capable of doing against five weak French battalions mingled with a disorderly peasantry. The soldiers must be attentive and obedient to their officers, and resolute in the execution of their duty.

Wolfe's last orders struck the right chord. To Johnson, they were 'couched in such tender and expressive terms, as was sufficient to inspire the most frozen constitution with the thirst for glory'. The corporal also remembered that the orders were issued 'in the most private manner imaginable': Wolfe was keeping his cards close to his chest – and for obvious reasons. Outlining his plan to Burton two days before, he had cautioned: 'be you careful not to drop it to any, for fear of desertion'. Such a breach of security had compromised the Montmorency assault. There must be no repetition of it now. Although they revealed no precise point of attack, with their reference to close support from Point Lévis Wolfe's orders left no doubt that he would strike close to Quebec, rather than in the upper river. One light infantryman concluded: 'By this day's orders it appears the general intends a most vigorous attack, supposed behind the town, where to appearance a landing is impracticable.' To maximize security, the orders had been issued at the last possible moment – quite literally on the eve of the attack. These precautions were warranted: a soldier of the Royal Americans *did* desert from St Nicholas on 12 September, but he absconded *before* the troops re-embarked – and before the orders were issued.[41]

The secrecy shrouding the operation was justifiable; but, from the perspective of Wolfe's brigadiers, it went too far. On 12 September, as the final preparations were made for the attack, they sent him a joint letter from aboard the *Lowestoft*, requesting more information regarding the precise role that each of them was to play, and the location or locations they were to attack – none of which they could establish from the public orders.[42] The brigadiers' request was respectfully worded. Wolfe's reply, addressed to his second-in-command, Monckton, betrayed some impatience. After all, Wolfe wrote, the reason he had recently asked Monckton to accompany him to Gorham's Post was to indicate the enemy's situation and the point of attack. As Monckton was responsible for directing the first landing wave, however, Wolfe gave him the clarification he wanted. Wolfe's letter was written at 8.30 p.m., just half an hour before the troops were expected to start climbing down from the transport ships into their boats, and his closing comment reveals mounting exasperation:

> It is not a usual thing to point out in the publick orders the direct spot of an attack, nor for any inferior officer not charg'd with a particular duty to ask instructions upon that point. I had the honour to inform you today, that it is my duty to attack the French Army, [and] to the best of my knowledge, and abilities, I have fix'd upon that spot, where we can act with most force,

and are most likely to succeed. If I am mistaken, I am sorry for it; and must be answerable to his Majesty and the publick for the consequences.

Wolfe sent a shorter note to Townshend, in which he explained his role in supporting Monckton with the second wave of troops carried aboard the fleet. He expressed his own belief in the army's ability to fight and beat the enemy – a task in which he did not doubt of enjoying Townshend's 'best assistance'.[43] Murray, the junior brigadier, received no reply; as he would be acting under Monckton, none was needed.

Wolfe has been taken to task for failing to keep his brigadiers fully briefed, his excuse of security undermined when it is remembered that he had already disclosed comprehensive details to Burton, a mere battalion commander.[44] Yet under the circumstances Wolfe's reluctance to take the brigadiers fully into his confidence is understandable. It is clear that his personal relations with Townshend and Murray remained dire; according to the journal kept by a member of his 'family', on 9 September, when the general was absent on his lone reconnaissance from Cap Rouge to Quebec, the pair 'came aboard the Admiral, and behaved very seditiously' towards him. Wolfe had long since learned to distrust the scheming Murray and Townshend, whilst taking pains to appease and reassure the cautious Monckton; but now, as the campaign reached its climax, he grew increasingly irate with all three brigadiers. According to the same officer, after he received their joint letter, 'Mr Wolfe said to his own family that the brigadiers had brought him up the river and now flinch'd. He did not hesitate to say that two of them were cowards and one a villain.'[45]

The manner in which Wolfe passed his last, tense hours aboard the *Sutherland* has prompted much imaginative speculation. When the brigadiers' letter arrived, it has been claimed, Wolfe 'was busy making what can only be interpreted as careful preparations for his death', which he expected to suffer soon, in the coming attack. In support of this intriguing theory, it is claimed that Wolfe had summoned his friend, Lieutenant John Jervis, the commander of the *Porcupine* sloop, to his cabin and there entrusted him with his will and personal papers, along with the miniature of his fiancée, Katherine Lowther.[46] Jervis was destined to achieve celebrity of his own as Earl St Vincent, and the story of this last meeting with Wolfe first surfaced in a later memoir of his illustrious career. In fact, Wolfe's will and papers, along with Miss

Lowther's picture, were placed in the care of his *aide-de-camp* Thomas Bell, not Jervis. And in 1798, when Jervis was quizzed about his relationship with Wolfe, he felt obliged to emphasize that, whilst the memory of the gallant general remained dear to him, their contacts had been all too fleeting. Both attended the Reverend Swinden's Academy at Greenwich, but as Wolfe was six years older than Jervis they were never pupils together. Their careers likewise diverged: Jervis saw Wolfe once in 1756, and 'not again until the Quebec campaign', when they met several times. He recalled nothing about any dramatic eve-of-battle conversation.[47]

The theory that Wolfe did not expect to survive the looming attack, and indeed was actively courting self-destruction, rests upon equally shaky footings. It presupposes that Wolfe expected his plan to fail, *and* that he believed himself to be mortally ill: he therefore preferred a swift and glorious exit courtesy of a French bullet, to an ignominious return to England, and a lingering death from consumption. But Wolfe's final orders, and also his last letters to Monckton and Townshend, breathe confidence in the daring, but meticulously planned, strike at the Foulon. And whilst Wolfe was certainly in very poor health, there is no evidence that he was *dying* – from consumption or anything else. However, the pain from his 'stone and gravel' was so excruciating, as one newspaper reported, that Wolfe 'had determined to resign his commission, on his return to England'. This claim that Wolfe intended to leave the army is supported by his own correspondence. Writing to Amherst from Louisbourg before the onset of the campaign, he maintained that, win or lose, he was 'fully determin'd never to take another command in the army'; and in his last letter to his mother, Wolfe again mentioned his 'plan of quitting the service' at the 'first opportunity'.[48]

Like any soldier on the constricted eighteenth-century battlefield, Wolfe faced the prospect of wounding or worse. But whilst proverbially fearless under fire, far from nursing some obsessive death wish, he had no intention of deliberately increasing those risks. Before the start of the campaign Wolfe told his Uncle Walter:

> You may be assured that I shall take all proper care of my own person, unless in case of the last importance, where it becomes a duty to do otherwise. I never put myself unnecessarily in the way of danger.[49]

In truth, Wolfe had much to live for, in both the short and long term.

Not only was it unthinkable that he – the 'soldiers' father' – should deliberately leave his men leaderless at the very crisis of the campaign, when the decisive clash he had hankered after for so long was at last imminent, but he was engaged to be married upon his return to England. There he would begin a new life outside the army, his 'latter days' comforted by the children he had long wished to father.[50] Taking all of these factors into consideration, the notion that Wolfe spent his last hours perfecting his own demise does not withstand scrutiny.

In any event, for Wolfe, the eve of his attack upon Quebec was scarcely a time for introspection. There was too much to be done – and too many interruptions. Not only was Wolfe obliged to respond to the brigadiers' belated request for information, he also had to pacify Captain Chads, who chose that moment to express his grave reservations about the landing – above all, that the 'heat of the tide wou'd hurry the boats beyond the object'. Wolfe was flabbergasted that the captain had not voiced his anxieties earlier, and it was suspected that someone had 'tampered' with him. Wolfe told Chads that all he could do was his best. If that was not enough, and the operation miscarried regardless, then *he* would take the blame. Finally, in his increasing vexation, Wolfe announced that he could do no more 'than lay his head to the block' to save Chads, and then turned on his heel and quit the cabin.[51]

Waiting aboard their transports for the order to climb down into the boats, the rank and file were oblivious to these disputes. To pass the time and ease the tension they busied themselves with final preparations – checking cartridges, adjusting flints and honing bayonets, or perhaps seeking out old comrades with whom to share some fellowship, and a swig or two of warming grog.

Wolfe had ordered that the troops should get into their boats 'during the latter part of the tide of flood' because the known strength of the ebb – the cause of Chads's concerns – would make the operation more difficult. At about 10.00 p.m. on 12 September, the men of the first wave – Howe's Light Infantry, Bragg's 28th Foot, Kennedy's 43rd, Lascelles's 47th, Anstruther's 58th, along with part of Fraser's Highlanders and fifty grenadiers of the Royal Americans – began to take their places in the boats.[52] When the *Sutherland* showed a single light in her main top-mast shrouds, the tightly packed landing craft were to rendezvous abreast of her, keeping close, and to minimize the risk of detection, lying between the ship and the south shore. The signal to cast loose and drop down the river would be two lanterns, one hoisted over the other.

The first boat of all included a hand picked forlorn hope of two dozen light infantrymen, commanded by Wolfe's close friend, Captain William De Laune. That evening, Colonel Howe had summoned all eight of the volunteers – or officer cadets – then serving in his corps, and ordered each to select another two men to go with him. Their task was a daunting one – to 'lead and land first', scrambling up the cliff face and fending off the enemy until the battalions behind had likewise gained the heights.[53]

Around midnight, the water at the St Nicholas anchorage grew slack, as the current gradually switched from flood to ebb. In their boats, the men of the first wave waited impatiently for the signal to go. All was deceptively tranquil: lapping water, creaking ropes, stifled coughs, the distant rumble of the tireless batteries at Pointe aux Pères – but beyond that, no noise, no movement. One of De Laune's volunteers described the conditions: 'Fine weather, the night calm, and silence over all.'[54]

By 2.00 a.m. on Thursday 13 September, the ebb tide was flowing strongly past the anchorage. Running at 2.4 knots, it could be expected to carry Wolfe's boats the nine miles to the Foulon in about two hours, so that they arrived just as the first hints of dawn showed. The moon was now in its last quarter in the eastern sky. Its position that night, no less than the timing and strength of the ebb, was crucial for the success of Wolfe's plan: the light it shed glittered down the river, outlining the black bulk of the northern shore, and providing a guiding path to follow in the darkness. But for French sentries squinting up the St Lawrence the moonlight afforded no such help; indeed, they would not even see the British boats until they were almost upon them.[55]

The time had come. Twin lanterns swung high above the *Sutherland*. Directly the signal was given the boats untied and moved off in 'pretty good order'. Wolfe went with them, although there is no evidence that he was in the first boat of all. According to perhaps the best known of all the stories told about Wolfe, it was now, as the flotilla finally slipped away down the river, that he quietly recited the words of Gray's *Elegy in a Country Churchyard*, before turning to his officers and declaring, 'Gentlemen, I would rather have written those lines than take Quebec.' Such is the version of events immortalized in Parkman's enduringly popular *Montcalm and Wolfe*.[56] Reluctantly, this must be dismissed: having issued strict orders for silence, it is unthinkable that Wolfe himself would have flouted them and thereby jeopardized his own plan.

But there are strong grounds for believing that this extraordinary episode really happened – with the proviso that it occurred shortly *before* the descent of the river, not whilst Wolfe was actually *en route* to the Foulon. Although mentioned in a letter dated 1804, the story first appeared in print in 1815. It rests upon the recollection of John Robison, who became Professor of Natural Philosophy at Edinburgh University. In 1759 he was tutor to the son of Admiral Knowles. When his pupil joined Saunders's flagship *Neptune* as a midshipman, Robison went too. Upon Knowles's promotion to lieutenant in the *Royal William*, Robison followed him and was rated as midshipman. On the eve of the final attack at Quebec, Robison maintained, he was aboard the boat in which Wolfe visited his outposts: the general repeated virtually all of the *Elegy* to the officer sitting next to him in the stern, 'adding, as he concluded, that he would prefer being the author of that poem to the glory of beating the French to-morrow'. Amongst those who heard Robison tell the same story was the novelist Sir Walter Scott. In 1830, upon learning that his friend the poet Robert Southey was writing a biography of Wolfe, Scott passed on his own recollection of the anecdote. This also fixed the episode on the evening of 12 September, but included minor variations – for example, that Wolfe produced a *copy* of the *Elegy* from his pocket, and then read it aloud.[57] As already established, there is no doubt that Wolfe was given a copy of Gray's poem by Katherine Lowther, and that he took it with him to the St Lawrence. Impossibly romantic as it seems, in essence the anecdote is likely to be authentic. In an ironic twist to the tale, there is no evidence that Thomas Gray, who died in 1771, ever learned of the circumstances by which his most famous poem was 'forever to be linked in cultural memory' with the momentous events at Quebec.[58]

Once the flat-bottomed boats were safely on their way, the armed sloops and vessels carrying ordnance stores and ammunition dropped downriver in their wake. Next, shortly before 3.00 a.m., Rear-Admiral Holmes followed with three frigates and two transport ships, all crammed with the troops of the second wave – Amherst's 15th Foot, Otway's 35th, the Louisbourg Grenadiers and the 3rd Battalion of the Royal Americans, plus more Highlanders and light infantry. The *Sutherland* hung back off Cap Rouge to keep an eye on the enemy there. Despite talk of a deliberate feint upriver, the ships' logs say nothing of such a move. But there is no doubt that an elaborate deception operation *was* staged along the Beauport shore and that it served its purpose admirably. Saunders laid buoys close inshore, suggesting moorings for men-of-war ordered to cover a landing there with their broadsides. According to the *Pembroke*'s master, James Cook, at midnight on 12 September all the rowing boats in the fleet 'made a faint to land at Beauport in order to draw the enemy's attention that way'.[59] Meanwhile, the British batteries flashed and thundered against Quebec throughout the night.

Whatever his misgivings about the difficulty of the task entrusted to him, Captain Chads now performed it with nerve and skill. Carried along by the current alone, with no assistance from their oars, the boats of the first wave approached within a mile of their objective without incident. But there was an anxious moment when they neared HMS *Hunter*, lying at anchor off Sillery.[60] Just hours earlier, two French deserters had come aboard the sloop. They revealed that a convoy of provisions was expected for Quebec that very night: as Wolfe's boats loomed out of the darkness there was a nerve-racking instant of hesitation before the *Hunter*'s watch confirmed their identity as friends. According to one report, it was Wolfe himself who persuaded the sloop's captain to hold his fire. The flotilla's passing gave a fleeting opportunity to whisper the deserters' intelligence about the anticipated convoy. Captain Simon Fraser heeded it well.[61]

As De Laune's boat maintained its course close to the north shore, 'followed by the rest in a string', it slipped past two sentries without being challenged by either. But a third was more alert. His cry of 'Qui vive?' was immediately answered 'according to the French manner' by Captain Fraser, who responded with 'La France' and 'Vive le Roi'. Like many of his countrymen, Fraser had served in the Dutch army and spoke French fluently. The quick-witted Scot explained that *they* were the provision boats from Montreal. In a finishing touch, he urgently cautioned the sentry to be silent, for fear of drawing the *Hunter*'s fire upon them. This was enough to satisfy the sentry and to send others scuttling along the shore announcing that the provision boats had arrived. Wolfe's men were luckier than they knew: in fact, the scheduled convoy had been postponed, but no notice of this change had been communicated to the outposts watching the northern shore. Neither had the French settled a password, and Fraser's inspired improvisations were sufficient.[62]

Minutes later, the first boats grounded upon the Foulon's narrow shingle beach. The current was as strong as Chads had warned, and it swept the light infantry slightly below their objective. Although intended to land just to the left of the barricaded path angling up from the cove, they struck to its right. According to De Laune, who must have glanced at his pocket watch, it was precisely 4.07 a.m.[63] Both the captain and his commander, Colonel Howe, rose to the occasion. Their priority was to push home the assault before the enemy even realized what was happening. Ordering De Laune to move back along the beach and scale the path, Howe led three companies of his men straight at the cliff that reared up in front of him. This was a formidable obstacle, no less than 175 feet high. Although not perpendicular, it looked daunting enough. Lieutenant Knox described it as 'one of the steepest precipices that can be conceived', whilst it reminded Colonel Murray of the rock behind Edinburgh Castle, 'at the West Kirk'.[64]

Slinging their muskets on their backs, the agile light infantry-men began to claw their way up the shifting shale, seeking purchase amongst the vegetation that clung to the surface. On reaching the sum-mit, Howe's men turned to their left, attacking and swiftly routing the picket posted to guard the path. The post's commander, Captain Louis Dupont de Chambon de Vergor, was wounded and captured. This coup owed much to the sheltering darkness – and the coolness and guile of another French-speaking officer of Fraser's Highlanders. Captain Don-ald McDonald, an erstwhile Jacobite who had previously served in King Louis's army, bought valuable time by convincing one of the cliff-top sentries that he was bringing a reinforcement to take post there.[65]

The battalions under Monckton and Murray struck the beach hard on the heels of the light infantry, who gave a resounding 'huzza' from on high to signal their success. By now more defenders were stirring; scattered militiaman and Indians were taking pot shots from the bushes along the cliff tops, and the four guns of the nearby Samos Battery at St Michel opened fire upon the boats, inflicting several casualties. Without delay, the redcoats of the first division followed the light infantry up to the heights. Some used the narrow path cleared by De Laune's volunteers; others clambered up wherever they could. One private soldier told his parents how he and his comrades 'mounted a hill one hundred yards high, being forced to creep on our hands and knees up it, and hold by the bushes that grew on it'.[66]

Like Monckton and Murray, Wolfe landed with the first division. When his boat reached the Foulon, his immediate task was to round up stray craft that had overshot the landing zone. On jumping ashore, Wolfe was jubilant at what had already been achieved by the indomitable Howe and his gallant advance guard: he 'wish'd that Mr Howe might outlive the day that he might have an opportunity of stamping his merit to the government'.[67] The Royal Navy had performed its share of the operation with equal coolness and professionalism. Holmes reported that the landing was 'the most hazardous and difficult task' that he had ever been obliged to undertake. As the officer responsible for the shipping, he feared that the blame for any 'miscarriage' would inevitably fall upon him; to his evident relief, thanks to 'the greatest good fortune' – and the efforts of Captain Chads – all 'was conducted very happily'. Admiral Saunders concurred, and conveyed his delight to Pitt: 'considering the darkness of the night, and the rapidity of the current', he wrote in his official despatch, 'this was a very critical operation, and very properly and successfully conducted'. Indeed, Holmes's ships had arrived at the Foulon exactly on schedule, in time to cover the landing with their guns.[68] In accordance with the rear-admiral's plan, the armed sloops lay closest inshore, with the frigates beyond them; ranged outside this protective cordon lay the transports, ready to offload their troops.

Now that the initial wave of redcoats was safely ashore, Wolfe decided to halt any further disembarkation until he had established the enemy's strength in the vicinity. As he explained, 'if the post was to be carry'd there were enough ashore for that purpose, if they were repuls'd a greater number would breed more confusion'.[69] Adjutant-General Isaac Barré was charged with delivering the order, but on reaching the shore found 'but very few boats there'. Most of them were now alongside the transports carrying the second wave and already full of troops waiting to land. From what he knew of Wolfe's plans, and aware that his general had not expected that the men could be brought ashore so swiftly, Barré seized the initiative. Instead of delivering his original orders, he urged on the disembarkation. When Barré reported this to Wolfe, he 'was much pleas'd to find himself established on shore with his army sooner than he expected'.[70]

Wolfe's order momentarily to halt the landing, and Barré's decision to disregard it, has provided ready ammunition for the general's critics. The episode is cited as evidence that Wolfe never intended his assault at the Foulon to be anything other than a face-saving exercise – concerned with satisfying the dictates of honour rather than bringing Montcalm to battle; it only evolved into something more decisive because of Barré's fortuitous disobedience.[71] But Barré himself never doubted the rationale behind Wolfe's orders. When asked about the incident years later, he declared,

> that it was notorious to every body, who had any the least knowledge of Mr Wolfe's wishes and intentions that campaign that they were most ardently bent on bringing the enemy to an action on any thing like equal terms, and that his ordering him [Barré] to stop the boats, could be only a temporary measure 'till he learned the enemys force in the neighbourhood of the landing place.

The second wave under Townshend landed smoothly, without delay. The empty boats were then rowed across the St Lawrence to collect the 48th and 2/60th from where they lay concealed along its wooded southern shoreline.[72] Crucially, Holmes's sailors began landing artillery and hauling it up the Foulon path; two light field pieces – short brass six pounders – would play an important part in coming events.

By about 6.00 a.m., at 'clear daylight', Wolfe and his first division had all gained the heights. A picket of French regulars hovered nearby; too late to intervene, they soon drew off. Whilst Brigadier Murray with the 58th Foot, and Colonel Howe and his light infantry, were detached to silence the troublesome Samos Battery, Wolfe marched his main body eastwards, towards Quebec.[73] In showery weather, the red-coated column snaked across the gently rising ground known as the 'Heights', or 'Plains', of Abraham. The latter term was something of a misnomer. In reality, the area bounded by the sheer drop to the St Lawrence on Wolfe's right, and the long slopes leading down to the St Charles on the left, was no level expanse of grass but a lumpy plateau, dotted with cornfields and mottled with patches of scrub. It was hardly Hyde Park, but it would be sufficient for what Wolfe had in mind.

Skirmishing now intensified as Montcalm's irregulars began sniping at the advancing redcoats. Grenadiers were sent out to clear a house of its defenders, and to flush some Indians from the coppice where they were 'skulking'. Wolfe's force had initially drawn up with its right to Quebec and its back to the St Lawrence; now the line pivoted, to face the east. There, about 600 yards away on the low ridge known as the Buttes-à-Neveu, the enemy could be seen assembling in ever-increasing numbers. A decisive clash was looming. Murray and Howe were recalled; and the battalions of the second division came up, to be joined soon after by the troops of the third. When these arrived, at 8.00 a.m., Wolfe's force reached its full strength of about 4500 men.[74] Wolfe now formed his army for battle. The extreme right was anchored upon the 35th Foot, which was angled back to face the bushy bank of the St Lawrence, where enemy skirmishers were creeping in an effort to outflank the British. The main battle line, from right to left, consisted of the Louisbourg Grenadiers, the 28th, 43rd, 47th, 78th and 58th regiments; behind them, in a slender reserve, were the 48th. Over on the left flank, where the enemy's irregulars were particularly numerous and troublesome, the 15th Foot, along with the 2nd and 3rd battalions of the 60th, formed up facing north, at ninety degrees to the front line. Returned from their mission to eradicate the Samos Battery, which they had found evacuated and with its guns spiked and useless, Howe's light infantry deployed to cover the army's rear. The two brass field pieces, crewed by the skilled gunners of the Royal Artillery, were dragged up into the front line.

Wolfe's frontage was extensive and it obliged him to stretch his line dangerously thin. That summer, Britain's troops in North America had practised fighting in a two-rank formation, instead of the customary three; this was justified on the grounds that the enemy in America fielded relatively few trained regulars. Indians and Canadians were unlikely to push home an attack against formed troops, however thin their line. But, as Corporal Johnson pointed out, given the smallness of his force on the Plains of Abraham, and the necessity of securing his flanks, Wolfe had little choice but to adopt the two-deep line. Indeed, to cover the chosen ground the men had to be placed in open order, with their files 'at least three feet asunder', and forty-yard intervals between each battalion.[75] Whatever the reasoning behind its adoption, that morning would witness the major battlefield debut of a formation that was destined to become synonymous with the British Army – 'the thin red line'.

Astonishingly, the first phase of Wolfe's daring plan had proceeded with scarcely a hitch; through a combination of luck, discipline, and bold and confident leadership – all underpinned by the consummate professionalism of soldiers and sailors alike – a British army was ranged where it had no right to be, within a mile of Quebec's walls. All now depended upon the response of Wolfe's opponents.

Duped by Saunders's feint, Montcalm and his men had spent a restless night, steeling themselves to repel the anticipated assault *below* Quebec. By the time they finally returned to their tents, to snatch some much-needed sleep, Wolfe had already landed above. The news that a formidable British force, complete with artillery, had scaled the heights west of the city was slow to arrive and even harder to credit. Vaudreuil and Montcalm did not learn of this stunning development until about 6.00 a.m.; by his own account, Bougainville, at Cap Rouge, only heard the tidings at nine.[76] For Montcalm, the realization that he had been totally outwitted struck like a thunderbolt. But the Marquis was a veteran, born of a family with a long and proud tradition as soldiers of the King, and he knew instinctively where his duty lay: he would gather his troops and sweep the British back to their boats before they could consolidate their position.

As the drummers beat the call to arms, the bleary-eyed French regulars and Canadian militiamen hastily grabbed weapons and accoutrements and formed up in their units. As a first measure, the battalion of Guyenne was ordered across the St Charles to hold the Buttes-à-Neveu between the redcoats and the city walls. It was a picket from Guyenne that had warily watched the movements of Wolfe's first division. In yet another of those extraordinary flukes of fate that cluster about this climactic phase of the Quebec campaign, just days before the entire battalion had been withdrawn from its position on the Heights of Abraham, where, had it proved more alert and determined than Vergor's militiamen, it might have transformed Wolfe's landing at the Foulon into a very bloody affair.

Because of the demand for manpower on other fronts, by now Mont-calm's Beauport army had been reduced to about 6000 men. Of these, 1500 militiamen of the Montreal brigade were ordered to guard the camp. Mounted upon his great dark horse, Montcalm placed himself at the head of the rest and led them at the double on a punishing march to meet the enemy. For some, this involved running 'nearly two leagues in one single race'.[77] By about 7.00 a.m. the first units were crossing the River St Charles, pounding through the charred suburb of St Roch and the rubble-strewn streets of Quebec before emerging from its western gates onto the open ground beyond. They came swarming, as one red-coat recalled, 'like bees out of a hive'.[78] Panting from their exertions, the regulars and militiamen formed up alongside the men of Guyenne, already ranged along the ridgeline facing the British army.

Armed with the element of surprise, Wolfe had had ample time to occupy the Buttes-à-Neveu himself. His failure to do so has drawn the ridicule of respected scholars. Surely, they exclaim, any general worth the name knows the importance of seizing the high ground. Indeed, from *his* chosen position, Wolfe could not even *see* the walls of Que-bec![79] But as the youngest British drummer boy could have told them, Wolfe knew exactly what he was doing: by leaving the ridge between his army and Quebec, and exploiting the shelter of the low-lying 'dead ground' behind it, he screened his men from the direct fire of the city's guns; had Wolfe arrayed his battalions atop the Buttes, as recommended by his critics, they would have become sitting targets.

It was with the same object of preserving the lives of his men that Wolfe ordered them to lie down in their ranks as they awaited the enemy attack, rather than stand stock-still under the fire of the Canadi-ans, Indians and colonial regulars who appeared in increasing numbers along his front and flanks, hunkering in the scrub as they took care-ful aim.[80] Although 'irregular', the fire of these marksmen was 'very galling'; more squads of redcoats were pushed forwards to keep them at bay. Clad in the same plain old red uniform that he had favoured throughout the campaign, Wolfe stalked the line, looking out over his prone battalions for signs of the attack upon which he had calculated. It must surely come soon.

Wolfe had read his opponent correctly. Across the Plains, Montcalm was marshalling his forces for the assault. Militiamen from Quebec,

Montreal and Trois Rivières clustered on the flanks, but the main strike force – intended to punch a hole through Wolfe's flimsy line – was composed of regular troops. All were clad in greyish-white coats, some turned up with facings of red or blue. The right comprised colonial regulars of the Compagnies Franches de La Marine, along with the battalions of La Sarre and Languedoc; the centre consisted of the Béarn and Guyenne; the left, of the Royal Rousillon and more men of La Marine. Silk colours – two to each of the five battalions of the Troupes de Terre – flared bravely in the breeze; the sun, which had broken through the clouds, reflected from fixed bayonets. Several iron field pieces, perhaps as many as four, were positioned on the flanks. In all, counting the skirmishers already harassing the British line, Montcalm's force numbered about 4500 men.[81]

The little armies that faced each other on the heights outside Quebec were comparable in size, but very different in quality. Wolfe's consisted entirely of trained professionals. As one of his subalterns proudly noted, every last man of them was a regular soldier.[82] This was true enough: all of the rangers were absent, off ravaging downriver with Major Scott, whilst the marines remained at the base installations on Point Lévis and the Isle of Orleans. Wolfe's ten redcoat battalions were tough, disciplined and drilled to perfection; with an open field to fight upon, they did not doubt their ability to drub whoever advanced against them.

By contrast, with its brigades of militiamen and bands of tribal warriors, Montcalm's army was far more diverse. Even his regular battalions were less homogeneous than appearances suggested. Before the onset of the campaign, in an effort to bolster their flagging numbers, and simultaneously forge links between the French metropolitan troops and the Canadians, Montcalm had reinforced them with some 600 militiamen. Although uniformed like their new comrades, these Canadians had now spent just three months with their units. This was a woefully inadequate time in which to master the parade-ground drill necessary to manoeuvre in the face of the enemy, and to acquire the iron discipline that enabled men to stand steady amidst the bloody mayhem of a close-quarter infantry fire fight.[83] In addition, the best soldiers of the battalions – including the fiercely moustachioed grenadiers who traditionally headed attacks – were still off with Bougainville's footsore command. Their aggressive leadership would be badly missed now.

Montcalm's decision to advance immediately with only the troops at hand attracted much censure at the time, and the criticism has continued ever since. Why did he not hold the high ground, and oblige the enemy to attack him? Why not allow his Canadians and Indians – skilled bush-fighters to a man – to grind down their enemy with guerrilla attacks? And above all, why not wait for Colonel Bougainville, who must surely be hastening on his way with the cream of the Quebec army, eager to crush the British between two fronts? But Montcalm adopted none of these courses; instead, it is argued, he minimized his own, very reasonable, prospects of victory by presenting Wolfe with exactly the kind of battle that he had sought in vain for so long. Of course, all such objections benefit from hindsight, a luxury denied to Montcalm, the commander on the spot and now unexpectedly facing the supreme crisis of the campaign. Well aware that Quebec was incapable of withstanding a siege, unsure of the enemy's strength, and convinced that they were already digging in and assembling more artillery, the Marquis resolved to attack whilst he still had a fighting chance. Shortly before 10.00 a.m., Montcalm flourished his drawn sword and led his motley army down the gentle slope towards the waiting redcoats.

When it became clear that the French attack was coming, Wolfe ordered his men to their feet. Although the fire of the lurking marksmen continued 'very hot', and wounded many men, the redcoats stood impassively with shouldered arms as their sergeants dressed the long, narrow line. At Wolfe's direction, each man loaded his musket with two balls; they were to hold their own fire until the enemy approached within forty yards – point blank range.[84] Whilst awaiting the French, Wolfe had walked up and down the line, checking his dispositions. He now took post on the right, with the Louisbourg Grenadiers, where a swell of ground provided a view over the battlefield.[85] Monckton, as senior brigadier, commanded the right of the line; Murray was in the centre and Townshend over on the left flank.

The French regulars came on gallantly at a brisk pace, waving their hats and shouting *Vive le Roi!* To British observers, they appeared to be massed in three dense columns; in fact, only the centre of Montcalm's line – the battalions of Béarn and Guyenne – was deliberately organized in assault formation, with the companies ranged behind each other. But the expanse of 'short brush' on the French right allowed scant room to manoeuvre, and other units, which had been ordered to attack in a more extended line formation, were obliged to compress their front-ages to squeeze past; whatever the cause, to one British sergeant major of grenadiers, the approaching enemy all looked 'at least six deep'.[86] According to John Knox, two of the French 'columns' veered towards the British left flank, the other to the right. At a range of about one hundred and thirty yards they opened fire, aiming 'obliquely' at the ends of Wolfe's line and maintaining the fusillade as they advanced, 'in a wild scattering manner'. Many of the balls flew harmlessly high over the heads of Wolfe's men.[87]

For all their brave appearance, Montcalm's regulars rapidly lost cohesion. The ground was rough, and the constricted flank units strug-gled to redeploy from column into line. Confusion only increased as groups of skirmishers, who had been peppering Wolfe's army for sev-eral hours, attempted to fall back through the advancing units. Worst of all, the Canadians recently drafted into the regular battalions swiftly reverted to their traditional mode of warfare: after firing their muskets, instead of maintaining formation and reloading in their ranks like dis-ciplined soldiers, they threw themselves on the ground, Indian fashion, and refused to rejoin the advance. All of these factors, exacerbated by well-directed blasts of canister from the two British field pieces, sowed disorder and weakened the impending blow.[88]

Urged on by their officers, the French regulars marched doggedly forward. Every step brought them closer to the British line: eighty, sixty, now fifty yards away, the redcoats stood ominously silent and still, their muskets shouldered. In strict obedience to orders, the British troops endured the enemy's fire with what John Knox characterized as 'the greatest intrepidity and firmness', all the while reserving their own. But the moment that Wolfe and his men had anticipated for so long was fast approaching. At last, when Montcalm's men were at the specified range of forty yards,[89] the orders rang out in swift succession. 'Make ready. Present. Fire!' Montcalm's musketry had been compromised by the poor discipline of his adulterated battalions. No such problem bedevilled the redcoats. That summer they had practised the simple 'alternate fire' long favoured by Wolfe, and they now demonstrated the results of their painstaking drill. With the remorseless rhythm of a smith working upon his anvil, their company volleys hammered the French, felling scores and forcing the rest to edge ever backwards.

In the centre of the British line two battalions – the 43rd and 47th – faced the dense column of the Béarn and Guyenne regiments. According to John Knox, the redcoats here had suffered little from the enemy's oblique fire. With 'great calmness', he recalled, they gave the enemy 'as remarkable a close and heavy discharge, as I ever saw performed at a private field of exercise, insomuch that better troops than we encountered could not possibly withstand it'.[90] The very techniques that Wolfe had recommended to his own 20th Foot back in 1755 had now been implemented on a battlefield with devastating effect. Angling their fire inwards against the sides of the column, the men of Kennedy's and Lascelles's raked their opponents with a storm of heavy lead balls. The issue was scarcely in doubt and the assault swiftly collapsed. French officers later testified that they had never before faced such regular and disciplined musketry – the shock was like the blast of a cannon, with every ball striking home. It was a classic confrontation between column and line, the precursor of a scenario that would be enacted many times over when British and French armies faced each other again during the Napoleonic Wars.

The rolling company volleys continued as the British battalions moved steadily forward over the battlefield. There followed a final crashing discharge – what Major Mackellar described as 'a general fire' – from the entire battle line.[91] Sustained firing had lasted for six or seven minutes – long enough to foul the air with the rotten-egg reek of gunpowder. When it ceased, and a breeze off the river began to disperse the fug, the French regulars could be seen retreating in utter confusion, 'running to all parts of the compass'.[92] The redcoats fixed bayonets; towards the left, on the orders of Brigadier Murray, Fraser's Highlanders drew their wicked, yard-long broadswords. With cheers, war cries and an intimidating line of sharpened steel, Wolfe's men advanced across the carpet of dead, dying and wounded to seal their victory. Most of the surviving French were too stunned to resist. Those who did, as Alexander Murray informed his wife, paid for their temerity: soon, several of his grenadiers' bayonets were bent, their very 'muzzles dipped in gore'.[93]

Over on the right wing, Wolfe led forward the Louisbourg Grenadiers and Bragg's 28th Foot. Close to the Canadian marksmen crouching in the bushes above the St Lawrence, this was a hazardous spot. Early in the action, Wolfe was shot through the right wrist; the wound, 'which tore the sinews much', must have been agonizing, but he bound it up with a handkerchief and ignored the pain. Soon after, he was struck again: a bullet scored the 'rim' of his belly, inflicting a gash that failed to stop him. But the third wound could not be shrugged off so lightly: as two balls simultaneously punched into his left breast, Wolfe reeled back out of the line.[94] Supported by volunteer James Henderson and Lieutenant Henry Browne of the Louisbourg Grenadiers, Wolfe had strength enough to wave his hat as a signal for Otway's 35th Foot to 'move up and flank the enemy'.[95] After staggering for about one hundred yards, Wolfe begged Henderson to set him down. When the volunteer opened Wolfe's coat he found his shirt soaked with blood. Lieutenant Browne had Wolfe's wounds dressed, but he was now haemorrhaging uncontrollably, and nothing more could be done for him.[96]

Various accounts of Wolfe's final moments soon circulated; as John Knox observed, 'many, from a vanity of talking, claimed the honour of being his supporters, after he was wounded'. Knox was not present either, but he went to great lengths to interview those who *were*. According to his informants, Browne and Henderson, it was they, helped only by a private soldier, who carried Wolfe to the rear. An artillery officer soon came to their assistance, and the four of them alone attended the general as he lay dying. There are grounds, however, for believing that others had some contact with the stricken Wolfe, if only briefly.[97] Irrespective of exactly who was present, it is clear that the scene bore little resemblance to Benjamin West's celebrated painting: there was no awed and respectful mourning chorus of senior officers, no artfully draped Union flag, no contemplative Noble Savage, just a knot of exhausted, bloody, smoke-grimed and grief-stricken soldiers, desperately seeking to comfort their young leader as best they could.

Wolfe's last words survive in differing versions, but Knox's account includes elements common to many and is far more credible than most. Asked if he wanted a surgeon, Wolfe replied, 'It is needless; it is all over with me.' Wolfe was rapidly losing consciousness, but when one of his attendants suddenly cried out, 'They run, see how they run', he reacted 'like a person roused from sleep' and urgently demanded '*Who* runs?' The officer answered: 'The enemy, Sir. Egad they give way everywhere.'

At this, Wolfe – a professional soldier to the very end – issued a final order: 'Go one of you, my lads, to Colonel Burton,' he gasped. 'Tell him to march Webb's regiment with all speed down to Charles's River, to cut off the retreat of the fugitives from the bridge.' Turning onto his side, he added, 'Now, God be praised, I will die in peace.' Wolfe lived long enough to know that his plan had succeeded, and that his men had done what he'd never doubted they would, and beaten the French. Safe in that knowledge, he quietly died, as volunteer Henderson recalled, with a smile fixed upon his face.

Montcalm's assault had been broken and rebuffed in a matter of minutes, but the fighting was far from over. Although the French regulars were shattered beyond rallying, the Canadian militia staged a stubborn rearguard action, fighting with a skill and determination that stemmed the redcoats' advance. Indeed, as several British participants noted, the combat that now followed over on the left, amongst the brush crowning the escarpment dropping down to the St Charles, was the hardest and costliest of the day. Fraser's Highlanders, who had discarded their carbines to give free play for swinging sword arms, suffered heavily as marksmen dropped them at close range.[98] Reinforcements from the 58th Foot and Royal Americans eventually obliged the militiamen to budge, but not before their stand had bought vital time for Montcalm's retreating regulars, many of whom streamed back to Quebec, and across the St Charles bridge to Beauport.

When Wolfe fell, command of his army had passed to Robert Monckton, although he had scant opportunity to exercise it. Within minutes, 'just as the French were giving way', the brigadier was himself shot through the lungs and obliged to leave the field. At 10.30 a.m., so the log of the *Lowestoft* reported, Monckton was brought on board, along with several other wounded officers; half an hour later the frigate received 'ye corps of General Wolf'.[99] The command now devolved upon Brigadier Townshend. Moving to the centre from the left flank, his priority was to recall the battalions that had chased the fleeing French regulars and organize a coherent line of battle. By Townshend's own account, this object was scarcely achieved before a new threat materialized. Sometime between noon and 1.00 p.m., Bougainville finally arrived from Cap Rouge, with about 2000 men and some artillery, to menace the

British army's rear; his advance troops had already sought to retake the Samos Battery, only to be fended off by the fifty-strong garrison of a nearby house, commanded by Lieutenant Daniel McAlpine of the Royal Americans. Bougainville's force formed up as if intending to attack; but it was soon all too obvious that 'the main point was already decided'. The arrival of Ralph Burton with the 35th and 48th Foot and some field pieces to reinforce the rearguard of Howe's Light Infantry and the 3/60th – which had dropped back early in the action to safeguard communications with the Foulon – deterred him from undertaking anything more ambitious. Bougainville promptly retraced his steps, leaving the British in undisputed possession of the battlefield.[100]

By mid afternoon, the last shots had been fired. The battle had been short but sharp, and the human cost was heavy enough. According to returns compiled next day, British casualties totalled 664 of all ranks, killed, wounded and missing.[101] French losses cannot be verified so exactly. British participants believed that the enemy had lost far more heavily, with 1500 killed and wounded, although one French witness put his army's casualties at just half that figure.[102] The senior ranks on both sides paid a high price for leading from the front. Montcalm was mortally wounded during his army's retreat, probably, as Colonel George Williamson claimed, by grapeshot from his six-pounders. The Marquis died next morning and was buried in a crater in the Ursuline Chapel, conveniently blasted by one of Williamson's thirteen-inch shells. Montcalm's second- and third-in-command likewise died of their wounds. Wolfe's staff also sustained heavy casualties. During the fighting, French officers were heard shouting 'Marquez bien les officiers', and their orders were clearly heeded. Besides Monckton, Wolfe's adjutant-general Isaac Barré, quartermaster-general Guy Carleton, and aide-de-camp Hervey Smyth were all hit. Indeed, despite later stories that Wolfe was mortally wounded by one of his own disgruntled men, there was more than enough lead emanating from the French firing line to account for such a conspicuous and tempting target.[103]

Wolfe had been felled during the battle's crisis; preoccupied with the business at hand, most of his men knew nothing of his death until after the fight was won. When they heard the news, the response was dramatic. Hard-bitten though they were, many of them broke down and wept openly for their lost leader. One officer attributed the depth

of these feelings to Wolfe's paternalism: 'the soldiers were inconsolable for the loss of their brave general,' he wrote, 'as they loved him
beyond measure; and well they might, for he was extremely tender to,
and careful of, them, and was called, *the Officer's Friend, and Soldier's
Father*'.[104] Lieutenant Browne, who had cradled Wolfe as he lay dying,
gave a similar explanation. He wrote:

> You can't imagine dear Father the sorrow of every individual in the army
> for so great a loss. Even the soldiers dropped tears, who were but the minute
> before driving their bayonets through the French. I can't compare it to any-
> thing better, than to a family in tears and sorrow which had just lost their
> father, their friend and their whole dependence.[105]

The letters and journals of officers and their men alike tell the same
poignant story: a 'glorious advantage' had been gained, but 'dearly purchased' by the death of the 'brave and never to be forgotten General
Wolfe', who was 'universally lamented' and 'much regretted by all his
little army'. It is tempting to see this wave of grief amongst the battle's
survivors as a collective post-traumatic reaction to the intense strain of
the past twenty-four hours. A similar phenomenon swept the British
fleet at Trafalgar, following the news of their admiral's death. It has
never been suggested that the grief of Nelson's men was anything but
heartfelt, and there is no reason to believe that Wolfe's redcoats were
any less sincere in their emotions. Weeks later, Colonel Murray of the
Louisbourg Grenadiers was unable to think about 'honest Wolfe' without shedding tears. He told his wife: 'I must own his death has given
me more affliction than anything I have met with, for I loved him with
a sincere and friendly affection.'[106]

Wolfe's men also mourned the loss of his aggressive leadership.
The battle of the Plains of Abraham was a clear-cut tactical victory
for the British army, but its strategic results fell short of what Wolfe
had wanted. He had envisaged the total elimination of Montcalm's
Beauport army, and had given instructions to block its retreat; instead,
many of the troops who had run from his redcoats escaped to fight
another day. This was partly a consequence of the French regulars'
swift collapse and rapid flight, which became a panicked rout after
Fraser's Highlanders were unleashed upon their heels. Ensign Malcolm
Fraser believed that Brigadier Murray's decision to order the clansmen

forward in full-blooded broadsword charge was a grave tactical error, as they never caught up with the enemy's main body; instead, the 'very well served' British artillery should have been allowed to 'play' for longer, with the whole army advancing in a more disciplined manner.[107] Of course, as the Highlanders themselves soon discovered, Montcalm's defeated regulars owed much to the resistance of the Canadian militia, but their escape also reflected a failure to implement the orders that Wolfe had issued as he lay dying – to advance the 48th Foot, and place it between Quebec and the fortified bridge over the St Charles, so blocking the French retreat.

Exactly why the 48th failed to move forward is unclear; perhaps, amidst the confusion of battle, Burton never received Wolfe's orders; and, as already noted, the same unit was subsequently swivelled around to help counter the belated threat from Bougainville. When Townshend assumed the command, he inherited a chaotic situation and responded as best he could. Yet there were those who felt that a golden opportunity had been lost. Had Wolfe survived, one officer believed, he and his army would have entered Quebec hard upon the enemy's heels, or crossed the River St Charles with them, either of which would have 'given such a blow to the French arms in Canada, as would have effectually prevented their striking another during this war'. But 'unhappily for his country, and to the great grief of the whole army', Wolfe had been 'taken off' before he could reap the full harvest of his victory.[108]

Before long, the bloodied battalions before Quebec had further cause to regret their general's untimely death. According to one of his inner circle of junior staff officers, Wolfe had anticipated taking post 'to the eastward of St Charles' and thereby trapping the remnants of Montcalm's army. Although the pontoon bridge over the St Charles was heavily defended, the river was easily fordable: with bold leadership, Wolfe's plan was a viable one. But rather than maintain pressure upon the beaten troops who now lay behind the walls of Quebec, or in their old camp at Beauport, Townshend instead consolidated his own position on the Heights. He secured his camp 'beyond insult' by constructing redoubts, improved the path up from the Foulon so that more artillery could be assembled, and began work on siege batteries. Meanwhile, his demoralized enemies were granted an unexpected respite, and they did not hesitate to use it. That same evening the French army stole away unmolested up the east bank of the St Charles; marching via Lorette, it bypassed Townshend's forces and next day reached Pointe-aux-Trembles. Vaudreuil went with the army, leaving instructions that the Chevalier de Ramezay, the city's commandant, should hold out while supplies lasted.[109]

By 17 September, work was progressing on the batteries intended to pound Quebec's landward defences, and a formidable train of siege artillery had been landed. In a calculated show of force, Admiral Saunders brought up 'seven of the best line of battle ships', powerful vessels that had never before entered the Basin, and disposed them ready to bombard the Lower Town with their menacing broadsides.[110] This was enough for Ramezay. At 3.00 p.m. that afternoon, he hoisted the white flag and proposed a capitulation. Most of his terms had already been accepted when fresh instructions arrived from Vaudreuil: a relief force under the Chevalier de Lévis was on its way. Ramezay was now to wait for him. But the negotiations were already far advanced, and the capitulation was signed on the morning of 18 September. The terms were unusually generous: unlike the garrison of Louisbourg, Quebec's defenders would return to France with the coveted honours of war; the inhabitants would enjoy their property, and full freedom to follow their Catholic faith. With winter fast approaching, and a new enemy massing in his rear, Townshend had good reason to be lenient. Lévis's advance troops under Bougainville were less than three miles away when they learned that Quebec had surrendered. 'Such was the end of what up to this moment was the finest campaign in the world,' reported the frustrated Bougainville.[111]

That evening, British troops entered Quebec. Alexander Murray and his grenadiers took formal possession of the city gates, whilst Colonel Williamson, at the head of fifty of the Royal Artillery, planted British colours upon the Grand Barbet Battery. As Williamson noted, a week before few would have credited such a sight. But now, after hanging in suspense for so long, Lieutenant John Brown of the Royal Americans wrote, their expedition had finally succeeded beyond all expectations. The redcoats who marched into the shell-torn city had no doubt who was responsible for this extraordinary outcome. In a letter that was sealed on 18 September, as he prepared to lead his own veteran battalion into Quebec's citadel, Lieutenant-Colonel Henry Fletcher of the

35th Foot attributed the crowning of all their labours to 'the great skill and indefatigable perseverance of General Wolfe'. Williamson likewise praised Wolfe's 'well laid' scheme; another officer gave all the 'glory' of the conquest to 'the brave Wolfe'; yet another was confident that it would 'prove as glorious to his memory, as anything ever performed by an English or Prussian general'.[112]

One especially fulsome tribute to the effectiveness of Wolfe's final stratagem came from an unexpected quarter. According to British officers held prisoner at Montreal, who met Vaudreuil after he was obliged to take fresh quarters there, the governor-general was full of admiration for Wolfe's decision to strike where, and when, he did: it was reported that he 'more than once declared in company, that at no other hour, and no other spot of ground', would the French army have been defeated. In Vaudreuil's opinion, 'no other general but Wolfe could have succeeded in an expedition of so great importance'.[113]

For a young colonel who had never expected to command an army of his own, this was as fine an epitaph as any.

10

Wolfe's Dust

What time great George who gallant actions priz'd,
And cowards from his inmost soul despis'd,
Was praising valiant Wolfe his actions great,
Whom death nor hell could ought intimidate,
Who on the Gauls Britannia's fury hurl'd,
And at his death bequeathed her a new World,
'May't please your Majesty' (exclaim'd his foes),
'The man was mad, which all his deeds disclose',
'Mad, then I wish he'd bit', the King reply'd,
'Some of my generals before he'd dy'd'.

John Mason, 'WOLFE, a Mad-man', 1759

Wolfe's despondent despatch to William Pitt, completed on 2 September during his final night at Montmorency camp, reached London early on the afternoon of Sunday 14 October 1759. It gave small cause to hope that Quebec would fall to British arms that year. According to the Duke of Newcastle, the King, with encouragement from Lord Anson, next morning remained 'very sanguine' that the city could still be taken. But, unlike Newcastle, Anson had not actually *read* Wolfe's despatch. 'If he had,' the Duke told Lord Hardwicke, 'I am sure it would have been impossible for him to have been of that opinion.' Neither did Pitt share Anson's optimism. There were signs that the Great Commoner now rued his decision to appoint the young and relatively untried Wolfe to command the crucial St Lawrence expedition. Newcastle added: 'Mr Pitt, with reason, gives it all over, and declares so publickly.' It seemed to the Duke that Pitt 'was not quite satisfied with Wolfe, in his heart'; indeed, although Wolfe's despatch, along with Admiral Saunders's of 5 September, was to be published by authority, several paragraphs – those detailing his ruthless scorched earth policy – would be omitted.[1]

The pessimistic reports from Quebec were duly printed on 16 October in an 'extraordinary' edition of the London Gazette. It was not only the administration that read them with trepidation for the fate of Wolfe and his army. Horace Walpole wrote warning his friend, Britain's ambassador in Florence, Sir Horace Mann, that the Quebec expedition would undoubtedly end in failure – and bloody failure at that.[2]

But these first reports had barely been digested before fresh bulletins arrived from the St Lawrence. That very same evening Pitt dashed off a breathless note to his colleague: 'Mr Secr[etar]y Pitt has the Pleasure to send the Duke of Newcastle the joyful news, that Quebec is taken, after a signal and compleat Victory over the French army.' Coming so hot on the heels of Wolfe's own glum despatch, this startling intelligence was hard to credit, but the reports from Quebec sent by Townshend, Monckton and Saunders left no doubt: next day, another 'extraordinary' edition of the Gazette was rushed out to broadcast the tidings. As Walpole informed Mann – who was now free to assume whatever airs he pleased – the juxtaposition of the successive despatches fuelled the drama of the moment: 'The notification of a probable disappointment at Quebec came only to heighten the pleasure of the conquest,' he wrote.[3]

There followed an explosion of public rejoicing such as few Britons could recall. Writing from London on 17 October, one of Wolfe's friends, who had heard 'the very unexpected news' of Quebec's surrender en route between Brentford and Kensington, told how the capital's streets were soon noisy with the clattering of 'marrowbones and cleavers' – those traditional percussion instruments of labouring folk – whilst 'bonfires and illuminations' were everywhere being prepared. The newspapers reported that the celebrations that followed in London had seldom been more general. Amongst the many 'testimonies of joy and loyalty', an illumination of six windows was particularly admired: the largest panel commemorated Wolfe – indeed, he was the only commander to be named of all those responsible for a recent glut of glorious victories in Europe, Asia, Africa and America.[4]

As the post boys sped out from London to spread the news, spontaneous celebrations erupted throughout the kingdom. From Norfolk, where the good folk not only gave thanks for 'the glorious and signal victory gained at Quebec', but also for the deliverance of their own Member of Parliament, George Townshend, came reports of the greatest rejoicings. In the market square at Fakenham, country gentry mingled with the town's tradesmen and freeholders to partake of a veritable feast – a spit-roasted ox, plus, for good measure, a sheep and a pig 'barbicu'd'. At Bath, where Wolfe had been well known, 'the joyful news of the taking of Quebec' arrived on Thursday 18 October. In honour of the occasion, 'Beau' Nash fired his cannon, and ordered a ball at 'Mr Simpson's'. Nearby, the humbler inhabitants of Bradford-upon-Avon marked the news in their own enthusiastic way with 'the greatest rejoicings ever known to the memory of man'. On Friday, when the news was confirmed by the arrival of the 'extraordinary' *Gazette* published in London two days earlier, the inhabitants met at 'The Swan'. After drinking many loyal healths, they progressed to the marketplace. There, before a great bonfire, they gave three cheers, toasting their 'brave countrymen in America, and the immortal memory of their late brave commander General Wolfe'. Remarkably, despite the 'large quantities of strong beer' freely on tap, there was no trouble; on the contrary, everything was conducted with 'the greatest order and regularity'.[5]

Indeed, as many reporters noted, the junketing for Quebec's capture was characterized by an unusual restraint. In London, it was claimed that the prudence of the magistrates and activity of the peace officers had prevented the outrages that typically marred such celebrations, after the gin and strong beer began to work their inevitable affects. In fact, much evidence suggests that the populace imposed its own controls. After all, this was no ordinary celebration. To be sure, a great victory had been won – but at a grievous cost. Britain's triumph came tinged with tragedy. Wolfe was dead, and even the members of the London mob, that most fickle and feared of Georgian institutions, showed 'by their behaviour, the night of the illuminations for the victory, that they felt for the loss of so brave a man'. At Blackheath, where Wolfe's devoted mother was inconsolable, all was still; her neighbours expressed their sympathy by forgoing any 'public rejoicings', lest they should add to her grief.[6]

In the provinces too, amidst all the quaffing and merriment, the crowds spared a thought for the man whose victory they were celebrating. At Salisbury, for example, the city's bells tolled a solemn knell for half an hour 'for the loss of the brave General Wolfe' before the inhabitants gave themselves over to 'spirited rejoicing'. Drums beat, the bells now pealed joyfully and bonfires blazed, whilst the Wiltshire militia drew up in the market place and fired volleys like seasoned veterans. That evening the city was 'more splendidly illuminated than was ever known on any former occasion'. At Oxford, too, they were not unmindful of 'the national loss sustained by the fall of General Wolfe; whose memory must ever be dear in this island, so long as military accomplishments, courage, and fidelity shall merit applause'.[7]

Press coverage of Wolfe extolled the same traits, as journals strove to satisfy readers' hunger for every detail of the fallen general's personality, background and service record. Much of this, as was recognized at the time, smacked of panegyric, but even after such 'froth' was blown away, there remained real virtues and concrete achievements to be remembered and applauded. It was clear that Wolfe's final victory rested upon deep foundations. Two widely published articles emphasized the roots of Wolfe's crowning triumph. There was his sterling performance throughout the War of the Austrian Succession, when the Duke of Cumberland himself had praised his conduct at Lauffeldt; and what he *would* have done at Rochefort if given the chance, and soon afterwards *did* at Louisbourg – where, although second-in-command, he was second to none in prosecuting the siege – were still fresh in everyone's memory. Wolfe's experience and dedication as a professional soldier had equipped him to face, and ultimately overcome, the greatest challenge of his career, where 'his abilities shone out in their brightest lustre'.[8]

The public's seemingly insatiable appetite for information about the dramatic events at Quebec was a gift to publishers, who spared no effort to exploit the demand. Before the end of October 1759, as the *London Magazine*'s monthly catalogue of publications noted, two works relating to the campaign were already in print. Many more were anticipated. As the same journal observed somewhat tiredly, 'everything relative to our late darling conquest will, no doubt, meet with purchasers'. Next month, it listed three poems relating to the death of Wolfe. The magazine's

11. *The attack at Montmorency, 31 July 1759.* 'Drawn on the spot' by Wolfe's *aide-de-camp* Captain Hervey Smyth, engraved by William Elliot and published in 1760, this image gives a strong sense of the daunting scale of the operations at Quebec (Library and Archives Canada, C–000782).

12. *The landing above Quebec, 13 September 1759.* Engraved c. 1761 by Pierre Charles Canot, from another Hervey Smyth sketch. Events that unfolded over a period of several hours are here shown simultaneously: the initial landing at the Anse au Foulon, the movement of Burton's troops from the south shore, the battle on the Plains of Abraham, and the defence of the house and battery at Samos against the counter-attack by advance elements of Bougainville's force are all depicted (Library and Archives Canada, C–000788).

13. *'Higher than before! Our General begins his day'*. Attributed to George
Townshend, and believed to have been executed during the Quebec campaign,
this convincing caricature in ink and watercolour shows Wolfe's reputation
being measured by the faithful Isaac Barré. It is unsparing in emphasising the
physical characteristics ('extremely thin, red-haired, and very ugly') reported
by a captive French woman who saw Wolfe in July 1759 (McCord Museum of
Canadian History, Montreal, Acc. No. M19857).

14. *Wolfe at Quebec in 1759*. Although similarly attributed to George Townshend, this ink and graphite cartoon differs markedly in style and handling from that shown opposite. Several characteristics, which are shared by five other associated caricatures in the same collection – for example, the handwriting and details of costume – raise doubts over its authenticity. Such considerations, and the fact that another cartoon in the series is executed on paper that was not manufactured before the 1770s, undermine the current attribution (McCord Museum of Canadian History, Montreal, Acc. No. M1793).

15. *The Death of General Wolfe, c. 1763–64 (detail).* The artist Edward Penny shows the stricken Wolfe attended by a surgeon believed to be Thomas Wilkins of the 35th Foot – one of several medical men mentioned in contemporary accounts as being present, or who later claimed to have been on hand. Other contenders include John Watson, the surgeon of the 48th Foot, and his mate 'Mr Treat'. Two of the Louisbourg Grenadiers who *were* with Wolfe during his last minutes, Volunteer James Henderson and Lieutenant Henry Browne, both feature in the foreground. Although Penny was apparently advised by Henderson himself, his painting cannot be regarded as an entirely accurate record of events. Some of the details, for example, Wolfe's uniform and the close proximity of the British firing line, do not tally with eyewitness evidence (Fort Ligonier Museum, Ligonier, Pennsylvania).

16. *The Death of General Wolfe*. William Woollett's engraving of Benjamin's West's celebrated painting was first issued in 1776 and enjoyed immense and lasting popularity. This was the image that shaped the enduring popular perception of Wolfe as imperial martyr, and fired the young Horatio Nelson to emulate him. Individuals identified in the published key include Captain Hervey Smyth, Major Isaac Barre, Brigadier-General Robert Monckton and Colonel George Williamson of the Royal Artillery. Although not named in the key, the soldier holding the Union flag is believed to be Lieutenant Henry Browne (New Brunswick Museum, Saint John, Acc. No. W1995).

17. *Colonel John Hale*. Engraved by Thomas Lupton from a painting by Sir Joshua Reynolds, this shows Hale in the uniform of the regiment of light dragoons that he raised after returning with the victory despatches from Quebec, where he had commanded the 47th Foot (Library and Archives Canada, C–004663).

THE VANITY OF HUMAN GLORY
A Design for the Monument of GENERAL WOLFE. 1760.

18. *The Vanity of Human Glory*. A savagely satirical comment on the competition to find a design for Wolfe's monument, this anonymous 1760 etching contrasts his unswerving pursuit of honour with the behaviour of Lord George Sackville, who was disgraced for failing to bring forward the British cavalry during the battle of Minden. Here, a hound wearing a collar marked 'Minden' is shown urinating upon a prostrated lion. Besides offering a powerful expression of the uncompromising honour code so dear to Wolfe, it offers an unflattering – but possibly accurate – profile view of the dead hero (New Brunswick Museum, Saint John, Acc. No. W1975).

19. *Major-General Robert Monckton, c. 1763–64.* Monckton, Wolfe's senior brigadier at Quebec, was subsequently promoted to command the British army that captured Martinique in 1762. The island's conquest features in the background of this much-admired portrait by the young Benjamin West, who would later include Monckton in his celebrated *Death of Wolfe* (National Army Museum, Chelsea, Neg. 55694).

critic found merit in *Daphnis and Menalcas: A Pastoral Sacred to the Memory of General Wolfe*. Another work, *A Monody, on the Death of General Wolfe*, however, drew forth a withering comment:

> We know too much of the unhappiness of many youths, who are cursed with a *singing in the head*, which they mistake for a poetical genius, to wonder at such a monody's being written: But we are greatly amazed, that a bookseller could be found who would print it.[9]

Nowhere had Wolfe's campaign on the St Lawrence been followed more closely than in British North America. There, too, the jubilant reaction to the news of Quebec's fall was mingled not only with grief but also with a palpable sense of relief. First tidings of victory reached New York on Thursday 11 October, and Boston next day. The celebrations that instantly followed, like those in Britain, afforded Wolfe the lion's share of the limelight. A window near Boston's Court House displayed an especially spectacular illumination depicting a monument inscribed to the dead general. Another window showed British colours flying over Quebec, and 'the French flag lying on the ground, with the staff broke; and over all, *Fame* sounding her trumpet'.[10]

In New England, where the long and bloody struggle with Catholic Canada had long since acquired a religious dimension, and the war itself the character of a crusade, Wolfe's victory and death held special significance. In his sermon on the reduction of Quebec, given in Boston on 16 October, Samuel Cooper accordingly lavished praise on the slain commander, observing that: 'No difficulty has arisen in this arduous service, superior to the skill of the leader.' Cooper added that Wolfe 'had died to live in the hearts of Britons, and especially in the hearts of British Americans, who are so peculiarly interested in this conquest'. The same theme was developed on 25 October – a day appointed for public thanksgiving throughout the province of Massachusetts Bay – when Jonathan Mayhew gave 'Two Discourses ... for the Success of His Majesty's Arms'. He exclaimed: 'We, I mean New-England, and all the British American plantations, had never so much cause for general joy as we have at present.' Wolfe had fallen far from his country of birth, 'yet near one which would glory might it be said that "this man was born here!"' Boston newspapers published a fulsome poetic tribute to Wolfe. Contributed by 'Americanus', this highlighted how Wolfe's role at Louisbourg and Quebec had secured the colonists' future safety. It trusted that even in death, he would continue to watch over them:

> Thus shall thy breast still fir'd with generous flame,
> Protect *America's* succeeding fame;
> Nor we by *treacherous foes* be more enslav'd,
> Whilst *thou* shalt guard that country *thou* hast sav'd.[11]

British Americans quickly claimed Wolfe for themselves; and as a martyr to a common cause he personified the remarkable extent to which the joint war effort against France had bonded mother country and colonies together as never before.[12]

Across the Atlantic the crabby old King was bombarded with addresses of congratulation from his loyal subjects. The first of all came from the lord mayor, aldermen and commons of the City of London, who waited upon their monarch at Kensington Palace on 20 October. The recorder, Sir William Moreton, delivered their 'humble but warmest congratulations ... upon the rapid and uninterrupted series of victories and successes, which, under the divine blessing, have attended Your Majesty's army by sea and land, within the compass of this distinguished and ever-memorable year'. By any accounting, 1759 was indeed a year of victories, a veritable *annus mirabilis*: it had opened encouragingly with news of the capture of Fort Duquesne, renamed Pittsburgh by its conqueror, the dying General Forbes. There had followed news of conquests at Goree in Africa, Guadeloupe in the West Indies, and Niagara, Ticonderoga and Crown Point in North America; added to this were triumphs in India, a great naval victory off Portugal's Cape Lagos, and, to cap it all, the sterling performance of the British infantry at Minden in Germany, where Ferdinand of Brunswick had drubbed the French on 1 August. These signal successes, but above all, the conquest of Quebec, 'against every advantage of situation and superior numbers', were such events as would for ever render His Majesty's 'auspicious reign the favourite era in the history of Great Britain'. Like the celebrations following the victory bulletins, the formal address included a sombre coda. Quebec's conquest had been attended by an immense loss 'in the death of that gallant general, whose abilities formed, whose courage attempted, and whose conduct happily effected the glorious enterprise in which he fell, leaving to future times an heroic example of military skill, discipline and fortitude ...' In coming weeks, the *London Gazette* was filled with addresses from all parts of the kingdom, mirroring such sentiments. This euphoric response offered a striking contrast to the wails of protest prompted by recent humiliations, of which Minorca's loss had been the hardest to endure. Indeed, for patriotic Britons, the bold and determined General Wolfe was the antithesis of the wretched Admiral Byng. By his glorious victory, won against the odds and at the cost of his own life, Wolfe had restored lustre to his country's tarnished honour.[13]

Pitt, who had sent Wolfe to Quebec, now received his share of plaudits for his chosen general's triumph. From Germany, Charles Manners, Marquess of Granby and commander of the British contingent serving under Ferdinand, reported how the army there had given a *feu de joie* for the news, while the Prince himself had expressed his 'joy in particular for this great success in taking Quebec in the strongest manner'. But Granby too felt obliged to condole with Pitt on the loss that king and country had sustained by the death of Wolfe. In Granby's opinion, had Wolfe lived, he 'would have done the greater honour to his country, as he would have been of the utmost service to it, nature having endow'd him with activity, resolution and perseverance, qualities absolutely necessary for executing great plans of operations, all which he had taken care to improve by great application'. This was high praise from a future commander-in-chief, who, like Wolfe, knew much about motivation and leadership. As the number of pub signs bearing his ruddy features and shining pate still testify, Granby too earned an enduring reputation as 'the soldier's friend'.[14]

Of course, there were those for whom the grief was far more personal. There was widespread sympathy for Wolfe's bereaved mother, and for his fiancée, Katherine Lowther. As a published 'Ode to Miss L—, on the Death of General Wolfe', put it, 'You, gentle maid, above the rest, his fate untimely mourn ...' Whilst sensible of the parent's loss, Lady Mary Wortley Montagu likewise considered the 'intended bride' to be the 'greatest sufferer'. As she told her daughter: 'Disappointments in youth are those that are felt with the greatest anguish, when we are all in expectation of happiness, perhaps not to be found in this life.' That autumn it was widely reported that Wolfe and Katherine Lowther were to have wed had he returned to England.

Miss Lowther, 'a young lady whose immense fortune' was 'her least recommendation', had been so uneasy at Wolfe's impending campaign in America that only the 'call of honour' had persuaded him to accept the command.[15]

Katherine Lowther only received 'tidings of the dreadful calamity' on 25 October, when she was staying at the remote Raby Castle in County Durham. Acting upon an impulse to mingle her own 'grief with that of the hero's mother', she immediately wrote to Blackheath. Miss Lowther did so with some trepidation, aware that a 'chasm' still yawned between her and Henrietta Wolfe. She wrote:

> Your displeasure at your noble son's partiality to one who is only too conscious of her own unworthiness has cost her many a pang. But you cannot without cruelty still attribute to me any coldness in his parting, for, madam, I always felt and express'd for you both reverence and affection, and desir'd you ever first to be consider'd.

Whatever had divided them in the past, surely both their hearts were 'now too deeply wrung for reproaches', Miss Lowther pleaded. It only remained to beg that any messages that might have been left for her would be forwarded, along with the portrait that Wolfe had taken with him to Quebec. She explained: 'There was a picture of me which I know it was his wish should, in case of fatality, come again into my hands.'[16]

Henrietta Wolfe, however, was in no mood for reconciliation, and the letter of condolence met a chilly response. When, after an interval of some weeks, Miss Lowther wrote again, the reply came from Mrs Wolfe's companion, Mrs Scott. She enclosed a letter that Katherine Lowther had written to Wolfe; this had followed him across the Atlantic, but he had not lived to read it. Miss Lowther felt more for Mrs Wolfe than words could express, and would gladly have exerted every power to alleviate her grief, but she would never dream of intruding upon it. 'I feel we are ye last people in the world who ought to meet', she wrote. She had not realized that Wolfe had willed that her picture was to be returned set with precious stones, but told Mrs Scott: 'I can't as a mark of his affection, refuse it; otherwise would willingly spare myself the pain of seeing a picture given under far different hopes and expectations.'[17] More than five years later, in April 1765, Miss Lowther married

Harry, the sixth Duke of Bolton. She outlived Wolfe by half a century, dying in 1809, at the age of seventy-five.

Katherine Lowther's portrait and unopened correspondence came back to England with Captain Thomas Bell. Along with William De Laune, Bell had the 'melancholy honour' of escorting his 'noble master to the grave'. Wolfe's body, which had been embalmed, wrapped in his embroidered dressing gown and then enclosed in a stone coffin or 'shell', taken from the shattered Ursuline's Convent in Quebec, was brought down to the *Royal William* at Isle Madame on 23 September. Two days later the seventy-four-gun man-of-war sailed for England.[18]

Bell and De Laune both bore raw scars from wounds sustained in the fighting on the St Lawrence. They went home in company with other casualties of the campaign – a score of disabled veterans of Fraser's Highlanders who hoped to secure pensions from the Royal Hospital at Chelsea. These men included sixty-year-old Donald Macleod of Skye. By his own account published decades later, Macleod had charged with Fraser's Highlanders on the Plains of Abraham, being sent limping to the rear with a musket ball through his arm and his shinbone shattered by grape. The old Highlander was amongst those men who claimed to have chanced upon the mortally wounded Wolfe. He offered his plaid to the dying general; slung within this swathe of tartan, so Macleod maintained, Wolfe was lugged off the field by four grenadiers.[19]

For Macleod and his comrades, the homeward passage was rough and perilous. Before the *Royal William* and her consorts had even left the St Lawrence, a 'brisk gale' threatened to send them to the bottom. According to Sergeant James Thompson of Fraser's Highlanders, who directed the party that conveyed Wolfe's body aboard the ship, she ran aground on Île aux Coudres; the shock knocked every man off his feet; but, as they were taking in no water, the voyage continued. It was only later, when the *Royal William* went into dry dock in Portsmouth, that this mysterious deliverance was explained: a rock as big as a table was found lodged fast in her hull, as snug and watertight as any plug.[20]

After four weeks at sea, the *Royal William* anchored at Spithead. On Saturday 17 November, at 7.00 a.m., she fired two guns to signal the removal of Wolfe's body. An hour later the corpse was lowered into a twelve-oared barge, towed by two others, and escorted by another dozen. It took an hour for the barge crews to row, 'in a train of gloomy silent pomp', to the landing place at Portsmouth Point. All the while, like the steady beat of a doleful drum, the warships at the anchorage fired minute guns. The Point was notorious for its numerous bawdy houses, where sailors habitually whored and drank away their hard-earned prize money. But at nine, when Wolfe's body was brought ashore, the atmosphere was subdued and solemn. The regiment of Invalids, accompanied by a company of Royal Artillery, marched from the Parade to receive the general's remains. The body was put into a travelling hearse, attended by a mourning coach, and then driven across the drawbridge spanning the ditch that divided the unruly Point from the disciplined Garrison. The fort's colours flew at half-mast, whilst muffled bells tolled in 'solemn concert' with the slow march. Their arms reversed, the Invalids and gunners escorted the cortège to the Landport gate, where it passed through on its way to London. Thousands had assembled to witness Wolfe's homecoming, but nothing was heard save for 'murmuring broken accents in praise of the dead hero'.[21]

Wolfe's body was taken to his parents' house in Blackheath; now encased within a black-cloth-covered coffin, it lay in the hall beneath wreaths of laurel. Mrs Wolfe was still too 'prostrated' to see Captain Bell, but he spoke at length with Mrs Scott 'about the general and his manner of dying'. Despite newspaper predictions of a great state funeral, the ceremony was a private and unpretentious affair. On the evening of 20 November, Wolfe's body was interred alongside his father in the fam-ily vault in St Alfege's Church, Greenwich – a medieval structure that had been rebuilt by the great Nicholas Hawksmoor. Just five mourners attended. Besides Captains Bell and De Laune, there were Wolfe's old schoolmaster, the Reverend Samuel Swinden, his army agent, Thomas Fisher, and Lieutenant Grant Scott, the son of Henrietta Wolfe's friend. The church's register recorded the burial of 'Major-General James Wolfe' with a simple single-line entry. It was no more than was afforded next day to the pauper Elizabeth Abbot.[22]

Despite the successes gained across the globe by British soldiers and sailors in 1759, the news of Quebec's conquest arrived at a time when Britain itself lay under fear of invasion. Increasingly desperate to compensate for its mounting colonial losses, France hoped to level the score by a last lunge at the very heart of the British Empire. Charles Edward Stuart, by now a brandy-sodden shadow of the Bonnie Prince of the '45, hovered unsteadily on the sidelines, hoping for some part in a venture that might finally restore his family's fortunes. But the plan that eventually evolved envisaged neither a Stuart restoration nor a total conquest of Britain. The objectives were more limited, although it was reasoned that they would nonetheless be enough to oblige the British to seek peace. Under the plan, the Toulon and Brest fleets were to concentrate off France's Atlantic coast and escort an invasion force to Western Scotland. Once those troops were safely ashore, the fleet would sail round the north of Scotland and then down the North Sea to France's Channel shore. There it would rendezvous with a second army and convoy it to Essex – within easy striking distance of the primary objective – London. In all, some 50,000 troops were earmarked for the venture. With Britain's regular army heavily committed to North America and Germany, it was reckoned that the landing forces would be sufficient to overwhelm such redcoats as remained for home defence and to brush aside the new, amateur militia.[23]

The scheme, which harked back to those of the war's opening year, rested upon the expedition's ability to evade the Royal Navy. Its prospects of doing so had already taken a battering in August, when Boscawen mauled the Toulon squadron off Lagos. But the Brest squadron, along with the formidable invasion forces secreted within Brittany's Quiberon Bay, remained intact. In the autumn of 1759, all that stood between Britain and a powerful French army was its own blockading fleet, under Sir Edward Hawke. If the Brest squadron could somehow give Hawke the slip, the long-threatened invasion might become a reality.

In this crisis atmosphere, when it was crucial to maintain the nation's morale, Wolfe's victory and death assumed still greater importance. Here was an opportune example for embattled Britons to emulate – one that recalled the glorious victories won by the outnumbered English during the *first* Hundred Years' War: 'In Wolfe', enthused the influential *Monitor* on 27 October 'was revived the courage of our Edwards and Henries, and that military skill and discipline, which enabled those puny armies, at Poictiers, Cressy and Agincourt, to defeat the vast armies of France.' Hogarth's prints satirizing the French preparations for invasion in 1756, and the carefree English response to them, were now reissued, as 'proper to be stuck up in publick places, both in town and country, at this juncture'. With a similar object of stiffening his countrymen's resolve, the defiant orders that Wolfe had issued to the 20th Foot back in 1755, 'in case the French land', were published at length in the press.[24]

Wolfe's fire-breathing spirit was infectious. Lieutenant-Colonel John Hale, who had commanded the 47th Foot on the Plains of Abraham, and collected a handsome gratuity of £500 for bringing the victory despatches from Quebec, harnessed it when he was promoted to the colonelcy of a new regiment of light horse. It was reported that Hale's dragoons were to be issued with a striking uniform: on the front of their caps and the left breast of their coats was a skull with crossed bones over it; underneath ran the uncompromising motto, 'Or Glory'. Originally numbered the 18th Light Dragoons, this unit soon became the 17th. Nearly a century later, when re-armed with lances, the 'Death or Glory Boys' would put their regimental code to the ultimate test during the Charge of the Light Brigade.[25]

In 1759, the troops guarding Britain's vulnerable coastline were not required to prove their resolution in such reckless fashion. Although the Brest fleet, under Admiral Hubert de Brienne, Marquis de Conflans, put to sea in mid-November after a gale buffeted Hawke's blockading squadron temporarily off station, it failed to get far. As Conflans headed for Quiberon Bay, to collect the transports destined for Scotland, Hawke gave chase. On 20 November, he overhauled his prey. In a confused pell-mell engagement, fought in a raging storm and off a treacherous rock-fringed and shoal-lined shore, Hawke's crews clawed their opponents to ribbons. When darkness came on, what remained of the Brest squadron had been scattered to the winds. Like Wolfe, Hawke had taken heavy risks in a single-minded pursuit of victory, calculating upon the proven quality of his men to balance the odds.[26]

The spectre of invasion dissipated with Conflans's fleet: battered and cowed, during the remainder of the war the French marine would never again venture out to challenge the Royal Navy. Immortalized in the stirring words and rollicking music of 'Heart of Oak', the battle of Quiberon Bay was an aptly dramatic and decisive climax to that 'wonderful year' of 1759. Its far-reaching strategic ramifications cemented Wolfe's conquest of Quebec: now virtually powerless at sea, France could offer no further hope of assistance to Canada. It was therefore fitting that at the very moment Hawke's crews were completing their remarkable victory, James Wolfe's body was being laid to rest in Greenwich.

Like many of its competitors, the popular *Scots Magazine* reprinted all of the despatches from Quebec that had been officially published by the ministry. It justified this page-filling policy on the grounds that the 'grand object' of the war in America had now been 'in a good measure attained', and such a momentous event could not be 'passed over without the most particular notice'. If further cause was needed, Wolfe's last, lengthy letter to Pitt deserved publication on its own merits, being 'perhaps the best written' composition of its kind to appear since the war began. The journal's editorial went further: the despatch's clarity, 'the difficulties that are foreseen and represented, the manly fortitude that is notwithstanding expressed, in order to surmount these difficulties, and the resignation with which the general persists in risking the greatest dangers for the honour and interest of his country, will leave a monument to his memory, more durable than marble, and more splendid than titles'.[27]

But given the unprecedented public reaction to Wolfe's death, there was never any doubt that, necessary or not, a monument would be erected to his name. On 21 November, the day following Wolfe's funeral, Pitt proposed this step to the House of Commons. The speech was not his best. According to Walpole, it was 'perhaps the worst harangue' that he'd ever uttered. In 'a low and plaintive voice', Pitt had 'pronounced a kind of funeral oration', drawing parallels from Greek and Roman history. In Walpole's opinion, these classical allusions fell flat, failing utterly to do justice to recent events: after all, Pitt himself had done more for Britain than any orator had achieved for Rome; and in three campaigns the British had overrun more territory than the legions had conquered in a century. As for the Greeks, Walpole scoffed, their history would seem all very well if St Albans was at war with Brentford, but it could not stand comparison with the high drama on the St Lawrence. Indeed,

> The horror of the night, the precipice scaled by Wolfe, the empire he with a handful of men added to England, and the glorious catastrophe of contentedly terminating life where his fame began – ancient story may be

ransacked, and ostentatious philosophy thrown into the account, before an episode can be found to rank with Wolfe's.[28]

Despite the deficiencies of Pitt's oratory, the Commons promptly resolved that Wolfe had earned a monument in Westminster Abbey, and that the public should pay for it. A competition was announced to find the best design. Given the prestige of the project, leading sculptors submitted proposals. They numbered the French Huguenot, Louis-François Roubiliac, widely regarded as the finest sculptor to work in eighteenth-century England, and his illustrious Flemish rival, John Michael Rysbrack. Both men had already created much-admired tombs for the Abbey, but the commission instead went to a relative newcomer, the young English artist Joseph Wilton. He had modelled a bust of Wolfe already, reputedly after viewing his corpse when it was landed at Portsmouth, but Wilton's nationality was another factor in his favour: the prospect of a Frenchman, however gifted, crafting the hero of Quebec's monument was more than most Britons could be expected to stomach. Wilton's winning design, upon which he started work in 1760, was enough to delight the most ardent patriot. As a Gallic visitor to the sculptor's studio noted with horror, the dying general's foot was pointedly shown trampling upon the *fleur de lis* of a French standard. Rumours that Wolfe's monument would displace others sparked the interest of Horace Walpole. Hearing that the Dean of Westminster, Dr Zachary Pearce, had agreed to shift the fourteenth-century tomb of Aymer de Valence, Earl of Pembroke – 'one of the finest and most ancient monuments in the Abbey' – he had written begging to erect and preserve it in his own Gothic mansion at Strawberry Hill, Twick-enham. But Pembroke stayed put, and Wilton's unwieldy marble edifice, which was finally unveiled in 1773, was placed in the Abbey's North Ambulatory.[29]

By then other impressive memorials to Wolfe had already been raised. As if determined to justify his title, Richard Grenville, Earl Temple, had continued the family tradition of scattering monuments throughout the extensive gardens of his countryseat at Stowe, near Buckingham. Temple's additions commemorated the spectacular spate of triumphs over which his brother-in-law Pitt had presided. The 'Tem-ple of Concord and Victory', completed in 1763, was festooned with medallions marking British successes from Louisbourg to Quebec, and Cherbourg to Pondicherry. Its portico gave a fine view of another, yet more prominent monument. Set high upon a hill, and soaring to over one hundred feet in height, this obelisk to the memory of Major-General Wolfe bore the inscription, 'The Fates but shew him to the world'. Such conspicuous glorification sits oddly alongside the story, supposedly spread by Temple himself, of Wolfe's boastful behaviour at his last meeting with him and Pitt.[30]

In New England, news of Wolfe's victory and death had scarcely registered before plans for a memorial were afoot. On 17 October 1759, the Lieutenant-Governor of Massachusetts Bay, Thomas Pownall, addressed the colony's Council and House of Representatives. As they had recently voted funds for a monument to Lord Howe – that other young British officer killed 'in the service of America' – he recommended that the province should likewise take the lead 'in expressing the unanimous sense of New-England towards the services of General Wolfe, who fell leading his brave army to the conquest of the capital of Canada'. A committee of both houses was immediately appointed to consider the matter and to report back. There was much talk, but nothing concrete came of it. Although it was reported in London that the Bostonians had 'voted a marble statue to be erected in King Street, at or near the east end of the town-house, in memory of the late General Wolfe', there is no evidence that it was ever raised. However, an obelisk dedicated to 'the memory of General Wolfe and others' *was* erected at New York, prominently sited at the end of the long lane leading north to Greenwich Village; it appears on a map of the city drawn in 1776 by British engineer Captain John Montresor, himself a veteran of the siege of Quebec.[31]

In London, talk of a publicly funded monument for 'the late brave General Wolfe' had gone hand in hand with claims that a 'handsome pension' would be settled upon his distraught mother.[32] Henrietta Wolfe certainly needed the money. Encouraged by expressions of sympathy from Pitt and his wife, Lady Hester, she took the liberty of addressing the Secretary of State to explain why. She wrote:

> My dear son, not knowing the disposition his father had made of his fortune – which was wholly settled on me for life, and magnified by fame greatly beyond what it really is – has left to his friends more than a third part of it; and, though I should have the greatest pleasure imaginable in

discharging these legacies in my lifetime, I cannot do it without distressing myself to the highest degree.

She now sought Pitt's advice about petitioning the King for a pension, to enable her to fulfil 'the generous and kind intentions' of her 'most dear lost son to his friends, and to live like the relict of General Wolfe and General Wolfe's mother'.[33]

Pitt's response was not what Henrietta Wolfe had anticipated. Whilst nothing would have given him greater satisfaction than to gratify her request, the matter fell within the Duke of Newcastle's department, and it was to him that such appeals should be addressed. If Mrs Wolfe should 'judge proper' to take that step – with regard to which Pitt could not possibly venture to advise – she would continue to command all his good offices and sincerest endeavours. Beyond that, it was clear, Pitt intended to do nothing.[34]

This rebuff was soon after followed by another, and even more crushing, disappointment. In February 1761, when warrants for the payment of staff officers on the Quebec expedition were at last made out, Wolfe's army agent, acting on behalf of Henrietta Wolfe, claimed a commander-in-chief's pay of £10 per day for her son, from the date of his final commission until his death. But the War Office maintained that Wolfe was entitled to no more than the ordinary daily pay of a major-general – £2; after all, it was reasoned, technically he had been serving under the overall command of Jeffery Amherst at the time. Mrs Wolfe was incredulous that her 'dear son's glorious death' should have raised up enemies who now sought to strike at 'a defenceless woman his mother, by withholding his proper reward'. Surely no one, she asked, least of all the King himself, could doubt that her son 'was appointed by his late majesty commander in chief?' The sheer injustice of it all goaded her to defiant rage: 'Am I to sue on my bended knees for what shou'd be given of right and would have been had he surviv'd the campaign which covered England with glory. But my pen fails me to describe such unlook'd for baseness as to rob me of what he so hardly earned ...'[35]

Henrietta Wolfe was surely correct to argue that if her son had lived to enjoy a hero's return, he would have been showered with honours and riches worth far more than the £2500 she was attempting to extract from the War Office. For his victory at Quiberon Bay, so the newspapers reported, the King had granted Admiral Hawke an annual pension of

£1500 for life, to descend to his son. It is unlikely that Wolfe would have received less.[36]

Nothing daunted, on the advice of her friends, the indomitable matron sent a memorial to the young King George III, who had succeeded to the throne after the death of his grandfather in October 1760. Despite the backing of influential men, including William Petty, Earl of Shelburne, her appeal failed to dent the bureaucratic resolve of Barrington and his successor at the War Office, George Townshend's brother, Charles. The shabby chapter only closed on 14 September 1764, when the new Secretary at War, Welbore Ellis, delivered the final verdict on the matter. Full details of the case had already been put before the King during Charles Townshend's sojourn at the War Office, he wrote: after considering these, His Majesty did not think Wolfe entitled to £10 a day for the Quebec expedition and could see no reason to change his mind. For Henrietta Wolfe, this was the final blow. She died just twelve days later, on 26 September, aged sixty. Her will honoured all of the bequests made by James, and directed that she should be interred in the family vault, between him and her husband.[37]

It was as well that Henrietta Wolfe never witnessed the unveiling of Wilton's towering monument to her beloved son: with supreme irony, its inscription commemorated him for posterity as 'Major-General and Commander-in-Chief of the British Land Forces on an Expedition Against Quebec'.

On 21 November 1759, during the same parliamentary session that voted funds for Wolfe's monument, members also agreed that the thanks of the House should go to the surviving admirals and generals employed against Quebec. This official recognition came amidst rumours that, although 'glorious and successful', the campaign on the St Lawrence had been dogged by bitter divisions between Wolfe and his brigadiers.

Evidence of such rifts had emerged after the publication of Townshend's victory despatch. This scarcely mentioned Wolfe. In Walpole's opinion, it 'said nothing in praise of him'; he maintained that Townshend, with the connivance of his friends in England, had tried to 'ravish the honour of the conquest from Wolfe', and to assume the laurels that rightfully belonged to his slain commander. Similar sentiments swiftly surfaced in the press. One anonymous army officer noted that Townshend had 'omitted ... to raise one stone to his rivalled merit'.[38]

Such criticism prompted the swift publication of a private letter, said to be from Townshend, which lavished plaudits upon Wolfe. In language that offers a marked contrast to the opinions that he had expressed when Wolfe was alive, Townshend could now hardly speak highly enough of his late 'friend' and commander. Amongst other tributes, he wrote: 'If the world were sensible at how dear a price we have purchased Quebec in his death, it would damp the general joy.'[39]

In some quarters the unseemly controversy was seen as a deliberate effort to diminish Pitt's triumph. Hence the *London Magazine* had nothing but praise for the *Monitor* of 27 October, which was 'levelled against that malignant, repining faction, who view with envy and malignity the glorious success of our arms, under the direction of our present great minister', and which had concluded with a 'spirited encomium on the general officers employed' at Quebec. Indeed, their alacrity in assuming command on the battlefield after Wolfe's death bade defiance to 'those scandalous reports of a disagreement between him and them in a council of war previous to that decisive engagement'.[40] Of course, such 'reports' were not without grounds; and, as fresh information emerged, Wolfe's independence of spirit would be recognized as a virtue, not a vice. According to one famous anecdote, those who subscribed to this view had included George II himself: if Wolfe was mad, as his critics maintained, then so much the better; the old King only wished he'd bitten some of his generals before he died.[41]

Whilst rumour and counter-rumour rippled through London, George Townshend was on passage from Canada to England. Eager to return to his family, he had left Quebec on 18 October, in company with Admiral Saunders, six men-of-war, and more than a score of transports. Monckton, who was still recovering from the wound received on the Plains of Abraham, sailed for New York on 26 October. Before leaving, he appointed Murray as governor of Quebec in command of the army that would garrison the ruined city.[42]

With winter fast approaching, Murray faced an unenviable task. Quebec was dangerously isolated. Its vulnerability stemmed from the failure of both Amherst and his subordinate, Brigadier Gage, to push forward against Montreal that summer. Gage had never budged beyond

Oswego – a woeful lack of initiative that drew a stinging reprimand from Amherst, and incurred the displeasure of Pitt and the King.[43] But when it finally resumed, the commander-in-chief's own lumbering offensive came too late to influence the outcome of the campaign. It was not until 11 October that the warships Amherst needed to master the French flotilla on Lake Champlain were ready for action. Heading north with 4500 men, he sought to destroy the enemy's fleet. As he told Sir John Ligonier, he also hoped to make a diversionary thrust against Isle-aux-Noix, to favour a surprise attack upon Montreal. Out on the vast waters of Lake Champlain in open whaleboats, Amherst's men were soon battling rough weather. Three French sloops were eliminated, but the expedition achieved nothing more. On 17 October, when the commander-in-chief finally received word that Quebec was in British hands, he promptly turned back for Crown Point. Justifying his decision, Amherst noted that Quebec's fall would inevitably bring Vaudreuil and the entire army of Canada to Montreal. He was wary of tackling such a powerful enemy so far from his own base; a defeat would risk losing all that he had already gained.[44]

Amherst's caution was understandable, but his dilemma need never have arisen if he and Gage had acted more vigorously when the bulk of New France's manpower was preoccupied with the defence of Quebec; but both men had expected Wolfe to be repulsed, and had failed miserably to support him. Set beside Wolfe's own determined pursuit of victory against the odds, their performances appear all the more feeble. Amidst the euphoria surrounding the unexpected conquest of Quebec, the disappointing results of Amherst's campaign were largely overlooked on both sides of the Atlantic. But their dangerous consequences would all too soon become apparent.

When George Townshend quit Quebec, he was oblivious of the unflattering stories circulating in London. But before they parted company, he and his 'brother brigadiers' took steps to counter some disagreeable gossip that had already gained currency within the victorious Quebec army and which now threatened to spread beyond it. In an effort to limit the damage, Townshend wrote anxiously to Amherst. If the commander-in-chief heard 'ill and malicious reports' concerning any 'negative' opinion that the brigadiers had given regarding 'poor

Mr Wolfe's' pursuit of the operations above Quebec, or his successful landing at the Foulon, he should not believe them. And if the three brigadiers received 'as little justice' in Amherst's army as Townshend understood they had met with from some members of their own, they were prepared to vindicate themselves, and were, thank God, ready with materials sufficient to do so. Monckton could state their case to Amherst in person, although it was a subject that neither he nor Townshend wished to revisit.[45]

It is significant that James Murray was excluded from those keen to let sleeping dogs lie. Murray had been Wolfe's fiercest critic during the Quebec campaign. The fact that his commander was now dead, and the city in British hands, did nothing to soften his feelings. On 5 October, Townshend had told Murray of the plan to collect all the 'negotiations' of the campaign. He intended to take the originals home himself – a move that would hopefully enable them to escape the 'censure of upright and rational men', if not 'that defamation which is ye offspring of ignorance and faction'. Approving heartily of Townshend's actions, Murray jumped at the opportunity to bestride his favourite hobbyhorse. Recalling the suddenness of Wolfe's decision to abandon the scheme of landing 'between Point au Tremble and St Augustin', in favour of the strike at the Foulon, Murray felt obliged to observe that the general's orders *throughout* the campaign had lacked 'stability, stratagem or fixt resolution'. He added: 'I wish his friends had not been so much our enemys, his memory would probably have been dearer to his country than now it can be.' Although the brigadiers were now 'acting on the defensive', Murray had no doubt that Townshend would execute their plan, and 'with as much tenderness to the memory of the poor Genll as the nature of things will admit of'.[46] With the aim of putting the record straight, as he saw it, Murray had kept a careful note of all the correspondence that passed between Wolfe and his brigadiers from late August to 12 September 1759.[47] Murray took it for granted that Wolfe would be discredited once the 'truth' about the Quebec campaign emerged. It was a hope that he would nurse for decades to come.

Once he had returned to England, Townshend lost little time in briefing his fellow brigadiers on the situation he found there, and on the outcome of the delicate affair that they'd entrusted to his care.[48] He had arrived long after the official despatches from Quebec – and the unofficial 'relations' of those men who had brought them. That these informal reports had been highly damaging is suggested by a story recorded by the poet Thomas Gray. When the Prince of Wales asked Colonel Hale how long Townshend had commanded after Wolfe's death, he had received a dismissive reply: 'A minute, Sir.' Gray himself added that all was not well between Townshend and Wolfe, 'who for some time had not cared to consult with him, or to communicate any of his designs to him'.[49]

From his brother Charles and others, Townshend soon learned that 'some artful insinuations had been industriously though secretly propagated'. These not only aimed to deprive the brigadiers of the least credit for the success of the campaign, but the same rumour which had circulated at Quebec – that they'd opposed Wolfe's final plan – had now crept into certain coffee houses. In addition, some of the newspapers, from 'a commendable excess of zeal for ye memory of a very gallant man', had shown an inclination 'to immolate to his manes the reputation of his brother officers'. As Townshend observed, the applause or disgust of his countrymen was inevitably taken to such extremes that it savoured of ferocity. Some of the printed panegyrics had imputed more than they could prove – that none of the brigadiers deserved any merit for the campaign's victorious outcome. Here Townshend was likely referring to the 'Character' of Wolfe in the *London Magazine*, which plagiarized an officer's letter to the *London Chronicle*. This had provided a boldly drawn, although far from fanciful, account of Wolfe's last days:

> In spite of many unforeseen difficulties, from the nature of the situation, from the great superiority of numbers, the strength of the place itself, and his own bad state of health, he persevered, with unwearied diligence, practising every stratagem of war to effect his purpose: At last, *singly and alone in opinion*, he formed, and executed, that great, that dangerous, yet necessary plan, which drew out the French to their defeat, and will for ever denominate him *The Conqueror of Canada*.[50]

Despite such public statements, and all the gossip and rumours, the documents that the brigadiers had laboriously collected to verify their 'honest endeavours to do ye best for ye service' were never even needed. Their vindication came instead from an unexpected, but unimpeachable, source – Wolfe's own letter to Pitt of 2 September 1759. For all the tensions between Wolfe and his senior subordinates, his much-admired

despatch had nothing but praise for the brigadiers: indeed, in closing his letter Wolfe had proclaimed his total confidence in them. In
consequence, as the relieved Townshend reported, Pitt, Newcastle and
Ligonier were fully satisfied with their conduct, and not 'liable to those
impressions which unprincipled intriguing men are often clandestinely
promoting to serve their own purposes or to gratify the views of their
party without any regard to truth and private justice'. In Townshend's
opinion, there was nothing more to be gained by taking things further
and entering 'into contest upon any circumstance with the memory
of a deceased man, deserving on so many accounts so much from his
country'.

Townshend, who for all his faults was not a vindictive man, was
clearly happy to let the matter drop. But he was not permitted to do
so. In the autumn of 1760, a pamphlet was published that rekindled the
controversy with a vengeance.[51] This was, as Walpole observed, 'the first
gust of faction' in the reign of George III. With a pen dipped in venom
and dripping with sarcasm, its anonymous author subjected Townshend
to a prolonged and bitter attack. The old issue of Townshend's victory
despatch was resurrected: this had failed to pay 'one civil compliment to
the memory of General *Wolfe*, or used one kind expression of esteem or
affection with regard to his person'. Of course, such neglect was scarcely
surprising, as Townshend had opposed Wolfe's plan of operations 'both
in public and private', and had 'protested in form' against his last desperate attempt. Despite this stance, Townshend had been quick to seize
the honour of accepting Quebec's surrender. That done, the brigadier
had returned home with indecent haste, preferring a 'peaceful walk
from Worcester to Norfolk' at the head of his beloved militia to the
hazardous 'snow-shoes expeditions of America'.

Turning to Townshend's own cautious handling of the final phase of
the fighting before Quebec, the letter writer accused him of cowardice
– what he styled 'Sackvillean prudence'. This was a pointed reference to
the notorious conduct of Lord George Sackville, who had commanded
the British cavalry at the battle of Minden. Sackville's failure to bring
forward his troopers, despite repeated orders from Prince Ferdinand,
had resulted in his recall from Germany in disgrace, and led to the
crushing court martial verdict – relayed to every far-flung unit of the
British Army – that he was unfit to exercise command in any capacity.

Although more pigheaded than pusillanimous, Lord George was swiftly stigmatized as 'the Coward of Minden', his craven behaviour offering a deplorable contrast to that of his former regimental major, James Wolfe, 'the Hero of Quebec'.[52]

As Walpole observed, the pamphlet's author felt fully justified 'in taking such freedom with a man whose ill-nature had seized every opportunity of ridiculing those he disliked by exhibiting their personal defects in caricatures'. Chief amongst Townshend's butts had been the Duke of Cumberland. Concluding that Cumberland was behind the letter, 'in the first blindness of his rage', Townshend rounded upon the Duke's favourite, Lord Albemarle. On 4 November 1760, a challenge was issued and accepted, only for the duel to be prevented by the prompt intervention of Captain Timothy Caswall of the Coldstream Guards.[53]

Denied the satisfaction of skewering Albemarle on the point of his small-sword, Townshend was obliged to content himself with a printed riposte.[54] This sought to parry the thrusts of the 'jumbled farraginous letter', and to land a few hits of its own. Attributed to 'an officer', the 'refutation' did not deny that Townshend had objected to an attack planned by Wolfe, but emphasized that this had been the package of proposals to assault the enemy's entrenchments at Beauport, 'a design ... so fraught with ruin, and so big with dangerous consequences, as rather to be declined than carried into execution'. This was true enough, although the statements that followed – that Townshend and his fellow brigadiers subsequently 'proposed attacking Quebec in the unexpected and surprising manner by which it was taken', and, 'like a true patriot', Wolfe had 'put into happy execution the plan of others' – were blatant falsehoods. The brigadiers had certainly advised their commander to shift his operations above Quebec, but the decision to land at the Foulon – as Murray had recently recalled with such indignation – was Wolfe's alone.

The 'refutation' closed with the hope that General Amherst, who had now completed the conquest of Canada, would return to a warmer reception than that encountered by Townshend, the 'reducer of *Quebec*'. That summer, Amherst's methodical campaign had proceeded with barely a hitch, as a trio of self-contained armies converged upon Montreal from the south, east and west. As ever, Britain's commander-in-chief in North America was taking no chances. But Amherst's customary caution was only heightened by an alarming development that spring, when Canada's outnumbered defenders had come close to retaking Quebec.

Separated from the nearest reinforcements by hundreds of miles of frozen wilderness, Governor Murray's garrison offered a tempting target for the Chevalier de Lévis, who had rebuilt and revitalized Montcalm's defeated army. With no British offensives to distract him on other fronts, he was able to concentrate almost the entire force of the colony, including ten battalions of regulars, and then move swiftly against Quebec. By 27 April Lévis was closing in upon his objective at the head of more than 7000 men. During the winter, Murray's army had been winnowed by frostbite and scurvy: fewer than four thousand redcoats were now fit for action. The odds were stacked heavily against Murray, but given the chance of fighting his own battle at last he had no intention of letting the longed-for opportunity slip. Next day, 28 April 1760, he marched out his sickly garrison, initially determined to deny Lévis the high ground that dominated Quebec. Murray's men carried entrenching tools and expected to dig in on the Buttes-à-Neveu, relying upon their superior artillery to compensate for lack of numbers. Instead, like Montcalm before him, Murray attacked. In the intensive fighting that followed, the outnumbered redcoats were gradually ground down. Lévis turned Murray's flanks and only narrowly missed severing his line of retreat to Quebec. It was a bloody affair for both sides. Nearly one thousand redcoats were killed or wounded. James Murray was a brave soldier, but as a battlefield commander he lacked judgement. His rashness and thirst for fame had risked squandering the fruits of Wolfe's victory on the same ground. His men judged him harshly. Malcolm Fraser believed Murray's 'passion for glory' had overcome his reason; John Johnson likewise blamed the needless loss of so many lives upon Murray's attempt to acquire 'great honour' for himself.[55]

Two days later, whilst Quebec lay under siege by Lévis's victorious army, Murray sent a despatch informing Amherst of developments. Its arrival caused the commander-in-chief considerable consternation. He informed Robert Monckton: 'this is a very unfortunate affair, and I think it is very uncertain whether it will end with or without the loss of the town'.[56] It was not only Amherst who was left hanging upon tenterhooks by Murray's bombshell. As the Annual Register reported, the 'blow was sensibly felt in England'. At the close of the triumphant 1759 campaign it had been assumed that the next would be a *fait accompli*. But Murray's defeat changed all that. 'Our sanguine hopes were at once sunk,' the same journal observed. 'If Quebec was lost, it was evident that the greatest difficulties must have arisen to our affairs in America; and the reduction of Canada must become the work of more than one campaign.'[57] That this dire situation did not come to pass was another consequence of Quiberon Bay, and the total eclipse of French sea-power: when the St Lawrence thawed in May, the first warships to reach Quebec flew British colours. Lévis had no option but to abandon his siege lines and withdraw to the west. Britons on both sides of the Atlantic could breathe again. Wolfe's legacies – the acquisition of Canada for the British Empire, and an English-speaking North America – were confirmed.

Montreal's fall did not end the American war. Canada had been conquered, but France's vulnerable Caribbean territories offered further tempting targets. Veterans of the mainland campaigns now joined an amphibious expedition against the rich sugar-island of Martinique. Command of the land forces went to Wolfe's senior brigadier, Robert Monckton. His army was formidable in numbers and experience, and it made short work of the island's intimidated defenders, who abandoned their strong entrenchments in the face of headlong assaults. By February 1762, Martinique and its dependencies were in British hands. As Spain's Bourbon monarchy had now belatedly edged into the conflict in support of the beleaguered French, it was decided that Britain's victorious 'American Army' should strike next against Havana. Command of this new expedition was entrusted to Wolfe's former colonel, George, Earl of Albemarle. Although he had seen no active service since Culloden, Albemarle was given the exalted rank of lieutenant-general. Such paper credentials failed to impress men who had soldiered with Wolfe. As Albemarle grumbled to his close friend Amherst, the North American army was 'a fine one, brave to the last degree', although 'almost spoilt by the expedition *up the River St Lawrence*'. He added: 'Your officers are all generals, with a thoro' contempt for everybody that has not served under *Mr Wolfe* ...'[58]

This fierce and exclusive *esprit de corps* testified to Wolfe's aggressive leadership, and to the devotion that he had inspired amongst his sub-ordinates. But it was not only within the 'American Army' that Wolfe's influence was felt. His long sojourn at the head of the 20th Foot had moulded a model regiment with standards of training and discipline that other units used as a yardstick to measure their own efficiency. The simplified drill that Wolfe had promoted was widely imitated. Its value had been obvious during the rigorous exercises staged before the Rochefort expedition of 1757; these techniques were mimicked again, and with happier results, in the British contingent that served in Germany two years later. At Minden, Kingsley's 20th had triumphed 'by practising what was familiar to them'. Indeed, it was reported, Wolfe

> introduced (without one act of inhumanity) such regularity and exactness of discipline into his corps, that, as long as the six British battalions on the plains of Minden are recorded in the annals of Europe, so long will Kingsley's stand amongst the foremost in the glory of that day.[59]

Already highlighted in the press in 1759, and further broadcast when his regimental 'Instructions' were published in book form in 1768, the importance of Wolfe's training methods were formally acknowledged in one of the era's most influential military manuals. According to Captain Bennett Cuthbertson of the crack 5th Foot, it was Wolfe who 'first pointed out to his countrymen, to what perfection and exactness an English soldier might be brought'. Cuthbertson advised every lieutenant-colonel to 'pursue all methods, which may, in the smallest degree, tend to the imitation of a plan designed by so able and respectable an officer'. In the next edition of his book Cuthbertson was still more specific about the origins of his own rules, many of which followed 'the regulations of Brigadier Wolfe, when lieutenant colonel of the XXth Regiment, which he formed for the use of that corps'.[60]

Cuthbertson credited Wolfe with introducing a much-needed professionalism into the British Army. It is possible to go further, and to give him a key role in restoring the reputation of the redcoats after decades in the doldrums. For a public whose expectations of its army had become based upon such débâcles as Cartagena, Falkirk, the Monongahela and Rochefort, the twin victories of Quebec and Minden went far to enhance the army's standing. This remarkable renaissance was epitomized in the changing fortunes of Bragg's 28th Foot. Bragg's had been slated for dissolution in 1748 because of its notorious inefficiency, but in 1759, as the newspapers reported, it had advanced to glory on the Plains of Abraham under Wolfe's personal command.

In Canada and Germany alike the redcoats had employed the utilitarian 'alternate fire' that Wolfe had ordered his own regiment to practise since 1755. Ever more widely adopted, the same system became enshrined in the 1764 drill regulations. Whilst there is no evidence that Wolfe was single-handedly responsible for introducing alternate fire into the British Army, he was certainly amongst its evangelists. Wolfe's emphasis upon simplicity, practicality and firepower was expounded in another military manual, written by one of Cuthbertson's brother officers. The author was none other than Wolfe's devoted *aide-de-camp* at Quebec, Thomas Bell, who had been rewarded with a captaincy in the 5th Foot in recognition of his services on the St Lawrence.[61] With his new unit, Bell soon saw much hard and bloody service in the war's German theatre. In the fierce action at Wilhelmsthal on 24 June 1762, his regiment famously worsted an elite force of French grenadiers. As Bell told his father, 'We have gained what we soldiers call immortal honour, all the whole army giving us the greatest praises.' Forwarding a copy of this letter to William Pitt, Bell's brother hoped that it would show not only that the Great Commoner's protection and patronage were justified, but that 'the memory of Mr Wolfe' had not been disgraced.[62]

In keeping with Wolfe's own doctrine, Bell's treatise was couched in direct and uncompromising language that reflected the reality of what actually mattered on the battlefield. As a reviewer noted, here were no 'dry and arbitrary rules of martial discipline' drawn from the parade ground, but a 'clear and rational' explanation of the 'military art'. Bell's *Essay* employed terms of unusual frankness: the essence of musketry drill was to make the soldier load as quickly as possible, and then to hit what he fired at – 'to be sure, as much as man can, to kill'. Indeed, 'A battalion whose fire is certain and deadly, kills, stops, and conquers; a battalion whose fire is unsure, is unkilling, will not stop, and may be conquered.'[63]

Whether presiding over a battalion or an army, Wolfe had succeeded in inculcating his officers and men with a rare fighting spirit – a readiness to push onwards, whatever the odds. This, more than any passing tactical fad, was his real legacy to the British Army. In the early 1770s, as that institution faced the prospect of a new, but very different, American war, Wolfe's ethos was invoked in an appeal to restore old virtues in a changing world. On the eve of that conflict, one young officer in the 35th Foot deployed the memory of Wolfe and his seasoned veterans as weapons in a satire upon the prevailing vogue for skin-tight uniforms and stately drill. Adopting the persona of an 'Old Soldier' wounded on the Plains of Abraham and now retired to Ireland on pension, Edward Drewe penned a whimsical attack upon the 'fame of modern discipline', by which the 'hardy veterans' of 'the American army' were processed in 'The School of Modern Military Virtue', to re-emerge, with nothing but their scars to distinguish them from the new breed of strutting popinjays. Drewe's extraordinary satire climaxed with the sudden, Jove-like appearance of Wolfe himself, who exclaimed in horror: 'Are these the troops of Britain? Is this the victorious army whom I led to conquest and renown? ... Where is now the manly look, the vigorous form, the iron body which alike defied the deadly engines of the foe, and the bitter inclemency of heaven?'[64]

Alongside this uncompromising emphasis upon courage and endurance, within the British Army Wolfe was remembered for his legendary paternalism – a personal concern for officers and men alike. In his *Memoirs* published in 1791, the 'Old Highlander', Sergeant Donald Macleod characterized Wolfe as 'the poor man's friend, and the determined patron of merit in whatever station he found it'.[65] This trait was highlighted in the closing lines of the popular ballad 'The Death of General Wolfe', by which Wolfe advised:

> So let all commanders do as I have done before,
> Be a soldier's friend, be a soldier's friend,
> My boys they'll fight for evermore.[66]

Wolfe's readiness to help the deserving, regardless of social rank, was highly unusual for an era in which such patronage was typically the preserve of the well connected. This fact was made brutally clear to junior officers who had flourished under Wolfe's command, only to see their professional prospects die with him. For them, grief at the loss of a venerated commander and friend was sharpened by resentment towards men who lacked his readiness to reward merit. Both sentiments merged when Henry Caldwell, who had served the Quebec campaign as one of Wolfe's assistant quartermaster-generals, sought the patronage of Pitt in December 1759. Captain Caldwell, who was well aware of how easily 'so little a person' as himself could be forgotten without someone to speak up on his behalf, therefore enclosed a letter that Wolfe had written to him in 1758. This would let Pitt know the general's honest assessment of his character, as 'insincerity', Caldwell added, 'was a vice unknown to that great man'.[67] But this 'honourable mention', and other testimonies of Caldwell's North American service, had no effect. In 1763 the disillusioned veteran wrote to Pitt once more, bitterly announcing his intention to resign his commission and relinquish the army to others who were more adept at creeping into the graces of powerful men. Before signing off, Caldwell asked a final favour, one that gave striking evidence of the enduring loyalty that Wolfe inspired amongst his followers. He wrote:

> as I shall allways look upon the opinion that great, that good man, had of me as the highest honour I could possibly receive, and as I esteem it tho' he is dead more than I should that of half the living world besides, I must request and intreat Sir that you will be so good as to give orders that that letter of his to me which I took the liberty of sending to you for your perusal may be looked for and inclosd to me ...[68]

Like Henry Caldwell, Wolfe's adjutant-general, Major Isaac Barré, had felt the general's loss keenly, both personally and professionally. Wolfe had plucked Barré from obscurity, and had assured him that if the Quebec campaign were crowned with success, *he* would have the honour of taking home the victory despatches. But as Barré explained to Pitt in April 1760, 'by one hapless stroke', the battle on the Plains of Abraham had baffled all his hopes, depriving him of his 'sole patron' and leaving him 'in all the distressful circumstances of an orphan'. Instead of promotion, the only trophies he could boast were the scars left by the musket ball that had smashed the bones of his nose and left cheek, and blinded his left eye, and which even now remained obstinately lodged in his head. Barré had informed Pitt of his pretensions to the rank of lieutenant-colonel, but notwithstanding all of his service and sufferings he had heard nothing from the War Office. Barré flattered himself that the mortifications he had undergone would pardon this intrusion upon the Secretary of State's precious time.[69]

Major Barré served the campaign of 1760 under Jeffery Amherst, and when Montreal fell, was entrusted with the general's despatches, which he delivered in London on 5 October. But the patronage and advancement that the major expected from Pitt did not immediately materialize. Caldwell had been powerless to do more than vent his frustration in a private letter; Barré exacted vengeance in a far more public fashion. As a newly elected MP, on 11 December 1761, the dis-gruntled veteran used his parliamentary debut to launch a blistering assault upon Pitt, who had recently resigned from office. Barré, whose wound bequeathed him what Walpole characterized as a 'savage glare', castigated Pitt as a 'profligate minister who'd thrust himself into power on the shoulders of the mob', only to desert the young King when his help was most needed.[70]

With time, Barré became one of Pitt's most devoted followers. In the fluid and volatile British political scene that followed the triumphant conclusion of the Seven Years' War in 1763, both men became known as 'friends' of the increasingly obstreperous inhabitants of Britain's North American colonies. In the wake of victory, spasmodic British attempts to claw back some of the costs incurred in dismantling New France had provoked mounting opposition. Its true scale was first apparent in 1765, when the Prime Minister George Grenville – Earl Temple's brother – attempted to tax the colonies through his Stamp Act. Rising to oppose this measure in a forceful speech, Barré had defended the British Americans, praising them as veritable 'Sons of Liberty'. When Barré's words were reported across the Atlantic, this label was embraced with enthusiasm by the men most determined to resist British taxes, and the one-eyed veteran became their hero.[71]

During these same years of escalating imperial crisis, the man to whose memory Barré remained devoted enjoyed an equally high repu-tation amongst British Americans. Of all the British soldiers who had fought to free Americans from their enemies, James Wolfe remained the most celebrated. In North America, as in Britain, his fame rested upon firm footings that predated his death in battle; for example, in April 1759, a New York-based privateer vessel was already named the *General Wolfe* in his honour.[72] So, in 1762, when the scale of Britain's victories over her enemies became fully apparent, it was only natural that 'Wolfe – The British Hero', should be included with William Pitt and George III in a triumvirate engraved by Nathaniel Hurd. The special significance of Wolfe's contribution had been highlighted in a broadsheet ballad, published in New England during the previous year, in celebration of a joyful jubilee – a release 'from wars, and bloody thralls, of popish and perfidious Gauls'. It added:

> Brave Wolfe who shar'd so large a part,
> In every loyal English heart,
> He to defend our liberties,
> Yielded his life a sacrifice.[73]

In coming years, Wolfe – like Barré – would continue to be regarded as the champion of American liberties. But whilst Wolfe had died to defend the colonists against *French* aggression, his memory was increasingly invoked to protect them from the tyrannical policies of *British* politicians. Even as mother country and colonies lurched from one crisis to another, Wolfe retained his high standing across the Atlantic. This phenomenon was epitomized in 1768, when Israel Putnam, a tough Connecticut-born veteran of the fighting on the New York frontier and Cuba, decided to name the tavern that he had opened in his native province in honour of the dead general. The sign of Putnam's inn, which has survived intact, carries a boldly painted image of Wolfe based upon the popular engraving made from a drawing by his *aide-de-camp*, Hervey Smyth.[74] In a year of determined colonial opposition to a fresh wave of imperial taxation, the fact that a red-coated British officer could be commemorated so publicly was powerful evidence of Wolfe's enduring popularity in America.

In Britain, where many pundits remained convinced that the quarrel between crown and colonies was no more than a passing family spat, Wolfe's stock likewise continued to rise. In 1769, when John Knox published an account of his North American campaigns, of which Wolfe's St Lawrence expedition provided a dramatic highpoint, commentators were given a fresh opportunity to reflect upon their significance. One reviewer observed that, although many of the details within Knox's hefty two-volume work might seem tedious and some trivial, they were amply compensated for by others of 'real importance, and of the most interesting nature, to every Briton'. This was especially true of 'the ever-memorable sieges of Quebec, etc'. Another believed that Knox's work offered a rich quarry of raw materials from which some future author would 'undertake to describe the most shining period, perhaps, in the British annals'. And it left no doubt about Wolfe's 'military genius, patience, and perseverance'.[75]

When the Pennsylvanian-born painter Benjamin West decided to portray the death of Wolfe, he was therefore embarking upon a project guaranteed to resonate in his homeland and in Britain alike. Indeed, when West began making preliminary sketches in 1765, the subject had already been tackled by George Romney and Edward Penny. Despite these precedents, West's canvas caused a sensation when it was unveiled in 1771, and has since generated a vast literature assessing its importance, particularly as a revolutionary development in 'history painting'.[76] Given its undoubted impact, it has also been suggested that West's painting was responsible for making Wolfe's reputation: the artist's vision granted iconic status to an otherwise insignificant and undeserving soldier, thereby propelling him into the pantheon of Britain's imperial heroes.[77] But, as a mass of evidence shows, during the very years when West's *Death of Wolfe* was conceived, painted and exhibited, its subject was *already* a household name, and in no danger of fading into obscurity: James Wolfe had no need of Benjamin West's brush to proclaim his fame; rather, it was Wolfe's celebrity that West exploited in a bid to secure his own.[78]

West's painting – or more accurately the best-selling engraving made from it five years later by William Woollett – was, however, undeniably influential in shaping how Wolfe would be perceived by future generations. By choosing, like Romney, Penny, and the sculptor Joseph Wilton before him, to depict Wolfe's final moments, West created an essentially passive image of a stoical soldier-martyr, lying limp like Christ taken down from the cross, and flanked by an equally static chorus of mourners. Minutes earlier, Wolfe had been leading his grenadiers in an adrenalin-fuelled bayonet charge; but West was not interested in capturing that dynamic moment. Owing to the extraordinary popularity of Woollett's engraving, which was destined to hang above thousands of parlour fireplaces for decades to come, undue emphasis was placed upon the 'nobility' of Wolfe's *death*, so deflecting attention from his achievements in life. On balance, West's painting has proved more damaging than beneficial to Wolfe's reputation.

To modern eyes, West's Wolfe can appear faintly ridiculous. It is interesting to speculate upon the very different impression of Wolfe that might have endured if he had survived the Quebec campaign to sit for the era's pre-eminent painter of British soldiers and sailors, Sir Joshua Reynolds. The immortalizer of Commodore Keppel and General Tarleton would surely have captured something at least of Wolfe's restless energy, and his formidable contemporary reputation for bold leadership.

Although West took considerable pains with the minutiae of military costume, he never intended to give a faithful reconstruction of historical events. Symbolism outweighed reality, and the result has been described as 'a classic of historical inaccuracy'.[79] It is notorious that the majority of those depicted by the artist were nowhere near Wolfe when he died, and that some of them were not even at Quebec. Others present on the Plains of Abraham when Wolfe was killed, and whose actions that day merited commemoration, are absent. The reasons for exclusion varied. According to his daughter, Colonel Hale indignantly refused to pay the one hundred guineas reputedly requested for the privilege of proving his presence on the battlefield; and to his lasting chagrin, Captain Samuel Holland, who claimed to have held Wolfe's wounded wrist as he lay dying, was not even asked to pose, for reasons 'best known to Mr West'.[80]

By contrast, Robert Monckton assumed a prominent place in the composition, gazing gravely down upon the recumbent Wolfe, even though he was himself being carried off the field, seriously wounded, at the time. Monckton's participation, and the fact that his family commissioned a copy of the painting, supports the contention that his attitude towards Wolfe was less antagonistic than that of his fellow brigadiers. Equally telling was James Murray's response to West's invitation to sit for him: he pointedly refused the offer, saying 'No, no! I was not by; I was leading the left'.[81] This was of course true, but there were other reasons why Murray had no desire to be pictured for all posterity alongside his old rival. Even now, he remained determined to hound him beyond the grave.

James Murray's abiding antipathy towards Wolfe is clear from a correspondence that he maintained with George Townshend in 1774.[82]

Murray was about to leave Britain to command the garrison of Minorca; but, despite the challenges ahead, the past, not the future, dominated his thoughts. Time had done nothing to alter Murray's belief that the real story of the Quebec campaign remained to be told; and that, when it was, *he* would finally receive his due share of recognition. As he had put it to Monckton back in 1761, the more that 'the history of that campaign' was known, the greater would be the honour given to the 'poor brigadiers', and the confusion meted out to their 'backbiters'. But such then was the 'popular rage' in Wolfe's favour that Murray accepted that 'truths must be allow'd to come out by degrees'.[83]

Thirteen years later, when Murray took up the cudgels once more, he discovered that the public's veneration for his old commander was undiminished. As Murray had yet to read a truthful account of the three American campaigns in which he'd fought, he was now putting together a narrative of his own. Once this labour was finished, Townshend and Monckton would each receive a copy of the section 'relative to the taking of Quebec' for their correction. With strict accuracy in mind, Murray had doggedly pursued the story, said to have originated in comments made by Isaac Barré, that Wolfe had never expected his landing at the Foulon to succeed. In Murray's opinion, only luck – as manifested in Barré's presence of mind – had delivered an unforeseen victory.

But Townshend had no intention of becoming embroiled in Murray's obsession; his own 'love of fame' having 'expired sooner than some other passions', he tactfully sought to deflect the Scot from his purpose. Although Barré's orders at the Foulon were 'not strictly correspondent with those of Mr Wolfe', Townshend wrote, they certainly reflected his intentions and had 'sprung from a zeal for the service'. Indeed, Barré had seconded his general's efforts, 'as every one else did, to the best of their abilities, on that important day'. Townshend also warned Murray against riling the pugnacious Barré, whose 'attachment to Mr Wolfe's memory' remained 'warm, honourable, and jealous'. He hoped that the episode should be made 'no matter of public discussion', not least because:

> the public admire Mr Wolfe, for many eminent qualities, and revere his
> memory; and therefore any distinction that may be made, upon the merits
> of a field where he fought, and died, will be but ill received; and in fact, be

deemed an irreverence to a tomb, where it is to be wished, the laurels may ever sprout.

Whilst wishing Murray well with his endeavours, Townshend was sadly unable to offer his assistance, having neither time nor inclination 'to recollect the different periods, and incidents, attending that expedition'. He confessed that if a book about the St Lawrence campaign lay before him alongside another recounting the little-known hostilities at Tanjour in India a decade earlier, he would pick up the latter first.

Murray was not to be deflected: Townshend's indifference left him more convinced than ever that 'truth must prevail at last'. He now unleashed a nonsensical tirade, based upon the bizarre belief that Wolfe had *never* intended to bring the enemy to 'a general action'. Murray had plainly never forgiven Wolfe for rejecting the plan, based upon his own reconnaissance, of landing above Quebec in early July, 'by means of the redans' – here he meant the clumsy *radeaux* or rafts – before any of Saunders's ships had passed into the upper river. Then there had been the general's refusal to assault the city itself from the river, and his 'absurd, visionary attack' upon the Beauport lines. Last, but not least, there was Wolfe's desertion of the 'sensible, well concerted' plan to land at Pointe-aux-Trembles, where, without opposition he could have entrenched his entire army across the enemy's supply line, for 'the almost impossible, tho successful attempt, thanks to Providence at the Foulon'. He closed his letter on a note of exasperation:

> God forbid my Lord I should interrupt your amusements: Tanjour you may quietly enjoy, while I am knocking my obstinate Scotch head, against the admiration, and reverence of the English mob for Mr Wolfe's memory...

Townshend had no truck with Murray's theories, finding it hard to credit 'that Mr Wolfe had any objection to bring the enemy to an engagement as early as possible'; the only question was to seek a fight under circumstances offering the best prospect of success. But he remained troubled by his old comrade's determination to rake up the past. In hopes of preventing a publication likely to have 'many disagreeable consequences', and possibly lead to 'mischief', Townshend decided to apprise Jeffery Amherst, who was now the British Army's commander-in-chief, of the situation. He enclosed copies of all the correspondence, so that his own conduct at least would be clear. Given the increasingly ominous political scene, such quibbling over the details of the Quebec campaign seemed all the more pointless. Now, as he told Amherst, the real issue at stake was not who had conquered *Canada* but who could preserve *America*.[84]

Townshend informed Murray that he had 'lived long enough to see people not only divided in their opinions upon those who served' at Quebec, but even upon the value of the conquest itself. His meaning was clear: by eliminating the long-standing threat from Canada, Britain had unwittingly created a situation in which its American colonies no longer needed the protection of the mother country, and nascent thoughts of independence could become a reality.

But even as the final crisis approached, Wolfe's own stock stood steady on *both* sides of the Atlantic. Early in 1775, the immigrant Thomas Paine, who would soon demonize George III in his devastating tract *Common Sense*, cast Wolfe as a defender of all English liberties – not least those of English Americans. Paine imagined a *Dialogue between General Wolfe and General Gage, in a Wood Near Boston*. Despite his lamentably lacklustre performance in 1759, Thomas Gage had succeeded Amherst as commander-in-chief in North America, and now faced the unenviable task of containing an increasingly volatile situation in New England. In Paine's article, published in the *Pennsylvania Journal and Weekly Advertiser* of 4 January, Wolfe announced that he had returned to earth to persuade Gage that his task of depriving his fellow subjects of their liberty was 'unworthy of a British soldier, and a freeman'.[85]

Of course, all of this was deeply ironic. Wolfe, more than any other British soldier, had created the essential preconditions for American independence, yet he was the last man to have foreseen, or wanted, such an outcome. Whilst enthusiastic about the massive potential of the American colonies, Wolfe had envisaged them loyally thriving within a mighty *British* Empire, not as some breakaway republic. Despite the colonists' abiding affection for *him*, had Wolfe lived long enough to be offered high command in America in 1775, it is unlikely that he would have spurned the task of pacification out of sympathy for the rebels, or 'spared the rod' when faced with their first, ramshackle armies. Whether Wolfe could have provided the kind of dynamic and aggressive leadership necessary to nip insurrection in the bud, or the determination and generalship capable of offsetting the daunting strategic challenge of crushing a widespread rebellion some 3000 miles from home, must remain matters for speculation. Beyond doubt, however, is the fact that the bitter Revolutionary War not only obliged George III to relinquish his prized American colonies, but also ended Wolfe's reign as transatlantic hero.

Within months of the conflict's opening shots at Lexington and Concord, a new recipient for Wolfe's mantle as soldier-martyr to shared English liberties had already stepped forward. Richard Montgomery was a former British Army officer who had served alongside Wolfe at Louisbourg in 1758, before settling in the colonies and attaining senior rank in Congress's fledgling Continental Army. The dashing young soldier was killed on 31 December 1775, leading a doomed assault on the British garrison of Quebec. The comparisons with Wolfe were obvious; and Montgomery too would be commemorated in a dramatic and influential painting, executed by Benjamin West's protégé, John Trumbull. In his adopted country, Montgomery swiftly became an icon of patriotic heroism.[86] By the Revolutionary War's close in 1783, many others had risked, or given, all in the cause of American liberty. Now amply supplied with *bona fide* patriots of their own, the citizens of the young American Republic had little further need of a long-dead British redcoat like James Wolfe, however valid his credentials.

Wolfe's fame in North America was circumscribed by the outcome of events that he had himself done much to instigate. But for Britons and their empire, his legacy proved more durable. It outlasted not only the loss of America, but also the victorious climactic bout of the 'Second Hundred Years' War' – the titanic and protracted struggle against Revolutionary and Napoleonic France.

Wolfe died young. Many of his contemporaries outlived him by half a century or more. As they reached senior rank, they carried Wolfe's ethos into this new era of intensified warfare with the old enemy. It was not only through West's celebrated canvas that Horatio Nelson imbibed Wolfe's spirit; he also came into contact with men who had known his hero in the flesh. At Jamaica in 1779, Nelson encountered the island's governor Major-General John Dalling, the same officer who had headed a corps of light infantry at Quebec, and who remained fond of discussing that campaign.[87] Neither did Sir William Hamilton, the husband of Nelson's great love Emma, forget the veteran officer who had befriended him when he was a callow young subaltern in Paris. But the link with Wolfe was strongest in the stern, venerable admirals who presided over Nelson's rise to prominence during the 1790s: 'Black Dick' Howe, who had captained the *Magnanime* at Rochefort in 1757, and capped a glittering fighting career in 1794 at the 'Glorious First of June'; and above all Nelson's tough old mentor, Sir John Jervis. 'Old Jarvie', who was proud to recall his friendship with Wolfe, and his early service at Quebec, did more than any man to set Nelson upon his own path of glory: it was under the wing of Jervis, the Royal Navy's commander-in-chief in the Mediterranean, that Commodore Nelson first reaped popular acclaim for his well-publicized exploits against the Spanish off Cape St Vincent on Valentine's Day 1797.[88]

The impact of Wolfe's example went far beyond Nelson's hankering after an equally heroic death – what has been styled his 'Wolfe moment'.[89] It was manifested in aggressive leadership, anchored upon professionalism, personal fearlessness and the hard-earned devotion of subordinates. Nowhere was Wolfe's legacy seen more clearly than at the climax of Nelson's career. The admiral's legendary pre-battle signal at Trafalgar – 'England expects that every man will do his duty' – echoed Wolfe's last orders before Quebec. And when Nelson's ships closed with the enemy, their opening broadsides were double-shotted for maximum effect – like the muskets of Wolfe's redcoats on the Plains of Abraham.[90] Whether these directives were deliberate imitations of Wolfe's is impossible to establish, although Nelson would certainly have had access to publications such as John Knox's *Journal* and Wolfe's own *Instructions*. The similarities are nonetheless striking: for both men, confidence of victory rested upon an unswerving belief in the unequalled morale and technical proficiency of their men.

Britain's enthusiastic celebration of the Trafalgar bicentenary suggests that 'Nelson's role model' is not a title to be taken lightly. But Wolfe deserves to be remembered for much more. Nelson, and other fighting men of his generation, like generals Sir John Moore and Arthur Wellesley, Duke of Wellington, inherited a tradition of British martial glory that Wolfe, above all others, had long since established. The Seven Years' War, and particularly Wolfe's conquest of Quebec, had proved a crucial stepping-stone on Britain's path to global power. In addition, the short sharp battle on the Plains of Abraham would take its place amongst the handful of truly decisive encounters to be fought during the 'Second Hundred Years' War', forming an illustrious triptych with Blenheim and Waterloo and, in chronological terms, falling almost exactly between those far larger and bloodier clashes. It was significant that in 1822, when the Scottish artist Sir David Wilkie unveiled a painting that celebrated Britain's recent crowning triumph over France, a direct link was made with the events of 1759: Wilkie's *Chelsea Pensioners Reading the Gazette of the Battle of Waterloo* acknowledged the symbolic importance of Wolfe's victory by including an aged veteran of Quebec as its pivotal, central figure.[91]

Wilkie's painting hints at the significance that Wolfe would assume for the Victorians and Edwardians as a founding father of the British Empire. For the many historians and writers who have since recoiled from this outmoded imperial perspective, Wolfe appears very differently – a brutal oddity and an incompetent soldier whose reputation rests upon little more than a moment of exceptionally good luck. In the process of transformation from hero to villain, from military genius to overrated mediocrity, Wolfe himself has become a palimpsest, his character scraped bare and repeatedly recut until scant trace of the original remains. It is only by stripping away these accumulated layers of opinion, and returning to the surviving testimonies of Wolfe's contemporaries, that something of his humanity can be restored, and a more balanced picture revealed. This evidence shows unequivocally that the achievements of Wolfe's life were no less remarkable than the consequences of his famous death.

James Wolfe was just thirty-two years old when he was killed in action. It can never be known whether, assuming of course that he could have been persuaded to forgo his plans to leave the army, he would have matured into a Marlborough or Wellington, acquiring a strategic vision to bolster his tactical flair. Any assessment of Wolfe's claim to greatness as a British general of the front rank must therefore hinge upon the conduct of his one and only independent command – that epic and momentous campaign against Quebec. The manifold problems that Wolfe faced upon the St Lawrence have been explored here; the fact that he ultimately overcame them in the teeth of discouraging setbacks is evidence of steely resolve. In contrast to his pessimistic brigadiers, Wolfe's officers and men never lost faith in him. Their performance on the last day of his life remains an extraordinary feat of arms, and a tribute to his inspirational leadership. Even if not a great general, Wolfe was undoubtedly a great soldier.

The true measure of Wolfe's worth is perhaps best expressed in the ballads that began circulating soon after his death. With their commemoration of paternalism, bravery and sacrifice, and fortitude in the face of adversity, they strike to the very heart of his character. The best known of them, 'Bold General Wolfe', lingered in the oral tradition long into the last century, its survival a striking testimony to its subject's enduring reputation.[92]

However heartfelt, by their very nature such manifestations of popular sentiment must be ephemeral. Today the old songs are rarely sung. Like the robust patriotism they exhale, they belong to another age, with different values. Yet even now, the qualities they celebrated are not totally redundant: as long as courage, determination and loyalty continue to be recognized and valued, James Wolfe, no less than Horatio Nelson, merits the 'immortal memory'.

Notes

Abbreviations

Add. MS Additional Manuscripts, British Library, London

CHR   *Canadian Historical Review*

CO   Colonial Office Papers, National Archives, Kew

DCB   *Dictionary of Canadian Biography*, ed. F. G. Halpenny (13 vols, Toronto, 1966–94).

EHR   *English Historical Review*

GD   Gifts and Deposits, National Archives of Scotland, Edinburgh

HMC   *Royal Commission on Historic Manuscripts*

JSAHR *Journal of the Society for Army Historical Research*

LAC   Library and Archives Canada (National Archives of Canada), Ottawa

LO   Loudoun Papers, Huntington Library, San Marino, California

MS   Manuscript

NAM   National Army Museum, Chelsea

NLS   National Library of Scotland, Edinburgh

NYCD *Documents Relative to the Colonial History of the State of New York*, ed. E. B. O'Callaghan and B. Fernow (15 vols, Albany, 1853–87).

PRO 30/8 Chatham Papers, National Archives, Kew

SP   State Papers, National Archives, Kew

WO   War Office Papers, National Archives, Kew

Note: Short forms are used for all sources after the first full citation in each chapter. Where manuscript materials must now be consulted on microfilm, reel (rl) references are given in addition to the original archival citations.

Notes to Introduction: The Changing Reputation of James Wolfe

1. T. Pocock, *Horatio Nelson* (London, 1987), pp. 114, 275–76.
2. For example, Wolfe fares badly in Fred Anderson's widely acclaimed *Crucible of War: The Seven Years' War and the Fate of Empire in British North America, 1754–1766* (New York, 2000), pp. 344–68. This stance reflects the increasingly harsh verdicts of historians and writers since the 1980s. Francis Jennings described Wolfe as one of the British Army's 'cruelest commanders', whose 'glamorous aura in the schoolbooks dims greatly when exposed to the facts of his commands'; for Angus Calder, Wolfe was a 'bloody' and 'priggish young man' who 'despised most sections of the human race'. See F. Jennings, *Empire of Fortune: Crowns, Colonies and Tribes in the Seven Years' War in America* (New York, 1988), p. 205; A. Calder, *Revolutionary Empire: The Rise of the English-Speaking Empires from the Fifteenth Century to the 1780s* (New York, 1981), pp. 607–10. Not surprisingly, this weight of opinion also coloured the depiction of Wolfe in the drama-documentary, *The War That Made America*, first shown on Public Broadcast Service television in the United States in January 2006.
3. J*** P****** [John Pringle] *The Life of General James Wolfe, the Conqueror of Canada: or The Elogium of that Renowned Hero, Attempted According to the Rules of Eloquence, with a Monumental Inscription, to Perpetuate his Memory* (London, 1760). For a discussion of this work, and critical reactions to it, see J. C. Webster, 'The First Published Life of James Wolfe', *CHR*, 11 (1930), pp. 328–32.
4. R. Wright, *The Life of Major-General James Wolfe* (London, 1864); B. Willson, *The Life and Letters of James Wolfe* (New York, 1909).
5. See news report: 'Mayor Attacks Generals in Battle of Trafalgar Square', *Guardian*, 20 October 2000.
6. Margaret Atwood, *The Robber Bride* (paperback edn, London, 1994), p. 23.
7. Wolfe to Captain William Rickson, Glasgow, 2 April 1749 ('Original Correspondence of General Wolfe'), in *The Siege of Quebec and the Battle of the Plains of Abraham*, ed. A. Doughty and G. W. Parmelee (6 vols, Quebec, 1901–2), vi, p. 2; given in full in Willson, *Life and Letters of Wolfe*, p. 93. For Wolfe's letter to his father, from Inverness, 12 January 1752, see the heavily edited version in ibid., p. 167; the original manuscript (carrying the Old Style date of 12 January 1751) is in 'General Wolfe's Letters to his Parents, 1740–1759' (held privately at Squerryes Court, Westerham, Kent), pp. 200–2. The transcription, complete with damning comment,

is in the accompanying volume misleadingly entitled 'General Wolfe's Letters to his Mother, 1740–1760', pp. 113–15. Accurate copies of the Wolfe family correspondence, made from the originals in 1913, are held in the Library and Archives Canada, Ottawa (LAC, 'James Wolfe Collection', MG 18 – L5, vol. 3).

8. E. R. Adair, 'The Military Reputation of Major-General James Wolfe', *Canadian Historical Association Report* (Ottawa, 1936), pp. 7–31.

9. C. Hibbert, *Wolfe at Quebec* (London, 1959); C. P. Stacey, *Quebec, 1759: The Siege and the Battle* (Toronto, 1959). Citations here refer to the 'revised edition' of this important work (Toronto, 2002), which includes additional editorial material by Donald E. Graves, and more illustrations.

10. C. P. Stacey, 'Wolfe, James', in *DCB*, iii, pp. 666–74; W. J. Eccles, 'Montcalm, Louis-Joseph de, Marquis de Montcalm', ibid., pp. 458–69.

11. 'Plains of Abraham II a Draw', *National Post*, 13 September 1999.

12. Pocock, *Horatio Nelson*, p. 276. This view is echoed by Andrew Lambert, who observes: 'Wolfe was an unknown who achieved fame by the manner of his death; Nelson had become a national deity in life, a hero in the Homeric mould'. See A. Lambert, *Nelson: Britannia's God of War* (London, 2004), p. 300.

13. Horace Walpole, *Memoirs of King George II*, ed. J. Brooke (3 vols, New Haven and London, 1985), iii, p. 75.

14. A. McNairn, *Behold the Hero: General Wolfe and the Arts in the Eighteenth Century* (Liverpool, 1997), p. xii.

Notes to Chapter 1: False Start

1. This section is compiled from reports published in the following newspapers: *Weekly Journal: or The British Gazeteer*, 19, 17 and 24 December 1726; *London Journal*, 3, 10 and 17 December 1726; and *Daily Journal*, 6, 9, 11 and 17 January 1727. Mary Tofts (or Toft) subsequently confessed her 'imposture' and was pardoned. Although now largely forgotten, her bizarre case made a deep impression upon her contemporaries. To satirists like the artist William Hogarth, Tofts epitomized the gullibility of his age. Her case drew his attention at the time, and as late as 1762 the 'rabbit woman' featured in the foreground of his print *Credulity, Superstition and Fanaticism*. See D. Jarrett, *England in the Age of Hogarth* (London, 1974), p. 182 and plate 31.

2. Evidence suggests that Henrietta Wolfe had been delivered of a child earlier in her marriage, but that the baby did not survive to be baptized – a far from rare occurrence in an age of high infant mortality. The son

of Wolfe's schoolmaster at Westerham, Thomas Lawrence, later recalled that his father was 'present at the christening and [spoke] of Mrs Wolfe telling him that James was not her first child'. See Thomas Lawrence junior to William Sutton, Reading, 2 September 1769, in McCord Museum, Montreal, C–173 ('Wolfe Collection'), box 1, MS 1432.

The date given here for Wolfe's birth, 2 January 1727, follows the New Style calendar. According to the Old Style calendar in use in England at that time, Wolfe was actually born on 22 December 1726, with his baptism following some three weeks later, on 11 January 1727 (O.S. 1726). As early as 1760, however, when Westerham residents erected a memorial tablet to Wolfe in their church, the New Style date was preferred. As this is also used in standard references, for example, E. M. Lloyd, 'Wolfe, James (1727–1759)', in *Dictionary of National Biography*, ed L. Stephen and S. Lee (63 vols, London, 1885–1900), lxii, pp. 296–304, it is followed here. For the full text of the memorial tablet see A. E. Wolfe-Aylward, *The Pictorial Life of Wolfe* (Plymouth, n.d., but *c.* 1924), pp. 178–79.

3. *London Magazine, 1759* (October), p. 568; *Scots Magazine, 1759* (October), p. 554; ibid., *1760* (January), p. 33. Wolfe's father was reputedly born in York and was certainly living in the city at the time of his marriage in 1724.

4. Daniel Defoe, *A Tour Through the Whole Island of Great Britain* (first published 1724–26), ed. P. Rogers (Harmondsworth, 1971), p. 165. Spiers still stands: renamed Quebec House in honour of its most celebrated tenant, it is now maintained as a museum by the National Trust. The old vicarage where Wolfe was born has also survived.

5. Ibid., pp. 43–44.

6. The literature on Britain's American colonies is vast. For useful overviews see. R. R. Johnson, 'Growth and Mastery: British North America, 1690–1748', and J. Shy, 'The American Colonies in War and Revolution, 1748–1783', chapters 13–14, in *The Oxford History of the British Empire*, ii, *The Eighteenth Century*, ed. P. J. Marshall (Oxford, 1998).

7. By 1775, on the eve of the American War of Independence, this figure had mushroomed to 2,500,000. See A. Taylor, *American Colonies: The Settlement of North America to 1800* (New York, 2001), pp. 426, 443. The population for England and Wales in 1731 has been estimated at 5,200,000, rising to 6,100,000 in 1760. The long reign of George III saw a population boom: the first census of 1801 recorded 8,800,000 inhabitants; that of 1821, no fewer than twelve million. See E. A. Wrigley and R. S. Schofield, *The Population History of England and Wales, 1541–1871: A Reconstruction* (2nd edn, Cambridge, 1989).

8. B. Willson, *The Life and Letters of James Wolfe* (New York, 1909), p. 7.

9. A. R. Wagner, 'The Genealogy of James Wolfe', in *Wolfe: Portraiture and Genealogy* (Westerham, 1959), pp. 45–56. The Wolfes nonetheless had close ties with Ireland. James's uncle, Major Walter Wolfe, retired to Dublin in the 1740s. In addition, his aunt Margaret was married to George Goldsmith of that city, a cousin of the celebrated poet and playwright Oliver Goldsmith.

10. Defoe, *Tour*, p. 113.

11. K. Wilson, *The Sense of the People: Politics, Culture and Imperialism in England, 1715–1785* (Cambridge, 1995), pp. 140–65.

12. D. Syrett, 'The Raising of American Troops for Service in the West Indies during the War of the Austrian Succession, 1740–41', *Historical Research*, 73 (2000), pp. 20–32; also D. E. Leach, *Roots of Conflict: British Armed Forces and Colonial Americans, 1677–1763* (Chapel Hill, North Carolina, 1986), pp. 49–61.

13. For the problems facing the Royal Navy, see in general, J. R. Jones, 'Limitations of British Seapower in the French Wars, 1689–1815', in *The British Navy and the Use of Naval Power in the Eighteenth Century*, ed. J. Black and P. Woodfine (Leicester, 1988), pp. 33–49. A more specific focus upon the War of Jenkins's Ear is provided by P. Woodfine, 'Ideas of Naval Power and the Conflict with Spain, 1737–1742', ibid., pp. 71–90. Naval shortcomings, and other problems that hampered prosecution of the conflict, are also addressed in R. Harding, 'Sir Robert Walpole's Ministry and the Conduct of the War with Spain, 1739–41', in *Historical Research*, 60 (1987), pp. 299–320.

14. For attitudes towards the army in eighteenth-century Britain see C. Barnett, *Britain and Her Army, 1509–1970: A Military, Political and Social History* (London, 1970), pp. 165–68. A useful brief survey is A. J. Guy, 'The Army of the Georges, 1714–1783', in *The Oxford Illustrated History of the British Army*, ed. D. Chandler and I. Beckett (Oxford, 1994), pp. 92–110.

15. J. Houlding, *Fit for Service: The Training of the British Army, 1715–1795* (Oxford, 1981), pp. 9–10.

16. Following Robert Wright, in his *The Life of Major-General James Wolfe* (London, 1864), p. 12, subsequent writers have stated that Edward Wolfe was appointed adjutant-general to the West Indian expedition. This key post, which conveyed responsibility for the training and discipline of the troops, was in fact given to Colonel Blakeney; he was sent across the Atlantic ahead of the main force to help organize the American volunteers. In Blakeney's absence, Brigadier-General Wentworth fulfilled the role of adjutant-general to the troops at Newport Camp.

See R. Harding, *Amphibious Warfare in the Eighteenth Century: The British Expedition to the West Indies, 1740–1742* (Woodbridge, Suffolk, 1991), pp. 45–47.

17. Houlding, *Fit for Service*, p. 69. For the army's police role, see T. Hayter, *The Army and the Crowd in Mid-Georgian England* (London, 1978).

18. Because of the chronic shortage of seamen, another two infantry regiments, the 34th and 36th of Foot, were assigned to the expedition before it sailed. Blakeney's rejected regiment eventually joined the West Indian force in February 1742 as part of a 3000-strong reinforcement from Britain that also included a battalion of the Royal Scots and the 6th Foot. See C. T. Atkinson, 'Jenkins' Ear, the Austrian Succession War and the Forty Five', in *JSAHR*, 22 (1944), p. 287; and J. W. Fortescue, *A History of the British Army*, ii (London, 1910), pp. 61, 75.

19. Letter of 6 August 1740, in Wright, *Life of Wolfe*, p. 13.

20. For a detailed account of these operations see Harding, *Amphibious Warfare*; also Fortescue, *History of the British Army*, ii, pp. 55–79.

21. Tobias Smollett, *The Adventures of Roderick Random* (first published 1748), ed. P. G. Boucé (Oxford, 1979), p. 186.

22. *The Life, Adventures and Surprising Deliverances of Duncan Cameron, Private Soldier* ... (3rd edn, Philadelphia, 1756), pp. 6–7.

23. McCord Museum, C–173, box 1, MS 1293: Wolfe to Weston, at Queen's College, Oxford, from Mr Swinden's, King Street, Greenwich, 24 January 1742.

24. Ibid., MS 1292 (Wolfe to Weston, Greenwich, 29 December 1741).

Notes to Chapter 2: First Campaign

1. For overviews of this conflict see M. S. Anderson, *The War of the Austrian Succession, 1740–1748* (London, 1995); also R. Browning, *The War of the Austrian Succession* (New York, 1993).

2. *Gentleman's Magazine*, 1742 (July), p. 390; 'The Life of Lieutenant-General Hawley', Hawley-Toovey Papers (copies of originals in Royal Archives, Windsor), NAM, MS 7411–24–101–1 (transcript), p. 16.

3. B. Willson, *The Life and Letters of James Wolfe* (New York, 1909) pp. 21–22.

4. NAM, MS 7704–81–1 (transcript): 'Diary of Ensign Hugh McKay, May 1742-February 1743'. All cited passages are readily located by date.

5. On desertion and discipline in the mid eighteenth-century British Army see S. Brumwell, *Redcoats: The British Soldier and War in the Americas, 1755–1763* (Cambridge, 2002), pp. 99–112.

6. See J. C. O'Callaghan, *History of the Irish Brigades in the Service of France* (Glasgow, 1870; reprint, Shannon, 1969).

7. For the prevalence of duelling in Georgian England see D. T. Andrew, 'The Code of Honour and its Critics: The Opposition to Duelling in England, 1700–1850', in *Social History*, 5 (1980), pp. 409–34.

8. From Ghent, 27 August and 12 September 1742, in Willson, *Life and Letters of Wolfe*, pp. 21–23.

9. J. W. Fortescue, *A History of the British Army*, ii (London, 1910), pp. 85–88; R. Whitworth, *Field Marshal Lord Ligonier: A Story of the British Army, 1702–1770* (Oxford, 1958), pp. 63–66.

10. James Wolfe to his mother, 'St Tron, in the Bishopric of Liège', 12 February 1743, and Edward Wolfe to his father, Bonn, 7 April 1743, in Willson, *Life and Letters of Wolfe*, pp. 25–27.

11. Fortescue, *History of the British Army*, ii, p. 89.

12. The account of Dettingen that follows draws upon: Anon, *British Glory Reviv'd: Being a Compleat Collection of all the Accounts, Papers, Expresses and Private Letters Relating to the Late Glorious Action at Dettingen* (London, 1743); Anon, *The Operations of the British and the Allied Arms, during the Campaigns of 1743 and 1744* (London, 1744), pp. 15–17; *Scots Magazine, 1743* (July), pp. 337–39; 'Military Memoirs of Lieutenant-General the Hon. Charles Colville: Part II', ed. J. O. Robson, in *JSAHR*, 26 (1948), pp. 117–20; M. Orr, *Dettingen 1743* (London, 1972), pp. 46–66; Whitworth, *Lord Ligonier*, pp. 73–77; R. Butler, *Choiseul*, i, *Father and Son, 1719–1754* (Oxford, 1980), pp. 414–18.

13. Extract from Townshend's journal in C. V. F. Townshend, *The Military Life of Field-Marshal George First Marquess Townshend, 1724–1807* (London, 1901), p. 29.

14. James Wolfe to his father, Höchst, 4 July 1743, in Willson, *Life and Letters of Wolfe*, pp. 36–38.

15. *British Glory Reviv'd*, pp. 21, 30–31.

16. For Trooper Brown's exploits see H. Bolitho, *The Galloping Third* (London, 1963), pp. 64–66. Brown was initially appointed to the prestigious, and well paid, First Troop of Horse Guards. But his Dettingen wounds left him too disabled to serve; indeed, his transfer may have been no more than a formality to guarantee him the higher pension rate available to a 'Private Gentleman' in the Horse Guards. On 31 January 1744 he came before the commissioners of Chelsea's Royal Hospital to be examined for his pension. The hospital's surviving 'Admissions Book' shows that Brown was then aged twenty-eight and had served for eight years. He was described as a shoemaker, from Kirkleatham in Yorkshire's North Riding.

His examiners noted 'several scars in his head, a cut in the forehead, nose and lip' (see WO/116/3, fol. 88).

17. R. Wright, *The Life of Major-General James Wolfe* (London, 1864), p. 49.

18. 1 September 1743 in Willson, *Life and Letters of Wolfe*, pp. 40–41.

19. Ostend, 21 March 1744 (OS), ibid., p. 43.

20. S. Reid, *Wolfe: The Career of General James Wolfe from Culloden to Quebec* (Staplehurst, Kent, 2000), pp. 59–61.

21. Whitworth, *Lord Ligonier*, p. 84.

22. Orders, Camp of Anstain, 10/20 August; 4 September 1744, in Amherst Family Papers, Centre for Kentish Studies, Maidstone, MS U1350/02/1 (unpaginated).

23. *Operations of the British and the Allied Arms*, p. 54.

24. See W. M. Parker, 'Wade's Campaign in Flanders', *Army Quarterly*, 86 (1963), p. 114.

25. Letter from Ghent, 29 October 1744 (OS), in Willson, *Life and Letters of Wolfe*, pp. 60–61.

26. Whitworth, *Lord Ligonier*, pp. 97–103; Fortescue, *History of the British Army*, ii, pp. 111–20; Wolfe to his father, Ghent, 4 May 1745 (OS), in Willson, *Life and Letters of Wolfe*, pp. 49–50.

27. 'Cumberland's Order Book' in Townshend, *Life of Townshend*, p. 81. The commission itself carried the Old Style date of 12 June 1745.

28. [George Townshend] *A Brief Narrative of the Late Campaigns in Germany and Flanders in a Letter to a Member of Parliament* (London, 1751), pp. 25–26; Lady Sarah Cowper to Mrs Dewes, cited in Wright, *Life of Wolfe*, pp. 64–65 (note).

Notes to Chapter 3: Rebellion

1. This overview follows W. A. Speck, *The Butcher: The Duke of Cumberland and the Suppression of the 45* (Oxford, 1981), pp. 27–31.

2. Wolfe to his father, 21 June 1743, in R. Wright, *The Life of Major-General James Wolfe* (London, 1864), p. 38; *London Gazette*, 9–12 July 1743.

3. See WO/120/4, p. 550. For other Prestonpans casualties see ibid., pp. 539–40, 545, 549–52.

4. Edward Wolfe to Mrs Wolfe, Newcastle, 3 November 1745 (McCord Museum, C–173, box 1, MS 1434); B. Willson, *The Life and Letters of James Wolfe* (New York, 1909), p. 53.

5. For Prince Charles's march south and the royalist efforts to thwart it, see C. Duffy, *The '45: Bonnie Prince Charlie and the Untold Story of the Jacobite Rising* (London, 2003), pp. 208–99.

6. 'The Life of Lieutenant-General Hawley' (NAM, MS 7411-24-101-1), pp. 1, 7, 13, 20.

7. Anon, *The Operations of the British and the Allied Arms, during the Campaigns of 1743 and 1744* (London, 1744), pp. 43-44.

8. Cited in F. Tomasson and K. Buist, *Battles of the '45* (London, 1967), pp. 93-94.

9. Cholmondeley to Edward Weston, Edinburgh, 21 January 1746, in *HMC: Reports of the Manuscripts of the Earl of Eglinton, Sir J. Stirling Maxwell, Bart, C. S. H. Drummond Moray, Esq., C. F. Weston Underwood, Esq., and G. Wingfield Digby, Esq.* (London, 1885), pp. 440-42; 'Life of Hawley', pp. 24-25. For general accounts of Falkirk see also S. Reid, *1745: A Military History of the Last Jacobite Rising* (Staplehurst, Kent, 1996), pp. 98-103; Duffy, *The '45*, pp. 409-26; Tomasson and Buist, *Battles of the '45*, pp. 97-111.

10. Ibid., p. 182.

11. Letter dated Edinburgh, 20 January 1746, in Willson, *Life and Letters of Wolfe*, pp. 56-7.

12. For Wolfe's views on Hawley, see letter to his mother, Canterbury, 5 November 1755, in ibid., p. 280. Wolfe was appointed to Hawley's staff at Edinburgh on 21 January 1746. See NLS, MS 303, copy of orderly book kept in the army of Wade (and also those of Hawley and Cumberland), 23 October 1745-14 August 1746, fol. 84.

13. See Mrs Gordon's correspondence in Robert Forbes, *The Lyon in Mourning*, ed. H. Paton (3 vols, Edinburgh, 1896), iii, pp. 167-80; also, J. T. Findlay, *Wolfe in Scotland in the '45 and from 1749 to 1753* (London, 1928), pp. 88-95; Wright, *Life of Wolfe*, pp. 78-81.

14. Letter dated Inverness, 17 April 1746, in Willson, *Life and Letters of Wolfe*, p. 65. For detailed accounts of Culloden, see J. Prebble, *Culloden* (London, 1961), pp. 79-141; Reid, *1745: A Military History*, pp. 145-72; Tomasson and Buist, *Battles of the '45*, pp. 126-77; Duffy, *The '45*, pp. 501-26.

15. Anon, *A Journey Through Part of England and Scotland Along with the Army under the Command of His Royal Highness the Duke of Cumberland ... By a Volunteer. Comprised in Several Letters to a Friend in London* (London, 1747), p. 164; 'Life of Hawley', p. 28.

16. Andrew Henderson, *The History of the Rebellion MDCCXLV and MDCCXLVI* (5th edn, revised and corrected, London, 1753), pp. 329-31; Speck, *The Butcher*, pp. 149-55; Willson, *Life and Letters of Wolfe*, p. 65; also Wolfe to Henry Delabene, Inverness, 17 April 1746 in ibid., p. 63. Cumberland's latest biographer believes that the 'no quarter' orders were genuine. See R. Whitworth, *William Augustus, Duke of Cumberland: A Life* (Barnsley,

1992), pp. 89–90. By contrast, the most recent scholarly account of the campaign concludes that the Jacobite orders were 'doctored', further to motivate the royal troops (Duffy, *The '45*, p. 511). Like Wolfe, trooper Enoch Bradshaw of Cobham's Dragoons credited the reports: on 11 May 1746, he told his brother that according to the rebels' 'orderly books, had they got the better, we were to be every soul of us cut off, and not have had one prisoner, and [as] for the Duke he was to have been cut as small as herbs for the pot' (*Lyon in Mourning*, i, p. 380).

17. *Anti-Jacobin Review*, 13 (1802), p. 125; *Lyon in Mourning*, iii, p. 56.
18. To Henry Delabene, in Willson, *Life and Letters of Wolfe*, p. 63.
19. See Speck, *The Butcher*, pp. 163–71; Prebble, *Culloden*, pp. 174–218; Allan I. Macinnes, *Clanship, Commerce and the House of Stuart, 1603–1788* (East Linton, 1996), pp. 211–17.
20. Prebble, *Culloden*, pp. 186–88. See also Wolfe's letters to Hamilton, Inverness, 19 May 1746; Fort Augustus, 11 June 1746; and undated, but *c.* July 1746, in Willson, *Life and Letters of Wolfe*, pp. 68–69.
21. On Lauffeldt see especially the following detailed accounts: 'Relation of the Action at the Village of Val [Lauffeldt]', republished from *London Gazette Extraordinary* in *Gentleman's Magazine, 1747* (July), pp. 315–18; Anon, 'Operations of the Campaigne 1748 [actually 1747]', NAM, MS 6807–149, pp. 20–27; R. Whitworth, *Field Marshal Lord Ligonier: A Story of the British Army, 1702–1770* (Oxford, 1958), pp. 150–60; R. Butler, *Choiseul, i, Father and Son, 1719–1754* (Oxford, 1980), pp. 689–95; Major Adolphus Oughton to –, Maastricht, 9 July (begun 5 July) 1747, in *By Dint of Labour and Perseverance . . .* , ed. S. Wood (Society for Army Historical Research, Special Publication No. 14, 1997), pp. 10–13; J. C. O'Callaghan, *History of the Irish Brigades in the Service of France* (Glasgow, 1870; reprint, Shannon, 1969), pp. 467–73; J. W. Fortescue, *A History of the British Army*, ii, (London, 1910), pp. 159–63.
22. [George Townshend] *A Brief Narrative of the Late Campaigns in Germany and Flanders in a Letter to a Member of Parliament* (London, 1751), pp. 44–45; *Remarks on the Military Operations of the English and French Armies, Commanded by His Royal Highness the Duke of Cumberland and Marshal Saxe, during the Campaign of 1747 . . . By an Officer* (London, 1760), pp. 56–90.
23. 'Memorandum' under 2 July, in 'Orders 19 June to 13 September 1747' (Amherst Family Papers, U1350/02/5); *Gunner at Large: The Diary of James Wood, R. A., 1746–1765*, ed. R. Whitworth (London, 1988), pp. 41–42. Despite Wood's use of the term 'grapeshot', the close-range ammunition concerned was more accurately 'case shot' or 'canister' – basically

a container (typically a tin case) packed with from forty to eighty-five large-calibre lead bullets, the number depending upon whether it was 'heavy' or 'light'. True grapeshot, which involved a bunch of just nine far weightier projectiles, was typically a naval armament. See B. P. Hughes, *Firepower: Weapons Effectiveness on the Battlefield, 1630–1850* (London, 1974), pp. 34–35. However, given the frequent references to 'grapeshot' in contemporary accounts of warfare – not least those written by artillerymen themselves – it is likewise used here as a synonym for case shot.

24. *Scots Magazine, 1747* (July), pp. 346–47.

25. The Scots Greys suffered 112 killed and forty-four wounded; the Inniskilling Dragoons eighty-four dead and thirty-one wounded; Cumberland's Dragoons reported seventeen killed and wounded, but no fewer than seventy missing. See 'Kill'd, wounded, etc in the battle near Kisselt', *Gentleman's Magazine, 1747* (June), p. 259.

26. 'Life of Hawley', p. 30.

27. Undated item entitled 'British Troops Brigaded 1747', in 'Orders 19 June to 13 September 1747'. The three battalions of Mordaunt's brigade together reported a total of 494 of all ranks killed, wounded or missing (*Gentleman's Magazine, 1747*, p. 259).

28. Wright, *Life of Wolfe*, p. 100; *London Gazette*, 30 June to 4 July 1747; Colonel Yorke to Colonel Barrington, camp at Richelt, 11 July 1747, in *HMC: Frankland-Russell-Astley Manuscripts* (London, 1900), p. 371.

29. 'Character, with Some Particulars, of the Late Major-General James Wolfe', in *London Magazine, 1759* (November), p. 579.

30. See under relevant dates in 'Orders 19 June to 13 September 1747'.

31. Letter from Glasgow, 2 April 1749, in Willson, *Life and Letters of Wolfe*, p. 93.

32. Cumberland's recommendation, contained in a letter dated 20 May 1747, is cited in Fortescue, *History of the British Army*, ii, p. 157.

33. See Wolfe to his father, Osterhout, 12 April 1748, in Willson, *Life and Letters of Wolfe*, pp. 79–80. On Wolfe's promotion frustrations see also S. Reid, *Wolfe: The Career of General James Wolfe from Culloden to Quebec* (Staplehurst, Kent, 2000), pp. 71–72, 74–75. Cumberland soon after made an unsuccessful attempt to 'break', or disband, Bragg's unruly regiment as a warning to others that failed to meet his high standards of efficiency. See Whitworth, *William Augustus, Duke of Cumberland*, p. 132.

34. For the Peace of Aix-La-Chapelle, see M. S. Anderson, *The War of the Austrian Succession, 1740–1748* (London, 1995), pp. 193–209.

Notes to Chapter 4: The Frustrations of Peace

1. J*** P****** [John Pringle] *The Life of General James Wolfe, the Conqueror of Quebec: or The Elogium of that Renowned Hero, Attempted According to the Rules of Eloquence, with a Monumental Inscription, to Perpetuate his Memory* (London, 1760), p. 6.

2. W. A. Speck, *The Butcher: The Duke of Cumberland and the Suppression of the 45* (Oxford, 1981), pp. 171–77; also, Bob Harris, *Politics and The Nation: Britain in the Mid-Eighteenth Century* (Oxford, 2002), pp. 165–80.

3. These General Orders, and others subsequently issued by Wolfe to the units under his command, were collected in *General Wolfe's Instructions to Young Officers . . .* (London, 1768; repr. 1780), p. 5. A battalion of 'marching foot' at this time consisted of ten companies, each composed of seventy privates, two drummers, three corporals, three sergeants, one ensign, one lieutenant and a captain. See J. Houlding, *Fit for Service: The Training of the British Army, 1715–1795* (Oxford, 1981), p. 418, table C.

4. For Wolfe's physical appearance, see especially the description by Lieutenant Henry Hamilton of the 15th Foot, given in J. S. McLennan, *Louisbourg from its Foundation to its Fall, 1713–1758* (London, 1918), p. 315. Some idea of the unusualness of Wolfe's height can be gauged from data taken from British units serving in North America in 1757. Of the 14,358 men for whom details are given, just 194 – less than 1.5 per cent – had a height of six feet or over. See S. Brumwell, *Redcoats: The British Soldier and War in the Americas, 1755–1763* (Cambridge, 2002), p. 316, table 3.

5. *Wolfe's Instructions*, p. 7.

6. T. M. Devine, *The Scottish Nation, 1700–2000* (London, 1999), pp. 58–59, 105.

7. Glasgow, 2 April 1749, in B. Willson, *The Life and Letters of James Wolfe* (New York, 1909), p. 94.

8. Wolfe to his mother, Glasgow, 14 April 1749 (ibid., pp. 97–98).

9. M. Fido, *Bodysnatchers: A History of the Resurrectionists, 1742–1832* (London, 1988), especially chapter 2, 'The Origins of Bodysnatching in Scotland'. On the mid eighteenth-century mob's antipathy towards dissection, see Peter Linebaugh, 'The Tyburn Riot Against the Surgeons', in Douglas Hay et al., *Albion's Fatal Tree: Crime and Society in Eighteenth-Century England* (London, 1975), pp. 65–117.

10. Wolfe to Churchill, 6 March 1747, in NLS, MS 307 ('Letter Book of General George Churchill, 5 April 1747–24 October 1749'), pp. 114–116. On 21 May, the two men arrested during the riot, who'd been sentenced to whipping and transportation, made a daring escape during the Sunday

church service, sliding from their high prison window by a rope. See Wolfe to Churchill, Glasgow, 22 May 1749 (ibid., p. 185).

11. Cited in J. T. Findlay, *Wolfe in Scotland in the '45 and from 1749 to 1753* (London, 1928), pp. 162–63.

12. *Wolfe's Instructions*, p. 11.

13. Sackville clearly had remarkable reserves of character. Ostracized following his court martial for disobedience at the battle of Minden in 1759, he slowly clawed his way back to power, and as Lord George Germain, the American Secretary, masterminded British strategy during the American War of Independence. See P. Mackesy, *The Coward of Minden: The Affair of Lord George Sackville* (London, 1978); and also his *The War for America, 1775–1783* (London, 1963).

14. Wolfe to his mother, 19 July 1749, and his father, 2 August 1749 (Willson, *Life and Letters of Wolfe*, pp. 102, 105).

15. Glasgow, 13 August 1749 (ibid., p. 107).

16. To his mother, Glasgow, 8 September 149 (ibid.).

17. 2 October 1749 (ibid., p. 109).

18. *Wolfe's Instructions*, p. 3; Wolfe to General Churchill's *aide-de-camp*, Captain James Stewart, Glasgow, 5 October 1749 (NLS, MS 307, p. 266).

19. To his father, Perth, 23 March 1750, and to his mother, 29 March 1750, in Willson, *Life and Letters of Wolfe*, pp. 117–18.

20. *Wolfe's Instructions*, pp. 7, 20.

21. Wolfe to Erskine, 16 March 1750, in NLS, MS 5076 ('Erskine-Murray Correspondence, 1747–51'), fol. 136. For Wolfe as 'military parent', see his letter to his mother from Banff, 17 September 1751 (Willson, *Life and Letters of Wolfe*, p. 153). On his legendary paternalism, see for example, *New-York Gazette*, 3 December 1759, under 'Philadelphia, 29 November'. Wolfe's role as 'parent' to his regimental 'family' is underlined by a petition addressed to him by Anne White, the wife of one of his sergeants, at Glasgow on 25 June 1752. Mrs White wrote: 'Collonel, Being a true Noble harted Pittifull gentleman and Officer yr worship will excuse these few lines concearning ye Husband of ye under sign'd, Sergt White who not from his own fault is not beehaving as Hee shoud towards mee and his Family although good and faithful until ye middle of November last' (besides the spelling, here the original punctuation and capitalization has also been retained). Wolfe acted upon this appeal. In a note on the petition he observed: 'The writer of the above is a most respectable young woman and the wife of a former servant of Cornwallis's whom I have since endeavour'd to wean from his evil ways!' See McCord Museum, C–173 ('Wolfe Collection'), box 1, MS 1218.

22. See Wolfe's letters to his father from Perth, 6 April, 27 April, 15 July and 1 September 1750, and to Rickson from Dundee, October 1750, and Banff, 9 June 1751, in Willson, *Life and Letters of Wolfe*, pp. 121–22, 127–28, 130–31, 135 and 144.

23. Glasgow, 2 April 1749 (ibid., p. 93).

24. This discussion draws heavily upon Lawrence Stone's *The Family, Sex and Marriage in England, 1500–1800* (London, 1977), especially chapter 7, 'Mating Arrangements'.

25. Wolfe to his mother, Glasgow, 19 July 1749, and Perth, 15 December 1749, in Willson, *Life and Letters of Wolfe*, pp. 103, 111.

26. Same to same, Perth, 6 and 29 February 1750, and to his father, Perth, 19 February 1750 (ibid., pp. 114–15, 118).

27. R. Wright, *The Life of Major-General James Wolfe* (London, 1864), p. 164. Wright notes that Miss Hoskins of Croydon – Henrietta Wolfe's favourite – married Wolfe's old Westerham friend John Warde in February 1751.

28. Wolfe to Rickson, Banff, 9 June 1751 (Willson, *Life and Letters of Wolfe*, p. 144).

29. E. R. Adair, 'The Military Reputation of Major-General James Wolfe', *Canadian Historical Association Report* (Ottawa, 1936), p. 10.

30. Wolfe to his father, Banff, 12 June 1751, and Peterhead, 29 July 1751 (Willson, *Life and Letters of Wolfe*, pp. 146, 150). Christopher Hibbert writes that the 'suppression and sublimation of [Wolfe's] homosexual tendencies is undoubtedly a reasonable explanation of the neurosis which complicated his character. That they were suppressed seems certain'. This same theme has been developed by another prominent popular historian, Frank McLynn, who characterizes Wolfe as 'a psychological oddity, what psychoanalysts would doubtless call an example of "masculine over-protest"'. He links Wolfe's bachelor status to over-identification with his parents. See C. Hibbert, *Wolfe at Quebec* (London, 1959), pp. 9–11; F. McLynn, *1759: The Year Britain Became Master of the World* (London, 2004), p. 205. By contrast, Professor Adair accepted that Wolfe fell in love with both Elizabeth Lawson, and later, Katherine Lowther ('Military Reputation', p. 10).

31. Banff, 12 August 1751 (Willson, *Life and Letters of Wolfe*, p. 151).

32. See Wolfe's letters to his mother, Glasgow, 19 July 1749, Perth, 9 March, 25 July and 23 September 1750, in ibid., pp. 102, 117, 128, 132–33; and to his father, Perth, 29 May and 15 July 1750 (ibid., pp. 126–27). Wolfe's health has attracted much interest. Although it is often stated that he was gradually succumbing to pulmonary tuberculosis, or 'consumption', there is no hard contemporary evidence for this. In addition, it is worth noting that,

even by the standards of their privileged class, Wolfe's parents lived long lives. For some very helpful insights into Wolfe's health and illnesses, I am much indebted to Lawrence Power, M.D., of Ann Arbor, Michigan, who generously allowed me to see a copy of his unpublished paper, 'A Good Spirit Carries'.

33. On the onset of Wolfe's gravel, see letters to his father from Peterhead, 29 July, and to his mother, 12 August 1751 (Willson, *Life and Letters of Wolfe*, pp. 150–51).

34. For growing Anglo-French tensions in North America, see especially T. R. Clayton, 'The Duke of Newcastle, the Earl of Halifax and the American Origins of the Seven Years' War', *Historical Journal*, 24 (1981), pp. 573–84; also F. Anderson, *Crucible of War: The Seven Years' War and the Fate of Empire in British North America, 1754–1766* (New York, 2000), pp. 22–41.

35. Wolfe to Rickson, Dundee, – October 1750, in Willson, *Life and Letters of Wolfe*, pp. 133–34.

36. To Rickson, Banff, 9 June 1751 (ibid., pp. 140–41).

37. Cited in James A. Henretta, *'Salutary Neglect': Colonial Administration under the Duke of Newcastle* (Princeton, New Jersey, 1972), p. 292.

38. Wolfe to his father, – October 1751, in Willson, *Life and Letters of Wolfe*, p. 157.

39. To his mother, Inverness, 6 November 1751 (ibid., pp. 158–61).

40. To his father, Inverness, 13 December 1751 (ibid., p. 163). For Keppoch's charge, see J. Prebble, *Culloden* (London, 1961), pp. 103–106.

41. Wolfe to his mother, Inverness 22–25 December 1751 (Willson, *Life and Letters of Wolfe*, pp. 164–66).

42. To his father, 1 February 1752 (ibid., p. 170); same to same, Inverness, 12 January 1752 ('General Wolfe's Letters to his Parents, 1740–1759', Squerryes Court, Westerham, pp. 199–202). The hazardous, and excruciatingly painful, surgery so dreaded by Wolfe had been undergone by the diarist Samuel Pepys in 1658. After an incision into the neck of his bladder, Pepys was finally relieved of a 'tennis ball'-sized 'stone' that had lodged there after migrating from a kidney. See Claire Tomalin, *Samuel Pepys: The Unequalled Self* (London, 2002), pp. 59–63.

43. Wolfe to his father, Inverness, 20 March 1752 (Willson, *Life and Letters of Wolfe*, p. 174).

44. See Wright, *Life of Wolfe*, pp. 202–3.

45. Willson, *Life and Letters of Wolfe*, pp. 176–77.

46. On these forts, see C. Duffy, *The '45: Bonnie Prince Charlie and the Untold Story of the Jacobite Rising* (London, 2003), pp. 149–52.

47. Wolfe to his father, Fort Augustus, 28 May 1752 (Willson, *Life and Letters of Wolfe*, pp. 179–89).
48. Wright, *Life of Wolfe*, pp. 212–13.
49. Cluny only quit his 'cage' in 1754, when Charles Edward finally summoned him to Paris. To the Prince's chagrin, the gold was long gone. See Frank McLynn, *Charles Edward Stuart: A Tragedy in Many Acts* (London, 1988), especially pp. 303–5, 432, 435–36.
50. GD 248, box 614: Commonplace book of John Grant for 1752–97 (kept whilst Grant was minister at Dundurglas and Elgin) under 'Anecdotes Relating to the American War and Other Memorable Matters', no. 76.
51. Letter from Exeter, 7 March 1755, in Willson, *Life and Letters of Wolfe*, p. 254.
52. For example, Wolfe's biographer Robin Reilly considered the plan 'indefensible and unworthy of him' – indeed, an operation that would have disgraced 'Hangman' Hawley himself. See *The Rest to Fortune: The Life of Major-General James Wolfe* (London, 1960), p. 100.
53. NLS, MS 308 ('Letter Book of General Churchill, 1751–52'), p. 218.
54. Wolfe to his father, Dublin, 13 July 1752, and to his mother, Canterbury, 27 December 1755, in Willson, *Life and Letters of Wolfe*, pp. 182–83, 284. The sketch of the 'Irish Venus', by George Townshend, the noted caricaturist and one of Wolfe's brigadiers at Quebec, is in the collections of the McCord Museum, Montreal. It is reproduced in A. McNairn, *Behold the Hero: General Wolfe and the Arts in the Eighteenth Century* (Liverpool, 1997), p. 50.
55. A banner bearing the slogan 'Give us our Eleven Days' features in the foreground of Hogarth's painting *The Banquet*, from his *Election* series of 1754.
56. Wolfe to his father, Paris, 9 October 1752 (Willson, *Life and Letters of Wolfe*, pp. 186–87). For the Saint-Cloud fête see R. Butler, *Choiseul*, i, *Father and Son, 1719–1754* (Oxford, 1980), pp. 921–23. On contemporary British attitudes towards the French see J. Black, *Natural and Necessary Enemies: Anglo-French Relations in the Eighteenth Century* (London, 1986).
57. Wolfe to his father, Paris, 2 November and 4 December 1752, in Willson, *Life and Letters of Wolfe*, pp. 189, 193.
58. To his mother, Paris, 2 January 1753 (ibid., pp. 197–98).
59. To his father, Paris, 10 January 1753 (ibid., p. 199).
60. For a breakdown of the library, see Nancy Mitford, *Madame de Pompadour* (London, 1954), pp. 154–55.

61. Wolfe to his mother, Paris, 19 January 1753, and to his father, Paris, 29 January 1753, in Willson, *Life and Letters of Wolfe*, pp. 200–1.
62. To his mother, Paris, 1 March 1753, and to his father, Paris, 22 February 1753 (ibid., 206, 204).
63. To his father, Paris, 9 March 1753 (ibid., pp. 206–7).
64. Same to same, Glasgow, 22 April 1753 (ibid., pp. 210–11).
65. To his mother, Glasgow, 13 May 1753 (ibid., p. 211).
66. Wolfe to his father, north-west side of Loch Lomond, 7 August 1753 (ibid., pp. 217–218).
67. For General Campbell's comments on the 20th, see WO/27/3 (Inspection Returns, 1753–55). Cumberland's observations – and Bury's reaction to them – are given in *Wolfe's Instructions*, pp. 31–32. See also Houlding, *Fit for Service*, p. 310 n. 67. Pulteney's 13th Foot clearly excelled at musketry: when seen at Carlisle in April 1753, the reviewing officer noted that it fired 'very quick, as close, and well, as it was possible for men to fire' (WO/27/3).
68. *Wolfe's Instructions* (Dover Castle, 23 December 1753), pp. 30–31. The seriousness of this problem is all too clear from a letter from Major-General Lord Charles Hay to the Secretary at War, Lord Barrington, on 12 February 1759. Hay had received a report from the commanding officer of the 33rd Regt of Foot in Hilsea Barracks, Portsmouth, that his men were 'continually infested with numbers of vagrants and dissolute women lying in the hedgerows round the barracks'. In consequence, many soldiers were 'distemper'd', others had 'become incapable of duty', and several had 'died under salivations' (WO/1/979, not paged or foliated).
69. *Wolfe's Instructions*, p. 31.
70. Wolfe to his mother, Sittingbourne, 24 March 1754 (Willson, *Life and Letters of Wolfe*, p. 236).
71. Same to same, Freefolk, 14 July 1754 (ibid., pp. 237–38).
72. See Wolfe from Exeter to his father and mother, 25 and 31 October 1754 (ibid., pp. 240–43).
73. Henry Fox to Major Wilkinson, War Office, 20 October 1754 (WO/4/50, p. 77).
74. See 'Sketch for the Operations in North America, November 16, 1754', in *Military Affairs in North America, 1748–1765: Selected Documents from the Cumberland Papers in Windsor Castle*, ed. Stanley Pargellis (New Haven, 1936), pp. 45–48.
75. *Wolfe's Instructions*, p. 38.

Notes to Chapter 5: Waiting in the Wings

1. See R. S. Neale, *Bath, 1680–1850: A Social History* (London, 1981); also Paul Langford, *A Polite and Commercial People: England, 1727–1783* (Oxford, 1989), pp. 105–107.

2. To his mother, Bristol, 19 January 1755, in B. Willson, *The Life and Letters of James Wolfe* (New York, 1909), p. 300.

3. *General Wolfe's Instructions to Young Officers ...* (London, 1768; repr. 1780), pp. 33–35.

4. Wolfe to his father, Winchester, 12 April 1755, in Willson, *Life and Letters of Wolfe*, pp. 260–61.

5. *Wolfe's Instructions*, p. 36.

6. *Gentleman's Magazine, 1755* (July), p. 327; Wolfe to his father, Winchester, 5 July 1755, in Willson, *Life and Letters of Wolfe*, p. 268. On Anson, see G. Williams, *The Prize of all the Oceans: The Triumph and Tragedy of Anson's Voyage Around the World* (London, 1999).

7. Wolfe to Captain Rickson, Lymington, 19 July 1755, in Willson, *Life and Letters of Wolfe*, pp. 270–71.

8. Wolfe to his father, Southampton, 14 August 1755 (ibid., pp. 272–73).

9. Wolfe to his mother, Southampton, 28 September 1755, and Cirencester, 30 December 1756 (ibid., pp. 276, 311–12).

10. See the reports in *London Gazette*, 23–26 August 1755, and *Gentleman's Magazine, 1755* (August), p. 380; Wolfe to his father, Southampton, 4 September 1755, in Willson, *Life and Letters of Wolfe*, p. 274. Willson omitted the 'ox' from 'pox', but the gap can be filled by consulting the original ('General Wolfe's Letters to his Parents, 1740–1759', Squerryes Court, Westerham, p. 635).

11. Letter of 15 September 1755, McCord Museum, C–173 ('Wolfe Collection'), box 1, MS 1290.

12. Winchester, 25 October 1755, in 'Some Unpublished Wolfe Letters, 1755–58', ed. R. H. Whitworth, in *JSAHR*, 53 (1975), p. 68.

13. Wolfe to his mother, Canterbury, 5 and 8 November, in Willson, *Life and Letters of Wolfe*, pp. 279–80.

14. 'Instructions for the 20th Regiment (in case the French land), given by Lieutenant-Colonel Wolfe at Canterbury', in *Wolfe's Instructions*, pp. 46–53.

15. For the 'ferocious recoil' from such double loading, see the discussion in David F. Harding, *Smallarms of the East India Company, 1600–1856* (4 vols, London, 1997–99), iii, p. 12.

16. Wolfe to his mother, Canterbury, 12 May 1756, in Willson, *Life and Letters of Wolfe*, p. 290.

17. On Minorca, see Lawrence Henry Gipson, *The British Empire Before the American Revolution* (15 vols, New York, 1936–70), vi, *The Great War for the Empire: The Years of Defeat, 1754–1757*, pp. 402–16; also J. W. Fortescue, *A History of the British Army*, ii, (London, 1910), pp. 297–301; Jonathan R. Dull, *The French Navy and the Seven Years' War* (Lincoln, Nebraska, 2005), pp. 50–54; N. A. M Rodger, *The Command of the Ocean: A Naval History of Britain, 1649–1815* (London, 2004), pp. 264–67.

18. See letters from Basingstoke, 1 June, Bristol, 7 June, Devizes, 27 June, 17 and 26 July 1756, in Willson, *Life and Letters of Wolfe*, pp. 292–93, 295, 300.

19. Wolfe to his mother, Devizes, 26 July 1756 (ibid., p. 299).

20. To Richmond, Devizes, 20 July 1756, *JSAHR* (1975), p. 76; to his father, Blandford Camp, 4 August 1756, and Winchester, 1 September 1756 (Willson, *Life and Letters of Wolfe*, pp. 300–1, 303).

21. On the Newcastle ministry's responses to the military manpower problem, see R. Middleton, 'The Recruitment of the British Army, 1755–1762', in *JSAHR*, 67 (1989), pp. 226–30.

22. Wolfe to Richmond, undated, but probably Canterbury, April / May 1756, in *JSAHR* (1975), p. 73.

23. Same to same, Devizes, 23 June and 20 July 1756 (ibid., pp. 74, 76).

24. Wolfe to his father, Winchester, 1 September 1756, in Willson, *Life and Letters of Wolfe*, p. 303.

25. For a detailed analysis of the military's response to the riots of 1756, see T. Hayter, *The Army and the Crowd in Mid-Georgian England* (London, 1978), pp. 75–92.

26. Wolfe to his father, Camp near Blandford, 19 October 1756 (Willson, *Life and Letters of Wolfe*, p. 304).

27. Wolfe to his mother, Sodbury, 24 October 1756 (ibid., pp. 304–5).

28. This overview draws upon Adrian Randall, *Before the Luddites: Custom, Community and Machinery in the English Woollen Industry, 1776–1809* (Cambridge, 1991), pp. 13–19.

29. Wolfe to Barrington, Stroud, 27 October, and 8 and 15 November 1756 (British Library, Egerton MS 3432, fos 9–10, 13–14, 16); Wolfe to his mother, Stroud, –November 1756, in Willson, *Life and Letters of Wolfe*, p. 306.

30. Wolfe to Lord George Henry Lennox, Stroud, 6 November 1756, *HMC: Bathurst Manuscripts* (London, 1923), p. 11; Hayter, *Army and Crowd in Mid-Georgian England*, pp. 96–97.

31. See Marie Peters, *The Elder Pitt* (London, 1998), pp. 66–68.

32. *London Magazine, 1757* (January), pp. 41–42; Wolfe to Richmond, Cirencester, 19 January 1757, in *JSAHR* (1975), p. 79.

33. Wolfe to Rickson, Banff, 9 June 1751, in Willson, *Life and Letters of Wolfe*, p. 141.

34. See E. M. Lloyd, 'The Raising of the Highland Regiments in 1757', in *EHR*, 17 (1902), pp. 466–69; also S. Brumwell, *Redcoats: The British Soldier and War in the Americas, 1755–1763* (Cambridge, 2002), pp. 268–70.

35. T. M. Devine, *Clanship to Crofters' War: The Social Transformation of the Scottish Highlands* (Manchester, 1994), pp. 91–92.

36. R. Wright, *The Life of Major-General James Wolfe* (London, 1864), pp. 367–68; Willson, *Life and Letters of Wolfe*, pp. 313–14.

37. Wolfe to his mother, Cirencester, 26 December 1756 (ibid., p. 311).

38. To his father, Cirencester, 6 and 19 February 1757 (ibid., pp. 314–15).

39. To Major Rickson, London, 21 July 1757 (ibid., p. 321).

40. To his father, London, 17 March 1757 (ibid., p. 317).

41. R. Whitworth, *William Augustus, Duke of Cumberland: A Life* (Barnsley, 1992), pp. 184–90.

42. On the planning and execution of the Rochefort raid, see Richard Middleton, 'The British Coastal Expeditions to France, 1757–1758', *JSAHR*, 81 (1993), pp. 74–82; also W. Kent Hackman, 'The British Raid on Rochefort, 1757', in *Mariner's Mirror*, 64 (1978), pp. 263–75.

43. Willson, *Life and Letters of Wolfe*, pp. 321–22; Wolfe to Richmond, Newport, 23 August 1757, in *JSAHR* (1975), p. 83. Wolfe's appointment to the expedition provided a convenient excuse for failing to take up his new Irish posting. He took pains, however, to inform the Duke of Bedford of the circumstances behind his absence. Writing from the Isle of Wight, on 6 August 1757, he explained: 'If this business did not stand in the way it would give me the highest satisfaction to endeavour to acquit myself so as to meet your Grace's approbation ...' (McCord Museum, C–173, box 1, MS 1289).

44. Murray to Jeffery Amherst, Newport Camp, 20 August 1757 (Amherst Family Papers, U1350/013/5).

45. To his mother, Newport, 10 and 22 August 1757 (Willson, *Life and Letters of Wolfe*, p. 324).

46. Richmond to Lennox, Barham Downs Camp, 9 September 1757, *HMC: Bathurst Manuscripts*, pp. 680–81.

47. Cumberland to Barrington, 28 August 1757, in *Military Affairs in North America, 1748–1765: Selected Documents from the Cumberland Papers in Windsor Castle*, ed. Stanley Pargellis (New Haven, 1936), p. 398. It has been suggested (Reid, *Wolfe*, p. 135) that the 'fertile genius' in question was Wolfe, although the context indicates that Cumberland aimed his broadside squarely at Mordaunt. The growing influence of Wolfe's preferred training methods is nonetheless striking.

48. Whitworth, *William Augustus, Duke of Cumberland*, pp. 190–99.
49. The narrative of the Rochefort expedition that follows draws upon the following sources: *The Report of the General Officers Appointed ... to Inquire into the Causes of the Failure of the Late Expedition to the Coasts of France* (London, 1758), especially Wolfe's evidence at pp. 28–31; General Court Martial of Lieutenant-General Sir John Mordaunt, 14–20 December 1757, in WO/71/23, pp. 1–125 (Wolfe's testimony at pp. 35–40); 'An Account of the Trial of Lieut. Gen. Sir John Mordaunt', in *Gentleman's Magazine, 1758* (January), pp. 26–33; letters from Wolfe to his mother, from onboard the *Ramillies*, 17 September 1757, and to his father from 'Off the Isles of Rhé and Oleron', 21 September 1757 (finished Isle of Aix, 23 September 1757) and 'Rade des Basques', 30 September 1757, in Willson, *Life and Letters of Wolfe*, pp. 326–30, 333; also Middleton, 'British Coastal Expeditions', *JSAHR* (1993) and Hackman, 'British Raid on Rochefort', *Mariner's Mirror* (1978).
50. Wolfe to his mother, Blackheath, 17 October 1757, and to Major Walter Wolfe, Blackheath, 18 October 1757 (Willson, *Life and Letters of Wolfe*, pp. 335–37).
51. 'Memoirs of an Invalid' (Amherst Family Papers, U1350/Z9A, pp. 8–9, 17).
52. See for example, *Gentleman's Magazine, 1757* (October), pp. 475–76, and *London Magazine, 1757* (October), p. 495.
53. Willson, *Life and Letters of Wolfe*, p. 337. Second battalions were authorized for a total of fifteen regiments. See Barrington to James West, War Office, 7 August 1756 (WO/4/52, p. 144). Each was to consist of 780 men, exclusive of officers. Wolfe's assessment of the 2/20th's first batch of recruits was typically hyperbolic and deprecating: they were ruffians, he told the Duke of Richmond, 'terrible dogs to look at', who must be taught to fight at night, so that the enemy might not see how bad they were. Equally typically, these flippant criticisms soon gave way to sincere praise. Within months, as Wolfe proudly informed his father, the battalion was 'in very good condition': its recruits were now 'healthy and forward in their exercise' – indeed, they constituted 'the soberest collection of young Englishmen' that he'd ever seen. See Wolfe to Richmond, Cirencester, 19 January 1757, in *JSAHR* (1975), pp. 79–80; and to his father, Gloucester, 13 May 1757 (Willson, *Life and Letters of Wolfe*, p. 319).
54. Horace Walpole, *Memoirs of King George II*, ed. J. Brooke (3 vols, New Haven and London, 1985), ii, p. 276; for Wolfe on Howe, see letters to his father, 21–23, and 30 September 1757, in Willson, *Life and Letters of Wolfe*, pp. 330, 333.

55. *Report of the General Officers*, pp. 61–62 (mispaginated as pp. 61–64).

56. Wolfe to Major Rickson, Blackheath, 5 November 1757, Willson, *Life and Letters of Wolfe*, p. 339.

57. *Gentleman's Magazine*, 1757 (November), p. 491.

58. From Bath, 29 December 1757, in Willson, *Life and Letters of Wolfe*, pp. 344–45.

Notes to Chapter 6: Louisbourg

1. On Pitt, Ligonier and the formation of the new American strategy see R. Middleton, *The Bells of Victory: The Pitt-Newcastle Ministry and the Conduct of the Seven Years' War, 1757–1762* (Cambridge, 1985), pp. 51–54; R. Whitworth, *Field Marshal Lord Ligonier: A Story of the British Army, 1702–1770* (Oxford, 1958), pp. 236–42.

2. C. P. Stacey, 'Amherst, Jeffery, 1st Baron Amherst', in *DCB*, iv, pp. 20–26.

3. Richmond to Lord George Lennox, Whitehall, 21 January 1758, in *HMC: Bathurst Manuscripts* (London, 1923), pp. 681–82.

4. LO 5092: Calcraft to Loudoun, 25 December 1757. I remain very grateful to Professor Geoffrey Plank for providing me with this reference.

5. See Wolfe's letters to his mother, Exeter, 7 January 1758; to his father, London, 8 January 1758; to Rickson, Blackheath, 12 January; and to Major Walter Wolfe, Blackheath, 21 January 1758, in B. Willson, *The Life and Letters of James Wolfe* (New York, 1909), pp. 347–51. Wolfe's letter of service as brigadier-general in North America, signed by George II, was dated 23 January 1758. With his new posting, Wolfe's recent Irish appointment fell vacant. Edward Sandford was soon after appointed 'Quarter Master General of all forces in Ireland and Barrack Master General in Ireland' in Wolfe's place. This suggests that despite his own statements to the contrary, Wolfe had held *both* positions. See SP/44/191, pp. 15–16, March (no date given) 1758.

6. Richmond to Lennox, *HMC: Bathurst Manuscripts*, pp. 681–82; Henry Fox to Lennox, 9 February 1758 (ibid., p. 684).

7. On Boscawen, see the sketch by W. A. B. Douglas in *DCB*, iii, pp. 70–71.

8. See Wolfe's letters from Portsmouth, of 7 February 1758 to Sackville, and 11 February 1758 to his mother, in Willson, *Life and Letters of Wolfe*, pp. 357, 361.

9. Wolfe to Sackville, Halifax, 12 May 1758, in *HMC: Stopford-Sackville Manuscripts* (2 vols, London, 1910), ii, pp. 257–58.

10. See PRO/30/8/96, fos 45–52: draft of instructions for Major-General Amherst, 3 March 1758 (especially fos 47–48).

11. See H. Boscawen, 'The Origins of the Flat-Bottomed Landing Craft 1757–58', in 'Army Museum '84' (National Army Museum Report, 1984), pp. 23–30; 'Lt Gordon's Journal of the Siege of Louisbourg', *Journal of the Royal United Service Institution*, 60 (1915), p. 121; James Cuninghame to Sackville, on board the *Ludlow Castle* at sea, 30 May 1758 (*HMC: Stopford-Sackville Manuscripts*, ii, p. 262).

12. For the bill to Wolfe from John Willis, the Great Pontac's proprietor, see 'A Dinner Given by Wolfe', in *Wolfiana: A Potpourri of Facts and Fantasies, Culled from Literature, Relating to the Life of James Wolfe*, ed. J. C. Webster (Shediac, New Brunswick, 1927), p. 27. 'Harry' Hamilton's vivid recollections can be found in J. S. McLennan, *Louisbourg: from its Foundation to its Fall, 1713–1758* (London, 1918), p. 315.

13. Wolfe to Sackville, Halifax, 24 May 1758 (*HMC: Stopford-Sackville Manuscripts*, ii, p. 259).

14. *The Journal of Jeffery Amherst, Recording the Military Career of General Amherst in America from 1758 to 1763*, ed. J. Clarence Webster (Toronto, 1931), pp. 33–46.

15. See McLennan, *Louisbourg*. For Drucour, see John Fortier, 'Boschenry de Drucour (Drucourt), Augustin de', in *DCB*, iii, pp. 71–74.

16. The following section draws upon J. Mackay Hitsman and C. C. J. Bond, 'The Assault Landing at Louisbourg, 1758', in *CHR*, 35 (1954), pp. 314–30.

17. 'Lt Gordon's Journal', *Journal of the Royal United Services Institution* (1915), p. 125.

18. Brigadier-General Lawrence to James Abercromby, Boston 2 April 1758, in AB (Abercromby Papers, Huntington Library, San Marino) 99; Wolfe to Sackville, Halifax, 12 May 1758 (*HMC: Stopford-Sackville Manuscripts*, ii, p. 258).

19. For the events of 8 June 1758, see in particular the lengthy extract from *An Authentick Account of the Reduction of Louisbourg*, given in the *London Magazine, 1758* (November), pp. 549–52, and the vivid eyewitness testimony contained in an 'Extract of a Letter from Louisbourg, in Cape-Breton, 8 August', printed in the *New-York Mercury*, 4 September 1758. For Miller's recollections, see 'Memoirs of an Invalid' (Amherst Family Papers, U1350/Z9A), pp. 20–21. See also, Murray to his wife, Camp before Louisbourg, 13 June 1758, in 'The Letters of Colonel Alexander Murray, 1742–59', ed. Col. H. C. Wylly, in *1926 Regimental Annual. The Sherwood Foresters, Nottinghamshire and Derbyshire Regiment* (London, 1927), p. 199; 'Journal of the Expedition Against Louisburg' in *The Northcliffe Collection* (Ottawa, 1926), pp. 91–92; Captain George Fletcher to [Brigadier-General John Forbes?], camp before

Louisbourg, 22 June 1758, in National Archives of Scotland, Edinburgh, rl RH4/86/1.

20. *Journal of Jeffery Amherst*, p. 51. Amherst's journal provides a detailed day-to-day account of the siege from the British perspective (ibid., pp. 50–72). For a useful modern overview, drawing heavily upon the French sources, see René Chartrand, *Louisbourg 1758: Wolfe's First Siege* (Botley, Oxford, 2000).

21. Letters from Louisbourg dated 27 and 30 July in Willson, *Life and Letters of Wolfe*, pp. 384–85, 387–88.

22. 'Journal of the Expedition Against Louisburg', *Northcliffe Collection*, p. 92.

23. 'Lt Gordon's Journal', *Journal of the Royal United Service Institution* (1915), p. 139.

24. NAM, 8001–30: 'Diary of Captain Philip Townsend, 22nd Foot' (no page or folio numbers); see also 'Extract of a Letter from an Officer on the Expedition against Louisbourg', 24 June 1758, in *Boston Gazette*, 14 August 1758.

25. Ibid. The besiegers did not lack pineapples: Amherst sent Madame Drucour two of them on 17 June 1758, to which she responded next day with a generous gift of wine. A further offering of pineapples from Amherst to the governor's wife, delivered with despatches under a flag of truce by a British drummer, earned the messenger a handsome tip, but no more wine was forthcoming. The wary Drucour observed that Amherst was apparently seeking to swap 'my wine cellar for pineapples' (Chartrand, *Louisbourg 1758*, pp. 56–57).

26. *Journal of William Amherst in America, 1758–1760*, ed. J. Clarence Webster (Shediac, New Brunswick, n.d.), p. 24.

27. *Journal of Jeffery Amherst*, p. 70.

28. 'Diary of Townsend', under entry for 22 July 1758.

29. *William Amherst's Journal*, p. 31; Wolfe to Amherst, 'Trenches, 25th [July 1758] at day break' (Amherst Family Papers, U1350/o31/12).

30. LO 5880: 'Plan of the Intended Attacks against Louisbourg under the Command of Brigadr. Gen Wolfe, July, 1758'.

31. Wolfe to Sackville, Halifax 12 May 1758 and Louisbourg 30 July 1758, in *HMC: Stopford-Sackville Manuscripts*, ii, 258, 262–63.

32. Undated note (but *c.* early June 1758), in Amherst Family Papers, U1350/o31/5.

33. LO 5654: Burton to John Calcraft, Louisbourg, *c.* 27 July 1758, enclosed in Calcraft to Loudoun, 19 August 1758 (LO 5890); 'Extract of a Letter, dated Chabarus-Bay, July 29', in *Boston News-Letter*, 24 August 1758; 'Memoirs of an Invalid', p. 24.

34. *Boston News-Letter*, 24 August 1758; *William Amherst's Journal*, pp. 33–35. On the widespread rejoicing in Britain see Bob Harris, *Politics and the Nation: Britain in the Mid-Eighteenth Century* (Oxford, 2002), pp. 113–14.

35. Wolfe to Richmond, Isle Royale, 28 July 1758, in 'Some Unpublished Wolfe Letters, 1755–58', ed. R. H. Whitworth, *JSAHR*, 53 (1975), p. 85.

36. To Sackville, July 1758 (*HMC: Stopford-Sackville Manuscripts*, ii, pp. 263–64).

37. Thomas Webb, *A Military Treatise on the Appointments of the Army* (Philadelphia, 1759), ii, pp. 107, 110. Webb dedicated his book to Boscawen.

38. LO 6975: Bell to John Calcraft (extract), Louisbourg, *c.* 27 July 1758, enclosed in Calcraft to Loudoun, 19 August 1758 (LO 5890). Some 800 men drawn from the second battalions of Duroure's 4th Foot, and Cornwallis's 24th Foot, were also allocated to the expedition to serve as marines aboard the fleet. See Wolfe to Sackville, Portsmouth, 11 February 1758 (*HMC: Stopford-Sackville Manuscripts*, ii, p. 257).

39. See letter dated Louisbourg, 30 July 1759, in *An Historical Journal of the Campaigns in North America for the Years 1757, 1758, 1759, and 1760, by Captain John Knox*, ed. A. G. Doughty (3 vols, Toronto, 1914), i, p. 253. See also the letter received by Knox on 2 August 1758, from 'Camp before Louisbourg, June 16' referring to Wolfe's 'prodigies of valour' (ibid., p. 184).

40. Wolfe to Sackville, Halifax, 12 May 1758 (*HMC: Stopford-Sackville Manuscripts*, ii, p. 258).

41. GD 45/3/422, fos 481–83: 'Anecdote of Wolfe's Army – Wolfe, the Soldier's Friend – as related by a volunteer of Fraser's Highlanders'. Thompson dictated his recollections in 1828, when he was in his ninety-sixth year, and it is tempting to discount them as nostalgic ramblings. Yet Thompson certainly served in Fraser's Highlanders as he claimed, and his memories of Wolfe's paternalism square with other, contemporary, accounts. Wolfe's use of the term '*Brother*-Soldier' is intriguing, and suggests the fraternity promoted by Freemasonry. Despite a lack of conclusive documentary evidence, there is a strong tradition that Wolfe was a Freemason. This is far from unlikely: by the mid eighteenth century Freemasonry was firmly established in the British Army; for example, of the fourteen infantry battalions serving at the siege of Louisbourg, nine – including Fraser's Highlanders – had travelling 'field lodges'. The same was already true of the 20th Foot when Wolfe became its major in 1749; indeed, the regiment's colonel and Wolfe's patron, Lord George Sackville, was also master of its lodge. Besides strengthening bonds between soldiers of all ranks, Freemasonry also served a social function and provided a useful

forum for professional contact making; although it offered no guarantee of accelerated promotion, membership was clearly seen as beneficial for an officer's career prospects. An involvement in Freemasonry *may* explain Wolfe's otherwise puzzling bequest of no less than £1000 to Colonel Adolphus Oughton; this was the same amount willed to Wolfe's close friends colonels Guy Carleton, William Howe and George Warde. Although both men had served at Falkirk, Culloden and Lauffeldt, Oughton does not feature anywhere in Wolfe's surviving correspondence. Oughton was a prominent and active Freemason, however, and this is one possible point of connection. Curiously enough, Oughton's memorial tablet in Westminster Abbey is located adjacent to Wolfe's monument, in the north ambulatory. For background on Freemasonry in the mid-Georgian British Army, see Michael Baigent and Richard Leigh, *The Temple and the Lodge* (London, 1989), pp. 203–11, 268; also A. J. B. Milborne, 'The Lodge in the 78ᵗʰ Regiment (Fraser's Highlanders)', in *Ars Quatuor Coronatorum*, 65 (1952), pp. 23–24; and S. Brumwell, *Redcoats: The British Soldier and War in the Americas, 1755–1763* (Cambridge, 2002), p. 119–20. On Oughton, see *By Dint of Labour and Perseverence . . .* , ed. S. Wood (1997), pp. 13, 22–23.

42. See *London Gazette*, 19 August 1758; *London Magazine, 1758* (August), pp. 379–83; *Gentleman's Magazine, 1758* (August), pp. 384–89. By the 1740s, both of these monthly periodicals already enjoyed a circulation of from 7000 to 13,000 copies (Harris, *Politics and the Nation*, p. 110).

43. *Scots Magazine, 1758* (August), p. 436; letter from 'Camp at the Light-House Point, the East Side of Louisbourg Harbour', 4 August 1758, in *New-York Mercury* and *New-York Gazette*, 4 September 1758, and *Boston Gazette*, 18 September 1758. See also 'Extract of a Letter from an Officer in the Camp before Louisbourg', 11 July 1758, in *New-York Gazette*, 7 August 1758.

44. This section follows Stephen Brumwell, 'The First Trans-Atlantic Hero? General James Wolfe and British North America', in *The Historian: The Magazine of the Historical Association*, 84 (Winter, 2004), pp. 8–15.

45. Although current in Boston and New York on 24 July – nearly a month before the first tidings of Louisbourg's conquest (received on 17 August) – news of Abercromby's defeat only reached London on 20 August, two days *after* Amherst's victory despatches.

46. To Major Walter Wolfe, Camp before Louisbourg, 27 July 1758, in R. Wright, *The Life of Major-General James Wolfe* (London, 1864), pp. 448–49.

47. *Boston News-Letter*, 27 July 1758. See also Howe's obituary in *Scots*

Magazine, 1758 (August), p. 442; and Wolfe to Sackville, 30 July / 7 August 1758, in Willson, *Life and Letters of Wolfe*, p. 390.

48. Abercromby to Pitt, Camp at Lake George, 12 July 1758, in *The Correspondence of William Pitt, when Secretary of State, with Colonial Governors and Military and Naval Commissioners in America*, ed. G. S. Kimball (2 vols, London, 1906; repr. New York, 1969), i, p. 298. For a fine account of this episode, see Ian McCulloch, '"Like Roaring Lions Breaking from their Chains": The Battle of Ticonderoga, 8 July 1758', in *Fighting for Canada: Seven Battles, 1758–1945*, ed. Donald E. Graves (Toronto, 2000), pp. 23–80.

49. Wolfe to Sackville, 30 July / 7 August 1758 (Willson, *Life and Letters of Wolfe*, p. 392).

50. 'Extract of a Letter from Albany', 14 August 1758, in *New-York Gazette*, 21 August 1758.

51. To Amherst, 'Tuesday morning', 8 August 1758, in Willson, *Life and Letters of Wolfe*, p. 394.

52. *Journal of Jeffery Amherst*, pp. 73–74.

53. Amherst to Wolfe, Louisbourg, 8 August 1758, in *The Correspondence of the Earl of Chatham* (4 vols, London, 1838), i, pp. 332–33.

54. 'Advices to the 12th of August', in *Boston News-Letter* (Supplement), 31 August 1758.

55. Louisbourg, 11 August 1758, in Willson, *Life and Letters of Wolfe*, pp. 395–96.

56. To his father, Louisbourg, 21 August 1758 (ibid., p. 396).

57. Thomas Bell, 'My Journal of the Gaspée Expedition and Other Matters' (unpaged), LAC, 'Northcliffe Collection', Separate Items (MG18-M/rl C–370). For this section, see also Wolfe's letters to Amherst from Louisbourg, 30 September 1758, in Willson, *Life and Letters of Wolfe*, pp. 396–97; and to Pitt, aboard the *Namur*, Spithead, 1 November 1758 (*Correspondence of Pitt*, i, pp. 379–82).

58. See A. McNairn, *Behold the Hero: General Wolfe and the Arts in the Eighteenth Century* (Liverpool, 1997), p. 31; F. McLynn, *1759: The Year Britain Became Master of the World* (London, 2004), pp. 203–4. For a more balanced view, see Geoffrey Plank, *Rebellion and Savagery: The Jacobite Rising of 1745 and the British Empire* (Philadelphia, 2006), pp. 169–70.

59. G. Fregault, *Canada: The War of the Conquest*, trans. Margaret M. Cameron (Toronto, 1969), p. 220.

60. PRO 30/8/96, fol. 102, 'Extract of a letter from Major-General Amherst to Brigadier-General Wolfe, dated Louisbourg August 15, 1758 and inclosed

in General Amherst's letter to Mr Secretary Pitt of August 28, 1758'; Barrington to Pitt and to Brigadier Wolfe, War Office, 2 October 1758 (WO/4/56, pp. 293, 312).

61. Major-General Wolfe to Barrington, *Neptune* at sea, 6 June 1759, in Willson, *Life and Letters of Wolfe*, pp. 433–34.

62. WO/1/975, p. 275: Wolfe to Barrington, Portsmouth, 4 November 1758. Barrington acted on Wolfe's plea, sending orders for the invalids to be provided with quarters and subsistence until they were sent up to Chelsea Hospital. See Barrington to Wolfe, War Office, 7 November 1758 (WO/4/57, p. 6).

63. McCord Museum, C–173 ('Wolfe Collection'), box 1, MS 1385: Wolfe to Captain Maitland, Guildford, 5 August 1757; Wolfe to Captain Parr, Salisbury, 6 December 1758 (Willson, *Life and Letters of Wolfe*, p. 404).

64. Ligonier to Wolfe, 9 November 1758, cited in Whitworth, *Lord Ligonier*, pp. 275–76.

65. WO/4/55, p. 491: Barrington to the commanding officers of fifteen regiments of foot, War Office, 5 May 1758.

66. 'An Authentick Account of the Reduction of Louisbourg', in *London Magazine, 1758*, (November), pp. 549–52; (December), pp. 615–17.

67. Wolfe to Amherst, Louisbourg, 30 September 1758 (Willson, *Life and Letters of Wolfe*, p. 397).

68. Brigadier-General Wolfe to Pitt, St James's Street, 22 November 1758 (*Chatham Correspondence*, i, p. 370).

69. WO/34/46B, fos 286–88: Wolfe to Amherst, Bath, 29 December 1758 (my italics). It is unclear whether Wolfe's letter to Pitt was sent before or after his meeting with Ligonier; however, Ligonier's communication of the strategy for the coming campaign – apparently unconfirmed when Wolfe approached Pitt – supports the first scenario.

70. Wolfe to Colonel Rickson, Salisbury, 1 December 1758 (Willson, *Life and Letters of Wolfe*, p. 403).

Notes to Chapter 7: To Quebec

1. Wolfe to Captain Parr, Salisbury, 6 December 1758, and to his father, Bath, 9 December 1758, in B. Willson, *The Life and Letters of James Wolfe* (New York, 1909), pp. 405–406. On the 'Bath' portrait of Wolfe, see J. Clarence Webster, *Wolfe and the Artists: A Study of his Portraiture* (Toronto, 1930), pp. 25–26.

2. Wolfe to Amherst, Bath, 29 December 1758 (WO/34/46B, fos 286–88). The fact that Wolfe was promoted beyond his own expectations and wishes

has rarely been recognized. A notable exception is Stanley Ayling, *The Elder Pitt: Earl of Chatham* (London, 1976), pp. 258–59.

3. S. Reid, *Wolfe: The Career of General James Wolfe from Culloden to Quebec* (Staplehurst, Kent, 2000), p. 162.

4. 'Proposals for the Expedition to Quebeck' (undated, but *c.* December 1758), LAC, 'Northcliffe Collection', xx (MG18-M / rl C–366). Wolfe was appointed 'to command a body of troops, destined for a particular service in North America', with the temporary rank of major-general, on 29 December 1758. See Barrington to Wolfe, War Office, WO/4/57, p. 136. His formal commission from the King, as 'Major-General and Commander-in-Chief of all and singular Our forces, employed, or to be employed on an expedition against Quebec' was issued at St James's on 12 January 1759 (SP/44/191, pp. 184, 501–4).

5. To Major Walter Wolfe, London, 29 January 1759, in Willson, *Life and Letters of Wolfe*, p. 418.

6. See Wolfe to Colonel Warde, Blackheath, 20 December 1758 (ibid., p. 407); in a list of memorandums given to Ligonier on 19 December 1758, Wolfe proposed that Warde should serve as his adjutant-general (PRO/30/8/1, fos 237–38). See also Wolfe to Pitt, Bath, 24 December 1758, enclosing letters from lieutenants Henry Caldwell and Matthew Leslie, Louisbourg 27 and 30 October 1758, in *The Correspondence of the Earl of Chatham* (4 vols, London, 1838), i, pp. 378–85.

7. Pitt to Amherst, Whitehall, 29 December 1758, in *The Correspondence of William Pitt, when Secretary of State, with Colonial Governors and Military and Naval Commissioners in America*, ed. G. S. Kimball (2 vols, London, 1906; repr. New York, 1969), i, pp. 432–42.

8. Wolfe to Amherst, Bath, 29 December 1758 (WO/34/46B, fos 286–88); Ligonier to Amherst, London, 12 February 1759 (Amherst Family Papers, U1350/O35/8).

9. Carleton was appointed on 30 December 1758, Barré on 13 January 1759 (see SP/44/191, pp. 170–71, 183–84).

10. See transcript of a letter from Wolfe to Barré, 10 January 1759 (sold at auction in London in 1849), in a manuscript notebook, *c.* 1851, containing notes, newspaper cuttings etc relating to Wolfe (McCord Museum, C–173, box 2, MS 13577, fos 177–81); also Major Barré to Pitt, New York, 28 April 1760, in *Chatham Correspondence*, ii, p. 42.

11. The staff appointments were formally announced in orders issued in Halifax, Nova Scotia, on 4 May 1759. See *An Historical Journal of the Campaigns in North America for the Years 1757, 1758, 1759, and 1760, by Captain John Knox*, ed. A. G. Doughty (3 vols, Toronto, 1914), i, pp. 328–32.

Wolfe had requested De Laune's services immediately after he accepted command of the Quebec expedition. See his memorandums to Ligonier of 19 December 1758 in PRO/30/8/1, fol. 237.

12. In the 'Proposals', a gap was left between the names of Monckton and Murray, suggesting an original intention to appoint *four* brigadiers.

13. See S. Brumwell, 'Monckton, Robert', in *Oxford Dictionary of National Biography*, ed. H. C. G. Matthew and B. Harrison (60 vols, Oxford 2004), xxxviii, pp. 597–99; Wolfe to Monckton, London, 16 January 1759, in LAC, 'Northcliffe Collection', xxii (MG18-M / rl C–366). Unless specified otherwise, this is the location of all Wolfe–Monckton correspondence cited in this chapter.

14. Major-General R. H. Mahon, *Life of General the Hon. James Murray: A Builder of Canada* (London, 1921), pp. 25–29, 43–45, 67–70; Wolfe to Sackville, Louisbourg, 30 July 1758, in *HMC: Stopford-Sackville Manuscripts* (2 vols, London, 1910) ii, p. 363. For Murray's commissions see 'General Return of the ... Fifteenth Regiment of Foot ... Shroton Camp, 13 October 1756' (in WO/27/4).

15. Murray to Amherst, Halifax, 11 February, 18 March and 26 April 1759 (WO/34/46B, fos 112, 114, 117).

16. Wolfe to Murray, London, 9 January, in LAC, 'James Murray Collection' (MG23-GII1 / rl C–2225).

17. Walpole to Henry Seymour Conway, Arlington Street, 19 September 1758, in *The Yale Edition of Horace Walpole's Correspondence*, ed. W. S. Lewis (London and Oxford, 48 vols, 1937–83), xxxvii, p. 572; *The History of Parliament: The House of Commons 1754–1790*, ii, *Members K-Y*, ed. Sir Lewis Namier and John Brooke (London, 1964), p. 549.

18. Townshend to Pitt, Bristol, 27 August 1758, in *Chatham Correspondence*, i, pp. 345–47; Walpole to Sir Horace Mann, Arlington Street, 9 February 1759, in *Walpole's Correspondence*, xxi, pp. 266–67.

19. Wolfe to Townshend, London, 6 January 1759, in C. V. F. Townshend, *The Military Life of Field-Marshal George First Marquess Townshend, 1724–1807* (London, 1901), pp. 143–44. See also C. P. Stacey, 'Townshend, George', in *DCB*, v, p. 823.

20. From Louisbourg, 19 May 1759, in Willson, *Life and Letters of Wolfe*, p. 427.

21. For Wolfe's secret instructions, see *The Northcliffe Collection* (Ottawa, 1926), pp. 131–32.

22. See William H. Whiteley, 'Saunders, Sir Charles', in *DCB*, iv, pp. 698–702.

23. Wolfe to Pitt, Bath, 24 December 1758 (*Chatham Correspondence*, i, p. 379);

W. A. B. Douglas, 'Durell, Philip', in *DCB*, iii, pp. 208–10; Pitt to Durell, Whitehall, 29 December 1758 (*Correspondence of Pitt*, i, pp. 444–45); Pitt to Saunders, Whitehall, 9 January 1759 (ibid., ii, p. 2).

24. On the naval preparations, see R. Middleton, *The Bells of Victory: The Pitt-Newcastle Ministry and the Conduct of the Seven Years' War, 1757–1762* (Cambridge, 1985), pp. 103–6.

25. For example, a version of the story was cited, as evidence of Wolfe's 'confidence in himself', in a footnote to Sir Denis Le Marchant's edition of Walpole's *Memoirs of the Reign of King George III* (London, 1845), i, pp. 21–22.

26. Philip Henry Stanhope, Lord Mahon, *The History of England from the Peace of Utrecht to the Peace of Versailles, 1713–1783* (7 vols, Leipzig, 1853–54), iv, p. 153; R. Wright, *The Life of Major-General James Wolfe* (London, 1864), pp. 482–87, and R. Reilly, *The Rest to Fortune: The Life of Major-General James Wolfe* (London, 1960), p. 217.

27. Wolfe to Richmond, Cirencester, 19 January 1757, in 'Some Unpublished Wolfe Letters, 1755–58', ed. R. H. Whitworth, *JSAHR*, 53 (1975), p. 80; Wolfe to his mother, Exeter, 7 January 1758 (Willson, *Life and Letters of Wolfe*, p. 348).

28. The original of Wolfe's will, dated 'Neptune at Sea, 8 June 1759', is in Somerset House, London. For a facsimile, see *Knox's Journal*, i, opposite p. 358.

29. This small quarto volume only came to light early last century. The title-page is inscribed 'From K. L. Neptune at Sea'. It was aboard the *Neptune* that Wolfe sailed for Quebec. See Beckles Willson, 'General Wolfe and Gray's "Elegy"', in *The Nineteenth Century and After*, 434 (April 1913), pp. 862–75. Wolfe's copy of Gray's *Elegy* is now in the University of Toronto's Fisher Rare Book Library.

30. Wolfe to his mother, 'London, Monday morn' (12 February 1759), in Willson, *Life and Letters of Wolfe*, p. 420.

31. Wolfe to Amherst, *Neptune*, 6 March 1759 (WO/34/46B, fols. 292–95).

32. See letters, all dated Halifax Harbour, 1 May 1759, from Saunders to Pitt (*Correspondence of Pitt*, ii, pp. 92–93), Wolfe to Pitt (*Chatham Correspondence*, i, pp. 403–6), and Wolfe to Amherst (Willson, *Life and Letters of Wolfe*, pp. 425–26).

33. The original of this journal is in the Public Record of Northern Ireland, Belfast (DOD, 162/77), with a copy in the Library and Archives Canada ('Paulus Aemilius Irving Fonds', MG18-N45 / rl A–652). Although anonymous, the journal is associated with other material relating to the family of Paulus Aemilius Irving, who served the 1759 Quebec campaign as

major of the 15th Foot. The LAC has attributed the journal to Irving, but examination of the document itself shows this identification to be incorrect: in the absence of its lieutenant-colonel, Brigadier James Murray, Major Irving was the battalion's field commander; his well-known activities and whereabouts during the Quebec campaign cannot be reconciled with those of the journal's author. In addition, the author's strident views, especially regarding the character of James Murray, are equally at odds with Irving's. Whilst handwriting is a notoriously problematic form of identification, Irving's eccentric hand bears no resemblance whatsoever to that of the journal's author; and as the journal is a 'rough' version, complete with deletions and corrections, rather than a final copy, there can be little doubt that it is in the hand of the originator.

As C. P. Stacey pointed out in an article that first drew attention to the journal's importance, *whoever* wrote it was clearly devoted to Wolfe, a junior officer, and probably amongst the general's immediate 'family' of personal staff. See his 'Quebec, 1759: Some New Documents', in *CHR*, 47 (1966), pp. 344–50. As Stacey also observed, the journal was likely composed in the winter of 1759–60. After other potential candidates have been eliminated because they are discussed within the text itself, the likeliest authors include Wolfe's *aides-de-camp*, Hervey Smyth and Thomas Bell, and his deputy (or 'assistant') quartermaster-generals, Henry Caldwell and Matthew Leslie. All four captains were amongst Wolfe's most loyal subordinates, and were remembered in his will, which left each of them £100 to buy mourning swords and rings in memory of their 'friend'.

Before considering this quartet, it is necessary to mention another possible author amongst the expedition's staff, albeit one who does not feature in Wolfe's will, Brigade Major Thomas Gwillim. Whilst at Halifax in May 1759, Gwillim was promoted major of his regiment, the 7th Foot, which was then at Gibraltar. In a letter sent from the War Office on 18 May, in which Lord Barrington informed Wolfe that Gwillim was therefore to rejoin his unit 'at the first opportunity', Gwillim was described as Wolfe's *aide-de-camp* (LAC, 'Robert Monckton Fonds', MG40-Q17 / rl A–1715). This is puzzling: Wolfe already had two *aides-de-camp* – one more than a major-general was allowed on the official establishment – and in his letter to Amherst, written aboard the *Neptune* on 6 March 1759, he described 'Gwillem', who had sailed with him, as 'Major of Brigade' (WO/34/46B, fol. 295). Gwillim served through the siege of Quebec and was apparently close to Wolfe. Many years later, one veteran officer bracketed 'Major Garwilliams' with Isaac Barré as Wolfe's 'confidant'.

See 'A New Account of the Death of Wolfe', ed. A. G. Doughty, *CHR*, 4 (1923), p. 48.

But frustratingly little else is known of Gwillim's activities in the summer of 1759, and this dearth of evidence makes it difficult to establish a convincing case for his authorship of the 'Irving' journal. Turning to the other candidates, the strong anti-navy prejudice of the journal's author was shared by Caldwell, who had come to North America with the detachment of the 2/24th Foot (subsequently regimented as the 69th Foot), serving onboard the fleet. This stance is clear from a letter he wrote to Wolfe from Louisbourg on 27 October 1758 (PRO 30/8/1, fos 231–32). The same prejudices were expressed by Bell, and colour *his* surviving journal of the Quebec campaign (LAC, 'Northcliffe Collection', Separate Items, MG18-M / rl C–370). It might seem unlikely that Bell would have kept *another* such account, although as the 'Irving' journal is retrospective rather than contemporaneous, and Bell, like Caldwell, Smyth and Gwillim, had ample opportunity to compile it during his lengthy return voyage to England after the conquest of Quebec, this is certainly not impossible. But the handwriting of Bell's journal, and of original letters from Caldwell and Smyth amongst the Chatham Papers in the National Archives, Kew, does not resemble that of the anonymous journal. By contrast, two surviving examples of Matthew Leslie's handwriting – a letter to Wolfe from Louisbourg on 30 October 1758 (PRO 30/8/1, fos 233–34) and another to Pitt dated 24 February 1767 (PRO 30/8/48, fols. 101–102) – show marked similarities. Leslie, of the 48th Foot, was an experienced officer who had survived Braddock's defeat in 1755. Of his devotion to Wolfe there is no doubt: in his 1767 letter to Pitt he proudly recalled his service at Louisbourg and Quebec, emphasizing that Wolfe had honoured him 'by a singular remembrance of his friendship, in his will'. Of the five potential authors considered here, Leslie alone remained at Quebec after its capture (see CO/5/51, fol. 123: 'Disposal of the Staff of the Army up the River St Lawrence'). Although Colonel Stacey believed otherwise, there is nothing to indicate that the journal was not written in Canada. And *if* Leslie was the journal's author, this *may* explain why it ended up amongst Irving's papers: by his own account, following Quebec's capture Leslie became quartermaster-general 'in the room of Colonel Carleton', who was recovering from wounds; in October 1759, soon after James Murray assumed command of the Quebec army, Leslie 'resigned' his staff appointment. Carleton, whose post Leslie had in practice occupied, was replaced by none other than Paulus Aemilius Irving (see *Knox's Journal*, ii, pp. 243, 246). Although a range of evidence supports Leslie's authorship of the journal, there remain some areas of uncertainty. Further analysis of this important document is therefore required to place the identity of its author beyond doubt. Until then, as it reflects views common to several of Wolfe's circle of trusted subordinates, it will be cited here as 'Wolfe "Family" Journal'. The quotation is at part 1, p. 2.

34. Jonathan R. Dull, *The French Navy in the Seven Years' War* (Lincoln, Nebraska, 2005), p. 143.

35. Wolfe to Pitt, Halifax, 1 May 1759 (*Chatham Correspondence*, i, pp. 403–6).

36. LO 6095: Lieutenant Brown to Loudoun, Halifax, 13 May 1759.

37. 'Wolfe's Journal' survives in several slightly different versions. The original, in Wolfe's own handwriting, and containing personal details missing from the others, is in the McCord Museum, Montreal, and available for consultation as a photo-copy (C–173, box 1, MS 255; microfilm copy in LAC, on rl M–1910). As pages are missing at either end, this only covers the period from 18 June to 7 August 1759. Another version – a copy made by Captain Thomas Bell (LAC, 'Northcliffe Collection', Separate Items, MG18-M / rl C–370), runs from 13 May to 16 August, so preserving some entries lost from Wolfe's incomplete original; this was published, in a slightly edited form, by Beckles Willson ('Fresh Light on the Quebec Campaign – From the Missing Journal of General Wolfe', in *The Nineteenth Century and After*, 397 (March, 1910), pp. 445–60). Yet another variant, also believed to be a copy by Bell, and covering 18 June to 16 August 1759, is in the Library of the Royal Military College, Kingston (also on LAC rl M–1910). Here, the McCord version has been followed, supplemented where necessary by the longer Bell copy. For the sake of simplicity, these notes cite 'Wolfe's Journal', followed by the entry date.

38. Saunders to Pitt, *Neptune* off Scatari, 6 June 1759 (*Correspondence of Pitt*, ii, pp. 115–18); *Knox's Journal*, i, p. 355.

39. From Louisbourg, 19 May 1759, in Willson, *Life and Letters of Wolfe*, p. 427.

40. 'Journal of Richard Humphrys' (Add. MS 45,662, pp. 28–29, 33). The army was organized into three brigades with Monckton commanding the first, Townshend the second and Murray the third. Their majors of brigade were, respectively, captains John Spittal of the 47th Foot, Thomas Gwillim of the 7th Foot and Richard Maitland of the 43rd (*Knox's Journal*, i, p. 333).

41. Ibid., pp. 348–49.

42. See L. S. Winstock, 'Hot Stuff', in *JSAHR*, 33 (1955), pp. 2–4; also, *The Rambling Soldier: Life in the Lower Ranks, 1750–1900, through Soldiers' Songs and Writings*, ed. Roy Palmer (Harmondsworth, 1977), pp. 145–47.

43. For the 'American Army' see Wolfe to Amherst, London, 20 January 1759 (WO/34/46B, fol. 291).
44. See S. Brumwell, *Redcoats: The British Soldier and War in the Americas, 1755–1763* (Cambridge, 2002), p. 318, table 5; WO/25/435 ('Succession Book, 58th Foot, 1756–1804') fos 67–68, 85–86, 98–99, 111–12 and 125–26. See also S. Brumwell, 'Rank and File: A Profile of One of Wolfe's Regiments', *JSAHR*, 79 (2001), pp. 3–24.
45. Wolfe to Major Walter Wolfe, Louisbourg, 19 May 1759, in Willson, *Life and Letters of Wolfe*, pp. 427–29.
46. 'Report on Quebec, by Major Patrick Mackellar', 12 July 1757 (given in *Knox's Journal*, iii, pp. 151–60).
47. 'Memoirs of the Siege of Quebec from the Journal of a French Officer', in *The Siege of Quebec and the Battle of the Plains of Abraham*, ed. A. Doughty and G. W. Parmelee (6 vols, Quebec, 1901–2), iv, p. 239.
48. G. Fregault, *Canada: The War of the Conquest*, trans. Margaret M. Cameron (Toronto, 1969), p. 240; *Adventure in the Wilderness: The American Journals of Louis Antoine de Bougainville, 1756–60*, ed. E. P. Hamilton (Norman, Oklahoma, 1964), p. 323.
49. 'Memoirs of the Siege of Quebec' (*Siege of Quebec*, iv, pp. 240–41).
50. See C. P. Stacey, *Quebec, 1759: The Siege and the Battle* (new edn, Toronto, 2002), pp. 47–54.
51. 'Extract of a Journal Kept at the Army Commanded by the Late Lieutenant-General de Montcalm', in *NYCD*, x, p. 1017. This gives a very precise total of 13,718 combatants. As Stacey (*Quebec, 1759*, p. 59) observes, this figure reflects Montcalm's 'field army'; *another* 2000 men garrisoned the city itself.
52. This important, although often overlooked, point was made by Stanley Pargellis in the invaluable introduction to his *Military Affairs in North America* (pp. xix–xx).
53. Saunders to Pitt, *Neptune* off Scatari, 6 June 1759 (*Correspondence of Pitt*, ii, pp. 115–18).
54. CO/5/51, fol. 67: 'Embarkation Return of His Majesty's Forces, destined for an Expedition in the River St Lawrence... Neptune at sea, June 5, 1759'. This tally was exclusive of staff and drummers, whilst another one hundred rangers were expected, and joined later. See also Wolfe to Pitt, *Neptune*, 6 June 1759 (*Correspondence of Pitt*, ii, pp. 118–20).
55. Stacey, *Quebec, 1759*, p. 27. The exact number of seamen and marines sent to Quebec has never been established. Marines available for service ashore, however, included a 1000-strong battalion under Lieutenant-Colonel Hector Boisrond, and some 250 soldiers, drawn from the 62nd

Foot and 69th Foot (originally the 2nd battalions of the 4th and 24th Foot), who had been seconded to the fleet.

56. *Knox's Journal*, i, p. 368.

57. 'Wolfe's Journal', 18 June 1759 (the original gives the date as 10 June, but this is clearly an error). For continuing criticism of Durell, see 'Bell's Quebec Journal' (18 June 1759).

58. See Glyndwr Williams, 'Cook, James', in *DCB*, iv, pp. 162–67; Wolfe to Richmond, Isle Royale, 28 July 1758, in 'Some Unpublished Wolfe Letters', *JSAHR* (1975), p. 84; Willis Chipman, 'The Life and Times of Major Samuel Holland, Surveyor General 1764–1801', in *Ontario Historical Society, Papers and Records*, 21 (1924), pp. 18–19.

59. J. C. Beaglehole, *The Life of Captain James Cook* (Stanford, California, 1974), pp. 43–44; 'Journal du Siège de Québec', in *Northcliffe Collection*, p. 225.

60. *Knox's Journal*, i, pp. 374–75, 378; 'Extract of a Letter from a Military Officer, Dated at King George's Battery at Point Levee, near Quebeck', 13 August 1759, in *Boston News-Letter*, 6 September 1759.

61. 'Journal du Siège de Québec' (*Northcliffe Collection*, p. 224).

62. 'Wolfe "Family" Journal', part 1, pp. 4–6; 'Wolfe's Journal' (27 June 1759).

63. See 'Journal of Major Moncrief (actually kept by Major Patrick Mackellar)', in *Siege of Quebec*, v, p. 37; 'Copy of a Letter from a Gentleman in the Expedition against Canada ... Isle Coudre, in the River St Lawrence', 10 July 1759, in *Edinburgh Chronicle*, 20–22 September 1759; 'Wolfe "Family" Journal', part 1, pp. 3–4; 'Wolfe's Journal' (27–28 June 1759); 'Journal of Humphrys', pp. 37–38; *Knox's Journal*, i, pp. 379–81. These dramatic events were naturally noted in the logs of Saunders's ships, for example, HMS *Pembroke*. See *The Logs of the Conquest of Canada*, ed. William H. Wood (Toronto, 1909), pp. 265–66.

64. 'Wolfe "Family" Journal', part 1, pp. 6–7. Here the author was reporting events at second hand.

65. 'Bell's Quebec Journal', and 'Wolfe's Journal' (both for 1 July 1759); see also 'The Capture of Quebec: a Manuscript Journal Relating to the Operations Before Quebec ... by Colonel Malcolm Fraser ...', ed. Brig. R. Alexander, *JSAHR*, 18 (1939), p. 141. For Sergeant Thompson see J. R. Harper, *The Fraser Highlanders* (Montreal, 1979), pp. 78–79.

66. 'Journal of Fraser', *JSAHR* (1939), p. 141.

67. 'Wolfe's Journal' (2 July 1759); John Warde to George Warde, received 16 November 1759 ('General Wolfe's Letters to his Parents, 1740–1759', Squerryes Court, Westerham, p. 946).

68. 'Wolfe's Journal' (3–5 July 1759); 'Orders, Camp at the Island of Orleans', 5 July 1759, in *Knox's Journals*, i, p. 399.

69. See Murray to Wolfe, and Wolfe to Murray, 22 July 1759 (LAC, 'Paulus Aemilius Irving Fonds', MG18-N45 / rl A–652). On the rafts see 'Journal of Moncrief [Mackellar]', in *Siege of Quebec*, v, p. 38, and *Knox's Journal*, i, p. 413. Knox (ibid., p. 427) considered them to be 'unwieldy, and not likely to answer the intended purposes'.

70. 'Extract of a Journal', in *NYCD*, x, p. 1021.

71. 'An Accurate and Authentic Journal of the Siege of Quebec 1759, by a Gentleman in an Eminent Station on the Spot', in *Siege of Quebec*, iv, p. 283; Wolfe to Pitt, 'Headquarters at Montmorenci, in the River St Lawrence', 2 September 1759 (CO/5/51, fos 72–85). This famous despatch is given in full in Stacey, *Quebec, 1759*, pp. 193–97.

72. 'Wolfe's Journal' (10 July 1759).

73. 'Memoirs of the Siege of Quebec and the Total Reduction of Canada... by John Johnson', in *Siege of Quebec*, v, p. 97.

74. 'A Journal of the Expedition Up the River St Lawrence by the Serjeant-Major of General Hopson's Grenadiers', in ibid., p. 3.

75. See Townshend's 'Journal of the Voyage to America and Campaign Against Quebec', in ibid., pp. 241–45.

76. Wolfe to Monckton, Falls of Montmorency, 12 July 1759.

77. 'Extract of a Letter from a Military Officer', in *Boston News-Letter*, 6 September 1759.

78. For Wolfe's 'terror' tactics see F. Jennings, *Empire of Fortune: Crowns, Colonies and Tribes in the Seven Years' War in America* (New York, 1988), pp. 203, 420–21; F. McLynn, *1759: The Year Britain Became Master of the World* (London, 2004), pp. 216–17. On the French removal of Quebec's inhabitants, see 'Memoirs of the Siege of Quebec', in *Siege of Quebec*, iv, p. 241; also 'Journal du Siège de Québec', in *Northcliffe Collection*, p. 244. This notes that between 9.00 p.m. on 13 July and noon on the 14th, 'near 300 bombs were flung into the town, without a single person being wounded; a proof of the houses in Quebec being deserted by the inhabitants' (ibid.).

79. 'Wolfe's Journal' (13–16 July 1759); Wolfe to Monckton, Camp of Montmorency, 16 July 1759;

80. 'Bell's Quebec Journal' (16 July 1759); *Logs of the Conquest*, pp. 212, 295–96, 317.

81. 'Wolfe "Family" Journal', part 1, p. 13.

82. Wolfe spoke to Holland in French. His words, as remembered by Holland (and given here with the Captain's original spelling and punctuation)

were: 'Voilà mon cher Holland, ce sera ma Derniere Rescource mais il faut avant que mes autres projects travailent, et manquent. Je vous parle en confidance; en attendant, il faut deguiser mon intention à qui que ce soit et tachez de faire croire l'impossibilité de montez.' See Samuel Holland to Lieutenant-Governor John Graves Simcoe, near Quebec, 10 June 1792, in 'A New Account of the Death of Wolfe', *CHR*, (1923), p. 48.

83. Wolfe to Monckton, Point Lévis, 20 July 1759.

84. Saunders to Townshend, onboard the *Stirling Castle*, 20 July 1759, in *HMC: Marquess of Townshend Manuscripts* (London, 1887), p 308; Wolfe to Monckton, '1 o'Clock', 20 July 1759.

85. Murray to Wolfe, Montmorency, 22 July 1759 (LAC, 'Paulus Aemilius Irving Fonds').

86. Wolfe to Murray, Point Levy, 22 July 1759 (ibid.).

87. 'Bell's Quebec Journal'. Bell dated this event to 22 July, but other sources, including Wolfe's own journal, place it on the following day. As the *Hunter*'s log reveals (*Logs of the Conquest*, p. 229) that the two vessels weighed anchor at 3.00 a.m. on 23 July, the confusion is understandable. See also Wolfe to Pitt, Montmorency, 2 September 1759. Although Wolfe did not specify whether his remarks referred to his first, or subsequent St Michel plan, the context strongly suggests the latter.

88. 'Extract of a Journal', *NYCD*, x, pp. 1024–25; 'Journal du Siège de Québec', *Northcliffe Collection*, p. 246; 'Relation du Siège de Québec', in *Siege of Quebec*, v, pp. 314–15; *Knox's Journal*, i, p. 435; see also *Logs of the Conquest*, pp. 296, 317–18.

89. N. A. M. Rodger, *The Command of the Ocean: A Naval History of Britain, 1649–1815* (London, 2004), p. 278; Dull, *French Navy in the Seven Years' War*, p. 149.

90. 'Memoirs of the Siege of Quebec', in *Siege of Quebec*, iv, p. 247; 'Extract of a Journal', *NYCD*, x, pp. 1025–26. For the testimony of Madame Saint-Villemin ('De Saint-Vilmé') see 'Journal Militaire Tenu par Nicolas Renaud d'Avène des Méloizes' in *Rapport de l'Archiviste de la Province de Québec pour 1928–1929* (1929), pp. 48–49. On the arrival of these captives at the Point of Orleans, see 'Bell's Quebec Journal' (3 July 1759).

91. See 'Extract of a Journal', in *NYCD*, x, pp. 1020, 1043.

92. On Montcalm's 'defeatism', see especially Eccles, 'Montcalm', in *DCB*, iii, p. 468; Fregault, *War of the Conquest*, p. 250. Such verdicts have been widely accepted by subsequent historians, for example, Jonathan Dull (*French Navy in the Seven Years' War*, p. 174), who observes that Montcalm was 'chronically pessimistic'.

93. See 'Journal du Siège de Québec' (*Northcliffe Collection*, pp. 243–44); also, Stacey, *Quebec, 1759*, pp. 78–79.
94. Gibson to Lawrence, 'Bason of Quebec', 1/10 August 1759, in *Siege of Quebec*, v, p. 165.
95. Stacey, *Quebec, 1759*, p. 86.
96. 'Wolfe's Journal' (6–8 July 1759); 'Bell's Quebec Journal' (7 July 1759).
97. See D. Grinnell-Milne, *Mad, is He? The Character and Achievements of James Wolfe* (London, 1963), pp. 12–13. These 'navigational realities' are also emphasized by Don Graves in Appendix G ('Justice to the Admirals: The Royal Navy and the Siege of Quebec, 1759') of his edition of Stacey, *Quebec, 1759*, especially pp. 227–29.
98. Wolfe to Pitt, Montmorency, 2 September 1759.
99. See 'Méloizes's Journal', p. 50.

Notes to Chapter 8: Deadlock on the St Lawrence

1. 'Wolfe's Journal' (23 July 1759); 'Bell's Quebec Journal' (24 July 1759), in LAC, 'Northcliffe Collection', Separate Items, MG18-M / rl C-370).
2. Wolfe to Pitt, Montmorency, 2 September 1759; Wolfe to Monckton, Montmorency Fall, 27 July 1757, in LAC, 'Northcliffe Collection', xxii, MG18-M / rl C-366 (unless specified otherwise, this is the location of all Wolfe–Monckton correspondence cited here); 'Wolfe's Journal' (26 July 1759); 'Wolfe "Family" Journal', part 1, p. 15–16 (LAC, 'Paulus Aemilius Irving Fonds', MG18-N45 / rl A-652); 'Bell's Quebec Journal' (26 July); NLS MS 16521, Lieutenant-Colonel Fletcher, 35th Foot, to his father, 'Montmorencie Camp, near Quebec', 10 August 1759; 'Journal of Moncrief [Mackellar]', in *The Siege of Quebec and the Battle of the Plains of Abraham*, ed. A. Doughty and G. W. Parmelee (6 vols, Quebec, 1901-2), v, pp. 39–41.
3. *An Historical Journal of the Campaigns in North America for the Years 1757, 1758, 1759, and 1760, by Captain John Knox*, ed. A. G. Doughty (3 vols, Toronto, 1914), i, p. 445; *The Logs of the Conquest of Canada*, ed. William H. Wood (Toronto, 1909), pp. 235, 309.
4. Wolfe to Monckton, undated, but likely 29 July 1759 (see note 6 below).
5. 'Wolfe's Journal' (28 July 1759); Wolfe to Monckton, aboard the *Stirling Castle*, 28 July 1759.
6. Although undated, this important letter (which is written on two oblong scraps of paper) was probably penned on 29 July: Wolfe's journal entry for that day uses almost identical language to justify the plan.
7. 'Orders, Camp at Montmorency, 29 July 1759', given in *Knox's Journal*, i, pp. 446–48; the codicil is reproduced ibid., facing p. 446.

8. 'Relation du Siège de Québec', in *The Northcliffe Collection* (Ottawa, 1926), p. 218; 'Wolfe's Journal' (30 July 1759).

9. The ensuing account of the events of 31 July 1759 draws upon the following sources: Wolfe to Pitt, 2 September 1759; Wolfe to Saunders, 30 August 1759, in R. Wright, *The Life of Major-General James Wolfe* (London, 1864), pp. 549–51; 'Wolfe's Journal' (31 July); 'Wolfe "Family" Journal', part 1, pp. 16–21; Lieutenant John Brown, 2/60ᵗʰ Foot, to Loudoun, Quebec, 28 September 1759 (LO 6144); 'Extract of a Letter from an Officer in Major Genl Wolfe's Army, Island of Orleans, 10 August 1759', in *Military Affairs in North America, 1748–1765: Selected Documents from the Cumberland Papers in Windsor Castle*, ed. Stanley Pargellis (New Haven, 1936), pp. 433–35; 'Accurate and Authentic Journal', in *Siege of Quebec*, iv, pp. 286–87; 'Serjeant-Major's Journal' (ibid., v, p. 4); 'Townshend's Journal' (ibid., 254–55); 'Townshend's Rough Notes', *Northcliffe Collection*, p. 423; *Journal des Campagnes au Canada de 1755 à 1760 par le Comte de Maurès de Malartic*, ed. Gabriel de Maurès de Malartic and Paul Gafferel (Dijon, 1890), pp. 260–62; *Logs of the Conquest*, pp. 211, 236, 267, 309–10. For Ochterlony see 'A Genuine Detail of a Remarkable Incident . . . on 31st July 1759', *British Magazine, 1760*, (January), pp. 19–22; also, 'Memoir of Major Patrick Murray', in Lewis Butler, *Annals of the King's Royal Rifle Corps*, i, *The Royal Americans* (London, 1913), p. 292.

10. 'Return of the Kill'd, Wounded and Missing, at the Attack of the Enemys Works, on the 31ˢᵗ of July', LAC, 'Northcliffe Collection', xxi (MG18-M / rl C-366); 'Extract of a Journal', in *NYCD*, x, p. 1030.

11. *Knox's Journal*, ii, pp. 3–4.

12. Wolfe to Saunders, 30 August 1759, in Wright, *Life of Wolfe*, p. 551.

13. 'Memoirs of the Quarter-Master Sergeant' (*Siege of Quebec*, v, pp. 93–94); C. P. Stacey, *Quebec, 1759: The Siege and the Battle* (new edn, Toronto, 2002), p. 183–86.

14. *Knox's Journal*, ii, p. 6; Martin L Nicolai, 'A Different Kind of Courage: The French Military and the Canadian Irregular Soldier during the Seven Years' War', *CHR*, 70 (1989), pp. 67–68.

15. Wolfe to Monckton, 1 August 1759; 'The Letters of Colonel Alexander Murray, 1742–59', ed. Col. H. C. Wylly, in *1926 Regimental Annual. The Sherwood Foresters, Nottinghamshire and Derbyshire Regiment* (London, 1927), p. 210.

16. Schomberg to Admiral Forbes, Boston, 5 September 1759, and 'Letter of James Gibson' (*Siege of Quebec*, v, pp. 60, 67); 'Letters of Colonel Murray', p. 212. Those senior officers who opposed the Montmorency attack apparently included Wolfe's friend and quartermaster-general, Guy Carleton:

under his brief journal entry for 31 July, Thomas Bell reported Carleton's 'abominable behaviour to ye General'.

17. The eight McCord Museum caricatures currently attributed to Townshend fall into two distinct groups. Six, which are executed in ink and graphite, bear no obvious stylistic resemblance to any of Townshend's many surviving works, and suggest a late nineteenth-century attempt to recreate mid eighteenth-century costume. As a watermark indicates that one of this series was executed on paper made by a firm that only *began* production in the 1770s, the suspicion that all are later works, produced specifically to exploit the growing interest in Wolfe amongst wealthy Canadian collectors, must be strong. The remaining two McCord caricatures, which were acquired subsequently and from a separate collection, and are executed in ink and watercolour, are strikingly different. Here there is nothing on stylistic, or any other grounds, to question a dating of 1759, and *they* may well be genuine products of Townshend's off-duty hours during the siege of Quebec. Surprisingly, not even specialist works about Wolfe's portraiture have questioned the authenticity of any of the cartoons, or even highlighted the clear differences between the two groups. It is to be hoped that further, specialized, analysis of these intriguing works of art will provide firm answers regarding their dating and authorship. Meanwhile, I remain extremely grateful to Conrad Graham, Curator of Collections at the McCord Museum, for showing me the original cartoons, discussing them with me, and establishing the date of the watermark; I should emphasize that the views on their authenticity expressed here are mine, not his.

18. Horace Walpole, *Memoirs of King George II*, ed. J. Brooke (3 vols, New Haven and London, 1985), ii, p. 51; *The Soldier's Companion, or Martial Recorder*, cited by Wright, *Life of Wolfe*, p. 560.

19. 'Wolfe "Family" Journal', part 1, pp. 1, 12–13; part 2, pp. 16–18, 34–35, 37.

20. Murray to his wife, Montmorency, 8 August 1759, in 'Letters of Colonel Murray', p. 212.

21. See the note at the end of Bell's transcription of 'Wolfe's Journal' (p. 38).

22. 'Wolfe "Family" Journal', part 2, p. 37; Wolfe to Murray, *Stirling Castle*, 5 August 1759 (in LAC, 'Paulus Aemilius Irving Fonds', MG18-N45 / rl A-652).

23. Saunders to Pitt, *Stirling Castle*, off Point Lévis, 5 September 1759, in *The Correspondence of William Pitt, when Secretary of State, with Colonial Governors and Military and Naval Commissioners in America*, ed. G. S. Kimball (2 vols, London, 1906; repr. New York, 1969), ii, pp. 160–61;

Knox's Journal, ii, p. 12; 'Journal du Siège de Québec' (*Northcliffe Collection*, p. 254).

24. See 'James Murray's Journal, 5–8 August 1759' (actually a report to Wolfe), in *Knox's Journal*, iii, p. 161.

25. PRO 30/8/50, fol. 164: Murray to Wolfe, 9 August 1759; *Adventure in the Wilderness: The American Journals of Louis Antoine de Bougainville, 1756–60*, ed. E. P. Hamilton (Norman, Oklahoma, 1964), p. 319.

26. On the Pointe-aux-Trembles attack see Murray's report to Wolfe in *Knox's Journal*, iii, pp. 161–63; 'Journal of the Particular Transactions', in *Siege of Quebec*, v, pp. 177–79. The author of this valuable memoir served as a volunteer in the light company of Fraser's Highlanders; 'Journal of Richard Humphrys' (Add. MS 45,662), pp. 49–53.

27. 'Wolfe's Journal' (11 August 1759); Wolfe to Murray, *Stirling Castle*, 11 August 1759 (LAC, 'James Murray Collection', MG23-GII1 / rl C–2225).

28. Murray to Wolfe, 9 August 1759 (PRO 30/8/50, fol. 164).

29. 'Report of Brigadier-General Murray to Major-General Wolfe', 28 August 1759, in *Knox's Journal*, iii, pp. 163–64.

30. 'Extract of a Letter from the Camp at Point Levee', 6 September 1759, in *Boston Gazette*, 8 October 1759; *Adventure in the Wilderness*, p. 320; 'Extract of a Journal', *NYCD*, x, pp. 1032–33.

31. Murray to Holmes, 'St Anthony', 11 August 1759 (LAC, 'James Murray Collection'); 'Accurate and Authentic Journal', in *Siege of Quebec*, iv, p. 289; 'Journal of Moncrief [Mackellar]', in ibid., v, p. 46.

32. 'Wolfe's Journal' (7 August 1759).

33. Wolfe to Murray, *Stirling Castle*, 11 August 1759 (LAC, 'James Murray Collection'); same to same, Montmorency, 13 and 15 August 1759 (LAC, 'Paulus Aemilius Irving Fonds').

34. Wolfe to Monckton, Falls of Montmorency, 12 August 1759; *Knox's Journal*, ii, pp. 36–37, 40.

35. WO/34/46B, fos 305–6: Wolfe to Whitmore, 'Camp near the Falls at Montmorency', 11 August 1759; *Knox's Journal*, ii, pp. 31–32, 40; 'Bell's Quebec Journal' (21 August 1759); Wolfe to Pitt, Montmorency, 2 September 1759.

36. Wolfe to Monckton, Montmorency, 5 August 1759.

37. 'Wolfe "Family" Journal', part 1, p. 1; part 2, pp. 16–17.

38. Wolfe to Monckton, 6 August 1759.

39. Same to same, Montmorency, 15 and 16 August 1759.

40. Same to same, 'at the Point of Levy', 19 August, and from Montmorency, 22 August 1759 (LAC, 'Robert Monckton Fonds', MG40-Q17 / rl A–1715).

41. 'Bell's Quebec Journal' (21 August 1759).

42. Barré to Monckton, 'Headquarters', 24 August 1759 (LAC, 'Robert Monckton Fonds').

43. *Knox's Journal*, ii, pp. 45–46.

44. WO/34/46B, fol. 309: Amherst to Wolfe, Albany, 6 May 1759.

45. 'Extract of a Journal' (*NYCD*, x, p. 1024).

46. 'Extract of a Letter from Point Levee', 29 July 1759, in *New-York Gazette*, 17 September 1759; 'Extract of a Letter from a Military Officer', 13 August 1759, in *Boston News-Letter*, 6 September 1759; and 'Extract of a Letter from the River St Lawrence', 15 August 1759, in *Boston Evening-Post*, 24 September 1759; *Knox's Journal*, ii, p. 10.

47. 'Extract of a Journal' (*NYCD*, x, pp. 1031–33); 'Journal du Siège de Québec' (*Northcliffe Collection*, p. 256). On Gage at Lake Ontario, see Gipson, *The British Empire before the American Revolution*, vii, *The Great War for Empire: The Victorious Years, 1758–1760*, pp. 357–60; and J. R. Alden, *General Gage in America* (Baton Rouge, 1947), pp. 49–52. Both of these historians take a sympathetic view of Gage's inactivity. For a harsher verdict, see John Shy, *Toward Lexington: The Role of the British Army in the Coming of the American Revolution* (Princeton, 1965), pp. 131–32.

48. CO/5/56, fol: 213: Amherst to Gage, Camp at Crown Point, 14 August 1759.

49. 'Extract of a Journal' (*NYCD*, x, pp. 1033–35). For a detailed analysis of this episode, and its consequences, see Stephen Brumwell, *White Devil: A True Story of War, Savagery and Vengeance in Colonial America* (London, 2004; Cambridge, Massachusetts, 2005).

50. 'Letter from Fort Edward', 6 August 1759, in *Edinburgh Chronicle*, 20–22 September 1759; Huck to Loudoun, 4 August, and Abercrombie to Loudoun, 13 August 1759 (LO 6134 and LO 6137).

51. Letter written onboard the *Neptune*, 6 March 1759 (WO/34/46B, fol. 293).

52. See the proclamation 'Given at Laurent in the island of Orleans, this 28th day of June, 1759', in *Knox's Journal*, i, pp. 387–89; also Geoffrey Plank, *Rebellion and Savagery: The Jacobite Rising of 1745 and the British Empire* (Philadelphia, 2006), pp. 170–71.

53. Wolfe to Pitt, Montmorency, 2 September 1759.

54. Letter from Quebec, 7 October 1759, in *Derby Mercury*, 30 November to 7 December 1759; 'Extract of a Letter, dated Point Levee Camp', 10 August 1759, in *New-York Gazette*, 17 September 1759.

55. Wolfe's opinions, as communicated to Vaudreuil by Barré on 26 July 1759, and Vaudreuil's response of the same date (expressed by Bougainville), are given within 'Extract of a Journal' (*NYCD*, x, pp. 1027–28); see also

Vaudreuil to Wolfe, 'Headquarters', 2 August 1759 (original in French; calendared in *Northcliffe Collection*, p. 137).

56. *Knox's Journal*, i, pp. 441, 443.

57. See Wolfe's two letters to Monckton of 25 July 1759, the second from Montmorency, 'at night'.

58. See 'Journal du Siége de Québec en 1759, par Jean Claude Panet', in *Literary and Historical Society of Quebec: Manuscripts Relating to the Early History of Canada* (4th Series, Quebec, 1875), item 4, pp. 18–19; *Knox's Journal*, i, p. 438; Wolfe to Pitt, Montmorency, 2 September 1759; Captain John Montresor to Colonel James Montresor, Montmorency, 10 August 1759, in *Siege of Quebec*, iv, p. 319.

59. 'Wolfe's Journal' (4 August 1759); Wolfe to Monckton, Montmorency, 4 August 1759; *Knox's Journal*, ii, p. 17.

60. 'Proceedings of the Company of Rangers, commanded by Capt. Gorham', Île aux Coudres, 16 August 1759, in *New-York Gazette*, 17 September 1759; Captain Joseph Gorham to Wolfe, *Beaver* transport, 19 August 1759 (LAC, 'Northcliffe Collection', xxi, MG18-M / rl C–366).

61. Wolfe to Monckton, 6 and 15 August 1759.

62. 'Extract of a Journal' (*NYCD*, x, p. 1033).

63. Wolfe to Monckton, Montmorency, 22 August 1759 (LAC, 'Robert Monckton Fonds'); 'Report of a Tour to the South Shore of the River St Lawrence', by Major George Scott, 19 September 1759 (LAC, 'Northcliffe Collection', xxi, MG18-M / rl C–366); *Knox's Journal*, ii, pp. 54–55.

64. 'Extract of a Letter Dated Quebec-Road, 6 September' in *Boston Gazette*, 8 October 1759; *Boston News-Letter*, 6 December 1759.

65. Add. MS 32,897, fol. 88: Duke of Newcastle to Lord Hardwicke, Newcastle House, 15 October 1759.

66. See F. McLynn, *1759: The Year Britain Became Master of the World* (London, 2004), pp. 287–90; F. Jennings, *Empire of Fortune: Crowns, Colonies and Tribes in the Seven Years' War in America* (New York, 1988), pp. 420–21; G. Fregault, *Canada: The War of the Conquest*, trans. Margaret M. Cameron (Toronto, 1969), p. 252; R. Chartrand, *Quebec 1759* (Botley, Oxford, 1999), p. 77. Fred Anderson observes: 'No one ever reckoned the numbers of rapes, scalpings, thefts and casual murders perpetrated during this month of bloody horror.' See *Crucible of War: The Seven Years' War and the Fate of Empire in British North America, 1754–1766* (New York, 2000), p. 344.

67. *Knox's Journals*, i, p. 438.

68. John Childs, *Armies and Warfare in Europe* (Manchester, 1982), pp. 151, 154–55.

69. Wolfe to the Earl of Holderness, on board the *Sutherland*, at anchor off Cap Rouge, 9 September 1759, in Wright, *Life of Wolfe*, p. 564.

70. 'General Orders in Wolfe's Army', *Literary and Historical Society of Quebec: Manuscripts Relating to the Early History of Canada* (1875), item 2, p. 29; 'Townshend's Journal', 11 August 1759, in *Siege of Quebec*, v, p. 258.

71. See 'The Capture of Quebec: a Manuscript Journal Relating to the Operations Before Quebec ... by Colonel Malcolm Fraser ...', ed. Brig. R. Alexander, *JSAHR*, 18 (1939), p. 148; *Knox's Journal*, ii, p. 45. For Thompson's recollection see: GD 45/3/422, fol. 479, 'Anecdote of Wolfe's Army – Captain Montgomery, Afterwards General in the American Service'. Thompson misidentified the officer involved in this episode as Richard Montgomery, the future Revolutionary War hero, who was actually serving in the 17th Foot under Amherst at the time.

72. *Knox's Journal*, i, p. 428.

73. 'General Orders in Wolfe's Army', p. 34.

74. See Wolfe to Holderness, 9 September 1759 (Wright, *Life of Wolfe*, p. 565).

75. *Knox's Journal*, ii, pp. 7, 40, 42, 47.

76. 'Extract of a Journal', *NYCD*, x, p. 1034; *Knox's Journal*, ii, 55, 74; Saunders to Pitt, *Stirling Castle*, off Point Lévis, 5 September 1759 (*Correspondence of Pitt*, ii, p. 163).

Notes to Chapter 9: The Heights of Abraham

1. See *The Siege of Quebec and the Battle of the Plains of Abraham*, ed. A. Doughty and G. W. Parmelee (6 vols, Quebec, 1901–2), ii, pp. 238–39. Although undated, a range of evidence suggests that Wolfe compiled this memorandum on, or shortly before, 27 August. For example, under his journal for that day, and before the next entry (31 August), Thomas Bell included the underlined note 'Consultations of the Brigadrs' (LAC, 'Northcliffe Collection', Separate Items, MG18-M / rl C-370). The timing of the discussions that followed also supports that date. C. P. Stacey considered that the memorandum was 'probably' written on the 27 August. See *Quebec, 1759: The Siege and the Battle* (new edn, Toronto, 2002), p. 111.

2. 'Townshend's Journal' (28 August 1759), in *Siege of Quebec*, v, p. 261, and also 'Townshend's Rough Notes', in *Northcliffe Collection* (Ottawa, 1926), p. 422; for the brigadiers' letter, dated Point Lévis, 29 August 1759, see PRO 30/8/50, fos 162–63.

3. See *Siege of Quebec*, ii, pp. 241–42.

4. Wolfe to Saunders, 30 August 1759, in R. Wright, *The Life of Major-General James Wolfe* (London, 1864), p. 551.

5. W. T. Waugh, *James Wolfe: Man and Soldier* (Montreal, 1928), p. 274; R. Reilly, *The Rest to Fortune: The Life of Major-General James Wolfe* (London, 1960), pp. 273–76.

6. See 'Journal du Siége de Québec' (*Northcliffe Collection*, pp. 260–61); 'Extract of a Journal', in *NYCD*, x, p. 1034; L. H. Gipson, *The British Empire before the American Revolution*, vii, *The Great War for Empire: The Victorious Years, 1758–1760*, pp. 404–405.

7. PRO 30/8/69, fos 32–33: Lieutenant-Colonel John Young to Brigadier-General James Murray, *Sutherland*, 27 August 1759.

8. *The Logs of the Conquest of Canada*, ed. William H. Wood (Toronto, 1909), pp. 230, 237; Saunders to Pitt, *Stirling Castle*, off Point Lévis, 5 September 1759, in *The Correspondence of William Pitt, when Secretary of State, with Colonial Governors and Military and Naval Commissioners in America*, ed. G. S. Kimball (2 vols, London, 1906; repr. New York, 1969), ii, p. 161.

9. 'Wolfe "Family" Journal', part 1, pp. 24–26 (LAC, 'Paulus Aemilius Irving Fonds', MG18-N45 / rl A–652).

10. 'Townshend's Journal' (*Siege of Quebec*, v, p. 253).

11. Saunders to Wolfe, *Stirling Castle*, 25 August 1759 (PRO 30/8/55, fos 91–92); Wolfe to Saunders, 30 August 1759 (Wright, *Life of Wolfe*, pp. 548–49).

12. Wolfe to his mother, Banks of the St Lawrence, 31 August 1759 (ibid. p. 553).

13. 'Letter to Mr J. W., from *Stirling Castle*, in the River St Lawrence, Two Miles below the City of Quebec, 2 September 1759', in 'Genuine Letters from a Volunteer in the British Service at Quebec' (*Siege of Quebec*, v, pp. 19–20). For the Royal Navy's build-up of strength above Quebec, see 'Journal of Moncrief [Mackellar]', ibid., p. 47; 'Bell's Quebec Journal' (27 and 31 August 1759).

14. 'A Journal of the Expedition up the River St Lawrence', in *Literary and Historical Society of Quebec: Manuscripts Relating to the Early History of Canada* (1875), item 1, p. 16; 'General Orders in Wolfe's Army' (1–3 September 1759), ibid., item 2, pp. 44–46; 'Extract of a Journal', *NYCD*, x, p. 1035.

15. 'Journal of Moncrief [Mackellar]', *Siege of Quebec*, v, p. 47; 'Wolfe "Family" Journal', part 2, pp. 1–2; *Logs of the Conquest*, pp. 272, 313.

16. See CO/5/51, fol. 86: 'Return of the Killed, Wounded & Missing', enclosed with Wolfe to Pitt, Montmorency 2 September 1759; 'State of the Troops', 24 August 1759, signed by Isaac Barré (LAC, 'James Murray Collection',

MG23-GIIı / rl C–2225). Barré's total of 7491 includes 153 men of the 62nd and 69th regiments, under the command of Major Thomas Hardy, who were serving as marines. Excluded from the total were another one hundred or so of Hardy's men on the Isle of Orleans, and a battalion of marines, under Lieutenant-Colonel Boisrond at Point Lévis, which was reckoned at 1095 of all ranks. See 'Weekly Return of the Marines at the Camp at Point Levi', 27 August 1759 (LAC, 'Northcliffe Collection', xxi, MG18-M / rl C–366). By early September, of course, *all* of Wolfe's rangers (estimated by Barré at 450 men) plus several hundred regulars and marines, were operating downriver under Major Scott.

17. CO/5/56, fos 201–202: Amherst to Wolfe, Camp of Crown Point, 7 August 1759; 'Extract of a Letter from Point-Levee', 4 September 1759, in *Boston Gazette*, 8 October 1759.

18. J. R. Alden, *General Gage in America* (Baton Rouge, 1947), p. 49. Gage's vacillation is clear from the 'Private Diary Kept by Sir William Johnson at Niagara and Oswego, 1759', given in *An Historical Journal of the Campaigns in North America for the Years 1757, 1758, 1759, and 1760, by Captain John Knox*, ed. A. G. Doughty (3 vols, Toronto, 1914), iii, pp. 197, 210–211.

19. For the original report, see 'Extract of a Letter from Crown Point', in *Boston News-Letter*, 13 September 1759. The response was first carried in *Boston Gazette*, 17 September 1759, and subsequently in *New-Hampshire Gazette*, 21 September 1759, and *New-York Gazette*, 24 September 1759.

20. Letter from 'Camp Levi', 6 September 1759, in *HMC: Marquess of Townshend Manuscripts* (London, 1887), pp. 308–9.

21. 'Letter of Admiral Holmes, *Lowestoft*, off Foulon in the River St Lawrence above Quebec, 18 September 1759' (*Siege of Quebec*, iv, p. 295); 'Journal of Moncrief [Mackellar]', ibid., v, pp. 47–48; 'Journal of the Particular Transactions', ibid., p. 185.

22. 'Journal du Siége de Québec' (*Northcliffe Collection*, p. 265); *Adventure in the Wilderness: The American Journals of Louis Antoine de Bougainville, 1756–60*, ed. E. P. Hamilton (Norman, Oklahoma, 1964), p. 320.

23. 'Townshend's Journal' (*Siege of Quebec*, v, p. 265); *Knox's Journal*, ii, p. 78.

24. 'General Orders in Wolfe's Army' (7 September 1759), pp. 48–49; 'Townshend's Journal' (*Siege of Quebec*, v, pp. 265–66); *Knox's Journal*, ii, p. 79; *Logs of the Conquest*, pp. 241, 293–94. Knox assumed that the operations of 7 September were no more than a feint – an interpretation shared by C. P. Stacey (*Quebec, 1759*, p. 118). Both Townshend's journal and the ships' logs indicate, however, that a landing was actually contemplated, only to be cancelled because the frigates were unable to give covering fire.

25. 'General Orders in Wolfe's Army' (8 September 1759), pp. 48–49; 'Journal of Moncrief [Mackellar]', in *Siege of Quebec*, v, p. 48.

26. Wolfe to Holderness, on board the *Sutherland*, at anchor off Cap Rouge, 9 September 1759 (Wright, *Life of Wolfe*, pp. 564–65).

27. 'Wolfe "Family" Journal', part 2, p. 3; 'The Last Advices from our Forces up the River St Lawrence', in *Boston News-Letter*, 11 October 1759.

28. 'Journal of Moncrief [Mackellar]', *Siege of Quebec*, v, p. 48.

29. Ibid., pp. 48–49; 'Wolfe "Family" Journal', part 2, p. 3.

30. 'Letter of Holmes', 18 September 1759 (*Siege of Quebec*, iv, p. 296).

31. See the discussions in W. J. Eccles, 'The Battle of Quebec: A Reappraisal', in his *Essays on New France* (Toronto, 1987), pp. 125–33; and E. R. Adair, 'The Military Reputation of Major-General James Wolfe', *Canadian Historical Association Report* (Ottawa, 1936), pp. 28–30.

32. Wolfe to Burton, *Sutherland*, 'above Carouge', 10 September 1759, in Wright, *Life of Wolfe*, p. 569.

33. Rollo to Murray, Louisbourg, 10 June 1759 (LAC, 'James Murray Collection').

34. *Memoirs of Major Robert Stobo of the Virginia Regiment* (London, 1800), p. 65. See also Robert C. Alberts, *The Most Extraordinary Adventures of Major Robert Stobo* (Boston, 1965), and his entry on Stobo in *DCB*, iii, pp. 600–2. As Alberts notes (ibid., p. 601), although Stobo's *Memoirs* were based upon a manuscript dated 1760, they 'do not seem to have been written by Stobo himself'.

35. 'Townshend's Journal' (*Siege of Quebec*, v, p. 267); 'Journal of the Expedition up the River St Lawrence', p. 17; *Knox's Journal*, ii, p. 85; Wolfe to Burton, 10 September 1759 (Wright, *Life of Wolfe*, pp. 569).

36. Ibid., pp. 568–70. See also *New-Hampshire Gazette*, 29 December 1759, under 'Philadelphia, December 13', and citing a letter from 'a Gentleman at Quebec'. This reported that 'General Wolfe effactually executed a plan, which he had not above forty eight hours to concert, and was formed on intelligence of Monsieur Levy being detached with 4 or 5000 men towards Montreal'.

37. See Donald W. Olson et al., 'Perfect Tide, Ideal Moon: An Unappreciated Aspect of Wolfe's Generalship at Quebec, 1759', in *William and Mary Quarterly* (3rd Series), 59 (2002), p. 973.

38. 'General Orders in Wolfe's Army', pp. 50–53; also, *Knox's Journal*, ii, pp. 86–89, and Holmes's letter of 18 September 1759 (*Siege of Quebec*, iv, p. 296).

39. *Knox's Journal*, ii, pp. 91–93.

40. 'Memoirs of the Quarter Master Sergeant', in *Siege of Quebec*, v, p. 101.

41. 'Journal of the Expedition up the River St Lawrence', p. 17; 'Townshend's Journal' (*Siege of Quebec*, v, p. 267).

42. In *Northcliffe Collection*, p. 425.

43. Ibid., pp. 412, 415,

44. Stacey, *Quebec, 1759*, pp. 123–26.

45. 'Wolfe "Family" Journal', part 2, pp. 3, 5. Given his proven combat record, it is safe to assume that Murray was the 'villain'.

46. F. Anderson, *Crucible of War: The Seven Years' War and the Fate of Empire in British North America, 1754–1766* (New York, 2000), p. 353.

47. See J. S. Tucker's *Memoirs of Earl St Vincent* (2 vols, 1844), i, p. 19. This story was followed by Robert Wright (*Life of Wolfe*, pp. 573–74) and Francis Parkman in *Montcalm and Wolfe* (2 vols, Boston, 1884), ii, p. 295, and repeated by Beckles Willson in *The Life and Letters of James Wolfe* (New York, 1909), pp. 482–83. Willson, however, subsequently revised his opinion. See his 'Fresh Light on the Quebec Campaign', *Nineteenth Century and After* (1910), p. 445; also his 'General Wolfe and Gray's "Elegy"', ibid., (1913), p. 873. For Jervis's own recollections, see McCord Museum, C–173, box 1, MS 1431: Jervis to —, Portsmouth, 18 July [1798].

48. See *New-York Gazette*, 25 February 1760; Wolfe to Amherst, Louisbourg, 27 May 1759 (WO/34/46B, fol. 300); Wolfe to his mother, 31 August 1759 (Wright, *Life of Wolfe*, p. 553).

49. Wolfe to Major Walter Wolfe, Louisbourg, 19 May 1759 (Willson, *Life and Letters of Wolfe*, p. 429).

50. For Wolfe's fondness for children and aspirations to fatherhood, see his letter to his mother, Inverness, 6 November 1751 (Willson, *Life and Letters of Wolfe*, p. 160).

51. 'Wolfe "Family" Journal', part 2, pp. 4–6. According to Townshend, Chads's concerns nonetheless prompted some last-minute adjustments to the plan. He had assured Captain Smith, 'a very active and intelligent officer of the light troops', that, if they proceeded along the south side of the river, the current was so strong that they would overshoot their objective. Smith communicated this information to the brigadiers. As there was no time to report back to Wolfe, they authorized Chads to take them down the north side of the river instead. See 'Townshend's Rough Notes' (*Northcliffe Collection*, p. 424).

52. 'Wolfe "Family" Journal', part 2, p. 6; 'Journal of the Expedition up the River St Lawrence', p. 17. This was kept by an officer in the 47th Foot – part of the first wave.

53. 'Journal of the Particular Transactions', in *Siege of Quebec*, v, p. 187. The author was himself one of the eight volunteers.

54. Ibid.
55. Olson et al., 'Perfect Tide, Ideal Moon', *William and Mary Quarterly* (2002), pp. 966, 968–69.
56. Parkman, *Montcalm and Wolfe*, ii, p. 297.
57. This discussion draws upon the evidence assembled in Willson, 'General Wolfe and Gray's "Elegy"', in *Nineteenth Century and After* (1913), pp. 862–75; Robert L. Mack, *Thomas Gray: A Life* (New Haven and London, 2000), pp. 508–10; and Stacey, *Quebec, 1759*, pp. 134–36.
58. Mack, *Thomas Gray*, p. 510. In the 1804 version, reported by one of Robison's students, the future professor was in a boat *near* to Wolfe's, and overheard a 'gentleman' repeating the poem to the general. Despite such variations, and the absence of the story in the eighteenth-century literature, Robert Mack finds no reason 'to doubt the essential substance of Robison's recollection of Wolfe's sentiments', which were perhaps 'the greatest and most sincerely felt flattery ever bestowed upon the Elegy' (ibid).
59. Letter from Quebec, 14 September 1759, in *New-York Gazette*, 3 December 1759; *Logs of the Conquest*, p. 269.
60. Ibid., p. 231–32.
61. 'Journal of Moncrief [Mackellar]', in *Siege of Quebec*, v, p. 50; 'Journal of the Particular Transactions' (ibid., p. 187); 'Anecdotes Relating to the Battle of Quebec', in *British Magazine, 1760* (March) pp. 146–47; 'Wolfe "Family" Journal', part 2, pp. 6–7.
62. Ibid.; 'Townshend's Rough Notes' (*Northcliffe Collection*, p. 424); 'Extract of a Journal' (*NYCD*, x, p. 1038). Evidence suggests that this was the same Simon Fraser, who, as a brigadier-general, was killed at Saratoga in 1777. See for example, GD 248, box 614, Commonplace book of John Grant for 1752–1797, under 'Anecdotes Relating to the American War and Other Memorable Matters', no. 2.
63. De Laune's comments survive as notes he made to the account of the assault published in the *London Gazette Extraordinary* of 17 October 1759. This was pasted inside a copy of Humphrey Bland's *Treatise of Military Discipline* (6th edn, 1746), which Wolfe gave to De Laune in 1752, when he was an ensign in the 20th Foot. See *Wolfiana: A Potpourri of Facts and Fantasies, Culled from Literature, Relating to the Life of James Wolfe*, ed. J. C. Webster (Shediac, New Brunswick, 1927), p. 18.
64. Murray to his wife, Quebec, 20 September 1759, in 'The Letters of Colonel Alexander Murray, 1742–59', ed. Col. H. C. Wylly, in *1926 Regimental Annual. The Sherwood Foresters, Nottinghamshire and Derbyshire Regiment* (London, 1927), p. 216; *Knox's Journal*, ii, p. 96.

65. Ibid.
66. Letter from Quebec, 7 October 1759, in *Derby Mercury*, 30 November to 7 December 1759.
67. 'Journal of Moncrief [Mackellar]', *Siege of Quebec*, v, p. 50; 'Wolfe "Family" Journal', part 2, pp. 7–8.
68. 'Letter of Holmes', 18 September 1759 (*Siege of Quebec*, v, pp. 296–97); Saunders to Pitt, 20 September 1759 (*Correspondence of Pitt*, ii, p. 171).
69. 'Wolfe "Family" Journal', part 2, p. 8. This vivid testimony is strong evidence for Captain Matthew Leslie's authorship of this key memoir. According to his 1767 letter to Pitt, on 13 September 1759 Leslie had 'the honour to conduct the embarkation and landing of the troops' (see PRO 30/8/48, fol. 101).
70. Barré's comments are included in a letter from Major Henry Caldwell (the same officer who served as one of Wolfe's deputy quartermaster-generals in 1759) to James Murray, dated London, 1 November 1772. Murray sent a copy of this to Jeffery Amherst. See Amherst Family Papers, U1350/C21; see also LAC, 'James Murray Collection'.
71. Gipson, *The Victorious Years*, pp. 415–16.
72. Townshend to Pitt, Camp before Quebec, 20 September 1759 (*Correspondence of Pitt*, ii, p. 165); Lieutenant John Brown, 2/60th Foot, to Lord Loudoun, Quebec, 28 September 1759 (LO: 6144).
73. 'Journal of Moncrief [Mackellar]', in *Siege of Quebec*, v, p. 50–51.
74. Although this is the generally accepted figure, there is some confusion over the exact number of Wolfe's army on the Plains of Abraham. In his *Journal* (ii, p. 104), Knox reproduced a return showing 4828 of all ranks. In another, enclosed with his despatch to Pitt of 20 September 1759, Townshend gave a total of 4441 (CO/5/51, fol. 102). The likeliest explanation for the discrepancy is that Knox included soldiers who participated in the operation but did not actually reach the battlefield – for example, some sixty men of Fraser's Highlanders were 'left on board' the transports 'for want of boats', and another thirty remained at the Foulon ('Journal of Fraser', p. 159) – whilst Townshend failed to list all of the men of Howe's Light Infantry, who *were* present, albeit detached from their parent units.
75. 'Memoirs of the Quarter Master Sergeant' (*Siege of Quebec*, v, p. 107). For the genesis of the 'thin red line', see S. Brumwell, *Redcoats: The British Soldier and War in the Americas, 1755–1763* (Cambridge, 2002), pp. 254–55;
76. For an overview of these frantic hours, see Stacey, *Quebec, 1759*, pp. 147–49.

77. 'Extract of a Journal' (*NYCD*, x, pp. 1038–39).

78. Letter from Quebec, 7 October 1759 (*Derby Mercury*, 30 November to 7 December 1759).

79. Eccles, 'Battle of Quebec', in *Essays on New France*, p. 133; Bruce Lenman, *Britain's Colonial Wars, 1688–1783* (Harlow, 2001), p. 151; Anderson, *Crucible of War*, p. 355.

80. *Knox's Journal*, ii, p. 99; 'Journal of the Particular Transactions' (*Siege of Quebec*, v, p. 188).

81. See Townshend to Pitt, 20 September 1759 (*Correspondence of Pitt*, ii, p. 166). Townshend's detailed breakdown of 'the French line' (CO/5/51, fol. 101) numbers the regulars at 1920, with another 1500 lurking militia, for a total force of 3420. Given the original size of Montcalm's army this seems unduly low, particularly for the militia: the figure of 4500, as cited by one of the most reliable French sources ('Extract of a Journal', in *NYCD*, x, p. 1039), and accepted by Stacey (*Quebec, 1759*, p. 153) is followed here.

82. Letter from Ensign William Johnston, 48th Foot, to his father, Quebec, 9 October 1759, given in Lieutenant-Colonel Russell Gurney, *History of the Northamptonshire Regiment, 1742–1934* (Aldershot, 1935), p. 355, note 8.

83. Martin L. Nicolai, 'A Different Kind of Courage: The French Military and the Canadian Irregular Soldier during the Seven Years' War', *CHR*, 70 (1989), pp. 65–67.

84. *Knox's Journal*, ii, p. 101; 'Memoirs of the Quarter Master Sergeant' (*Siege of Quebec*, v, p. 104).

85. 'Journal of Moncrief [Mackellar]', ibid., p. 52.

86. See for example, 'Journal of the Expedition up the River St Lawrence', p. 18; 'Journal of Fraser', *JSAHR* (1939), p. 155; 'Serjeant-Major's Journal' (*Siege of Quebec*, v, p. 9).

87. *Knox's Journal*, ii, p. 101; 'Journal of Moncrief [Mackellar]', *Siege of Quebec*, v, p. 53; 'Letters of Colonel Murray', p. 216.

88. See 'Journal abrégé de la campagne de 1759 en Canada' (*Siege of Quebec*, v, p. 296); *Journal des Campagnes au Canada de 1755 à 1760 par le Comte de Maurès de Malartic*, ed. Gabriel de Maurès de Malartic and Paul Gafferel (Dijon, 1890), p. 285.

89. Townshend to Pitt, Quebec, 20 September 1759 (*Correspondence of Pitt*, ii, p. 166).

90. Knox's account, and the evidence of French survivors, suggests that these two units gave their first, devastating fire as massed battalion volleys, rather than by the 'alternate fire' of platoons or companies. This is supported by the statement of an officer in the 47th Foot, who described

how, 'by command', the troops 'threw in their *whole* fire' ('Journal of the Expedition up the River St Lawrence', p. 18; my italics).

91. 'Journal of Moncrief [Mackellar]', *Siege of Quebec*, v, p. 53. See also 'Letters of Colonel Murray', p. 216.

92. 'Journal of the Particular Transactions', in *Siege of Quebec*, v, p. 188.

93. Letter from Quebec, 20 September 1759, in 'Letters of Colonel Murray', p. 216.

94. For Wolfe's wounds, see 'Copy of a Letter from an Officer to his Friend, Off Point Levi, near Quebec', in *Gentleman's Magazine, 1759* (December), p. 556; *Scots Magazine, 1759* (October), p. 554; 'Extract of a Letter from an Officer at Quebec', 20 September 1759, in *Edinburgh Chronicle*, 22–24 October 1759; and a letter 'from a young gentleman ... from on board his Majesty's ship Scarborough off the Isle of Coudre', 23 September 1759 (ibid., 27–29 October 1759).

95. 'Wolfe "Family" Journal', part 2, p. 11.

96. For James Henderson to his uncle, Quebec, 7 October 1759, see 'A Letter Describing the Death of General Wolfe', *EHR*, 12 (1897), pp. 762–63; Henry Browne to his father, Louisbourg, 17 November 1759 (NAM, MS 7808-93-2).

97. See *Knox's Journal*, ii, p. 114. Newspaper reports claimed that, after receiving his fatal wound, Wolfe leaned upon Captain Ralph Corry of Bragg's 28th Foot, 'complaining that his eyesight and strength failed him', and asked 'how the day went'. On being told the enemy was routed, he replied 'God be praised – I die in peace' (*Scots Magazine, 1759*, p. 554; *Edinburgh Chronicle*, 27–29 October 1759). Others with a credible claim to have witnessed Wolfe's death include Captain Samuel Holland. His contention that 'Mr Treat', the surgeon's mate of the 48th Foot, was the only medical man at the scene, receives support from the return of Wolfe's army on 13 September given by John Knox: this shows that the 48th Foot was the sole unit to muster a surgeon's mate on the field. See 'A New Account of the Death of Wolfe', ed. A. G. Doughty, *CHR*, 4 (1923) pp. 53–54; *Knox's Journal* (ii, p. 104).

98. 'Journal of Fraser', *JSAHR* (1939), pp. 156–57.

99. Monckton to Pitt, Point Lévis, 15 September 1759, in *Correspondence of Pitt*, ii, p. 163; *Logs of the Conquest*, p. 242.

100. Townshend to Pitt, Quebec, 20 September 1759, in *Correspondence of Pitt*, ii, pp. 167–68; 'Journal of Fraser', *JSAHR* (1939), p. 157; 'Journal of Moncrief [Mackellar]', in *Siege of Quebec*, v, p. 54; *British Magazine, 1760* (March), p. 147; *Boston Evening-Post*, 22 October 1759.

101. CO/5/51, fol. 97.

102. 'Extract of a Journal' (*NYCD*, x, p. 1040).

103. See *Edinburgh Chronicle*, 27–29 October 1759. Of the reports that Wolfe was mortally wounded by one of his own men, the best known only surfaced in print nearly thirty years later, in the *London Chronicle* of 16–19 August 1788. This maintained that Wolfe was shot by 'a deserter from his own regiment' – a sergeant who nursed a grudge after the general threatened to reduce him to the ranks for striking a 'good soldier'. At the Battle of the Plains, this 'miscreant' fought on the enemy's left wing, opposite to Wolfe's position on the British right, and sniped him with a 'rifle piece'. After the French army's defeat, the story continues, all the deserters were sent to Crown Point; upon that post's conquest by the British, the entire garrison was captured and the sergeant hanged, but not before confessing his awful crime. The account 'was had from a gentleman who heard the confession'. Unfortunately for the story's credibility, although William De Laune of Wolfe's own 67th Foot served at Quebec, his regiment did not come with him; more glaringly, when Amherst took Crown Point on 4 August 1759 – more than a month *before* Wolfe's death – the garrison had already been evacuated. In addition, the extensive court martial papers of the British Army make no mention of any such sensational case.

More intriguing is a story published in the *Boston Evening-Post* of 2 March 1761, under 'London, December 20 [1760]'. This stated how:

A report has been current, that a convict who was lately executed at Salisbury, had, at the place of execution, made a voluntary confession, that he was present, as a private man in his Majesty's troops, at the action last year before Quebec, and did then, from a motive of revenge, fire twice at General Wolfe, and gave him two wounds, and that the latter of which proved mortal.

Whether there was any more to this tale than a condemned man's craving for some last notoriety cannot be established from the available evidence, although the killing of officers by their own men – a practice dubbed 'fragging' during the Vietnam War – was not unknown in the eighteenth century. But, as emphasized here, the French army at Quebec included skilled marksmen with orders to target the enemy's officers: whilst the smoke and confusion of a lively fire fight would make it well nigh impossible to establish exactly *who* hit Wolfe, Samuel Holland's claim that 'the fatal shot' was fired by a 'Canadian boy from Jacques Carthier' is probably as valid as any. See 'A New Account of the Death of Wolfe', *CHR* (1923), p. 52.

104. *New-York Gazette*, 3 December 1759, under 'Philadelphia, November 29', citing letter from Quebec, 14 September 1759.

105. Browne to his father, Louisbourg, 17 November 1759 (NAM, MS 7808-93-2).
106. See 'Journal of the Expedition up the St Lawrence', p. 19; letter from Quebec, 7 October 1759, in *Derby Mercury*, 30 November to 7 December 1759; Lieutenant Brown to Loudoun, Quebec, 28 September 1759 (LO 6144); 'Serjeant-Major's Journal', in *Siege of Quebec*, v, p. 10; 'Journal of the Particular Transactions' (ibid., p. 189); 'Letters of Colonel Murray', pp. 218–19. For the post-battle reaction of Nelson's men at Trafalgar, see, for example, A. Lambert, *Nelson: Britannia's God of War* (London, 2004), p. 307.
107. 'Journal of Fraser', *JSAHR* (1939), p. 156.
108. *New-Hampshire Gazette*, 29 December 1759 (under 'Philadelphia 13 December'); also, 'Extract of a Letter from an Officer at Quebec to his Friend', 20 September 1759, in *London Chronicle*, 23–25 October 1759. Had Wolfe lived, this correspondent wrote, Quebec would have been stormed immediately: however, 'his death threw a damp upon the whole army'.
109. 'Wolfe "Family" Journal', part 2, pp. 13–15; Townshend to Pitt, 20 September 1759 (*Correspondence of Pitt*, ii, p. 168); Stacey, *Quebec, 1759*, pp. 172–74; 'Journal of Moncrief [Mackellar]', in *Siege of Quebec*, v, p. 55.
110. Letter of Holmes, 18 September 1759 (ibid., p. 299).
111. *Adventure in the Wilderness*, p. 321.
112. Orders, 'Camp before Quebec' (18 September 1759), in *Northcliffe Collection*, p. 170; Williamson (to Jeffery Amherst?), undated, but from Quebec, *c*. late September 1759, in Amherst Family Papers (U1350/O33/4); also, Williamson to the Principal Officers of His Majesty's Ordnance, Quebec, 21 September 1759, given in *Knox's Journal*, iii, p. 339; Brown to Loudoun, Quebec, 28 September 1759 (LO 6144); Fletcher to his father, Camp before Quebec, 14/18 September 1759 (NLS, MS 16521); 'Extract of a Letter ...', Quebec, 20 September 1759 (*London Chronicle*, 23–25 October 1759); *New-Hampshire Gazette*, 29 December 1759 (under 'Philadelphia 13 December').
113. Reported in *New-York Gazette*, 10 December 1759 and *Boston Gazette*, 17 December 1759.

Notes to Chapter 10: Wolfe's Dust

1. Pitt to Newcastle, Whitehall, 14 October 1759; [John] Ibbetson to John Clevland, Admiralty Office, Sunday '¼ past 2.00 pm', 14 October 1759; Newcastle to Lord Hardwicke, Newcastle House, 15 October 1759 (Newcastle Papers, Add MS 32,897, fols. 73, 75–76, 88).
2. Walpole to Mann, Arlington Street, 16 October 1759, in *The Yale Edition of*

Horace Walpole's Correspondence, ed. W. S. Lewis (London and Oxford, 48 vols, 1937–83), xxi, pp. 335–36.

3. Add. MS 32,897, fol. 115: Pitt to Newcastle, 'Tuesday night past Eleven', 16 October 1759; Walpole to Mann, Strawberry Hill, 19 October 1759 (*Walpole's Correspondence*, xxi, p. 337).

4. Mrs Clayton to her daughter, London, 17 October 1759 ('General Wolfe's Letters to his Parents, 1740–1759', Squerryes Court, Westerham, pp. 939–40); *London Magazine, 1759* (October), p. 569.

5. *London Chronicle*, 20–23 October 1759; *Boddely's Bath Journal*, 22 October 1759.

6. *London Chronicle*, 25–27 October 1759, and 30 October to 1 November 1759.

7. *London Chronicle* and *London Evening Post*, 20–23 October 1759.

8. See for example, *London Magazine, 1759* (October), p. 568 – an initial sketch expanded by 'Character, with Some Particulars, of the Late Major-General James Wolfe', ibid., (November), p. 579. The latter was published in the often-reprinted *Annual Register for 1759* (pp. 281–82).

9. *London Magazine, 1759* (November), p. 631.

10. See *New-York Gazette*, 15 October 1759; *Boston News-Letter*, 18 and 26 October 1759.

11. Ibid., 18 October 1759; *Boston Evening-Post*, 22 October 1759.

12. For these links, see for example, J. Shy, 'The American Colonies, 1748–1783', in *The Oxford History of the British Empire*, ii, *The Eighteenth Century*, ed. P. J. Marshall (Oxford, 1998), pp. 306, 308; also, Fred Anderson, *The War that Made America: A Short History of the French and Indian War* (New York, 2005), pp. 207–9.

13. *London Magazine, 1759* (October), p. 569. The *Scots Magazine* of December 1759 (p. 657) noted that 'Congratulatory addresses on the success of the British arms continue still to appear in the gazette'. On Wolfe's importance for expunging the shame of Minorca, and more generally, for the 'recovery of British patriotism and manliness', see Kathleen Wilson, 'Empire of Virtue: The Imperial Project and Hanoverian Culture, c. 1720–1785', in *An Imperial State at War: Britain From 1688 to 1815*, ed. Lawrence Stone (London and New York, 1994), pp. 148–50.

14. PRO 30/8/33, fol. 120: Granby to Pitt, Koosfoort, 25 October 1759.

15. See the *London Magazine's* poetical essays for November 1759 (p. 613). Although published anonymously, this ode was written by Wolfe's acquaintance, John Mason of Greenwich. See McCord Museum, C–173, box 1, MS 263, 'Poems Dedicated to Mrs Wolfe'; Lady Montagu to Lady

Bute, 9 November 1759, in *The Complete Letters of Lady Mary Wortley Montagu*, ed. Robert Halsband (3 vols, Oxford, 1965–67), iii; *Scots Magazine, 1759* (October), p. 554.

16. Katherine Lowther to Mrs Wolfe, Raby Castle, 25 October 1759, given in Beckles Willson, 'General Wolfe and Gray's "Elegy"', in *The Nineteenth Century and After*, 434 (April, 1913), p. 874.

17. Ibid.; Katherine Lowther (to Mrs Scott), Raby Castle, 18 December 1759, in R. Wright, *The Life of Major-General James Wolfe* (London, 1864), p. 597.

18. See De Laune's notes, in *Wolfiana: A Potpourri of Facts and Fantasies, Culled from Literature, Relating to the Life of James Wolfe*, ed. J. C. Webster (Shediac, New Brunswick, 1927), p. 18; also 'Bell's Quebec Journal' (23 September 1759), in LAC, 'Northcliffe Collection', Separate Items (MG18-M / rl C-370).

19. Anon, *Memoirs of the Life and Gallant Exploits of the Old Highlander, Sergeant Donald Macleod* (London, 1791), pp. 73–74. The Chelsea register confirms that Macleod was indeed admitted, as an 'out-pensioner', on 4 December 1759 (WO/116/5, fol. 40).

20. 'Anecdote of Wolfe's Army – Wolfe, the Soldier's Friend' (GD 45/3/422, fos 481–83).

21. *London Magazine, 1759* (November), p. 580. For Portsmouth Point, see Lieutenant-Colonel Theodore Dury to Secretary at War Barrington, 13 September 1758 (WO/1/976, p. 373).

22. 'Bell's Quebec Journal'; *London Chronicle*, 17–20 November 1759; *London Evening-Post*, 22–24 November 1759. A copy of the register page including Wolfe's burial is on display at St Alfege's Church, Greenwich.

23. R. Middleton, *The Bells of Victory: The Pitt-Newcastle Ministry and the Conduct of the Seven Years' War, 1757–1762* (Cambridge, 1985) pp. 107–108; Jeremy Black, *Pitt the Elder* (Cambridge, 1992), pp. 186–88.

24. For Hogarth's prints, see *London Chronicle*, 23–25 October 1759; for Wolfe's orders, ibid., 3–6 November 1759. These were also reprinted in John Entick's popular *General History of the Late War* (5 vols, London, 1763–64), iv, pp. 92–97.

25. *Scots Magazine, 1759* (November), p. 607. On Hale's dragoons, see J. W. Fortescue, *A History of the British Army*, ii, (London, 1910), 509–10. Captain Sir James Douglas of the *Alcide*, who brought Saunders's victory despatches, received the same gratuity as Hale.

26. On Quiberon Bay, see N. A. M. Rodger, *The Command of the Ocean: A Naval History of Britain, 1649–1815* (London, 2004), pp. 281–83; Jonathan R. Dull, *The French Navy and the Seven Years' War* (Lincoln, Nebraska,

2005), pp. 161–62; F. McLynn, *1759: The Year Britain Became Master of the World* (London, 2004), pp. 354–87.

27. *Scots Magazine, 1759* (October), p. 541.

28. Horace Walpole, *Memoirs of King George II*, ed. J. Brooke (3 vols, New Haven and London, 1985), iii, p. 80.

29. See A. McNairn, *Behold the Hero: General Wolfe and the Arts in the Eighteenth Century* (Liverpool, 1997), pp. 71–88; Matthew Craske, *Art in Europe, 1700–1830* (Oxford, 1997), p. 263; Walpole to Henry Seymour Conway, Strawberry Hill, 5 August 1761 (*Walpole's Correspondence*, xxxviii, p. 110).

30. Anon, *Stowe: A Description of the House and Gardens of the Most Noble and Puissant Prince, George Grenville Nugent Temple, Marquis of Buckingham* (Buckingham, 1797), pp. 27–30.

31. See *Journal of the House of Representatives of Massachusetts*, xxxvi (1759–60), (Portland, Maine, 1964), pp. 89, 97, 112–13, 232, 239; *Annual Register for 1760*, p. 69, citing news from Boston of 26 October. The province's proposed monument to Lord Howe in Westminster Abbey *was* erected, on 14 July 1762. See *Boston Evening-Post*, 23 October 1762, under 'London, 15 July'. Montresor's 'Plan of the City of New-York and its Environs' is reproduced in *Atlas of the American Revolution*, ed. Kenneth Nebenzahl (New York, 1974), pp. 84–85.

32. *London Chronicle*, 20–23 October 1759.

33. Mrs Wolfe to Pitt, Blackheath, 30 November 1759, in *The Correspondence of the Earl of Chatham*, (4 vols, London, 1838), i, p. 462.

34. Pitt to Mrs Scott Whitehall, 15 January 1760 (McCord Museum, C–173, box 1, MS 1428); Pitt to Mrs Wolfe, St James's Square, 17 January 1760 (ibid., MS 1427).

35. Mrs Wolfe to Thomas Fisher, Bath, 22 February 1761 (ibid., MS 1435). According to Barrington, upon his appointment to the Quebec expedition Wolfe had expressed concern that his pay as major-general would be insufficient to meet the expenses arising from command of that army. To cover these therefore, a royal warrant for £500 was authorized, with which sum 'Mr Wolfe declared himself perfectly satisfied'. See Barrington to Secretary at War Charles Townshend, Cavendish Square, 7 May 1761, cited in Wright, *Life of Wolfe*, p. 479.

36. On Hawke's pension, see *Boddely's Bath Journal*, 17 December 1759, reporting London news of 13 December. Hawke actually got £2000.

37. See Wright, *Life of Wolfe*, pp. 609–11.

38. Walpole, *Memoirs of George II*, iii, p. 76; 'An Officer's Address to the Publick', in *London Chronicle*, 27–30 October 1759.

39. See *London Chronicle*, 30 October to 1 November 1759, and *Public Advertiser*, 2 November 1759. There was certainly a concerted campaign to extol Townshend at this time. For example, the *Scots Magazine* of January 1760 (p. 33) published 'A CALL TO THE POETS. On the Taking of Quebec'. The author felt that 'brave Wolfe' should share the limelight with Monckton, but more especially with Townshend, 'who, for his country, and great George's cause, forsook the fullness of domestic joys ...' Indeed, both the living and the dead should be celebrated 'in immortal verse'.

40. *London Magazine, 1759* (October), p. 517.

41. This story has been linked to Wolfe's supposed bragging to Pitt and Temple on the eve of his departure for Quebec (see, for example, Reilly, *Rest to Fortune*, pp. 217–18). But a poem written that autumn by Wolfe's friend John Mason (in McCord Museum, C–173, box 1, MS 263, and given at the head of this chapter), indicates that it originated in the partisan bickering that followed his death. Mason's poem is inscribed 'Oct 14, 1759'. This was the date of the arrival of Wolfe's own despatch from Quebec, two days *before* the news of his victory and death. This discrepancy is puzzling, although it is possible that Mason used the earlier date deliberately in a symbolic, commemorative, fashion. Whatever, the poem – and the anecdote it recalls – clearly post-dates Wolfe's death. It is also interesting that early versions of the story attribute the 'mad' assertion to Newcastle – George Townshend's uncle.

42. *An Historical Journal of the Campaigns in North America for the Years 1757, 1758, 1759, and 1760, by Captain John Knox*, ed. A. G. Doughty (3 vols, Toronto, 1914), ii, pp. 238, 241, 243.

43. See Amherst to Gage, Camp at Crown Point, 21 September 1759 (CO/5/56, fol. 223); Amherst to Pitt, Crown Point, 22 October 1759, in *The Correspondence of William Pitt, when Secretary of State, with Colonial Governors and Military and Naval Commissioners in America*, ed. G. S. Kimball (2 vols, London, 1906; repr. New York, 1969), ii, p. 196; Pitt to Amherst, Whitehall, 11 December 1759 (ibid., pp. 216–217).

44. Amherst to Ligonier, Camp of Crown Point, 22 October 1759 (Amherst Family Papers, U1350/035/13); *The Journal of Jeffery Amherst, Recording the Military Career of General Amherst in America from 1758 to 1763*, ed. J. Clarence Webster (Toronto, 1931), pp. 178–83.

45. WO/34/46B, fos 217–18: Townshend to Amherst, Quebec, 7 October 1759.

46. Townshend to Murray, Quebec, 5 October 1759 (LAC, 'James Murray Collection', MG23-GII1 / rl C–2225); Murray to Townshend, Quebec, 5

October 1759, in *HMC: Marquess of Townshend Manuscripts* (London, 1887), p. 316.

47. See 'Copies of Some Papers which Passed between General Wolfe and the Brigadiers, with Regard to the Operations of the Army, employed up the River St Lawrence'. These are included within a small leather-bound volume containing Murray's manuscript journal of events in Canada from 18 September 1759 to 9 September 1760 (NLS, MS 4853, pp. 1–14 from rear of book).

48. For Townshend's verdicts on the mood in the capital, see his letters from London to Murray, undated, but clearly spring 1760 (LAC, 'James Murray Collection'); and to Monckton, Audley Square, 1 May 1760 (LAC, 'Robert Monckton Fonds', MG40-Q17 / rl A–1715).

49. Gray to Thomas Wharton, London, 23 January 1760, in *The Correspondence of Thomas Gray*, ed. P. Toynbee and L. Whibley (3 vols, Oxford, 1971), ii, pp. 656–57.

50. *London Magazine*, 1759 (November), p. 579; *London Chronicle*, 27–30 October 1759.

51. *A Letter to an Honourable Brigadier-General, Commander in Chief of His Majesty's Forces in Canada . . .* (1760), in C. V. F. Townshend, *The Military Life of Field-Marshal George First Marquess Townshend, 1724–1807* (London, 1901), pp. 253–61.

52. For an impartial account, see P. Mackesy, *The Coward of Minden: The Affair of Lord George Sackville* (London, 1978).

53. Horace Walpole, *Memoirs of the Reign of George III*, ed. Sir Denis Le Marchant (London, 1845), i, pp. 20–24; Walpole to George Montagu, Arlington Street, 4 November 1760 (*Walpole's Correspondence*, ix, pp. 318–19).

54. *A Refutation of the Letter to an Honble. Brigadier General, Commander of His Majesty's Forces in Canada, By An Officer* (1760), in Townshend, *Life of Townshend*, pp. 261–74.

55. CO/5/58, fos 191–93: Murray to Amherst, Quebec, 30 April 1760. For the French perspective see 'Bataille Gagnée Par L'Armee Française Commandée Par M. De Lévis Sur Les Troupes Angloises, Le 28 Avril, Près De Quebec', in *Collection des Manuscripts du Maréchal de Lévis, i, Journal des Campagnes du Chevalier de Lévis en Canada De 1756 a 1760*, ed. H. R. Casgrain (Montreal, 1889), pp. 263–68. See also 'The Capture of Quebec: A Manuscript Journal Relating to the Operations Before Quebec . . . by Colonel Malcolm Fraser . . .', ed. Brig. R. Alexander, *JSAHR*, 18 (1939), p. 166; 'Memoirs of the Quartermaster-Sergeant', in *The Siege of Quebec and the Battle of the Plains of Abraham*, ed. A. Doughty and G. W. Parmelee (6 vols, Quebec, 1901–2), v, pp. 120–23.

56. Amherst to Monckton, Albany, 29 May 1760 (LAC, 'Robert Monckton Fonds').

57. *Annual Register for 1759*, p. 45, and ibid., *1760*, p. 8.

58. Albemarle to Amherst, 6 May 1762 (WO/34/55, fos 139–40).

59. *London Magazine, 1759* (October), pp. 568, and (November), p. 579. For the influence of Kingsley's 20th Foot, see J. Houlding, *Fit for Service: The Training of the British Army, 1715–1795* (Oxford, 1981), pp. 371–72.

60. Bennett Cuthbertson, *A System for the Complete Interior Management and Oeconomy of a Battalion of Infantry* (new edition with corrections, Bristol 1776), p. viii; and second edition (London, 1779), pp. ix–x.

61. Reporting Bell's promotion on 10 May 1760, the *London Chronicle* described him as 'late Aide-de-Camp to the great General Wolfe'.

62. PRO 30/8/19, fos 188–89: Bell to his father, Kalle, near Cassel, 26 June 1762; J. Bell to Pitt, 7 July 1762 (ibid., fol. 190). In recognition of its services at Wilhelmsthal the 5th Foot was granted the privilege of wearing French-style fur grenadier caps. See Fortescue, *History of the British Army*, ii, pp. 559–61.

63. *A Short Essay on Military First Principles, by Major Thomas Bell* (London, 1770?), as discussed in *Critical Review*, 29 (1770), pp. 462–64. No copy of Bell's book has yet come to light.

64. *[Dedicated to the British Army] Military Sketches: By Edward Drewe, Late Major of the 35th Regt of Foot* (Exeter, 1784). Drewe's article, intended for publication in the *Hibernian Chronicle*, was written in 1774 or early 1775, when his regiment was in Dublin. As captain of the 35th's light company, Drewe was soon after severely wounded at Bunker Hill, in June 1775.

65. *Memoirs of the Old Highlander*, p. 71.

66. From 'The Death of General Wolfe', a version of a popular ballad probably printed between 1802 and 1815, but highly likely to have circulated orally from 1759. See Roy Palmer, *A Ballad History of England from 1588 to the Present Day* (London, 1979), p. 64.

67. Caldwell to Pitt, Clarges Street, London, 2 December 1759 (PRO 30/8/25, fos 77–78).

68. Caldwell to Pitt, Dublin, 23 January 1763 (ibid., fol. 81).

69. Barré to Pitt (via Mr Wood, Under-Secretary of State), New York, 28 April 1760 (PRO 30/8/18, fos 166–67).

70. Stanley Ayling, *The Elder Pitt: Earl of Chatham* (London, 1976), pp. 274–75, 295–96; Black, *Pitt the Elder*, p. 232.

71. F. Anderson, *Crucible of War: The Seven Years' War and the Fate of Empire in British North America, 1754–1766* (New York, 2000), pp. 643–44.

72. See *Newport* [Rhode Island] *Mercury*, 17 April 1759.

73. 'A Final Conquest of Canada, or God Reigning over His and Our Enemies', by Martha Brewster, dated Lebanon, Connecticut, 6 February 1761, reproduced in W. T. Waugh, *James Wolfe: Man and Soldier* (Montreal, 1928), p. 320.

74. The inn sign, which is now in the Connecticut Historical Society Museum, Hartford, Connecticut, is illustrated in R. S. Stephenson, *Clash of Empires: The British, French and Indian War, 1754–1763* (Pittsburgh, 2005), p. 76.

75. See *Monthly Review*, 41 (1769, part 2), pp. 395–96; and *Critical Review*, 28 (1769), pp. 56–60. The subscribers for Knox's book included Lieutenant-General Sir Jeffery Amherst, 'Mr Thomas Bell', Major-General Ralph Burton, colonels John Hale and William Howe and Lieutenant-Colonel Matthew Leslie, who placed his order from the far-flung 'East-Indies'. Of Wolfe's three brigadiers at Quebec, only Major-General Robert Monckton was amongst the subscribers. See *Knox's Journal*, i, pp. 9–14.

76. For a useful introduction see 'The Apotheosis of General Wolfe', chapter 8 in Ann Uhry Abrams's, *The Valiant Hero: Benjamin West and Grand-Style History Painting* (Washington, 1985); also, William Vaughan, *British Painting: The Golden Age from Hogarth to Turner* (London, 1999), pp. 115–17.

77. This viewpoint is forcefully expressed in C. P. Stacey, 'Benjamin West and the "Death of Wolfe"', in *National Gallery of Canada Annual Bulletin*, 7 (1966), pp. 1–5.

78. McNairn, *Behold the Hero*, p. 144.

79. See J. F. Kerslake, 'The Likeness of Wolfe', in *Wolfe: Portraiture and Genealogy* (Westerham, 1959), p. 17.

80. See letter from General Hale's daughter to *Literary Gazette*, 11 December 1847, cited in *Siege of Quebec*, iii, p. 222. As McNairn (*Behold the Hero*, pp. 139–40) points out, the fee to which Hale objected was demanded for identification in the published key that accompanied Woollett's engraving; it follows that Hale must be amongst the currently unidentified figures in West's painting. On Holland, see Willis Chipman, 'The Life and Times of Major Samuel Holland, Surveyor-General 1764–1801', *Ontario Historical Society, Papers and Records*, 21 (1924), p. 20.

81. Wright, *Life of Wolfe*, p. 604.

82. See Murray to Townshend, 55 Margaret Street, Cavendish Square, London, 25 October and 5 November 1774; Townshend to Murray, Rainham, 29 October and 7 November 1774 (Amherst Family Papers, U1350/073/8, 11, 9 and 14); also Barré's recollections, as quoted in Major Caldwell's letter to Murray of 1 November 1772 (U1350/C21).

83. Murray to Monckton, Quebec, 28 January 1761 (LAC, 'Robert Monckton Fonds').

84. Townshend to Amherst, Rainham, 2 and 7 November 1774 (U1350/073/10 and 15).

85. See McNairn, *Behold the Hero*, pp. 215–16.

86. On Montgomery see C. Royster, *A Revolutionary People at War: The Continental Army and American Character, 1775-1783* (Chapel Hill, North Carolina, 1979), pp. 120–26.

87. T. Pocock, *Horatio Nelson* (London, 1987), p. 30.

88. See Kathleen Wilson, 'How Nelson Became a Hero', in *The Historian: The Magazine of the Historical Association*, 87 (Autumn, 2005), pp. 8–9.

89. A. Lambert, *Nelson: Britannia's God of War* (London, 2004), p. 54.

90. See for example, ibid., pp. 296, 301. Nelson's famous signal originally ran 'England *confides* that every man will do his duty'; 'expects' was substituted because of the lack of a simple code for 'confides'. However, the tone of Nelson's message to his men – with its very personal expression of trust in them – remains remarkably similar to Wolfe's.

91. H. A. D. Miles and D. Blayney Brown, *Sir David Wilkie of Scotland (1785-1841)*, (Raleigh, North Carolina, 1987), pp. 184–92.

92. See Roy Palmer, *The Sound of History: Songs and Social Comment* (Oxford, 1988), pp. 274–75; also, the same author's *Ballad History of England* (p. 64); and his edited collection, *The Rambling Soldier: Life in the Lower Ranks, 1750-1900, through Soldiers' Songs and Writings* (Harmondsworth, 1977), pp. 148–51. Known also as 'Brave Wolfe', and 'The Death of General Wolfe', this ballad was still 'vastly popular ... throughout England' at the end of the nineteenth century, with a version discovered in oral circulation in Canada as recently as 1957. A fine recording of 'Brave Wolfe', based upon a version collected in Dorset, can be heard on *The Watersons: Early Days* (Topic Records, London, 1994: TSCD472).

Index